2005 | LITTLE DATA BOOK

The World Bank

Copyright ©2005 by the International Bank for Reconstruction and
Development/THE WORLD BANK
1818 H Street N.W., Washington, D.C. 20433, U.S.A.

All rights reserved
Manufactured in the United States of America
First printing April 2005

ISBN 0-8213-6075-2

The Little Data Book 2005 is a product of the Development Data Group of the
World Bank's Development Economics Vice Presidency.

Editing, design, and layout by Meta de Coquereaumont, Christopher Trott, and
Elaine Wilson of Communications Development Incorporated, Washington, D.C.
Cover design by Grundy & Northedge, London.

Photo credits: Front cover, top, Penny Tweedie/Getty Images, left, Photodisc;
back cover, top, Fredrik Naumann/Panos Pictures, bottom, Steven Harris/World
Bank.

Contents

Acknowledgments

The Little Data Book 2005 was prepared by a team coordinated by M. H. Saeed Ordoubadi. Team members are Mehdi Akhlaghi, David Cieslikowski, Mahyar Eshragh-Tabary, Richard Fix, Amy Heyman, Masako Hiraga, Raymond Muhula, Murat Omur, Sulekha Patel, Juan Carlos Rodriguez, Eric Swanson, K. M. Vijayalakshmi, Vivienne Wang, and Estela Zamora. The work was carried out under the management of Shaida Badiee.

Richard Fix, with the assistance of Azita Amjadi and Gonca Okur, coordinated all stages of production with Meta de Coquereaumont, Christopher Trott, and Elaine Wilson of Communications Development Incorporated, who provided design, editing, and layout. Communications Development's London partner, Grundy & Northedge, designed the cover. Staff from External Affairs oversaw publication and dissemination of the book.

Introduction

The Little Data Book 2005 is a pocket edition of *World Development Indicators*. It is intended as a quick reference for users of the *World Development Indicators 2005* book and CD-ROM and *WDI Online,* our electronic subscription database. Together, they cover more than 600 indicators and span 40 years.

The 207 country pages in *The Little Data Book* present the latest available data for World Bank member countries and other economies with populations of more than 30,000. The 14 summary pages cover regional and income group aggregates.

For more information about these data or other World Bank data publications, visit our data web site at www.worldbank.org/data; e-mail us at data@worldbank.org; or call our data hotline at 800 590 1906 or 202 473 7824, fax 202 522 1498.

To order *World Development Indicators 2005* or the *World Development Indicators 2005* CD-ROM, visit the publications web site at www.worldbank.org/publications or call 800 645 7247 or 703 661 1580, fax 703 661 1501.

Data notes

The data in this book are for 1990, 2002, and 2003 or the most recent year for which data are available unless otherwise noted in the glossary.

- Growth rates are proportional changes from the previous year unless otherwise noted.

- Regional aggregates include data for low- and middle-income economies only.

- Figures in italics indicate data for years or periods other than those specified.

Symbols used:

    ..   means that data are not available or that aggregates cannot be calculated because of missing data.

  0 or 0.0   means zero or less than half the unit shown.

    $ means current U.S. dollars.

Data are shown for economies with populations greater than 30,000 and for smaller economies if they are members of the World Bank. The term *country* (used interchangeably with *economy*) does not imply political independence or official recognition by the World Bank but refers to any economy for which the authorities report separate social or economic statistics.

In keeping with *World Development Indicators 2005, The Little Data Book 2005* uses terminology in line with the 1993 System of National Accounts (SNA). In particular, gross national product (GNP) is replaced by gross national income (GNI).

Since 2003 the selection of indicators in these pages has been updated to include some of the indicators being used to monitor progress toward the Millennium Development Goals. For more information about the eight goals—halving poverty and increasing well-being by 2015—please visit the web site www.developmentgoals.org or see the other books in the *World Development Indicators* series.

Regional tables

The country composition of regions is based on the World Bank's analytical regions and may differ from common geographic usage.

East Asia and Pacific

American Samoa, Cambodia, China, Fiji, Indonesia, Kiribati, Korea, Dem. Rep., Lao PDR, Malaysia, Marshall Islands, Micronesia, Fed. Sts., Mongolia, Myanmar, Northern Mariana Islands, Palau, Papua New Guinea, Philippines, Samoa, Solomon Islands, Thailand, Timor-Leste, Tonga, Vanuatu, Vietnam

Europe and Central Asia

Albania, Armenia, Azerbaijan, Belarus, Bosnia and Herzegovina, Bulgaria, Croatia, Czech Republic, Estonia, Georgia, Hungary, Kazakhstan, Kyrgyz Republic, Latvia, Lithuania, Macedonia, FYR, Moldova, Poland, Romania, Russian Federation, Serbia and Montenegro, Slovak Republic, Tajikistan, Turkey, Turkmenistan, Ukraine, Uzbekistan

Latin America and Caribbean

Antigua and Barbuda, Argentina, Aruba, Barbados, Belize, Bolivia, Brazil, Chile, Colombia, Costa Rica, Cuba, Dominica, Dominican Republic, Ecuador, El Salvador, Grenada, Guatemala, Guyana, Haiti, Honduras, Jamaica, Mexico, Nicaragua, Panama, Paraguay, Peru, St. Kitts and Nevis, St. Lucia, St. Vincent and the Grenadines, Suriname, Trinidad and Tobago, Uruguay, Venezuela, RB

Middle East and North Africa

Algeria, Djibouti, Egypt, Arab Rep., Iran, Islamic Rep., Iraq, Jordan, Lebanon, Libya, Morocco, Oman, Saudi Arabia, Syrian Arab Republic, Tunisia, West Bank and Gaza, Yemen, Rep.

South Asia

Afghanistan, Bangladesh, Bhutan, India, Maldives, Nepal, Pakistan, Sri Lanka

Sub-Saharan Africa

Angola, Benin, Botswana, Burkina Faso, Burundi, Cameroon, Cape Verde, Central African Republic, Chad, Comoros, Congo, Dem. Rep., Congo, Rep., Côte d'Ivoire, Equatorial Guinea, Eritrea, Ethiopia, Gabon, The Gambia, Ghana, Guinea, Guinea-Bissau, Kenya, Lesotho, Liberia, Madagascar, Malawi, Mali, Mauritania, Mauritius, Mayotte, Mozambique, Namibia, Niger, Nigeria, Rwanda, São Tomé and Principe, Senegal, Seychelles, Sierra Leone, Somalia, South Africa, Sudan, Swaziland, Tanzania, Togo, Uganda, Zambia, Zimbabwe

World

Population (millions)	6,273	Population growth (%)		1.2
Surface area (1,000 sq. km)	133,942	National poverty rate (% pop.)		..
GNI ($ billions)	34,577	GNI per capita ($)		5,510

	1990	2002	2003
People			
Life expectancy at birth (years)	65	67	67
Fertility rate (births per woman)	3.1	2.6	2.6
Infant mortality rate (per 1,000 live births)	64	..	57
Under-five mortality rate (per 1,000)	95	..	86
Births attended by skilled health staff (% of total)	..	..	57
Child malnutrition, underweight (% of under age 5)	..	..	..
Child immunization, measles (% of ages 12–23 mon.)	73	76	77
HIV prevalence rate (% of ages 15–49)	..	*1.1*	1.1
Adult literacy, male (% of ages 15 and older)	74	*80*	..
Adult literacy, female (% of ages 15 and older)	63	*73*	..
Primary completion rate, total (% of age group)	..	..	..
Primary completion rate, female (% of age group)	..	..	..
Net primary enrollment (% of age group)	84	*87*	..
Net secondary enrollment (% of age group)	..	..	..
Environment			
Forests (1,000 sq. km)	39,551	*38,611*	..
Deforestation (average annual %, 1990–2000)		*0.2*	
Freshwater use (% of internal resources)			8
Carbon dioxide emissions (metric tons per capita)	3.9	*3.8*	..
Access to improved water source (% of total pop.)	75	82	..
Access to improved sanitation (% of urban pop.)	77	79	..
Energy use per capita (kg oil equivalent)	1,686	1,699	..
Electricity use per capita (kilowatt-hours)	1,743	2,225	..
Economy			
GDP ($ billions)	21,688	32,492	36,461
GDP growth (annual %)	2.9	1.8	2.8
GDP implicit price deflator (annual % growth)	..	..	..
Value added in agriculture (% of GDP)	5	*4*	..
Value added in industry (% of GDP)	34	*28*	..
Value added in services (% of GDP)	61	*68*	..
Exports of goods and services (% of GDP)	19	24	..
Imports of goods and services (% of GDP)	19	24	..
Gross capital formation (% of GDP)	23	21	..
Central government revenue (% of GDP)	..	*25.8*	..
Cash surplus/deficit (% of GDP)	..	..	..
Technology and infrastructure			
Fixed-line and mobile subscribers (per 1,000 people)	102	364	406
Cost of 3-minute local call ($)	0.06	0.06	0.05
Personal computers (per 1,000 people)	25.1	100.8	..
Internet users (per 1,000 people)	2	131	150
Paved roads (% of total)	37.5	*47.4*	..
Aircraft departures (thousands)	14,641	21,954	21,372
Trade and finance			
Trade in goods (% of GDP)	32.5	40.4	41.5
Trade growth less GDP growth (avg. %, 1990–2003)			..
High-technology exports (% of manufactured exports)	17	21	18
Net barter terms of trade (2000 = 100)	..	*64*	..
Foreign direct investment ($ billions)	201	699	573
Present value of debt ($ millions)			..
Total debt service (% of goods and services exports)	..	..	..
Short-term debt ($ millions)	..	..	..
Aid per capita ($)	11	11	12

East Asia & Pacific

Population (millions)	1,855	Population growth (%)	0.8
Surface area (1,000 sq. km)	16,302	National poverty rate (% pop.)	..
GNI ($ billions)	1,988	GNI per capita ($)	1,070

	1990	2002	2003
People			
Life expectancy at birth (years)	67	69	70
Fertility rate (births per woman)	2.4	2.1	2.1
Infant mortality rate (per 1,000 live births)	44	..	32
Under-five mortality rate (per 1,000)	59	..	41
Births attended by skilled health staff (% of total)	..	91	87
Child malnutrition, underweight (% of under age 5)	19	15	..
Child immunization, measles (% of ages 12–23 mon.)	89	82	82
HIV prevalence rate (% of ages 15–49)	..	0.2	0.2
Adult literacy, male (% of ages 15 and older)	88	90	..
Adult literacy, female (% of ages 15 and older)	72	86	..
Primary completion rate, total (% of age group)	..	..	..
Primary completion rate, female (% of age group)	..	..	..
Net primary enrollment (% of age group)	96	93	..
Net secondary enrollment (% of age group)	..	..	..
Environment			
Forests (1,000 sq. km)	4,354	4,284	..
Deforestation (average annual %, 1990–2000)		0.2	
Freshwater use (% of internal resources)			8
Carbon dioxide emissions (metric tons per capita)	1.9	2.1	..
Access to improved water source (% of total pop.)	71	78	..
Access to improved sanitation (% of urban pop.)	64	71	..
Energy use per capita (kg oil equivalent)	721	904	..
Electricity use per capita (kilowatt-hours)	383	891	..
Economy			
GDP ($ billions)	666	1,816	2,033
GDP growth (annual %)	5.5	7.2	8.1
GDP implicit price deflator (annual % growth)	..	..	..
Value added in agriculture (% of GDP)	25	15	14
Value added in industry (% of GDP)	40	48	49
Value added in services (% of GDP)	35	37	36
Exports of goods and services (% of GDP)	23	39	42
Imports of goods and services (% of GDP)	22	35	39
Gross capital formation (% of GDP)	34	35	38
Central government revenue (% of GDP)	9.3	11.4	..
Cash surplus/deficit (% of GDP)	..	..	..
Technology and infrastructure			
Fixed-line and mobile subscribers (per 1,000 people)	8	273	357
Cost of 3-minute local call ($)	0.08	0.03	0.03
Personal computers (per 1,000 people)	0.9	26.3	..
Internet users (per 1,000 people)	0	48	68
Paved roads (% of total)	17.2	22.5	..
Aircraft departures (thousands)	804	1,615	1,576
Trade and finance			
Trade in goods (% of GDP)	47.0	63.3	70.5
Trade growth less GDP growth (avg. %, 1990–2003)			..
High-technology exports (% of manufactured exports)	16	31	33
Net barter terms of trade (2000 = 100)	..	58	..
Foreign direct investment ($ billions)	11	56	60
Present value of debt ($ millions)			..
Total debt service (% of goods and services exports)	17.6	12.2	10.5
Short-term debt ($ billions)	37	99	125
Aid per capita ($)	5	4	4

Europe & Central Asia

Population (millions)	472	Population growth (%)	0.1
Surface area (1,000 sq. km)	24,207	National poverty rate (% pop.)	..
GNI ($ billions)	1,217	GNI per capita ($)	2,580

	1990	2002	2003
People			
Life expectancy at birth (years)	69	69	68
Fertility rate (births per woman)	2.3	1.6	1.6
Infant mortality rate (per 1,000 live births)	39	25	29
Under-five mortality rate (per 1,000)	46	30	36
Births attended by skilled health staff (% of total)	..	..	..
Child malnutrition, underweight (% of under age 5)	..	..	..
Child immunization, measles (% of ages 12–23 mon.)	84	93	92
HIV prevalence rate (% of ages 15–49)	..	..	0.7
Adult literacy, male (% of ages 15 and older)	98	98	..
Adult literacy, female (% of ages 15 and older)	94	96	..
Primary completion rate, total (% of age group)	..	..	..
Primary completion rate, female (% of age group)	..	..	..
Net primary enrollment (% of age group)	90	..	..
Net secondary enrollment (% of age group)	..	..	..
Environment			
Forests (1,000 sq. km)	9,379	9,463	..
Deforestation (average annual %, 1990–2000)		–0.1	
Freshwater use (% of internal resources)			7
Carbon dioxide emissions (metric tons per capita)	10.2	6.7	..
Access to improved water source (% of total pop.)	..	91	..
Access to improved sanitation (% of urban pop.)	94	93	..
Energy use per capita (kg oil equivalent)	3,725	2,697	..
Electricity use per capita (kilowatt-hours)	3,311	2,808	..
Economy			
GDP ($ billions)	1,109	1,140	1,403
GDP growth (annual %)	–1.8	4.7	5.8
GDP implicit price deflator (annual % growth)	..	..	..
Value added in agriculture (% of GDP)	16	8	8
Value added in industry (% of GDP)	43	31	31
Value added in services (% of GDP)	41	60	61
Exports of goods and services (% of GDP)	24	38	35
Imports of goods and services (% of GDP)	24	38	35
Gross capital formation (% of GDP)	27	22	22
Central government revenue (% of GDP)	..	..	..
Cash surplus/deficit (% of GDP)	..	..	..
Technology and infrastructure			
Fixed-line and mobile subscribers (per 1,000 people)	125	438	..
Cost of 3-minute local call ($)	0.01	0.06	0.10
Personal computers (per 1,000 people)	4.3	73.4	..
Internet users (per 1,000 people)	0	95	161
Paved roads (% of total)	74.2	89.7	..
Aircraft departures (thousands)	..	823	867
Trade and finance			
Trade in goods (% of GDP)	49.7	64.2	66.7
Trade growth less GDP growth (avg. %, 1990–2003)			..
High-technology exports (% of manufactured exports)	..	10	12
Net barter terms of trade (2000 = 100)	..	..	..
Foreign direct investment ($ billions)	1	35	36
Present value of debt ($ millions)			..
Total debt service (% of goods and services exports)	..	21.2	19.8
Short-term debt ($ billions)	40	88	135
Aid per capita ($)	8	24	22

Latin America & Caribbean

Population (millions)	533	Population growth (%)		1.4
Surface area (1,000 sq. km)	20,418	National poverty rate (% pop.)		..
GNI ($ billions)	1,747	GNI per capita ($)		3,280

	1990	2002	2003
People			
Life expectancy at birth (years)	68	71	71
Fertility rate (births per woman)	3.1	2.4	2.4
Infant mortality rate (per 1,000 live births)	43	..	28
Under-five mortality rate (per 1,000)	53	..	33
Births attended by skilled health staff (% of total)	..	..	..
Child malnutrition, underweight (% of under age 5)	..	..	..
Child immunization, measles (% of ages 12–23 mon.)	76	92	93
HIV prevalence rate (% of ages 15–49)	..	0.6	0.7
Adult literacy, male (% of ages 15 and older)	83	86	..
Adult literacy, female (% of ages 15 and older)	83	88	..
Primary completion rate, total (% of age group)	..	..	..
Primary completion rate, female (% of age group)	..	..	..
Net primary enrollment (% of age group)	86	95	..
Net secondary enrollment (% of age group)	29	64	..
Environment			
Forests (1,000 sq. km)	10,019	9,552	..
Deforestation (average annual %, 1990–2000)		0.5	
Freshwater use (% of internal resources)			2
Carbon dioxide emissions (metric tons per capita)	2.2	2.7	..
Access to improved water source (% of total pop.)	82	89	..
Access to improved sanitation (% of urban pop.)	83	84	..
Energy use per capita (kg oil equivalent)	1,055	1,156	..
Electricity use per capita (kilowatt-hours)	1,144	1,506	..
Economy			
GDP ($ billions)	1,103	1,704	1,741
GDP growth (annual %)	0.5	–0.9	1.6
GDP implicit price deflator (annual % growth)	..	..	..
Value added in agriculture (% of GDP)	9	7	7
Value added in industry (% of GDP)	36	27	27
Value added in services (% of GDP)	55	66	66
Exports of goods and services (% of GDP)	17	23	24
Imports of goods and services (% of GDP)	15	21	21
Gross capital formation (% of GDP)	19	19	18
Central government revenue (% of GDP)	19.4	18.9	..
Cash surplus/deficit (% of GDP)	31.7	–1.3	..
Technology and infrastructure			
Fixed-line and mobile subscribers (per 1,000 people)	62	359	416
Cost of 3-minute local call ($)	0.04	0.08	..
Personal computers (per 1,000 people)	5.8	67.4	..
Internet users (per 1,000 people)	0	93	106
Paved roads (% of total)	21.5	26.9	..
Aircraft departures (thousands)	1,213	1,712	1,530
Trade and finance			
Trade in goods (% of GDP)	23.2	40.7	42.2
Trade growth less GDP growth (avg. %, 1990–2003)			..
High-technology exports (% of manufactured exports)	7	15	14
Net barter terms of trade (2000 = 100)	..	..	..
Foreign direct investment ($ billions)	8	46	37
Present value of debt ($ millions)			..
Total debt service (% of goods and services exports)	23.8	30.2	30.7
Short-term debt ($ billions)	74	79	83
Aid per capita ($)	12	10	12

Middle East & North Africa

Population (millions)	312	Population growth (%)	1.9
Surface area (1,000 sq. km)	11,141	National poverty rate (% pop.)	..
GNI ($ billions)	744	GNI per capita ($)	2,390

	1990	2002	2003
People			
Life expectancy at birth (years)	64	69	69
Fertility rate (births per woman)	4.8	3.1	3.1
Infant mortality rate (per 1,000 live births)	58	..	43
Under-five mortality rate (per 1,000)	77	..	53
Births attended by skilled health staff (% of total)	..	..	80
Child malnutrition, underweight (% of under age 5)	..	..	..
Child immunization, measles (% of ages 12–23 mon.)	84	92	92
HIV prevalence rate (% of ages 15–49)	..	..	0.1
Adult literacy, male (% of ages 15 and older)	71	82	..
Adult literacy, female (% of ages 15 and older)	40	61	..
Primary completion rate, total (% of age group)	..	..	..
Primary completion rate, female (% of age group)	..	..	..
Net primary enrollment (% of age group)	83	*87*	..
Net secondary enrollment (% of age group)	..	..	..
Environment			
Forests (1,000 sq. km)	165	*168*	..
Deforestation (average annual %, 1990–2000)		*–0.1*	
Freshwater use (% of internal resources)			102
Carbon dioxide emissions (metric tons per capita)	3.3	*4.2*	..
Access to improved water source (% of total pop.)	87	88	..
Access to improved sanitation (% of urban pop.)	88	90	..
Energy use per capita (kg oil equivalent)	1,107	1,504	..
Electricity use per capita (kilowatt-hours)	890	1,412	..
Economy			
GDP ($ billions)	421	665	745
GDP growth (annual %)	7.3	2.7	5.7
GDP implicit price deflator (annual % growth)	..	..	..
Value added in agriculture (% of GDP)	14	11	11
Value added in industry (% of GDP)	38	41	43
Value added in services (% of GDP)	48	48	47
Exports of goods and services (% of GDP)	31	33	34
Imports of goods and services (% of GDP)	33	28	27
Gross capital formation (% of GDP)	23	23	25
Central government revenue (% of GDP)	..	..	..
Cash surplus/deficit (% of GDP)	..	..	..
Technology and infrastructure			
Fixed-line and mobile subscribers (per 1,000 people)	38	180	237
Cost of 3-minute local call ($)	*0.03*	0.04	0.05
Personal computers (per 1,000 people)	..	38.2	..
Internet users (per 1,000 people)	0	42	48
Paved roads (% of total)	67.0	*63.8*	..
Aircraft departures (thousands)	328	430	416
Trade and finance			
Trade in goods (% of GDP)	46.6	50.5	50.4
Trade growth less GDP growth (avg. %, 1990–2003)			..
High-technology exports (% of manufactured exports)	*0*	2	..
Net barter terms of trade (2000 = 100)	..	..	..
Foreign direct investment ($ millions)	741	3,808	4,756
Present value of debt ($ millions)			..
Total debt service (% of goods and services exports)	20.9	12.2	12.2
Short-term debt ($ billions)	20	18	20
Aid per capita ($)	44	20	24

South Asia

Population (millions)	1,425	Population growth (%)	1.7
Surface area (1,000 sq. km)	5,140	National poverty rate (% pop.)	..
GNI ($ billions)	733	GNI per capita ($)	510

	1990	2002	2003
People			
Life expectancy at birth (years)	58	63	63
Fertility rate (births per woman)	4.1	3.2	3.1
Infant mortality rate (per 1,000 live births)	89	67	66
Under-five mortality rate (per 1,000)	130	93	92
Births attended by skilled health staff (% of total)	..	43	36
Child malnutrition, underweight (% of under age 5)	64	48	..
Child immunization, measles (% of ages 12–23 mon.)	56	67	67
HIV prevalence rate (% of ages 15–49)	..	0.7	0.8
Adult literacy, male (% of ages 15 and older)	64	73	..
Adult literacy, female (% of ages 15 and older)	34	44	..
Primary completion rate, total (% of age group)	..	..	..
Primary completion rate, female (% of age group)	..	..	..
Net primary enrollment (% of age group)	..	83	..
Net secondary enrollment (% of age group)	..	..	..
Environment			
Forests (1,000 sq. km)	790	780	..
Deforestation (average annual %, 1990–2000)		0.1	
Freshwater use (% of internal resources)			40
Carbon dioxide emissions (metric tons per capita)	0.7	0.9	..
Access to improved water source (% of total pop.)	70	84	..
Access to improved sanitation (% of urban pop.)	50	64	..
Energy use per capita (kg oil equivalent)	393	468	..
Electricity use per capita (kilowatt-hours)	225	344	..
Economy			
GDP ($ billions)	401	657	765
GDP growth (annual %)	5.6	4.4	7.5
GDP implicit price deflator (annual % growth)	..	..	..
Value added in agriculture (% of GDP)	31	23	22
Value added in industry (% of GDP)	27	26	26
Value added in services (% of GDP)	43	51	51
Exports of goods and services (% of GDP)	9	16	16
Imports of goods and services (% of GDP)	12	18	18
Gross capital formation (% of GDP)	23	22	23
Central government revenue (% of GDP)	13.6	12.2	11.8
Cash surplus/deficit (% of GDP)	–3.4	–4.1	–3.8
Technology and infrastructure			
Fixed-line and mobile subscribers (per 1,000 people)	6	45	61
Cost of 3-minute local call ($)	0.05	0.02	0.02
Personal computers (per 1,000 people)	0.4	6.8	..
Internet users (per 1,000 people)	0	14	10
Paved roads (% of total)	37.5	42.9	..
Aircraft departures (thousands)	245	309	347
Trade and finance			
Trade in goods (% of GDP)	16.5	23.7	24.1
Trade growth less GDP growth (avg. %, 1990–2003)			..
High-technology exports (% of manufactured exports)	2	4	4
Net barter terms of trade (2000 = 100)	..	..	..
Foreign direct investment ($ millions)	536	4,779	5,163
Present value of debt ($ millions)			..
Total debt service (% of goods and services exports)	27.5	13.7	16.2
Short-term debt ($ billions)	12	7	7
Aid per capita ($)	5	5	4

Sub-Saharan Africa

Population (millions)	705	Population growth (%)	2.2
Surface area (1,000 sq. km)	24,265	National poverty rate (% pop.)	..
GNI ($ billions)	351	GNI per capita ($)	500

	1990	2002	2003
People			
Life expectancy at birth (years)	50	46	46
Fertility rate (births per woman)	6.1	5.2	5.2
Infant mortality rate (per 1,000 live births)	110	..	101
Under-five mortality rate (per 1,000)	187	..	171
Births attended by skilled health staff (% of total)	..	..	39
Child malnutrition, underweight (% of under age 5)	..	..	..
Child immunization, measles (% of ages 12–23 mon.)	57	57	61
HIV prevalence rate (% of ages 15–49)	..	7.3	7.2
Adult literacy, male (% of ages 15 and older)	59	71	..
Adult literacy, female (% of ages 15 and older)	40	58	..
Primary completion rate, total (% of age group)	..	..	..
Primary completion rate, female (% of age group)	..	..	..
Net primary enrollment (% of age group)	53	..	..
Net secondary enrollment (% of age group)	..	..	..
Environment			
Forests (1,000 sq. km)	6,965	*6,435*	..
Deforestation (average annual %, 1990–2000)		*0.8*	
Freshwater use (% of internal resources)			2
Carbon dioxide emissions (metric tons per capita)	0.9	*0.7*	..
Access to improved water source (% of total pop.)	49	58	..
Access to improved sanitation (% of urban pop.)	53	55	..
Energy use per capita (kg oil equivalent)	693	667	..
Electricity use per capita (kilowatt-hours)	451	457	..
Economy			
GDP ($ billions)	298	337	439
GDP growth (annual %)	1.1	3.4	3.9
GDP implicit price deflator (annual % growth)	..	..	..
Value added in agriculture (% of GDP)	19	18	17
Value added in industry (% of GDP)	34	30	31
Value added in services (% of GDP)	47	51	52
Exports of goods and services (% of GDP)	27	33	32
Imports of goods and services (% of GDP)	26	34	33
Gross capital formation (% of GDP)	17	18	19
Central government revenue (% of GDP)	..	..	..
Cash surplus/deficit (% of GDP)	..	..	..
Technology and infrastructure			
Fixed-line and mobile subscribers (per 1,000 people)	10	52	62
Cost of 3-minute local call ($)	0.09	0.09	..
Personal computers (per 1,000 people)	..	11.9	..
Internet users (per 1,000 people)	0	17	20
Paved roads (% of total)	16.0	*13.3*	..
Aircraft departures (thousands)	317	328	348
Trade and finance			
Trade in goods (% of GDP)	42.4	52.9	52.7
Trade growth less GDP growth (avg. %, 1990–2003)			..
High-technology exports (% of manufactured exports)	..	*4*	..
Net barter terms of trade (2000 = 100)	..	..	..
Foreign direct investment ($ billions)	1	9	10
Present value of debt ($ millions)			..
Total debt service (% of goods and services exports)	13.7	10.6	8.5
Short-term debt ($ billions)	21	29	31
Aid per capita ($)	35	27	34

Income group tables

For operational and analytical purposes the World Bank's main criterion for classifying economies is gross national income (GNI) per capita. Every economy is classified as low income, middle income (subdivided into lower middle and upper middle), or high income. Low- and middle-income economies are sometimes referred to as developing economies. The use of the term is convenient; it is not intended to imply that all economies in the group are experiencing similar development or that other economies have reached a preferred or final stage of development. Note that classification by income does not necessarily reflect development status.

Low-income economies are those with a GNI per capita of $765 or less in 2003.

Middle-income economies are those with a GNI per capita of more than $765 but less than $9,386.

Lower-middle-income and **upper-middle-income** economies are separated at a GNI per capita of $3,035.

High-income economies are those with a GNI per capita of $9,386 or more.

The 12 participating member countries of the **European Monetary Union** are Austria, Belgium, Finland, France, Germany, Greece, Ireland, Italy, Luxembourg, Netherlands, Portugal, and Spain.

Low income

Population (millions)	2,312	Population growth (%)	1.8
Surface area (1,000 sq. km)	31,551	National poverty rate (% pop.)	..
GNI ($ billions)	1,021	GNI per capita ($)	440

	1990	2002	2003
People			
Life expectancy at birth (years)	56	58	58
Fertility rate (births per woman)	4.7	3.7	3.7
Infant mortality rate (per 1,000 live births)	95	..	80
Under-five mortality rate (per 1,000)	149	..	123
Births attended by skilled health staff (% of total)	..	..	38
Child malnutrition, underweight (% of under age 5)	..	44	..
Child immunization, measles (% of ages 12–23 mon.)	58	64	65
HIV prevalence rate (% of ages 15–49)	..	2.1	2.1
Adult literacy, male (% of ages 15 and older)	60	68	..
Adult literacy, female (% of ages 15 and older)	38	48	..
Primary completion rate, total (% of age group)	..	..	..
Primary completion rate, female (% of age group)	..	..	..
Net primary enrollment (% of age group)	..	77	..
Net secondary enrollment (% of age group)	..	..	..
Environment			
Forests (1,000 sq. km)	8,541	7,939	..
Deforestation (average annual %, 1990–2000)		0.7	
Freshwater use (% of internal resources)			11
Carbon dioxide emissions (metric tons per capita)	0.8	0.8	..
Access to improved water source (% of total pop.)	64	75	..
Access to improved sanitation (% of urban pop.)	49	61	..
Energy use per capita (kg oil equivalent)	463	493	..
Electricity use per capita (kilowatt-hours)	191	312	..
Economy			
GDP ($ billions)	619	947	1,103
GDP growth (annual %)	4.3	4.2	6.9
GDP implicit price deflator (annual % growth)	..	..	..
Value added in agriculture (% of GDP)	32	25	24
Value added in industry (% of GDP)	26	27	27
Value added in services (% of GDP)	41	48	49
Exports of goods and services (% of GDP)	13	21	21
Imports of goods and services (% of GDP)	17	23	24
Gross capital formation (% of GDP)	21	22	23
Central government revenue (% of GDP)	13.9	12.5	11.9
Cash surplus/deficit (% of GDP)	–3.6	–4.0	–3.8
Technology and infrastructure			
Fixed-line and mobile subscribers (per 1,000 people)	6	39	56
Cost of 3-minute local call ($)	0.07	0.07	..
Personal computers (per 1,000 people)	..	6.9	..
Internet users (per 1,000 people)	0	8	16
Paved roads (% of total)	15.4	13.3	..
Aircraft departures (thousands)	538	616	637
Trade and finance			
Trade in goods (% of GDP)	24.6	33.3	34.9
Trade growth less GDP growth (avg. %, 1990–2003)			..
High-technology exports (% of manufactured exports)	..	4	..
Net barter terms of trade (2000 = 100)	..	..	..
Foreign direct investment ($ billions)	2	15	16
Present value of debt ($ millions)			..
Total debt service (% of goods and services exports)	22.9	11.3	12.0
Short-term debt ($ billions)	38	31	33
Aid per capita ($)	13	12	14

Middle income

Population (millions)	2,989	Population growth (%)	0.9
Surface area (1,000 sq. km)	69,921	National poverty rate (% pop.)	..
GNI ($ billions)	5,756	GNI per capita ($)	1,930

	1990	2002	2003
People			
Life expectancy at birth (years)	68	70	70
Fertility rate (births per woman)	2.6	2.1	2.1
Infant mortality rate (per 1,000 live births)	42	..	30
Under-five mortality rate (per 1,000)	55	..	37
Births attended by skilled health staff (% of total)	..	..	87
Child malnutrition, underweight (% of under age 5)	..	*11*	..
Child immunization, measles (% of ages 12–23 mon.)	87	87	87
HIV prevalence rate (% of ages 15–49)	..	0.7	0.7
Adult literacy, male (% of ages 15 and older)	85	*89*	..
Adult literacy, female (% of ages 15 and older)	75	*87*	..
Primary completion rate, total (% of age group)	..	..	..
Primary completion rate, female (% of age group)	..	..	..
Net primary enrollment (% of age group)	92	*93*	..
Net secondary enrollment (% of age group)	..	..	..
Environment			
Forests (1,000 sq. km)	23,132	*22,743*	..
Deforestation (average annual %, 1990–2000)		*0.2*	
Freshwater use (% of internal resources)			6
Carbon dioxide emissions (metric tons per capita)	3.6	*3.2*	..
Access to improved water source (% of total pop.)	77	83	..
Access to improved sanitation (% of urban pop.)	79	81	..
Energy use per capita (kg oil equivalent)	1,372	1,338	..
Electricity use per capita (kilowatt-hours)	764	1,422	..
Economy			
GDP ($ billions)	3,377	5,373	6,023
GDP growth (annual %)	1.7	3.1	4.9
GDP implicit price deflator (annual % growth)	..	..	..
Value added in agriculture (% of GDP)	15	10	10
Value added in industry (% of GDP)	39	36	36
Value added in services (% of GDP)	46	54	54
Exports of goods and services (% of GDP)	22	32	33
Imports of goods and services (% of GDP)	21	29	30
Gross capital formation (% of GDP)	26	24	25
Central government revenue (% of GDP)	16.0	*17.1*	..
Cash surplus/deficit (% of GDP)	..	..	..
Technology and infrastructure			
Fixed-line and mobile subscribers (per 1,000 people)	41	324	403
Cost of 3-minute local call ($)	0.04	0.04	0.04
Personal computers (per 1,000 people)	2.4	42.9	..
Internet users (per 1,000 people)	0	82	116
Paved roads (% of total)	51.1	*54.0*	..
Aircraft departures (thousands)	2,600	4,601	4,447
Trade and finance			
Trade in goods (% of GDP)	35.5	54.5	58.3
Trade growth less GDP growth (avg. %, 1990–2003)			..
High-technology exports (% of manufactured exports)	..	18	21
Net barter terms of trade (2000 = 100)	..	..	..
Foreign direct investment ($ billions)	20	139	136
Present value of debt ($ millions)			..
Total debt service (% of goods and services exports)	19.3	19.2	17.8
Short-term debt ($ billions)	166	290	369
Aid per capita ($)	10	9	9

Lower middle income

Population (millions)	2,655	Population growth (%)	0.9
Surface area (1,000 sq. km)	57,002	National poverty rate (% pop.)	..
GNI ($ billions)	3,944	GNI per capita ($)	1,490

	1990	2002	2003
People			
Life expectancy at birth (years)	67	69	69
Fertility rate (births per woman)	2.6	2.1	2.1
Infant mortality rate (per 1,000 live births)	44	..	31
Under-five mortality rate (per 1,000)	57	..	39
Births attended by skilled health staff (% of total)	..	..	86
Child malnutrition, underweight (% of under age 5)	..	11	..
Child immunization, measles (% of ages 12–23 mon.)	87	86	86
HIV prevalence rate (% of ages 15–49)	..	0.7	0.7
Adult literacy, male (% of ages 15 and older)	84	88	..
Adult literacy, female (% of ages 15 and older)	74	86	..
Primary completion rate, total (% of age group)	..	..	..
Primary completion rate, female (% of age group)	..	..	..
Net primary enrollment (% of age group)	93	93	..
Net secondary enrollment (% of age group)	..	..	..
Environment			
Forests (1,000 sq. km)	20,555	20,316	..
Deforestation (average annual %, 1990–2000)		0.1	
Freshwater use (% of internal resources)			6
Carbon dioxide emissions (metric tons per capita)	3.4	2.9	..
Access to improved water source (% of total pop.)	77	82	..
Access to improved sanitation (% of urban pop.)	78	80	..
Energy use per capita (kg oil equivalent)	1,286	1,227	..
Electricity use per capita (kilowatt-hours)	620	1,289	..
Economy			
GDP ($ billions)	2,467	3,637	4,168
GDP growth (annual %)	0.8	5.4	5.7
GDP implicit price deflator (annual % growth)	..	..	..
Value added in agriculture (% of GDP)	19	12	11
Value added in industry (% of GDP)	39	37	37
Value added in services (% of GDP)	43	51	52
Exports of goods and services (% of GDP)	19	29	31
Imports of goods and services (% of GDP)	19	27	29
Gross capital formation (% of GDP)	28	27	28
Central government revenue (% of GDP)	15.1	16.2	..
Cash surplus/deficit (% of GDP)	..	..	..
Technology and infrastructure			
Fixed-line and mobile subscribers (per 1,000 people)	35	302	381
Cost of 3-minute local call ($)	0.02	0.03	0.03
Personal computers (per 1,000 people)	1.5	35.6	..
Internet users (per 1,000 people)	0	45	63
Paved roads (% of total)	54.5	53.0	..
Aircraft departures (thousands)	1,709	3,245	3,159
Trade and finance			
Trade in goods (% of GDP)	31.3	49.3	53.8
Trade growth less GDP growth (avg. %, 1990–2003)			..
High-technology exports (% of manufactured exports)	..	17	20
Net barter terms of trade (2000 = 100)	..	..	..
Foreign direct investment ($ billions)	11	93	100
Present value of debt ($ millions)			..
Total debt service (% of goods and services exports)	23.1	20.6	18.1
Short-term debt ($ billions)	109	191	238
Aid per capita ($)	9	8	8

Upper middle income

Population (millions)	333	Population growth (%)	1.2
Surface area (1,000 sq. km)	12,919	National poverty rate (% pop.)	..
GNI ($ billions)	1,812	GNI per capita ($)	5,440

	1990	2002	2003
People			
Life expectancy at birth (years)	71	74	74
Fertility rate (births per woman)	3.1	2.3	2.3
Infant mortality rate (per 1,000 live births)	27	18	18
Under-five mortality rate (per 1,000)	34	21	22
Births attended by skilled health staff (% of total)	..	..	..
Child malnutrition, underweight (% of under age 5)	..	..	..
Child immunization, measles (% of ages 12–23 mon.)	80	94	94
HIV prevalence rate (% of ages 15–49)	..	0.7	0.6
Adult literacy, male (% of ages 15 and older)	88	90	..
Adult literacy, female (% of ages 15 and older)	86	90	..
Primary completion rate, total (% of age group)	..	..	..
Primary completion rate, female (% of age group)	..	..	..
Net primary enrollment (% of age group)	91	91	..
Net secondary enrollment (% of age group)	50	68	..
Environment			
Forests (1,000 sq. km)	2,577	2,427	..
Deforestation (average annual %, 1990–2000)		0.6	
Freshwater use (% of internal resources)			6
Carbon dioxide emissions (metric tons per capita)	5.2	6.3	..
Access to improved water source (% of total pop.)	..	..	..
Access to improved sanitation (% of urban pop.)	89	..	..
Energy use per capita (kg oil equivalent)	2,072	2,232	..
Electricity use per capita (kilowatt-hours)	1,859	2,496	..
Economy			
GDP ($ billions)	919	1,737	1,856
GDP growth (annual %)	3.7	–1.2	3.3
GDP implicit price deflator (annual % growth)	..	..	..
Value added in agriculture (% of GDP)	8	6	6
Value added in industry (% of GDP)	39	33	35
Value added in services (% of GDP)	52	61	59
Exports of goods and services (% of GDP)	29	38	37
Imports of goods and services (% of GDP)	25	33	32
Gross capital formation (% of GDP)	21	19	19
Central government revenue (% of GDP)	..	..	..
Cash surplus/deficit (% of GDP)	..	..	..
Technology and infrastructure			
Fixed-line and mobile subscribers (per 1,000 people)	89	501	594
Cost of 3-minute local call ($)	0.05	0.08	0.09
Personal computers (per 1,000 people)	9.4	100.6	..
Internet users (per 1,000 people)	0	141	208
Paved roads (% of total)	48.3	72.3	..
Aircraft departures (thousands)	891	1,356	1,289
Trade and finance			
Trade in goods (% of GDP)	45.0	65.1	68.4
Trade growth less GDP growth (avg. %, 1990–2003)			..
High-technology exports (% of manufactured exports)	11	19	22
Net barter terms of trade (2000 = 100)	..	..	..
Foreign direct investment ($ billions)	9	47	36
Present value of debt ($ millions)			..
Total debt service (% of goods and services exports)	14.8	17.7	18.0
Short-term debt ($ billions)	56	98	130
Aid per capita ($)	14	10	11

Low and middle income

Population (millions)	5,300	Population growth (%)	1.3
Surface area (1,000 sq. km)	101,473	National poverty rate (% pop.)	..
GNI ($ billions)	6,777	GNI per capita ($)	1,280

	1990	2002	2003
People			
Life expectancy at birth (years)	63	65	65
Fertility rate (births per woman)	3.4	2.8	2.8
Infant mortality rate (per 1,000 live births)	69	..	59
Under-five mortality rate (per 1,000)	103	..	87
Births attended by skilled health staff (% of total)	..	..	57
Child malnutrition, underweight (% of under age 5)	..	..	..
Child immunization, measles (% of ages 12–23 mon.)	72	75	76
HIV prevalence rate (% of ages 15–49)	..	1.2	1.2
Adult literacy, male (% of ages 15 and older)	73	79	..
Adult literacy, female (% of ages 15 and older)	62	73	..
Primary completion rate, total (% of age group)	..	..	..
Primary completion rate, female (% of age group)	..	..	..
Net primary enrollment (% of age group)	82	86	..
Net secondary enrollment (% of age group)	..	..	..
Environment			
Forests (1,000 sq. km)	31,673	30,682	..
Deforestation (average annual %, 1990–2000)		0.3	
Freshwater use (% of internal resources)			7
Carbon dioxide emissions (metric tons per capita)	2.4	2.2	..
Access to improved water source (% of total pop.)	72	79	..
Access to improved sanitation (% of urban pop.)	71	75	..
Energy use per capita (kg oil equivalent)	1,020	990	..
Electricity use per capita (kilowatt-hours)	533	970	..
Economy			
GDP ($ billions)	3,998	6,320	7,125
GDP growth (annual %)	2.0	3.3	5.2
GDP implicit price deflator (annual % growth)	..	..	..
Value added in agriculture (% of GDP)	18	12	12
Value added in industry (% of GDP)	37	35	35
Value added in services (% of GDP)	45	54	53
Exports of goods and services (% of GDP)	21	31	31
Imports of goods and services (% of GDP)	20	28	29
Gross capital formation (% of GDP)	25	24	25
Central government revenue (% of GDP)	15.7	16.4	..
Cash surplus/deficit (% of GDP)	..	..	..
Technology and infrastructure			
Fixed-line and mobile subscribers (per 1,000 people)	27	200	249
Cost of 3-minute local call ($)	0.05	0.05	..
Personal computers (per 1,000 people)	1.7	28.4	..
Internet users (per 1,000 people)	0	53	75
Paved roads (% of total)	27.2	30.8	..
Aircraft departures (thousands)	3,138	5,216	5,084
Trade and finance			
Trade in goods (% of GDP)	33.6	51.4	54.7
Trade growth less GDP growth (avg. %, 1990–2003)			..
High-technology exports (% of manufactured exports)	..	17	20
Net barter terms of trade (2000 = 100)	..	..	..
Foreign direct investment ($ billions)	22	154	152
Present value of debt ($ millions)			..
Total debt service (% of goods and services exports)	19.7	18.3	17.2
Short-term debt ($ billions)	203	321	402
Aid per capita ($)	13	12	14

Europe EMU

Population (millions)	307	Population growth (%)
Surface area (1,000 sq. km)	2,507	National poverty rate (% pop.)
GNI ($ billions)	6,999	GNI per capita ($)

	1990	2002	2003
People			
Life expectancy at birth (years)	76	79	79
Fertility rate (births per woman)	1.5	1.5	1.5
Infant mortality rate (per 1,000 live births)	8	5	4
Under-five mortality rate (per 1,000)	9	5	..
Births attended by skilled health staff (% of total)	..	..	..
Child malnutrition, underweight (% of under age 5)	..	..	..
Child immunization, measles (% of ages 12–23 mon.)	73	88	89
HIV prevalence rate (% of ages 15–49)	..	0.3	0.3
Adult literacy, male (% of ages 15 and older)	..	..	..
Adult literacy, female (% of ages 15 and older)	..	..	..
Primary completion rate, total (% of age group)	..	..	..
Primary completion rate, female (% of age group)	..	..	..
Net primary enrollment (% of age group)	95	99	..
Net secondary enrollment (% of age group)	..	91	
Environment			
Forests (1,000 sq. km)	823	853	..
Deforestation (average annual %, 1990–2000)		–0.4	
Freshwater use (% of internal resources)			21
Carbon dioxide emissions (metric tons per capita)	6.9	7.9	..
Access to improved water source (% of total pop.)	..	..	..
Access to improved sanitation (% of urban pop.)	..	..	..
Energy use per capita (kg oil equivalent)	3,583	3,895	..
Electricity use per capita (kilowatt-hours)	4,769	5,912	..
Economy			
GDP ($ billions)	5,504	6,662	8,196
GDP growth (annual %)	3.7	0.9	0.5
GDP implicit price deflator (annual % growth)	..	..	..
Value added in agriculture (% of GDP)	4	2	2
Value added in industry (% of GDP)	34	28	28
Value added in services (% of GDP)	62	69	70
Exports of goods and services (% of GDP)	27	36	33
Imports of goods and services (% of GDP)	28	34	31
Gross capital formation (% of GDP)	24	20	20
Central government revenue (% of GDP)	..	35.9	..
Cash surplus/deficit (% of GDP)	..	–1.8	..
Technology and infrastructure			
Fixed-line and mobile subscribers (per 1,000 people)	419	1,335	1,386
Cost of 3-minute local call ($)	0.15	0.13	0.16
Personal computers (per 1,000 people)	62.4	317.2	..
Internet users (per 1,000 people)	1	336	378
Paved roads (% of total)	92.8	99.5	..
Aircraft departures (thousands)	1,793	3,430	3,507
Trade and finance			
Trade in goods (% of GDP)	44.9	56.3	..
Trade growth less GDP growth (avg. %, 1990–2003)			..
High-technology exports (% of manufactured exports)	12	17	14
Net barter terms of trade (2000 = 100)	..	..	..
Foreign direct investment ($ billions)	61	351	281
Present value of debt ($ millions)			..
Total debt service (% of goods and services exports)	..	..	..
Short-term debt ($ millions)	..	..	..
Aid per capita ($)	..	..	..

High income

Population (millions)	972	Population growth (%)	0.5
Surface area (1,000 sq. km)	32,469	National poverty rate (% pop.)	..
GNI ($ billions)	27,806	GNI per capita ($)	28,600

	1990	2002	2003
People			
Life expectancy at birth (years)	76	78	78
Fertility rate (births per woman)	1.8	1.6	1.6
Infant mortality rate (per 1,000 live births)	8	5	..
Under-five mortality rate (per 1,000)	10	7	..
Births attended by skilled health staff (% of total)	..	..	..
Child malnutrition, underweight (% of under age 5)	..	..	..
Child immunization, measles (% of ages 12–23 mon.)	83	91	92
HIV prevalence rate (% of ages 15–49)	..	0.3	0.4
Adult literacy, male (% of ages 15 and older)	..	..	..
Adult literacy, female (% of ages 15 and older)	..	..	..
Primary completion rate, total (% of age group)	..	..	..
Primary completion rate, female (% of age group)	..	..	..
Net primary enrollment (% of age group)	97	96	..
Net secondary enrollment (% of age group)	87	90	..
Environment			
Forests (1,000 sq. km)	7,878	7,929	..
Deforestation (average annual %, 1990–2000)		–0.1	
Freshwater use (% of internal resources)			10
Carbon dioxide emissions (metric tons per capita)	11.8	12.4	..
Access to improved water source (% of total pop.)	..	99	..
Access to improved sanitation (% of urban pop.)	..	..	..
Energy use per capita (kg oil equivalent)	4,859	5,395	..
Electricity use per capita (kilowatt-hours)	7,050	8,693	..
Economy			
GDP ($ billions)	17,691	26,176	29,341
GDP growth (annual %)	3.1	1.5	2.2
GDP implicit price deflator (annual % growth)	..	..	..
Value added in agriculture (% of GDP)	3	2	..
Value added in industry (% of GDP)	33	27	..
Value added in services (% of GDP)	65	71	..
Exports of goods and services (% of GDP)	19	22	..
Imports of goods and services (% of GDP)	19	23	..
Gross capital formation (% of GDP)	23	20	..
Central government revenue (% of GDP)	..	25.7	..
Cash surplus/deficit (% of GDP)	..	–1.9	..
Technology and infrastructure			
Fixed-line and mobile subscribers (per 1,000 people)	470	1,250	1,268
Cost of 3-minute local call ($)	0.13	0.07	0.10
Personal computers (per 1,000 people)	111.6	466.5	..
Internet users (per 1,000 people)	3	364	377
Paved roads (% of total)	86.3	94.8	..
Aircraft departures (thousands)	11,503	16,737	16,289
Trade and finance			
Trade in goods (% of GDP)	32.3	37.8	38.3
Trade growth less GDP growth (avg. %, 1990–2003)			..
High-technology exports (% of manufactured exports)	18	22	18
Net barter terms of trade (2000 = 100)	..	..	..
Foreign direct investment ($ billions)	179	545	421
Present value of debt ($ millions)			..
Total debt service (% of goods and services exports)	..	..	..
Short-term debt ($ millions)	..	..	..
Aid per capita ($)	3	2	1

Country tables

China. On July 1, 1997, China resumed its exercise of sovereignty over Hong Kong, and on December 20, 1999, it resumed its exercise of sovereignty over Macao. Unless otherwise noted, data for China do not include data for Hong Kong, China; Taiwan, China; or Macao, China.

Democratic Republic of Congo. Data for the Democratic Republic of Congo (Congo, Dem. Rep., in the table listings) refer to the former Zaire. (The Republic of Congo is referred to as Congo, Rep., in the table listings.)

Czech Republic and Slovak Republic. Data are shown whenever possible for the individual countries formed from the former Czechoslovakia—the Czech Republic and the Slovak Republic.

Eritrea. Data are shown for Eritrea whenever possible, but in most cases before 1992 Eritrea is included in the data for Ethiopia.

Germany. Data for Germany refer to the unified Germany unless otherwise noted.

Serbia and Montenegro. On February 4, 2003, the Federal Republic of Yugoslavia changed its name to Serbia and Montenegro.

Timor-Leste. On May 20, 2002, Timor-Leste became an independent country. Data for Indonesia include Timor-Leste through 1999 unless otherwise noted.

Union of Soviet Socialist Republics. In 1991 the Union of Soviet Socialist Republics came to an end. Available data are shown for the individual countries now existing on its former territory (Armenia, Azerbaijan, Belarus, Estonia, Georgia, Kazakhstan, Kyrgyz Republic, Latvia, Lithuania, Moldova, Russian Federation, Tajikistan, Turkmenistan, Ukraine, and Uzbekistan). External debt data presented for the Russian Federation prior to 1992 are for the former Soviet Union. The debt of the former Soviet Union is included in the Russian Federation data after 1992 on the assumption that 100 percent of all outstanding external debt as of December 1991 has become a liability of the Russian Federation. Beginning in 1993 the data for the Russian Federation have been revised to include obligations to members of the former Council for Mutual Economic Assistance and other countries in the form of trade-related credits amounting to $15.4 billion as of the end of 1996.

República Bolivariana de Venezuela. In December 1999 the official name of Venezuela was changed to República Bolivariana de Venezuela (Venezuela, RB, in the table listings).

Republic of Yemen. Data for the Republic of Yemen refer to that country from 1990 onward; data for previous years refer to aggregated data for the former People's Democratic Republic of Yemen and the former Yemen Arab Republic unless otherwise noted.

Afghanistan

South Asia			Low income

Population (millions)	..	Population growth (%)	..
Surface area (1,000 sq. km)	652	National poverty rate (% pop.)	..
GNI ($ millions)	..	GNI per capita ($)	..

	1990	2002	2003
People			
Life expectancy at birth (years)	42	43	43
Fertility rate (births per woman)	6.9	..	..
Infant mortality rate (per 1,000 live births)	168	..	..
Under-five mortality rate (per 1,000)	260	..	..
Births attended by skilled health staff (% of total)		12	14
Child malnutrition, underweight (% of under age 5)	..	49	..
Child immunization, measles (% of ages 12–23 mon.)	20	44	50
HIV prevalence rate (% of ages 15–49)	..	..	..
Adult literacy, male (% of ages 15 and older)	..	..	..
Adult literacy, female (% of ages 15 and older)	..	..	..
Primary completion rate, total (% of age group)	..	..	..
Primary completion rate, female (% of age group)	..	..	..
Net primary enrollment (% of age group)	27	..	..
Net secondary enrollment (% of age group)	..	..	..
Environment			
Forests (1,000 sq. km)	14	14	..
Deforestation (average annual %, 1990–2000)		0.0	
Freshwater use (% of internal resources)			47
Carbon dioxide emissions (metric tons per capita)	0.1	0.0	..
Access to improved water source (% of total pop.)	..	13	..
Access to improved sanitation (% of urban pop.)	..	16	..
Energy use per capita (kg oil equivalent)	..	..	..
Electricity use per capita (kilowatt-hours)	..	..	..
Economy			
GDP ($ millions)	..	4,002	4,708
GDP growth (annual %)	..	..	..
GDP implicit price deflator (annual % growth)	..	..	..
Value added in agriculture (% of GDP)	..	52	..
Value added in industry (% of GDP)	..	24	..
Value added in services (% of GDP)	..	24	..
Exports of goods and services (% of GDP)	..	57	..
Imports of goods and services (% of GDP)	..	89	..
Gross capital formation (% of GDP)	..	16	..
Central government revenue (% of GDP)	..	..	..
Cash surplus/deficit (% of GDP)	..	..	..
Technology and infrastructure			
Fixed-line and mobile subscribers (per 1,000 people)	2	2	12
Cost of 3-minute local call ($)	..	..	..
Personal computers (per 1,000 people)	..	..	..
Internet users (per 1,000 people)	..	0	1
Paved roads (% of total)	13.3	13.3	..
Aircraft departures (thousands)	5	3	..
Trade and finance			
Trade in goods (% of GDP)	..	26.0	28.1
Trade growth less GDP growth (avg. %, 1990–2003)			..
High-technology exports (% of manufactured exports)	..	..	..
Net barter terms of trade (2000 = 100)	..	..	..
Foreign direct investment ($ millions)	..	..	..
Present value of debt ($ millions)			..
Total debt service (% of goods and services exports)	..	..	..
Short-term debt ($ millions)	..	..	..
Aid per capita ($)	7	15	..

Albania

Population (millions)	3	Population growth (%)	0.6
Surface area (1,000 sq. km)	29	National poverty rate (% pop.)	25
GNI ($ millions)	5,509	GNI per capita ($)	1,740

	1990	2002	2003
People			
Life expectancy at birth (years)	72	74	74
Fertility rate (births per woman)	3.0	2.2	2.2
Infant mortality rate (per 1,000 live births)	37	22	18
Under-five mortality rate (per 1,000)	45	25	21
Births attended by skilled health staff (% of total)	..	94	..
Child malnutrition, underweight (% of under age 5)	..	14	..
Child immunization, measles (% of ages 12–23 mon.)	88	96	93
HIV prevalence rate (% of ages 15–49)	..	..	..
Adult literacy, male (% of ages 15 and older)	87	99	..
Adult literacy, female (% of ages 15 and older)	67	98	..
Primary completion rate, total (% of age group)	..	101	101
Primary completion rate, female (% of age group)	..	101	100
Net primary enrollment (% of age group)	95	97	..
Net secondary enrollment (% of age group)	..	74	
Environment			
Forests (1,000 sq. km)	11	10	..
Deforestation (average annual %, 1990–2000)		0.8	
Freshwater use (% of internal resources)			5
Carbon dioxide emissions (metric tons per capita)	2.2	0.9	..
Access to improved water source (% of total pop.)	97	97	..
Access to improved sanitation (% of urban pop.)	99	99	..
Energy use per capita (kg oil equivalent)	812	617	..
Electricity use per capita (kilowatt-hours)	513	1,390	..
Economy			
GDP ($ millions)	2,102	4,835	6,124
GDP growth (annual %)	–9.6	4.7	6.0
GDP implicit price deflator (annual % growth)	–0.5	6.0	3.9
Value added in agriculture (% of GDP)	36	25	25
Value added in industry (% of GDP)	48	19	19
Value added in services (% of GDP)	16	56	56
Exports of goods and services (% of GDP)	15	19	19
Imports of goods and services (% of GDP)	23	43	42
Gross capital formation (% of GDP)	29	26	25
Central government revenue (% of GDP)	..	21.6	..
Cash surplus/deficit (% of GDP)	..	–9.5	..
Technology and infrastructure			
Fixed-line and mobile subscribers (per 1,000 people)	13	348	441
Cost of 3-minute local call ($)	0.01	0.02	..
Personal computers (per 1,000 people)	..	11.7	..
Internet users (per 1,000 people)	..	4	10
Paved roads (% of total)	..	39.0	..
Aircraft departures (thousands)	..	4	4
Trade and finance			
Trade in goods (% of GDP)	29.0	37.9	37.8
Trade growth less GDP growth (avg. %, 1990–2003)			13.1
High-technology exports (% of manufactured exports)	..	1	1
Net barter terms of trade (2000 = 100)	..	..	..
Foreign direct investment ($ millions)	0	135	178
Present value of debt ($ millions)			1,032
Total debt service (% of goods and services exports)	4.3	3.4	2.6
Short-term debt ($ millions)	425	29	149
Aid per capita ($)	3	98	108

Algeria

Middle East & North Africa		Lower middle income
Population (millions)	32	Population growth (%) 1.6
Surface area (1,000 sq. km)	2,382	National poverty rate (% pop.) 12
GNI ($ billions)	62	GNI per capita ($) 1,930

	1990	2002	2003
People			
Life expectancy at birth (years)	67	71	71
Fertility rate (births per woman)	4.5	2.8	2.7
Infant mortality rate (per 1,000 live births)	54	37	35
Under-five mortality rate (per 1,000)	69	45	41
Births attended by skilled health staff (% of total)	77	92	..
Child malnutrition, underweight (% of under age 5)	9	6	..
Child immunization, measles (% of ages 12–23 mon.)	83	81	84
HIV prevalence rate (% of ages 15–49)	..	0.1	0.1
Adult literacy, male (% of ages 15 and older)	64	78	..
Adult literacy, female (% of ages 15 and older)	41	60	..
Primary completion rate, total (% of age group)	80	96	..
Primary completion rate, female (% of age group)	74	95	..
Net primary enrollment (% of age group)	93	95	..
Net secondary enrollment (% of age group)	54	67	..
Environment			
Forests (1,000 sq. km)	19	21	..
Deforestation (average annual %, 1990–2000)		–1.3	
Freshwater use (% of internal resources)			36
Carbon dioxide emissions (metric tons per capita)	3.2	2.9	..
Access to improved water source (% of total pop.)	95	87	..
Access to improved sanitation (% of urban pop.)	99	99	..
Energy use per capita (kg oil equivalent)	954	985	..
Electricity use per capita (kilowatt-hours)	492	662	..
Economy			
GDP ($ billions)	62	56	67
GDP growth (annual %)	0.8	4.1	6.8
GDP implicit price deflator (annual % growth)	30.3	1.0	8.2
Value added in agriculture (% of GDP)	11	10	10
Value added in industry (% of GDP)	48	53	55
Value added in services (% of GDP)	40	37	35
Exports of goods and services (% of GDP)	23	35	39
Imports of goods and services (% of GDP)	25	26	24
Gross capital formation (% of GDP)	29	30	30
Central government revenue (% of GDP)	..	36.0	..
Cash surplus/deficit (% of GDP)	..	1.2	..
Technology and infrastructure			
Fixed-line and mobile subscribers (per 1,000 people)	32	74	115
Cost of 3-minute local call ($)	0.08	0.02	0.04
Personal computers (per 1,000 people)	1.0	7.7	..
Internet users (per 1,000 people)	..	16	..
Paved roads (% of total)	67.0	68.9	..
Aircraft departures (thousands)	44	46	44
Trade and finance			
Trade in goods (% of GDP)	36.6	55.2	56.6
Trade growth less GDP growth (avg. %, 1990–2003)			0.0
High-technology exports (% of manufactured exports)	1	1	2
Net barter terms of trade (2000 = 100)	74	90	..
Foreign direct investment ($ millions)	0	1,065	634
Present value of debt ($ billions)			23
Total debt service (% of goods and services exports)	63.4	..	..
Short-term debt ($ millions)	791	108	146
Aid per capita ($)	5	10	7

American Samoa

East Asia & Pacific		Upper middle income

Population (thousands)	57	Population growth (%)	..
Surface area (sq. km)	200	National poverty rate (% pop.)	..
GNI ($ millions)	..	GNI per capita ($)	..

	1990	2002	2003
People			
Life expectancy at birth (years)	..	..	..
Fertility rate (births per woman)	..	..	..
Infant mortality rate (per 1,000 live births)	..	..	..
Under-five mortality rate (per 1,000)	..	..	..
Births attended by skilled health staff (% of total)	..	..	..
Child malnutrition, underweight (% of under age 5)	..	..	..
Child immunization, measles (% of ages 12–23 mon.)	..	..	..
HIV prevalence rate (% of ages 15–49)	..	..	..
Adult literacy, male (% of ages 15 and older)	..	..	..
Adult literacy, female (% of ages 15 and older)	..	..	..
Primary completion rate, total (% of age group)	..	..	..
Primary completion rate, female (% of age group)	..	..	..
Net primary enrollment (% of age group)	..	..	..
Net secondary enrollment (% of age group)	..	..	..
Environment			
Forests (1,000 sq. km)	0	*0*	..
Deforestation (average annual %, 1990–2000)		*0.0*	
Freshwater use (% of internal resources)			..
Carbon dioxide emissions (metric tons per capita)	..	..	..
Access to improved water source (% of total pop.)	..	..	..
Access to improved sanitation (% of urban pop.)	..	..	..
Energy use per capita (kg oil equivalent)	..	..	..
Electricity use per capita (kilowatt-hours)	..	..	..
Economy			
GDP ($ millions)	..	..	..
GDP growth (annual %)	..	..	..
GDP implicit price deflator (annual % growth)	..	..	..
Value added in agriculture (% of GDP)	..	..	..
Value added in industry (% of GDP)	..	..	..
Value added in services (% of GDP)	..	..	..
Exports of goods and services (% of GDP)	..	..	..
Imports of goods and services (% of GDP)	..	..	..
Gross capital formation (% of GDP)	..	..	..
Central government revenue (% of GDP)	..	..	..
Cash surplus/deficit (% of GDP)	..	..	..
Technology and infrastructure			
Fixed-line and mobile subscribers (per 1,000 people)	*138*	*290*	..
Cost of 3-minute local call ($)	..	*0.00*	..
Personal computers (per 1,000 people)	..	..	..
Internet users (per 1,000 people)	..	..	..
Paved roads (% of total)	..	..	..
Aircraft departures (thousands)	..	..	..
Trade and finance			
Trade in goods (% of GDP)	..	..	..
Trade growth less GDP growth (avg. %, 1990–2003)			..
High-technology exports (% of manufactured exports)	..	..	..
Net barter terms of trade (2000 = 100)	..	..	..
Foreign direct investment ($ millions)	..	..	..
Present value of debt ($ millions)			..
Total debt service (% of goods and services exports)	..	..	..
Short-term debt ($ millions)	..	..	..
Aid per capita ($)	..	..	..

Andorra

High income

Population (thousands)	66	Population growth (%)	..
Surface area (sq. km)	468	National poverty rate (% pop.)	..
GNI ($ millions)	..	GNI per capita ($)	..

	1990	2002	2003
People			
Life expectancy at birth (years)	..	..	..
Fertility rate (births per woman)	..	..	..
Infant mortality rate (per 1,000 live births)	..	6	6
Under-five mortality rate (per 1,000)	..	7	7
Births attended by skilled health staff (% of total)	..	..	..
Child malnutrition, underweight (% of under age 5)	..	..	..
Child immunization, measles (% of ages 12–23 mon.)	..	97	96
HIV prevalence rate (% of ages 15–49)	..	..	..
Adult literacy, male (% of ages 15 and older)	..	..	..
Adult literacy, female (% of ages 15 and older)	..	..	..
Primary completion rate, total (% of age group)	..	..	..
Primary completion rate, female (% of age group)	..	..	..
Net primary enrollment (% of age group)	..	..	..
Net secondary enrollment (% of age group)	..	..	..
Environment			
Forests (1,000 sq. km)	..	..	..
Deforestation (average annual %, 1990–2000)		..	
Freshwater use (% of internal resources)			..
Carbon dioxide emissions (metric tons per capita)	..	..	
Access to improved water source (% of total pop.)	100	100	..
Access to improved sanitation (% of urban pop.)	100	100	..
Energy use per capita (kg oil equivalent)	..	..	..
Electricity use per capita (kilowatt-hours)	..	..	..
Economy			
GDP ($ millions)	..	..	..
GDP growth (annual %)	..	..	..
GDP implicit price deflator (annual % growth)	..	..	..
Value added in agriculture (% of GDP)	..	..	..
Value added in industry (% of GDP)	..	..	..
Value added in services (% of GDP)	..	..	..
Exports of goods and services (% of GDP)	..	..	..
Imports of goods and services (% of GDP)	..	..	..
Gross capital formation (% of GDP)	..	..	..
Central government revenue (% of GDP)	..	..	..
Cash surplus/deficit (% of GDP)	..	..	..
Technology and infrastructure			
Fixed-line and mobile subscribers (per 1,000 people)	414	740	..
Cost of 3-minute local call ($)	0.04	0.08	..
Personal computers (per 1,000 people)	..	..	..
Internet users (per 1,000 people)	..	90	..
Paved roads (% of total)	..	..	..
Aircraft departures (thousands)	..	..	..
Trade and finance			
Trade in goods (% of GDP)	..	..	..
Trade growth less GDP growth (avg. %, 1990–2003)			..
High-technology exports (% of manufactured exports)	..	17	..
Net barter terms of trade (2000 = 100)	..	..	..
Foreign direct investment ($ millions)	..	..	..
Present value of debt ($ millions)			..
Total debt service (% of goods and services exports)	..	..	..
Short–term debt ($ millions)	..	..	..
Aid per capita ($)	..	..	..

Angola

Sub-Saharan Africa			Low income

Population (millions)	14	Population growth (%)	3.0
Surface area (1,000 sq. km)	1,247	National poverty rate (% pop.)	..
GNI ($ billions)	10	GNI per capita ($)	740

	1990	2002	2003
People			
Life expectancy at birth (years)	45	47	47
Fertility rate (births per woman)	7.2	7.0	7.0
Infant mortality rate (per 1,000 live births)	154	*154*	154
Under-five mortality rate (per 1,000)	260	*260*	260
Births attended by skilled health staff (% of total)	..	45	..
Child malnutrition, underweight (% of under age 5)	20	*31*	..
Child immunization, measles (% of ages 12–23 mon.)	38	74	62
HIV prevalence rate (% of ages 15–49)	..	*3.7*	3.9
Adult literacy, male (% of ages 15 and older)	..	..	..
Adult literacy, female (% of ages 15 and older)	..	..	..
Primary completion rate, total (% of age group)	39	..	..
Primary completion rate, female (% of age group)	..	..	..
Net primary enrollment (% of age group)	58	*61*	..
Net secondary enrollment (% of age group)	..	..	..
Environment			
Forests (1,000 sq. km)	710	*698*	..
Deforestation (average annual %, 1990–2000)		0.2	
Freshwater use (% of internal resources)			0
Carbon dioxide emissions (metric tons per capita)	0.5	*0.5*	..
Access to improved water source (% of total pop.)	32	50	..
Access to improved sanitation (% of urban pop.)	62	56	..
Energy use per capita (kg oil equivalent)	672	672	..
Electricity use per capita (kilowatt-hours)	63	109	..
Economy			
GDP ($ billions)	10	11	13
GDP growth (annual %)	–0.3	15.3	4.5
GDP implicit price deflator (annual % growth)	10.9	103.3	92.3
Value added in agriculture (% of GDP)	18	8	9
Value added in industry (% of GDP)	41	68	65
Value added in services (% of GDP)	41	24	27
Exports of goods and services (% of GDP)	39	77	71
Imports of goods and services (% of GDP)	21	70	67
Gross capital formation (% of GDP)	12	32	32
Central government revenue (% of GDP)	..	..	..
Cash surplus/deficit (% of GDP)	..	..	..
Technology and infrastructure			
Fixed-line and mobile subscribers (per 1,000 people)	8	15	..
Cost of 3-minute local call ($)	0.13	0.09	..
Personal computers (per 1,000 people)	..	1.9	..
Internet users (per 1,000 people)	..	3	..
Paved roads (% of total)	*25.0*	*10.4*	..
Aircraft departures (thousands)	7	4	5
Trade and finance			
Trade in goods (% of GDP)	53.5	93.0	98.0
Trade growth less GDP growth (avg. %, 1990–2003)			..
High-technology exports (% of manufactured exports)	..	..	..
Net barter terms of trade (2000 = 100)	94	125	..
Foreign direct investment ($ millions)	–335	1,672	1,415
Present value of debt ($ millions)			9,474
Total debt service (% of goods and services exports)	8.1	16.3	14.9
Short–term debt ($ millions)	989	1,209	1,122
Aid per capita ($)	29	32	37

Antigua and Barbuda

Latin America & Caribbean   **Upper middle income**

Population (thousands)	79	Population growth (%)	2.7
Surface area (sq. km)	440	National poverty rate (% pop.)	..
GNI ($ millions)	719	GNI per capita ($)	9,160

	1990	2002	2003
People			
Life expectancy at birth (years)	74	75	75
Fertility rate (births per woman)	1.8	1.7	1.7
Infant mortality rate (per 1,000 live births)	..	13	11
Under-five mortality rate (per 1,000)	..	15	12
Births attended by skilled health staff (% of total)	..	100	..
Child malnutrition, underweight (% of under age 5)	..	..	..
Child immunization, measles (% of ages 12–23 mon.)	89	99	99
HIV prevalence rate (% of ages 15–49)	..	..	..
Adult literacy, male (% of ages 15 and older)	..	..	..
Adult literacy, female (% of ages 15 and older)	..	..	..
Primary completion rate, total (% of age group)	..	..	..
Primary completion rate, female (% of age group)	..	..	..
Net primary enrollment (% of age group)	..	..	..
Net secondary enrollment (% of age group)	..	..	..
Environment			
Forests (1,000 sq. km)	0	0	..
Deforestation (average annual %, 1990–2000)		0.0	
Freshwater use (% of internal resources)			..
Carbon dioxide emissions (metric tons per capita)	4.7	4.9	..
Access to improved water source (% of total pop.)	..	91	
Access to improved sanitation (% of urban pop.)	98	98	..
Energy use per capita (kg oil equivalent)	..	..	..
Electricity use per capita (kilowatt-hours)	..	..	..
Economy			
GDP ($ millions)	392	721	757
GDP growth (annual %)	2.5	2.9	3.2
GDP implicit price deflator (annual % growth)	2.3	0.4	1.7
Value added in agriculture (% of GDP)	4	4	..
Value added in industry (% of GDP)	20	22	..
Value added in services (% of GDP)	76	75	..
Exports of goods and services (% of GDP)	89	60	..
Imports of goods and services (% of GDP)	87	68	..
Gross capital formation (% of GDP)	32	30	..
Central government revenue (% of GDP)	..	..	..
Cash surplus/deficit (% of GDP)	..	..	..
Technology and infrastructure			
Fixed-line and mobile subscribers (per 1,000 people)	174	978	..
Cost of 3-minute local call ($)	0.06	0.06	..
Personal computers (per 1,000 people)	..	..	..
Internet users (per 1,000 people)	..	128	..
Paved roads (% of total)	..	..	..
Aircraft departures (thousands)	58	63	67
Trade and finance			
Trade in goods (% of GDP)	70.5	57.4	43.0
Trade growth less GDP growth (avg. %, 1990–2003)			–2.6
High-technology exports (% of manufactured exports)	..	1	..
Net barter terms of trade (2000 = 100)	..	..	..
Foreign direct investment ($ millions)	..	..	..
Present value of debt ($ millions)			..
Total debt service (% of goods and services exports)	..	..	..
Short-term debt ($ millions)	..	..	..
Aid per capita ($)	73	183	64

Argentina

Latin America & Caribbean		Upper middle income	
Population (millions)	37	Population growth (%)	0.8
Surface area (1,000 sq. km)	2,780	National poverty rate (% pop.)	..
GNI ($ billions)	140	GNI per capita ($)	3,810

	1990	2002	2003
People			
Life expectancy at birth (years)	72	74	74
Fertility rate (births per woman)	2.9	2.4	2.4
Infant mortality rate (per 1,000 live births)	25	17	17
Under-five mortality rate (per 1,000)	28	20	20
Births attended by skilled health staff (% of total)	96	98	99
Child malnutrition, underweight (% of under age 5)	..	..	..
Child immunization, measles (% of ages 12–23 mon.)	93	97	97
HIV prevalence rate (% of ages 15–49)	..	0.7	0.7
Adult literacy, male (% of ages 15 and older)	96	97	..
Adult literacy, female (% of ages 15 and older)	96	97	..
Primary completion rate, total (% of age group)	..	103	..
Primary completion rate, female (% of age group)	..	105	..
Net primary enrollment (% of age group)	94	..	..
Net secondary enrollment (% of age group)	..	81	..
Environment			
Forests (1,000 sq. km)	375	346	..
Deforestation (average annual %, 1990–2000)		0.8	
Freshwater use (% of internal resources)			10
Carbon dioxide emissions (metric tons per capita)	3.4	3.9	..
Access to improved water source (% of total pop.)	94	..	..
Access to improved sanitation (% of urban pop.)	87	..	..
Energy use per capita (kg oil equivalent)	1,428	1,543	..
Electricity use per capita (kilowatt-hours)	1,250	2,024	..
Economy			
GDP ($ billions)	141	102	130
GDP growth (annual %)	–2.4	–10.9	8.8
GDP implicit price deflator (annual % growth)	2,076.8	30.6	10.7
Value added in agriculture (% of GDP)	8	11	11
Value added in industry (% of GDP)	36	32	35
Value added in services (% of GDP)	56	57	54
Exports of goods and services (% of GDP)	10	28	25
Imports of goods and services (% of GDP)	5	13	14
Gross capital formation (% of GDP)	14	12	15
Central government revenue (% of GDP)	..	13.7	..
Cash surplus/deficit (% of GDP)	..	–5.8	..
Technology and infrastructure			
Fixed-line and mobile subscribers (per 1,000 people)	93	396	..
Cost of 3-minute local call ($)	0.11	0.03	0.02
Personal computers (per 1,000 people)	7.2	82.0	..
Internet users (per 1,000 people)	0	112	..
Paved roads (% of total)	28.5	29.4	..
Aircraft departures (thousands)	114	101	92
Trade and finance			
Trade in goods (% of GDP)	11.6	34.0	33.3
Trade growth less GDP growth (avg. %, 1990–2003)			4.5
High-technology exports (% of manufactured exports)	7	7	9
Net barter terms of trade (2000 = 100)	64	99	..
Foreign direct investment ($ millions)	1,836	1,093	1,020
Present value of debt ($ billions)			187
Total debt service (% of goods and services exports)	37.0	16.6	37.9
Short-term debt ($ billions)	10	15	23
Aid per capita ($)	5	2	3

Armenia

Europe & Central Asia   **Lower middle income**

Population (millions)	3	Population growth (%)	–0.4
Surface area (1,000 sq. km)	30	National poverty rate (% pop.)	51
GNI ($ millions)	2,888	GNI per capita ($)	950

	1990	2002	2003
People			
Life expectancy at birth (years)	72	75	75
Fertility rate (births per woman)	2.6	1.1	1.1
Infant mortality rate (per 1,000 live births)	52	33	30
Under-five mortality rate (per 1,000)	60	37	33
Births attended by skilled health staff (% of total)	..	97	..
Child malnutrition, underweight (% of under age 5)	..	3	..
Child immunization, measles (% of ages 12–23 mon.)	93	91	94
HIV prevalence rate (% of ages 15–49)	..	0.1	0.1
Adult literacy, male (% of ages 15 and older)	99	100	..
Adult literacy, female (% of ages 15 and older)	96	99	..
Primary completion rate, total (% of age group)	..	103	110
Primary completion rate, female (% of age group)	..	101	108
Net primary enrollment (% of age group)	..	94	..
Net secondary enrollment (% of age group)	..	84	..
Environment			
Forests (1,000 sq. km)	3	4	..
Deforestation (average annual %, 1990–2000)		–1.3	
Freshwater use (% of internal resources)			32
Carbon dioxide emissions (metric tons per capita)	1.1	1.1	..
Access to improved water source (% of total pop.)	..	92	..
Access to improved sanitation (% of urban pop.)	96	96	..
Energy use per capita (kg oil equivalent)	1,231	632	..
Electricity use per capita (kilowatt-hours)	1,786	1,113	..
Economy			
GDP ($ millions)	2,257	2,376	2,805
GDP growth (annual %)	–11.7	13.2	13.9
GDP implicit price deflator (annual % growth)	79.4	2.4	4.6
Value added in agriculture (% of GDP)	17	26	24
Value added in industry (% of GDP)	52	35	39
Value added in services (% of GDP)	31	39	37
Exports of goods and services (% of GDP)	35	29	32
Imports of goods and services (% of GDP)	46	47	50
Gross capital formation (% of GDP)	47	22	25
Central government revenue (% of GDP)	..	..	17.7
Cash surplus/deficit (% of GDP)	..	..	–0.7
Technology and infrastructure			
Fixed-line and mobile subscribers (per 1,000 people)	157	162	178
Cost of 3-minute local call ($)	0.00	0.02	0.02
Personal computers (per 1,000 people)	..	15.8	..
Internet users (per 1,000 people)	..	16	37
Paved roads (% of total)	99.2	96.8	..
Aircraft departures (thousands)	..	3	4
Trade and finance			
Trade in goods (% of GDP)	..	63.0	69.4
Trade growth less GDP growth (avg. %, 1990–2003)			–9.1
High-technology exports (% of manufactured exports)	..	2	1
Net barter terms of trade (2000 = 100)	..	..	..
Foreign direct investment ($ millions)	0	111	121
Present value of debt ($ millions)			733
Total debt service (% of goods and services exports)	..	8.3	8.8
Short-term debt ($ billions)	..	0	0
Aid per capita ($)	1	96	81

Aruba

High income

Population (thousands)	99	Population growth (%)	..
Surface area (sq. km)	190	National poverty rate (% pop.)	..
GNI ($ millions)	..	GNI per capita ($)	..

	1990	2002	2003
People			
Life expectancy at birth (years)	..	..	..
Fertility rate (births per woman)	..	..	..
Infant mortality rate (per 1,000 live births)	..	..	..
Under-five mortality rate (per 1,000)	..	..	..
Births attended by skilled health staff (% of total)	..	..	..
Child malnutrition, underweight (% of under age 5)	..	..	..
Child immunization, measles (% of ages 12–23 mon.)	..	..	..
HIV prevalence rate (% of ages 15–49)	..	..	..
Adult literacy, male (% of ages 15 and older)	..	..	..
Adult literacy, female (% of ages 15 and older)	..	..	..
Primary completion rate, total (% of age group)	..	97	..
Primary completion rate, female (% of age group)	..	102	..
Net primary enrollment (% of age group)	..	98	..
Net secondary enrollment (% of age group)	..	78	..
Environment			
Forests (1,000 sq. km)	..	..	..
Deforestation (average annual %, 1990–2000)		..	
Freshwater use (% of internal resources)			..
Carbon dioxide emissions (metric tons per capita)	..	..	..
Access to improved water source (% of total pop.)	100	100	..
Access to improved sanitation (% of urban pop.)	..	..	..
Energy use per capita (kg oil equivalent)	..	..	..
Electricity use per capita (kilowatt-hours)	..	..	..
Economy			
GDP ($ millions)	872	1,875	..
GDP growth (annual %)	..	..	..
GDP implicit price deflator (annual % growth)	5.7	..	..
Value added in agriculture (% of GDP)	..	..	..
Value added in industry (% of GDP)	..	..	..
Value added in services (% of GDP)	..	..	..
Exports of goods and services (% of GDP)	101	81	..
Imports of goods and services (% of GDP)	161	109	..
Gross capital formation (% of GDP)	..	..	..
Central government revenue (% of GDP)	..	..	..
Cash surplus/deficit (% of GDP)	..	..	..
Technology and infrastructure			
Fixed-line and mobile subscribers (per 1,000 people)	282	850	..
Cost of 3-minute local call ($)	0.09	0.09	0.09
Personal computers (per 1,000 people)	..	..	..
Internet users (per 1,000 people)	..	226	..
Paved roads (% of total)	..	..	..
Aircraft departures (thousands)	..	..	..
Trade and finance			
Trade in goods (% of GDP)	58.1	51.7	..
Trade growth less GDP growth (avg. %, 1990–2003)			..
High-technology exports (% of manufactured exports)	..	..	5
Net barter terms of trade (2000 = 100)	..	..	..
Foreign direct investment ($ millions)	131	269	186
Present value of debt ($ millions)			..
Total debt service (% of goods and services exports)	..	..	..
Short-term debt ($ millions)	..	..	..
Aid per capita ($)	..	..	..

Australia

	High income

Population (millions)	20	Population growth (%)	1.1
Surface area (1,000 sq. km)	7,741	National poverty rate (% pop.)	..
GNI ($ billions)	436	GNI per capita ($)	21,950

	1990	2002	2003
People			
Life expectancy at birth (years)	77	80	80
Fertility rate (births per woman)	1.9	1.8	1.8
Infant mortality rate (per 1,000 live births)	8	5	..
Under-five mortality rate (per 1,000)	10	6	..
Births attended by skilled health staff (% of total)	*100*	*100*	..
Child malnutrition, underweight (% of under age 5)	..	..	..
Child immunization, measles (% of ages 12–23 mon.)	86	94	93
HIV prevalence rate (% of ages 15–49)	..	*0.1*	0.1
Adult literacy, male (% of ages 15 and older)	..	..	..
Adult literacy, female (% of ages 15 and older)	..	..	..
Primary completion rate, total (% of age group)	..	..	..
Primary completion rate, female (% of age group)	..	..	..
Net primary enrollment (% of age group)	99	97	..
Net secondary enrollment (% of age group)	79	88	..
Environment			
Forests (1,000 sq. km)	1,574	*1,545*	..
Deforestation (average annual %, 1990–2000)		*0.2*	
Freshwater use (% of internal resources)			3
Carbon dioxide emissions (metric tons per capita)	15.6	*18.0*	..
Access to improved water source (% of total pop.)	100	100	..
Access to improved sanitation (% of urban pop.)	100	100	..
Energy use per capita (kg oil equivalent)	5,130	5,732	..
Electricity use per capita (kilowatt-hours)	7,572	9,663	..
Economy			
GDP ($ billions)	311	409	522
GDP growth (annual %)	–0.1	2.8	3.8
GDP implicit price deflator (annual % growth)	3.5	2.6	..
Value added in agriculture (% of GDP)	4	3	..
Value added in industry (% of GDP)	29	26	..
Value added in services (% of GDP)	67	71	..
Exports of goods and services (% of GDP)	17	20	..
Imports of goods and services (% of GDP)	17	22	..
Gross capital formation (% of GDP)	22	25	..
Central government revenue (% of GDP)	..	26.0	26.5
Cash surplus/deficit (% of GDP)	..	–0.5	0.8
Technology and infrastructure			
Fixed-line and mobile subscribers (per 1,000 people)	467	1,178	1,262
Cost of 3-minute local call ($)	*0.19*	0.12	0.19
Personal computers (per 1,000 people)	149.8	565.1	..
Internet users (per 1,000 people)	6	534	567
Paved roads (% of total)	35.0	*38.7*	..
Aircraft departures (thousands)	256	537	530
Trade and finance			
Trade in goods (% of GDP)	26.3	33.7	30.7
Trade growth less GDP growth (avg. %, 1990–2003)			3.2
High-technology exports (% of manufactured exports)	8	16	14
Net barter terms of trade (2000 = 100)	116	106	106
Foreign direct investment ($ billions)	8	16	7
Present value of debt ($ millions)			..
Total debt service (% of goods and services exports)	..	..	..
Short-term debt ($ millions)	..	..	..
Aid per capita ($)	..	..	..

Austria

High income

Population (millions)	8	Population growth (%)	0.3
Surface area (1,000 sq. km)	84	National poverty rate (% pop.)	..
GNI ($ billions)	217	GNI per capita ($)	26,810

	1990	2002	2003
People			
Life expectancy at birth (years)	76	79	79
Fertility rate (births per woman)	1.5	1.4	1.4
Infant mortality rate (per 1,000 live births)	8	4	5
Under-five mortality rate (per 1,000)	10	6	..
Births attended by skilled health staff (% of total)	..	..	..
Child malnutrition, underweight (% of under age 5)	..	..	..
Child immunization, measles (% of ages 12–23 mon.)	60	78	79
HIV prevalence rate (% of ages 15–49)	..	0.2	0.3
Adult literacy, male (% of ages 15 and older)	..	..	..
Adult literacy, female (% of ages 15 and older)	..	..	..
Primary completion rate, total (% of age group)	..	101	..
Primary completion rate, female (% of age group)	..	101	..
Net primary enrollment (% of age group)	88	90	..
Net secondary enrollment (% of age group)	..	89	..
Environment			
Forests (1,000 sq. km)	38	39	..
Deforestation (average annual %, 1990–2000)		–0.2	
Freshwater use (% of internal resources)			4
Carbon dioxide emissions (metric tons per capita)	7.4	7.6	..
Access to improved water source (% of total pop.)	100	100	..
Access to improved sanitation (% of urban pop.)	100	100	..
Energy use per capita (kg oil equivalent)	3,270	3,774	..
Electricity use per capita (kilowatt-hours)	5,536	6,838	..
Economy			
GDP ($ billions)	162	205	253
GDP growth (annual %)	4.7	1.4	0.7
GDP implicit price deflator (annual % growth)	3.3	1.4	2.0
Value added in agriculture (% of GDP)	4	2	2
Value added in industry (% of GDP)	34	32	32
Value added in services (% of GDP)	62	66	66
Exports of goods and services (% of GDP)	40	53	52
Imports of goods and services (% of GDP)	38	51	50
Gross capital formation (% of GDP)	25	22	23
Central government revenue (% of GDP)	..	39.1	..
Cash surplus/deficit (% of GDP)	..	–1.0	..
Technology and infrastructure			
Fixed-line and mobile subscribers (per 1,000 people)	427	1,275	1,360
Cost of 3-minute local call ($)	0.18	0.19	0.19
Personal computers (per 1,000 people)	64.8	369.3	..
Internet users (per 1,000 people)	1	415	462
Paved roads (% of total)	100.0	100.0	..
Aircraft departures (thousands)	42	136	128
Trade and finance			
Trade in goods (% of GDP)	55.9	76.4	76.7
Trade growth less GDP growth (avg. %, 1990–2003)			4.2
High-technology exports (% of manufactured exports)	8	15	13
Net barter terms of trade (2000 = 100)	..	..	..
Foreign direct investment ($ millions)	653	319	7,276
Present value of debt ($ millions)			..
Total debt service (% of goods and services exports)	..	..	..
Short-term debt ($ millions)	..	..	..
Aid per capita ($)	..	..	..

Azerbaijan

Europe & Central Asia		Lower middle income
Population (millions)	8	Population growth (%)	0.7
Surface area (1,000 sq. km)	87	National poverty rate (% pop.)	49
GNI ($ millions)	6,713	GNI per capita ($)	820

	1990	2002	2003
People			
Life expectancy at birth (years)	71	65	..
Fertility rate (births per woman)	2.7	2.1	2.1
Infant mortality rate (per 1,000 live births)	84	77	75
Under-five mortality rate (per 1,000)	105	93	91
Births attended by skilled health staff (% of total)	..	84	..
Child malnutrition, underweight (% of under age 5)	..	7	..
Child immunization, measles (% of ages 12–23 mon.)	66	97	98
HIV prevalence rate (% of ages 15–49)	..	..	0.1
Adult literacy, male (% of ages 15 and older)	..	..	..
Adult literacy, female (% of ages 15 and older)	..	..	..
Primary completion rate, total (% of age group)	..	103	106
Primary completion rate, female (% of age group)	..	102	104
Net primary enrollment (% of age group)	100	80	..
Net secondary enrollment (% of age group)	..	76	..
Environment			
Forests (1,000 sq. km)	10	11	..
Deforestation (average annual %, 1990–2000)		–1.3	
Freshwater use (% of internal resources)			206
Carbon dioxide emissions (metric tons per capita)	6.4	3.6	..
Access to improved water source (% of total pop.)	66	77	..
Access to improved sanitation (% of urban pop.)	..	73	..
Energy use per capita (kg oil equivalent)	2,259	1,435	..
Electricity use per capita (kilowatt-hours)	1,645	1,878	..
Economy			
GDP ($ millions)	8,858	6,236	7,138
GDP growth (annual %)	–0.7	10.6	11.2
GDP implicit price deflator (annual % growth)	..	3.2	4.0
Value added in agriculture (% of GDP)	29	15	14
Value added in industry (% of GDP)	33	50	55
Value added in services (% of GDP)	38	35	31
Exports of goods and services (% of GDP)	44	43	43
Imports of goods and services (% of GDP)	39	50	67
Gross capital formation (% of GDP)	27	32	49
Central government revenue (% of GDP)	..	17.6	..
Cash surplus/deficit (% of GDP)	..	–4.7	..
Technology and infrastructure			
Fixed-line and mobile subscribers (per 1,000 people)	86	220	242
Cost of 3-minute local call ($)	..	0.10	..
Personal computers (per 1,000 people)	..	..	..
Internet users (per 1,000 people)	..	37	..
Paved roads (% of total)	..	92.4	..
Aircraft departures (thousands)	..	8	9
Trade and finance			
Trade in goods (% of GDP)	..	61.5	73.1
Trade growth less GDP growth (avg. %, 1990–2003)			14.8
High-technology exports (% of manufactured exports)	..	8	5
Net barter terms of trade (2000 = 100)	..	..	..
Foreign direct investment ($ millions)	0	1,392	3,285
Present value of debt ($ millions)			1,357
Total debt service (% of goods and services exports)	..	5.9	7.5
Short-term debt ($ billions)	..	0	0
Aid per capita ($)	0	43	36

Bahamas, The

High income

Population (thousands)	317	Population growth (%)	1.1
Surface area (1,000 sq. km)	14	National poverty rate (% pop.)	..
GNI ($ millions)	..	GNI per capita ($)	..

	1990	2002	2003
People			
Life expectancy at birth (years)	69	70	70
Fertility rate (births per woman)	2.1	2.1	2.1
Infant mortality rate (per 1,000 live births)	24	14	11
Under-five mortality rate (per 1,000)	29	17	14
Births attended by skilled health staff (% of total)	99	..	..
Child malnutrition, underweight (% of under age 5)	..	..	..
Child immunization, measles (% of ages 12–23 mon.)	86	94	90
HIV prevalence rate (% of ages 15–49)	..	3.0	3.0
Adult literacy, male (% of ages 15 and older)	..	..	..
Adult literacy, female (% of ages 15 and older)	..	..	..
Primary completion rate, total (% of age group)	..	78	..
Primary completion rate, female (% of age group)	..	83	..
Net primary enrollment (% of age group)	90	86	..
Net secondary enrollment (% of age group)	..	76	..
Environment			
Forests (1,000 sq. km)	8	8	..
Deforestation (average annual %, 1990–2000)		0.0	
Freshwater use (% of internal resources)			..
Carbon dioxide emissions (metric tons per capita)	7.6	5.9	..
Access to improved water source (% of total pop.)	..	97	..
Access to improved sanitation (% of urban pop.)	100	100	..
Energy use per capita (kg oil equivalent)	..	..	..
Electricity use per capita (kilowatt-hours)	..	..	..
Economy			
GDP ($ millions)	3,105	5,050	5,260
GDP growth (annual %)	1.1	0.7	..
GDP implicit price deflator (annual % growth)	3.2	1.3	..
Value added in agriculture (% of GDP)	..	..	..
Value added in industry (% of GDP)	..	..	..
Value added in services (% of GDP)	..	..	..
Exports of goods and services (% of GDP)	..	..	..
Imports of goods and services (% of GDP)	..	..	..
Gross capital formation (% of GDP)	..	..	..
Central government revenue (% of GDP)	16.0	17.6	17.1
Cash surplus/deficit (% of GDP)	–1.9	–2.6	–3.2
Technology and infrastructure			
Fixed-line and mobile subscribers (per 1,000 people)	281	796	782
Cost of 3-minute local call ($)	0.00	..	..
Personal computers (per 1,000 people)	..	..	..
Internet users (per 1,000 people)	..	43	265
Paved roads (% of total)	52.0	57.4	..
Aircraft departures (thousands)	19	27	25
Trade and finance			
Trade in goods (% of GDP)	89.8	44.2	43.2
Trade growth less GDP growth (avg. %, 1990–2003)			..
High-technology exports (% of manufactured exports)	..	1	..
Net barter terms of trade (2000 = 100)	..	..	..
Foreign direct investment ($ millions)	–17	153	147
Present value of debt ($ millions)			..
Total debt service (% of goods and services exports)	..	..	..
Short-term debt ($ millions)	..	..	..
Aid per capita ($)	14	17	12

Bahrain

High income

Population (thousands)	712	Population growth (%)	2.0
Surface area (sq. km)	710	National poverty rate (% pop.)	..
GNI ($ millions)	..	GNI per capita ($)	..

	1990	2002	2003
People			
Life expectancy at birth (years)	71	73	73
Fertility rate (births per woman)	3.8	2.3	2.3
Infant mortality rate (per 1,000 live births)	15	13	12
Under-five mortality rate (per 1,000)	19	16	15
Births attended by skilled health staff (% of total)	94	..	..
Child malnutrition, underweight (% of under age 5)	7	..	..
Child immunization, measles (% of ages 12–23 mon.)	87	99	100
HIV prevalence rate (% of ages 15–49)	..	0.1	0.2
Adult literacy, male (% of ages 15 and older)	87	92	..
Adult literacy, female (% of ages 15 and older)	75	84	..
Primary completion rate, total (% of age group)	95	100	..
Primary completion rate, female (% of age group)	96	94	..
Net primary enrollment (% of age group)	99	90	..
Net secondary enrollment (% of age group)	85	87	..
Environment			
Forests (1,000 sq. km)	..	..	
Deforestation (average annual %, 1990–2000)	..		
Freshwater use (% of internal resources)			..
Carbon dioxide emissions (metric tons per capita)	23.3	29.1	..
Access to improved water source (% of total pop.)	..	..	
Access to improved sanitation (% of urban pop.)	100	100	..
Energy use per capita (kg oil equivalent)	9,600	9,837	..
Electricity use per capita (kilowatt-hours)	5,964	9,248	..
Economy			
GDP ($ millions)	4,230	7,683	..
GDP growth (annual %)	4.4	5.1	..
GDP implicit price deflator (annual % growth)	4.8	–7.9	..
Value added in agriculture (% of GDP)	1	..	..
Value added in industry (% of GDP)	46	..	..
Value added in services (% of GDP)	53	..	..
Exports of goods and services (% of GDP)	116	81	..
Imports of goods and services (% of GDP)	95	65	..
Gross capital formation (% of GDP)	16	17	..
Central government revenue (% of GDP)	29.5	34.2	..
Cash surplus/deficit (% of GDP)	–0.6	–0.4	..
Technology and infrastructure			
Fixed-line and mobile subscribers (per 1,000 people)	202	846	906
Cost of 3-minute local call ($)	0.08	0.06	0.05
Personal computers (per 1,000 people)	..	160.4	..
Internet users (per 1,000 people)	..	183	216
Paved roads (% of total)	75.4	76.7	..
Aircraft departures (thousands)	11	20	29
Trade and finance			
Trade in goods (% of GDP)	176.7	140.2	..
Trade growth less GDP growth (avg. %, 1990–2003)			..
High-technology exports (% of manufactured exports)	..	0	0
Net barter terms of trade (2000 = 100)	..	..	..
Foreign direct investment ($ millions)	..	..	..
Present value of debt ($ millions)			..
Total debt service (% of goods and services exports)	..	..	..
Short-term debt ($ millions)	..	..	..
Aid per capita ($)	272	101	53

Bangladesh

South Asia   **Low income**

Population (millions)	138	Population growth (%)	1.7
Surface area (1,000 sq. km)	144	National poverty rate (% pop.)	50
GNI ($ billions)	55	GNI per capita ($)	400

	1990	2002	2003
People			
Life expectancy at birth (years)	55	62	62
Fertility rate (births per woman)	4.1	3.0	2.9
Infant mortality rate (per 1,000 live births)	96	*54*	46
Under-five mortality rate (per 1,000)	144	*82*	69
Births attended by skilled health staff (% of total)	..	12	14
Child malnutrition, underweight (% of under age 5)	66	52	..
Child immunization, measles (% of ages 12–23 mon.)	65	77	77
HIV prevalence rate (% of ages 15–49)	..	..	..
Adult literacy, male (% of ages 15 and older)	44	50	..
Adult literacy, female (% of ages 15 and older)	24	31	..
Primary completion rate, total (% of age group)	*46*	73	..
Primary completion rate, female (% of age group)	..	76	..
Net primary enrollment (% of age group)	71	85	..
Net secondary enrollment (% of age group)	19	44	..
Environment			
Forests (1,000 sq. km)	12	13	..
Deforestation (average annual %, 1990–2000)		*–1.3*	
Freshwater use (% of internal resources)			14
Carbon dioxide emissions (metric tons per capita)	0.1	*0.2*	..
Access to improved water source (% of total pop.)	71	75	..
Access to improved sanitation (% of urban pop.)	71	75	..
Energy use per capita (kg oil equivalent)	116	155	..
Electricity use per capita (kilowatt-hours)	43	100	..
Economy			
GDP ($ billions)	30	48	52
GDP growth (annual %)	5.9	4.4	5.3
GDP implicit price deflator (annual % growth)	6.3	3.2	4.5
Value added in agriculture (% of GDP)	30	23	22
Value added in industry (% of GDP)	21	26	26
Value added in services (% of GDP)	48	51	52
Exports of goods and services (% of GDP)	6	14	14
Imports of goods and services (% of GDP)	14	19	20
Gross capital formation (% of GDP)	17	23	23
Central government revenue (% of GDP)	..	10.2	10.1
Cash surplus/deficit (% of GDP)	..	–0.2	–0.1
Technology and infrastructure			
Fixed-line and mobile subscribers (per 1,000 people)	2	13	16
Cost of 3-minute local call ($)	0.05	*0.03*	0.03
Personal computers (per 1,000 people)	..	3.4	7.8
Internet users (per 1,000 people)	..	2	2
Paved roads (% of total)	*7.2*	*9.5*	..
Aircraft departures (thousands)	13	7	7
Trade and finance			
Trade in goods (% of GDP)	17.6	29.4	31.6
Trade growth less GDP growth (avg. %, 1990–2003)			4.6
High-technology exports (% of manufactured exports)	0	*0*	0
Net barter terms of trade (2000 = 100)	111	*100*	..
Foreign direct investment ($ millions)	3	52	102
Present value of debt ($ billions)			13
Total debt service (% of goods and services exports)	25.8	7.4	6.0
Short-term debt ($ millions)	156	572	617
Aid per capita ($)	19	7	10

Barbados

Latin America & Caribbean   **Upper middle income**

Population (thousands)	271	Population growth (%)	0.4
Surface area (sq. km)	430	National poverty rate (% pop.)	..
GNI ($ millions)	2,507	GNI per capita ($)	9,260

	1990	2002	2003
People			
Life expectancy at birth (years)	75	75	75
Fertility rate (births per woman)	1.7	1.8	1.8
Infant mortality rate (per 1,000 live births)	14	12	11
Under-five mortality rate (per 1,000)	16	14	13
Births attended by skilled health staff (% of total)	..	91	..
Child malnutrition, underweight (% of under age 5)	..	..	..
Child immunization, measles (% of ages 12–23 mon.)	87	91	90
HIV prevalence rate (% of ages 15–49)	..	1.5	1.5
Adult literacy, male (% of ages 15 and older)	99	100	..
Adult literacy, female (% of ages 15 and older)	99	100	..
Primary completion rate, total (% of age group)	..	110	..
Primary completion rate, female (% of age group)	..	109	..
Net primary enrollment (% of age group)	80	100	..
Net secondary enrollment (% of age group)	..	90	..
Environment			
Forests (1,000 sq. km)	0	0	..
Deforestation (average annual %, 1990–2000)		0.0	
Freshwater use (% of internal resources)			..
Carbon dioxide emissions (metric tons per capita)	4.2	4.4	..
Access to improved water source (% of total pop.)	100	100	..
Access to improved sanitation (% of urban pop.)	99	99	..
Energy use per capita (kg oil equivalent)	..	..	..
Electricity use per capita (kilowatt-hours)	..	..	..
Economy			
GDP ($ millions)	1,710	2,535	2,627
GDP growth (annual %)	–4.8	–2.1	1.3
GDP implicit price deflator (annual % growth)	5.5	2.1	2.0
Value added in agriculture (% of GDP)	7	6	..
Value added in industry (% of GDP)	20	21	..
Value added in services (% of GDP)	73	73	..
Exports of goods and services (% of GDP)	49	52	..
Imports of goods and services (% of GDP)	52	55	..
Gross capital formation (% of GDP)	19	17	..
Central government revenue (% of GDP)	..	..	43.1
Cash surplus/deficit (% of GDP)	..	..	–0.6
Technology and infrastructure			
Fixed-line and mobile subscribers (per 1,000 people)	281	679	1,016
Cost of 3-minute local call ($)	0.00	0.00	..
Personal computers (per 1,000 people)	..	104.1	..
Internet users (per 1,000 people)	..	112	371
Paved roads (% of total)	86.8	98.6	..
Aircraft departures (thousands)	1	..	..
Trade and finance			
Trade in goods (% of GDP)	53.8	49.1	51.1
Trade growth less GDP growth (avg. %, 1990–2003)			0.6
High-technology exports (% of manufactured exports)	20	16	14
Net barter terms of trade (2000 = 100)	..	..	..
Foreign direct investment ($ millions)	112	17	58
Present value of debt ($ millions)			8,025
Total debt service (% of goods and services exports)	15.1	5.7	5.2
Short-term debt ($ millions)	178	0	0
Aid per capita ($)	11	13	74

Belarus

Europe & Central Asia   **Lower middle income**

Population (millions)	10	Population growth (%)		−0.4
Surface area (1,000 sq. km)	208	National poverty rate (% pop.)		42
GNI ($ billions)	16	GNI per capita ($)		1,600

	1990	2002	2003
People			
Life expectancy at birth (years)	71	68	68
Fertility rate (births per woman)	1.9	1.3	1.3
Infant mortality rate (per 1,000 live births)	14	14	13
Under-five mortality rate (per 1,000)	17	17	17
Births attended by skilled health staff (% of total)	..	100	..
Child malnutrition, underweight (% of under age 5)	..	..	..
Child immunization, measles (% of ages 12–23 mon.)	94	99	99
HIV prevalence rate (% of ages 15–49)	..	..	..
Adult literacy, male (% of ages 15 and older)	100	100	..
Adult literacy, female (% of ages 15 and older)	99	100	..
Primary completion rate, total (% of age group)	94	99	..
Primary completion rate, female (% of age group)	97	98	..
Net primary enrollment (% of age group)	86	94	..
Net secondary enrollment (% of age group)	..	85	..
Environment			
Forests (1,000 sq. km)	68	94	..
Deforestation (average annual %, 1990–2000)		−3.2	
Freshwater use (% of internal resources)			7
Carbon dioxide emissions (metric tons per capita)	9.3	5.9	..
Access to improved water source (% of total pop.)	100	100	..
Access to improved sanitation (% of urban pop.)	..	..	..
Energy use per capita (kg oil equivalent)	3,886	2,496	..
Electricity use per capita (kilowatt-hours)	3,325	2,657	..
Economy			
GDP ($ billions)	17	15	17
GDP growth (annual %)	−1.2	5.0	6.8
GDP implicit price deflator (annual % growth)	103.6	45.0	28.7
Value added in agriculture (% of GDP)	24	12	10
Value added in industry (% of GDP)	47	37	30
Value added in services (% of GDP)	29	51	60
Exports of goods and services (% of GDP)	46	64	66
Imports of goods and services (% of GDP)	44	67	70
Gross capital formation (% of GDP)	27	22	24
Central government revenue (% of GDP)	31.5	26.6	..
Cash surplus/deficit (% of GDP)	−4.8	1.1	..
Technology and infrastructure			
Fixed-line and mobile subscribers (per 1,000 people)	154	346	424
Cost of 3-minute local call ($)	..	0.01	..
Personal computers (per 1,000 people)	..	..	..
Internet users (per 1,000 people)	..	82	141
Paved roads (% of total)	95.8	86.7	..
Aircraft departures (thousands)	..	6	6
Trade and finance			
Trade in goods (% of GDP)	..	116.8	122.7
Trade growth less GDP growth (avg. %, 1990–2003)			−2.8
High-technology exports (% of manufactured exports)	..	4	4
Net barter terms of trade (2000 = 100)	..	..	..
Foreign direct investment ($ millions)	0	247	172
Present value of debt ($ millions)			2,659
Total debt service (% of goods and services exports)	..	2.6	2.2
Short-term debt ($ billions)		2	2
Aid per capita ($)	18	4	3

Belgium

High income

Population (millions)	10	Population growth (%)		0.4
Surface area (1,000 sq. km)	31	National poverty rate (% pop.)		..
GNI ($ billions)	267	GNI per capita ($)		25,760

	1990	2002	2003
People			
Life expectancy at birth (years)	76	78	78
Fertility rate (births per woman)	1.6	1.6	1.6
Infant mortality rate (per 1,000 live births)	8	5	4
Under-five mortality rate (per 1,000)	9	6	5
Births attended by skilled health staff (% of total)	..	..	..
Child malnutrition, underweight (% of under age 5)	..	..	..
Child immunization, measles (% of ages 12–23 mon.)	85	75	75
HIV prevalence rate (% of ages 15–49)	..	0.2	0.2
Adult literacy, male (% of ages 15 and older)	..	..	..
Adult literacy, female (% of ages 15 and older)	..	..	..
Primary completion rate, total (% of age group)	..	..	..
Primary completion rate, female (% of age group)	..	..	..
Net primary enrollment (% of age group)	96	100	..
Net secondary enrollment (% of age group)	87	95	..
Environment			
Forests (1,000 sq. km)	7	7	..
Deforestation (average annual %, 1990–2000)		0.2	
Freshwater use (% of internal resources)			..
Carbon dioxide emissions (metric tons per capita)	10.1	10.0	..
Access to improved water source (% of total pop.)	..	..	..
Access to improved sanitation (% of urban pop.)	..	..	..
Energy use per capita (kg oil equivalent)	4,884	5,505	..
Electricity use per capita (kilowatt-hours)	5,817	7,592	..
Economy			
GDP ($ billions)	197	245	302
GDP growth (annual %)	3.1	0.7	1.1
GDP implicit price deflator (annual % growth)	2.8	1.7	1.7
Value added in agriculture (% of GDP)	2	1	1
Value added in industry (% of GDP)	33	27	26
Value added in services (% of GDP)	65	72	72
Exports of goods and services (% of GDP)	71	84	82
Imports of goods and services (% of GDP)	69	80	80
Gross capital formation (% of GDP)	22	20	20
Central government revenue (% of GDP)	..	43.1	..
Cash surplus/deficit (% of GDP)	..	0.0	..
Technology and infrastructure			
Fixed-line and mobile subscribers (per 1,000 people)	397	1,280	1,282
Cost of 3-minute local call ($)	0.18	0.14	0.17
Personal computers (per 1,000 people)	87.9	241.4	318.1
Internet users (per 1,000 people)	0	328	386
Paved roads (% of total)	81.2	78.2	..
Aircraft departures (thousands)	67	134	133
Trade and finance			
Trade in goods (% of GDP)	120.4	179.1	172.3
Trade growth less GDP growth (avg. %, 1990–2003)			2.4
High-technology exports (% of manufactured exports)	..	8	8
Net barter terms of trade (2000 = 100)	..	101	101
Foreign direct investment ($ billions)	8	16	32
Present value of debt ($ millions)			..
Total debt service (% of goods and services exports)	..	..	..
Short-term debt ($ millions)	..	..	..
Aid per capita ($)	..	..	..

Belize

Latin America & Caribbean   **Upper middle income**

Population (thousands)	274	Population growth (%)	3.2
Surface area (1,000 sq. km)	23	National poverty rate (% pop.)	..
GNI ($ millions)	923	GNI per capita ($)	3,370

	1990	2002	2003
People			
Life expectancy at birth (years)	73	71	71
Fertility rate (births per woman)	4.5	3.2	3.1
Infant mortality rate (per 1,000 live births)	39	*34*	33
Under-five mortality rate (per 1,000)	49	*41*	39
Births attended by skilled health staff (% of total)	77	83	..
Child malnutrition, underweight (% of under age 5)	6	..	..
Child immunization, measles (% of ages 12–23 mon.)	86	89	96
HIV prevalence rate (% of ages 15–49)	..	2.1	2.4
Adult literacy, male (% of ages 15 and older)	90	77	..
Adult literacy, female (% of ages 15 and older)	88	77	..
Primary completion rate, total (% of age group)	*92*	89	..
Primary completion rate, female (% of age group)	*92*	92	..
Net primary enrollment (% of age group)	94	99	..
Net secondary enrollment (% of age group)	31	68	..
Environment			
Forests (1,000 sq. km)	17	*13*	..
Deforestation (average annual %, 1990–2000)		2.3	
Freshwater use (% of internal resources)			1
Carbon dioxide emissions (metric tons per capita)	1.6	*3.1*	..
Access to improved water source (% of total pop.)	..	91	..
Access to improved sanitation (% of urban pop.)	..	71	..
Energy use per capita (kg oil equivalent)	..	..	..
Electricity use per capita (kilowatt-hours)	..	..	..
Economy			
GDP ($ millions)	413	926	988
GDP growth (annual %)	10.6	4.2	9.4
GDP implicit price deflator (annual % growth)	2.8	2.4	−2.4
Value added in agriculture (% of GDP)	20	15	..
Value added in industry (% of GDP)	22	20	..
Value added in services (% of GDP)	58	65	..
Exports of goods and services (% of GDP)	62	53	54
Imports of goods and services (% of GDP)	60	67	67
Gross capital formation (% of GDP)	27	24	21
Central government revenue (% of GDP)	25.4	*21.4*	..
Cash surplus/deficit (% of GDP)	−0.6	−2.9	..
Technology and infrastructure			
Fixed-line and mobile subscribers (per 1,000 people)	92	328	317
Cost of 3-minute local call ($)	*0.08*	0.15	0.15
Personal computers (per 1,000 people)	..	138.3	..
Internet users (per 1,000 people)	..	109	..
Paved roads (% of total)	..	*17.0*	..
Aircraft departures (thousands)	..	..	..
Trade and finance			
Trade in goods (% of GDP)	77.2	74.9	76.6
Trade growth less GDP growth (avg. %, 1990–2003)			0.5
High-technology exports (% of manufactured exports)	..	0	..
Net barter terms of trade (2000 = 100)	..	..	..
Foreign direct investment ($ millions)	17	25	40
Present value of debt ($ millions)			1,240
Total debt service (% of goods and services exports)	7.5	36.7	24.5
Short-term debt ($ millions)	6	45	65
Aid per capita ($)	161	84	44

Benin

Sub-Saharan Africa — **Low income**

Population (millions)	7	Population growth (%)	2.5
Surface area (1,000sq. km)	113	National poverty rate (% pop.)	29
GNI ($ millions)	2,972	GNI per capita ($)	440

	1990	2002	2003
People			
Life expectancy at birth (years)	52	53	53
Fertility rate (births per woman)	6.6	5.3	5.2
Infant mortality rate (per 1,000 live births)	111	95	91
Under-five mortality rate (per 1,000)	185	160	154
Births attended by skilled health staff (% of total)	..	66	..
Child malnutrition, underweight (% of under age 5)	..	23	..
Child immunization, measles (% of ages 12–23 mon.)	79	78	83
HIV prevalence rate (% of ages 15–49)	..	1.9	1.9
Adult literacy, male (% of ages 15 and older)	38	55	..
Adult literacy, female (% of ages 15 and older)	15	26	..
Primary completion rate, total (% of age group)	22	51	..
Primary completion rate, female (% of age group)	14	37	..
Net primary enrollment (% of age group)	45	71	..
Net secondary enrollment (% of age group)	..	20	..
Environment			
Forests (1,000 sq. km)	33	27	..
Deforestation (average annual %, 1990–2000)		2.3	
Freshwater use (% of internal resources)			1
Carbon dioxide emissions (metric tons per capita)	0.1	0.3	..
Access to improved water source (% of total pop.)	60	68	..
Access to improved sanitation (% of urban pop.)	31	58	..
Energy use per capita (kg oil equivalent)	356	340	..
Electricity use per capita (kilowatt-hours)	37	76	..
Economy			
GDP ($ millions)	1,845	2,695	3,476
GDP growth (annual %)	3.2	6.0	4.8
GDP implicit price deflator (annual % growth)	1.6	1.9	2.6
Value added in agriculture (% of GDP)	36	36	36
Value added in industry (% of GDP)	13	14	14
Value added in services (% of GDP)	51	50	50
Exports of goods and services (% of GDP)	14	14	14
Imports of goods and services (% of GDP)	26	27	27
Gross capital formation (% of GDP)	14	18	18
Central government revenue (% of GDP)	..	..	..
Cash surplus/deficit (% of GDP)	..	..	..
Technology and infrastructure			
Fixed-line and mobile subscribers (per 1,000 people)	3	41	43
Cost of 3-minute local call ($)	0.23	0.28	0.11
Personal computers (per 1,000 people)	..	2.2	3.7
Internet users (per 1,000 people)	..	7	10
Paved roads (% of total)	20.0	20.0	..
Aircraft departures (thousands)	1	1	..
Trade and finance			
Trade in goods (% of GDP)	30.0	41.8	37.4
Trade growth less GDP growth (avg. %, 1990–2003)			–2.6
High-technology exports (% of manufactured exports)	..	2	..
Net barter terms of trade (2000 = 100)	107	102	..
Foreign direct investment ($ millions)	62	41	51
Present value of debt ($ millions)			797
Total debt service (% of goods and services exports)	8.2	7.9	..
Short-term debt ($ millions)	55	74	29
Aid per capita ($)	57	33	44

Bermuda

High income

Population (thousands)	64	Population growth (%)	0.3
Surface area (sq. km)	50	National poverty rate (% pop.)	..
GNI ($ millions)	..	GNI per capita ($)	..

	1990	2002	2003
People			
Life expectancy at birth (years)	..	77	..
Fertility rate (births per woman)	..	1.9	..
Infant mortality rate (per 1,000 live births)	8	..	..
Under-five mortality rate (per 1,000)	..	..	..
Births attended by skilled health staff (% of total)	..	..	..
Child malnutrition, underweight (% of under age 5)	..	..	..
Child immunization, measles (% of ages 12–23 mon.)	..	..	..
HIV prevalence rate (% of ages 15–49)	..	..	..
Adult literacy, male (% of ages 15 and older)	..	..	..
Adult literacy, female (% of ages 15 and older)	..	..	..
Primary completion rate, total (% of age group)	..	106	..
Primary completion rate, female (% of age group)	..	..	..
Net primary enrollment (% of age group)	..	100	..
Net secondary enrollment (% of age group)	..	86	..
Environment			
Forests (1,000 sq. km)	..	..	..
Deforestation (average annual %, 1990–2000)		..	
Freshwater use (% of internal resources)			..
Carbon dioxide emissions (metric tons per capita)	9.8	7.2	..
Access to improved water source (% of total pop.)	..	..	..
Access to improved sanitation (% of urban pop.)	..	..	..
Energy use per capita (kg oil equivalent)	..	..	..
Electricity use per capita (kilowatt-hours)	..	..	..
Economy			
GDP ($ millions)	1,592	2,253	..
GDP growth (annual %)	..	..	..
GDP implicit price deflator (annual % growth)	6.0	2.1	..
Value added in agriculture (% of GDP)	..	..	..
Value added in industry (% of GDP)	..	..	..
Value added in services (% of GDP)	..	..	..
Exports of goods and services (% of GDP)	..	..	..
Imports of goods and services (% of GDP)	..	..	..
Gross capital formation (% of GDP)	..	..	..
Central government revenue (% of GDP)	..	..	..
Cash surplus/deficit (% of GDP)	..	..	..
Technology and infrastructure			
Fixed-line and mobile subscribers (per 1,000 people)	635	1,323	..
Cost of 3-minute local call ($)	0.15	0.20	0.20
Personal computers (per 1,000 people)	..	523.1	..
Internet users (per 1,000 people)	..	464	..
Paved roads (% of total)	..	..	..
Aircraft departures (thousands)	..	..	..
Trade and finance			
Trade in goods (% of GDP)	41.1	30.0	..
Trade growth less GDP growth (avg. %, 1990–2003)		..	
High-technology exports (% of manufactured exports)	..	..	..
Net barter terms of trade (2000 = 100)	..	..	..
Foreign direct investment ($ millions)	..	..	..
Present value of debt ($ millions)			..
Total debt service (% of goods and services exports)	..	..	..
Short-term debt ($ millions)	..	..	..
Aid per capita ($)	697	0	0

Bhutan

South Asia   **Low income**

Population (thousands)	874	Population growth (%)	2.6
Surface area (1,000 sq. km)	47	National poverty rate (% pop.)	..
GNI ($ millions)	554	GNI per capita ($)	630

	1990	2002	2003
People			
Life expectancy at birth (years)	*58*	63	64
Fertility rate (births per woman)	*5.8*	5.1	5.1
Infant mortality rate (per 1,000 live births)	107	*77*	70
Under-five mortality rate (per 1,000)	166	*100*	85
Births attended by skilled health staff (% of total)	..	24	..
Child malnutrition, underweight (% of under age 5)	*38*	19	..
Child immunization, measles (% of ages 12–23 mon.)	93	78	88
HIV prevalence rate (% of ages 15–49)	..	..	..
Adult literacy, male (% of ages 15 and older)	..	..	..
Adult literacy, female (% of ages 15 and older)	..	..	..
Primary completion rate, total (% of age group)	*18*	45	46
Primary completion rate, female (% of age group)	..	44	46
Net primary enrollment (% of age group)	..	..	..
Net secondary enrollment (% of age group)	..	..	..
Environment			
Forests (1,000 sq. km)	30	*30*	..
Deforestation (average annual %, 1990–2000)		*0.0*	
Freshwater use (% of internal resources)			0
Carbon dioxide emissions (metric tons per capita)	0.2	*0.5*	..
Access to improved water source (% of total pop.)	..	62	..
Access to improved sanitation (% of urban pop.)	..	65	..
Energy use per capita (kg oil equivalent)	..	..	..
Electricity use per capita (kilowatt-hours)	..	..	..
Economy			
GDP ($ millions)	285	603	697
GDP growth (annual %)	7.7	6.7	6.7
GDP implicit price deflator (annual % growth)	5.6	7.9	7.6
Value added in agriculture (% of GDP)	43	34	33
Value added in industry (% of GDP)	25	39	39
Value added in services (% of GDP)	32	27	27
Exports of goods and services (% of GDP)	28	22	..
Imports of goods and services (% of GDP)	32	43	..
Gross capital formation (% of GDP)	32	53	..
Central government revenue (% of GDP)	17.9	17.3	15.2
Cash surplus/deficit (% of GDP)	–6.1	–3.3	–7.4
Technology and infrastructure			
Fixed-line and mobile subscribers (per 1,000 people)	4	28	45
Cost of 3-minute local call ($)	*0.04*	0.02	0.02
Personal computers (per 1,000 people)	..	14.5	13.6
Internet users (per 1,000 people)	..	14	20
Paved roads (% of total)	77.1	*60.7*	..
Aircraft departures (thousands)	1	2	2
Trade and finance			
Trade in goods (% of GDP)	53.0	45.2	45.9
Trade growth less GDP growth (avg. %, 1990–2003)			..
High-technology exports (% of manufactured exports)	..	0	..
Net barter terms of trade (2000 = 100)	..	..	..
Foreign direct investment ($ millions)	2	0	0
Present value of debt ($ millions)			394
Total debt service (% of goods and services exports)	5.5	4.6	..
Short-term debt ($ millions)	3	1	7
Aid per capita ($)	78	86	88

Bolivia

Latin America & Caribbean | **Lower middle income**

Population (millions)	9	Population growth (%)	1.9
Surface area (1,000 sq. km)	1,099	National poverty rate (% pop.)	63
GNI ($ millions)	7,924	GNI per capita ($)	900

	1990	2002	2003
People			
Life expectancy at birth (years)	58	64	64
Fertility rate (births per woman)	4.8	3.8	3.7
Infant mortality rate (per 1,000 live births)	85	59	53
Under-five mortality rate (per 1,000)	120	75	66
Births attended by skilled health staff (% of total)	43	65	..
Child malnutrition, underweight (% of under age 5)	11	8	..
Child immunization, measles (% of ages 12–23 mon.)	53	64	64
HIV prevalence rate (% of ages 15–49)	..	0.1	0.1
Adult literacy, male (% of ages 15 and older)	87	93	..
Adult literacy, female (% of ages 15 and older)	70	81	..
Primary completion rate, total (% of age group)	71	102	101
Primary completion rate, female (% of age group)	64	99	99
Net primary enrollment (% of age group)	91	95	..
Net secondary enrollment (% of age group)	29	71	..
Environment			
Forests (1,000 sq. km)	547	531	..
Deforestation (average annual %, 1990–2000)		0.3	
Freshwater use (% of internal resources)			0
Carbon dioxide emissions (metric tons per capita)	0.8	1.3	..
Access to improved water source (% of total pop.)	72	85	..
Access to improved sanitation (% of urban pop.)	49	58	..
Energy use per capita (kg oil equivalent)	416	499	..
Electricity use per capita (kilowatt-hours)	270	419	..
Economy			
GDP ($ millions)	4,868	7,801	7,867
GDP growth (annual %)	4.6	2.8	2.5
GDP implicit price deflator (annual % growth)	16.3	2.7	5.1
Value added in agriculture (% of GDP)	17	15	15
Value added in industry (% of GDP)	35	30	30
Value added in services (% of GDP)	48	56	55
Exports of goods and services (% of GDP)	23	22	24
Imports of goods and services (% of GDP)	24	27	25
Gross capital formation (% of GDP)	13	15	11
Central government revenue (% of GDP)	..	18.6	19.3
Cash surplus/deficit (% of GDP)	..	–8.8	–7.8
Technology and infrastructure			
Fixed-line and mobile subscribers (per 1,000 people)	28	172	224
Cost of 3-minute local call ($)	..	0.09	..
Personal computers (per 1,000 people)	2.2	22.8	..
Internet users (per 1,000 people)	..	32	..
Paved roads (% of total)	4.3	6.6	..
Aircraft departures (thousands)	16	21	29
Trade and finance			
Trade in goods (% of GDP)	33.1	39.3	40.5
Trade growth less GDP growth (avg. %, 1990–2003)			1.3
High-technology exports (% of manufactured exports)	7	7	8
Net barter terms of trade (2000 = 100)	102	98	..
Foreign direct investment ($ millions)	27	677	167
Present value of debt ($ millions)			2,896
Total debt service (% of goods and services exports)	38.6	27.5	20.9
Short-term debt ($ millions)	154	370	116
Aid per capita ($)	82	79	105

Bosnia and Herzegovina

Europe & Central Asia			Lower middle income	

Population (millions)	4	Population growth (%)	0.7
Surface area (1,000 sq. km)	51	National poverty rate (% pop.)	20
GNI ($ millions)	6,352	GNI per capita ($)	1,530

	1990	2002	2003
People			
Life expectancy at birth (years)	71	74	74
Fertility rate (births per woman)	1.7	1.3	1.3
Infant mortality rate (per 1,000 live births)	18	15	14
Under-five mortality rate (per 1,000)	22	18	17
Births attended by skilled health staff (% of total)	97	100	..
Child malnutrition, underweight (% of under age 5)	..	4	..
Child immunization, measles (% of ages 12–23 mon.)	52	89	84
HIV prevalence rate (% of ages 15–49)	..	..	0.1
Adult literacy, male (% of ages 15 and older)	..	98	..
Adult literacy, female (% of ages 15 and older)	..	91	..
Primary completion rate, total (% of age group)	..	..	..
Primary completion rate, female (% of age group)	..	..	..
Net primary enrollment (% of age group)	..	..	..
Net secondary enrollment (% of age group)	..	..	..
Environment			
Forests (1,000 sq. km)	23	23	..
Deforestation (average annual %, 1990–2000)		0.0	
Freshwater use (% of internal resources)			3
Carbon dioxide emissions (metric tons per capita)	..	4.8	..
Access to improved water source (% of total pop.)	98	98	..
Access to improved sanitation (% of urban pop.)	99	99	..
Energy use per capita (kg oil equivalent)	..	1,052	..
Electricity use per capita (kilowatt-hours)	..	1,633	..
Economy			
GDP ($ millions)	..	5,599	6,973
GDP growth (annual %)	..	3.9	2.7
GDP implicit price deflator (annual % growth)	..	2.1	1.2
Value added in agriculture (% of GDP)	..	18	15
Value added in industry (% of GDP)	..	37	32
Value added in services (% of GDP)	..	45	53
Exports of goods and services (% of GDP)	..	25	25
Imports of goods and services (% of GDP)	..	61	59
Gross capital formation (% of GDP)	..	20	20
Central government revenue (% of GDP)	..	..	..
Cash surplus/deficit (% of GDP)	..	..	..
Technology and infrastructure			
Fixed-line and mobile subscribers (per 1,000 people)	140	433	519
Cost of 3-minute local call ($)	..	0.03	0.02
Personal computers (per 1,000 people)	..	..	..
Internet users (per 1,000 people)	..	26	..
Paved roads (% of total)	54.0	52.3	..
Aircraft departures (thousands)	..	4	5
Trade and finance			
Trade in goods (% of GDP)	..	88.3	83.7
Trade growth less GDP growth (avg. %, 1990–2003)			–3.7
High-technology exports (% of manufactured exports)	..	..	..
Net barter terms of trade (2000 = 100)		..	..
Foreign direct investment ($ millions)	0	268	382
Present value of debt ($ millions)			2,247
Total debt service (% of goods and services exports)	..	6.1	5.6
Short-term debt ($ billions)	..	0	0
Aid per capita ($)	..	137	130

Botswana

Sub-Saharan Africa   **Upper middle income**

Population (millions)	2	Population growth (%)		0.6
Surface area (1,000 sq. km)	582	National poverty rate (% pop.)		..
GNI ($ millions)	6,075	GNI per capita ($)		3,530

	1990	2002	2003
People			
Life expectancy at birth (years)	57	38	38
Fertility rate (births per woman)	5.1	3.8	3.7
Infant mortality rate (per 1,000 live births)	45	74	82
Under-five mortality rate (per 1,000)	58	101	112
Births attended by skilled health staff (% of total)	78	99	..
Child malnutrition, underweight (% of under age 5)	..	13	..
Child immunization, measles (% of ages 12–23 mon.)	87	90	90
HIV prevalence rate (% of ages 15–49)	..	38.0	37.3
Adult literacy, male (% of ages 15 and older)	66	76	..
Adult literacy, female (% of ages 15 and older)	70	82	..
Primary completion rate, total (% of age group)	91	91	..
Primary completion rate, female (% of age group)	99	96	..
Net primary enrollment (% of age group)	85	81	..
Net secondary enrollment (% of age group)	29	54	..
Environment			
Forests (1,000 sq. km)	136	124	..
Deforestation (average annual %, 1990–2000)		0.9	
Freshwater use (% of internal resources)			3
Carbon dioxide emissions (metric tons per capita)	1.7	2.3	..
Access to improved water source (% of total pop.)	93	95	..
Access to improved sanitation (% of urban pop.)	61	57	..
Energy use per capita (kg oil equivalent)	..	..	..
Electricity use per capita (kilowatt-hours)	..	..	..
Economy			
GDP ($ millions)	3,791	5,394	7,530
GDP growth (annual %)	6.8	4.4	5.4
GDP implicit price deflator (annual % growth)	6.3	7.9	3.6
Value added in agriculture (% of GDP)	5	2	2
Value added in industry (% of GDP)	57	47	45
Value added in services (% of GDP)	39	50	52
Exports of goods and services (% of GDP)	55	46	44
Imports of goods and services (% of GDP)	50	36	34
Gross capital formation (% of GDP)	37	28	27
Central government revenue (% of GDP)	50.8	..	..
Cash surplus/deficit (% of GDP)	19.1	..	..
Technology and infrastructure			
Fixed-line and mobile subscribers (per 1,000 people)	21	328	372
Cost of 3-minute local call ($)	0.05	0.02	0.02
Personal computers (per 1,000 people)	..	40.7	..
Internet users (per 1,000 people)	0	35	..
Paved roads (% of total)	32.0	55.0	..
Aircraft departures (thousands)	6	7	8
Trade and finance			
Trade in goods (% of GDP)	98.4	77.3	70.6
Trade growth less GDP growth (avg. %, 1990–2003)			–1.7
High-technology exports (% of manufactured exports)	..	0	..
Net barter terms of trade (2000 = 100)	98	101	..
Foreign direct investment ($ millions)	96	403	86
Present value of debt ($ millions)			438
Total debt service (% of goods and services exports)	4.3	2.0	1.3
Short-term debt ($ millions)	6	16	29
Aid per capita ($)	115	22	17

Brazil

Latin America & Caribbean		Lower middle income	
Population (millions)	177	Population growth (%)	1.2
Surface area (1,000 sq. km)	8,515	National poverty rate (% pop.)	22
GNI ($ billions)	480	GNI per capita ($)	2,720

	1990	2002	2003
People			
Life expectancy at birth (years)	66	69	69
Fertility rate (births per woman)	2.7	2.1	2.1
Infant mortality rate (per 1,000 live births)	50	35	33
Under-five mortality rate (per 1,000)	60	39	35
Births attended by skilled health staff (% of total)	72	..	..
Child malnutrition, underweight (% of under age 5)	7	..	..
Child immunization, measles (% of ages 12–23 mon.)	78	99	99
HIV prevalence rate (% of ages 15–49)	..	0.6	0.7
Adult literacy, male (% of ages 15 and older)	83	86	..
Adult literacy, female (% of ages 15 and older)	81	87	..
Primary completion rate, total (% of age group)	97	113	112
Primary completion rate, female (% of age group)	..	114	..
Net primary enrollment (% of age group)	86	97	..
Net secondary enrollment (% of age group)	15	72	..
Environment			
Forests (1,000 sq. km)	5,670	5,439	..
Deforestation (average annual %, 1990–2000)		0.4	
Freshwater use (% of internal resources)			1
Carbon dioxide emissions (metric tons per capita)	1.4	1.8	..
Access to improved water source (% of total pop.)	83	89	..
Access to improved sanitation (% of urban pop.)	82	83	..
Energy use per capita (kg oil equivalent)	902	1,093	..
Electricity use per capita (kilowatt-hours)	1,425	1,776	..
Economy			
GDP ($ billions)	462	461	492
GDP growth (annual %)	–4.3	1.9	–0.2
GDP implicit price deflator (annual % growth)	2,509.5	10.2	12.8
Value added in agriculture (% of GDP)	8	6	6
Value added in industry (% of GDP)	39	21	19
Value added in services (% of GDP)	53	74	75
Exports of goods and services (% of GDP)	8	15	17
Imports of goods and services (% of GDP)	7	13	13
Gross capital formation (% of GDP)	20	20	18
Central government revenue (% of GDP)	22.8	24.2	..
Cash surplus/deficit (% of GDP)	–3.4	–0.9	..
Technology and infrastructure			
Fixed-line and mobile subscribers (per 1,000 people)	65	424	486
Cost of 3-minute local call ($)	..	0.03	..
Personal computers (per 1,000 people)	3.1	74.8	..
Internet users (per 1,000 people)	0	82	..
Paved roads (% of total)	9.7	5.5	..
Aircraft departures (thousands)	416	628	487
Trade and finance			
Trade in goods (% of GDP)	11.7	23.9	25.1
Trade growth less GDP growth (avg. %, 1990–2003)			4.7
High-technology exports (% of manufactured exports)	7	17	12
Net barter terms of trade (2000 = 100)	66	97	..
Foreign direct investment ($ billions)	1	17	10
Present value of debt ($ billions)			254
Total debt service (% of goods and services exports)	22.2	68.9	63.8
Short-term debt ($ billions)	24	23	20
Aid per capita ($)	1	2	2

Brunei

High income

Population (thousands)	356	Population growth (%)	1.6
Surface area (1,000 sq. km)	6	National poverty rate (% pop.)	..
GNI ($ millions)	..	GNI per capita ($)	..

	1990	2002	2003
People			
Life expectancy at birth (years)	74	77	77
Fertility rate (births per woman)	3.2	2.5	2.5
Infant mortality rate (per 1,000 live births)	10	6	5
Under-five mortality rate (per 1,000)	11	7	6
Births attended by skilled health staff (% of total)	..	99	..
Child malnutrition, underweight (% of under age 5)	..	..	..
Child immunization, measles (% of ages 12–23 mon.)	99	99	99
HIV prevalence rate (% of ages 15–49)	..	0.1	0.1
Adult literacy, male (% of ages 15 and older)	91	..	..
Adult literacy, female (% of ages 15 and older)	79	..	..
Primary completion rate, total (% of age group)	98	105	..
Primary completion rate, female (% of age group)	..	101	..
Net primary enrollment (% of age group)	90	..	..
Net secondary enrollment (% of age group)	..	..	..
Environment			
Forests (1,000 sq. km)	5	4	..
Deforestation (average annual %, 1990–2000)		0.2	
Freshwater use (% of internal resources)			..
Carbon dioxide emissions (metric tons per capita)	22.6	14.2	..
Access to improved water source (% of total pop.)	..	..	..
Access to improved sanitation (% of urban pop.)	..	..	..
Energy use per capita (kg oil equivalent)	5,677	6,149	..
Electricity use per capita (kilowatt-hours)	3,934	6,563	..
Economy			
GDP ($ millions)	..	..	..
GDP growth (annual %)	..	..	..
GDP implicit price deflator (annual % growth)	..	..	..
Value added in agriculture (% of GDP)	..	..	..
Value added in industry (% of GDP)	..	..	..
Value added in services (% of GDP)	..	..	..
Exports of goods and services (% of GDP)	..	..	..
Imports of goods and services (% of GDP)	..	..	..
Gross capital formation (% of GDP)	..	..	..
Central government revenue (% of GDP)	..	..	..
Cash surplus/deficit (% of GDP)	..	..	..
Technology and infrastructure			
Fixed-line and mobile subscribers (per 1,000 people)	143	659	..
Cost of 3-minute local call ($)	0.00	0.00	..
Personal computers (per 1,000 people)	11.2	76.7	..
Internet users (per 1,000 people)	..	90	..
Paved roads (% of total)	31.4	100.0	..
Aircraft departures (thousands)	4	12	12
Trade and finance			
Trade in goods (% of GDP)	..	..	..
Trade growth less GDP growth (avg. %, 1990–2003)			..
High-technology exports (% of manufactured exports)	..	0	0
Net barter terms of trade (2000 = 100)	..	..	..
Foreign direct investment ($ millions)	..	..	..
Present value of debt ($ millions)			..
Total debt service (% of goods and services exports)	..	..	..
Short-term debt ($ millions)	..	..	..
Aid per capita ($)	15	–5	1

Bulgaria

Europe & Central Asia		Lower middle income

Population (millions)	8	Population growth (%)	–0.6
Surface area (1,000 sq. km)	111	National poverty rate (% pop.)	13
GNI ($ billions)	17	GNI per capita ($)	2,130

	1990	2002	2003
People			
Life expectancy at birth (years)	72	72	72
Fertility rate (births per woman)	1.8	1.2	1.2
Infant mortality rate (per 1,000 live births)	15	13	12
Under-five mortality rate (per 1,000)	19	17	..
Births attended by skilled health staff (% of total)	..	..	..
Child malnutrition, underweight (% of under age 5)	..	..	..
Child immunization, measles (% of ages 12–23 mon.)	99	92	96
HIV prevalence rate (% of ages 15–49)	..	..	0.1
Adult literacy, male (% of ages 15 and older)	98	99	..
Adult literacy, female (% of ages 15 and older)	96	98	..
Primary completion rate, total (% of age group)	90	96	97
Primary completion rate, female (% of age group)	92	94	96
Net primary enrollment (% of age group)	86	90	..
Net secondary enrollment (% of age group)	63	87	..
Environment			
Forests (1,000 sq. km)	35	37	..
Deforestation (average annual %, 1990–2000)		–0.6	
Freshwater use (% of internal resources)			66
Carbon dioxide emissions (metric tons per capita)	8.6	5.3	..
Access to improved water source (% of total pop.)	100	100	..
Access to improved sanitation (% of urban pop.)	100	100	..
Energy use per capita (kg oil equivalent)	3,306	2,417	..
Electricity use per capita (kilowatt-hours)	4,046	3,060	..
Economy			
GDP ($ billions)	21	16	20
GDP growth (annual %)	–9.1	4.9	4.3
GDP implicit price deflator (annual % growth)	26.2	3.8	2.1
Value added in agriculture (% of GDP)	17	12	12
Value added in industry (% of GDP)	49	30	31
Value added in services (% of GDP)	34	58	58
Exports of goods and services (% of GDP)	33	53	53
Imports of goods and services (% of GDP)	37	60	63
Gross capital formation (% of GDP)	26	20	22
Central government revenue (% of GDP)	47.1	33.0	35.4
Cash surplus/deficit (% of GDP)	–5.0	–0.5	0.2
Technology and infrastructure			
Fixed-line and mobile subscribers (per 1,000 people)	242	701	847
Cost of 3-minute local call ($)	0.09	0.02	0.03
Personal computers (per 1,000 people)	10.5	51.9	..
Internet users (per 1,000 people)		81	206
Paved roads (% of total)	91.6	92.0	..
Aircraft departures (thousands)	37	2	1
Trade and finance			
Trade in goods (% of GDP)	48.9	88.2	92.8
Trade growth less GDP growth (avg. %, 1990–2003)			6.6
High-technology exports (% of manufactured exports)		4	4
Net barter terms of trade (2000 = 100)	100	..	..
Foreign direct investment ($ millions)	0	905	1,419
Present value of debt ($ billions)			14
Total debt service (% of goods and services exports)	6.6	16.7	10.5
Short-term debt ($ millions)	1,567	1,839	2,663
Aid per capita ($)	2	42	53

Burkina Faso

Sub-Saharan Africa		Low income

Population (millions)	12	Population growth (%)	2.3
Surface area (1,000 sq. km)	274	National poverty rate (% pop.)	45
GNI ($ millions)	3,587	GNI per capita ($)	300

	1990	2002	2003
People			
Life expectancy at birth (years)	45	43	43
Fertility rate (births per woman)	7.0	6.3	6.2
Infant mortality rate (per 1,000 live births)	118	107	107
Under-five mortality rate (per 1,000)	210	207	207
Births attended by skilled health staff (% of total)	..	31	..
Child malnutrition, underweight (% of under age 5)	..	34	38
Child immunization, measles (% of ages 12–23 mon.)	79	64	76
HIV prevalence rate (% of ages 15–49)	..	4.2	1.8
Adult literacy, male (% of ages 15 and older)	25	..	..
Adult literacy, female (% of ages 15 and older)	8	..	..
Primary completion rate, total (% of age group)	19	29	..
Primary completion rate, female (% of age group)	14	24	..
Net primary enrollment (% of age group)	26	36	..
Net secondary enrollment (% of age group)	..	9	..
Environment			
Forests (1,000 sq. km)	72	71	..
Deforestation (average annual %, 1990–2000)		0.2	
Freshwater use (% of internal resources)			3
Carbon dioxide emissions (metric tons per capita)	0.1	0.1	..
Access to improved water source (% of total pop.)	39	51	..
Access to improved sanitation (% of urban pop.)	47	45	..
Energy use per capita (kg oil equivalent)	..	..	..
Electricity use per capita (kilowatt-hours)	..	..	..
Economy			
GDP ($ millions)	3,120	3,203	4,182
GDP growth (annual %)	–1.5	4.4	6.5
GDP implicit price deflator (annual % growth)	1.4	3.7	2.2
Value added in agriculture (% of GDP)	28	31	31
Value added in industry (% of GDP)	20	18	19
Value added in services (% of GDP)	52	51	50
Exports of goods and services (% of GDP)	11	8	9
Imports of goods and services (% of GDP)	24	22	23
Gross capital formation (% of GDP)	18	18	19
Central government revenue (% of GDP)	..	..	..
Cash surplus/deficit (% of GDP)	..	..	..
Technology and infrastructure			
Fixed-line and mobile subscribers (per 1,000 people)	2	13	24
Cost of 3-minute local call ($)	..	0.10	..
Personal computers (per 1,000 people)	0.1	1.6	2.1
Internet users (per 1,000 people)	..	2	4
Paved roads (% of total)	16.6	16.0	..
Aircraft departures (thousands)	2	1	1
Trade and finance			
Trade in goods (% of GDP)	22.0	30.5	28.0
Trade growth less GDP growth (avg. %, 1990–2003)			–2.0
High-technology exports (% of manufactured exports)	..	2	..
Net barter terms of trade (2000 = 100)	119	110	..
Foreign direct investment ($ millions)	0	9	11
Present value of debt ($ millions)			662
Total debt service (% of goods and services exports)	6.8	14.9	11.2
Short-term debt ($ millions)	84	55	68
Aid per capita ($)	37	40	37

Burundi

Sub-Saharan Africa		Low income

Population (millions)	7	Population growth (%)	1.9
Surface area (1,000 sq. km)	28	National poverty rate (% pop.)	..
GNI ($ millions)	628	GNI per capita ($)	90

	1990	2002	2003
People			
Life expectancy at birth (years)	44	42	42
Fertility rate (births per woman)	6.8	5.8	5.7
Infant mortality rate (per 1,000 live births)	114	114	114
Under-five mortality rate (per 1,000)	190	190	190
Births attended by skilled health staff (% of total)	..	25	..
Child malnutrition, underweight (% of under age 5)	..	45	..
Child immunization, measles (% of ages 12–23 mon.)	74	75	75
HIV prevalence rate (% of ages 15–49)	..	6.2	6.0
Adult literacy, male (% of ages 15 and older)	48	58	..
Adult literacy, female (% of ages 15 and older)	27	44	..
Primary completion rate, total (% of age group)	47	31	..
Primary completion rate, female (% of age group)	43	26	..
Net primary enrollment (% of age group)	53	57	..
Net secondary enrollment (% of age group)	..	9	..
Environment			
Forests (1,000 sq. km)	2	1	..
Deforestation (average annual %, 1990–2000)		9.0	
Freshwater use (% of internal resources)			3
Carbon dioxide emissions (metric tons per capita)	0.0	0.0	..
Access to improved water source (% of total pop.)	69	79	..
Access to improved sanitation (% of urban pop.)	42	47	..
Energy use per capita (kg oil equivalent)	..	..	..
Electricity use per capita (kilowatt-hours)	..	..	..
Economy			
GDP ($ millions)	1,132	628	595
GDP growth (annual %)	3.5	4.5	–1.2
GDP implicit price deflator (annual % growth)	6.0	–2.2	11.6
Value added in agriculture (% of GDP)	56	49	49
Value added in industry (% of GDP)	19	19	19
Value added in services (% of GDP)	25	31	32
Exports of goods and services (% of GDP)	8	8	7
Imports of goods and services (% of GDP)	28	22	18
Gross capital formation (% of GDP)	15	9	15
Central government revenue (% of GDP)	18.2	17.9	..
Cash surplus/deficit (% of GDP)	–2.3	..	..
Technology and infrastructure			
Fixed-line and mobile subscribers (per 1,000 people)	1	11	12
Cost of 3-minute local call ($)	0.08	0.02	0.07
Personal computers (per 1,000 people)	..	0.7	1.8
Internet users (per 1,000 people)	0	1	2
Paved roads (% of total)	..	..	..
Aircraft departures (thousands)	1	1	..
Trade and finance			
Trade in goods (% of GDP)	27.0	25.3	32.7
Trade growth less GDP growth (avg. %, 1990–2003)			7.1
High-technology exports (% of manufactured exports)	..	22	..
Net barter terms of trade (2000 = 100)	128	82	..
Foreign direct investment ($ millions)	1	0	0
Present value of debt ($ millions)			936
Total debt service (% of goods and services exports)	43.4	61.1	65.8
Short-term debt ($ millions)	13	96	48
Aid per capita ($)	48	24	31

Cambodia

East Asia & Pacific | **Low income**

Population (millions)	13	Population growth (%)
Surface area (1,000 sq. km)	181	National poverty rate (% pop.)
GNI ($ millions)	4,088	GNI per capita ($)

	1.7
	36
	300

	1990	2002	2003
People			
Life expectancy at birth (years)	50	54	54
Fertility rate (births per woman)	5.6	3.9	3.9
Infant mortality rate (per 1,000 live births)	80	95	97
Under-five mortality rate (per 1,000)	115	135	140
Births attended by skilled health staff (% of total)	..	32	..
Child malnutrition, underweight (% of under age 5)	..	45	..
Child immunization, measles (% of ages 12–23 mon.)	34	52	65
HIV prevalence rate (% of ages 15–49)	..	2.7	2.6
Adult literacy, male (% of ages 15 and older)	78	81	..
Adult literacy, female (% of ages 15 and older)	49	59	..
Primary completion rate, total (% of age group)	..	69	81
Primary completion rate, female (% of age group)	..	64	76
Net primary enrollment (% of age group)	67	93	..
Net secondary enrollment (% of age group)	..	18	..
Environment			
Forests (1,000 sq. km)	99	93	..
Deforestation (average annual %, 1990–2000)		0.6	
Freshwater use (% of internal resources)			0
Carbon dioxide emissions (metric tons per capita)	0.0	0.0	..
Access to improved water source (% of total pop.)	..	34	..
Access to improved sanitation (% of urban pop.)	..	53	..
Energy use per capita (kg oil equivalent)	..	..	..
Electricity use per capita (kilowatt-hours)	..	..	..
Economy			
GDP ($ millions)	1,115	4,000	4,228
GDP growth (annual %)	..	5.5	5.2
GDP implicit price deflator (annual % growth)	..	2.1	2.3
Value added in agriculture (% of GDP)	..	36	34
Value added in industry (% of GDP)	..	28	30
Value added in services (% of GDP)	..	36	36
Exports of goods and services (% of GDP)	6	59	62
Imports of goods and services (% of GDP)	13	67	71
Gross capital formation (% of GDP)	8	22	22
Central government revenue (% of GDP)	..	..	..
Cash surplus/deficit (% of GDP)	..	..	..
Technology and infrastructure			
Fixed-line and mobile subscribers (per 1,000 people)	0	30	38
Cost of 3-minute local call ($)	0.00	0.03	0.03
Personal computers (per 1,000 people)	..	2.0	2.3
Internet users (per 1,000 people)	..	2	2
Paved roads (% of total)	7.5	16.2	..
Aircraft departures (thousands)	..	5	4
Trade and finance			
Trade in goods (% of GDP)	22.4	76.6	80.5
Trade growth less GDP growth (avg. %, 1990–2003)			10.7
High-technology exports (% of manufactured exports)	..	..	..
Net barter terms of trade (2000 = 100)	..	..	..
Foreign direct investment ($ millions)	0	145	87
Present value of debt ($ millions)			2,683
Total debt service (% of goods and services exports)	4.0	0.9	0.9
Short-term debt ($ millions)	136	217	221
Aid per capita ($)	4	37	38

Cameroon

Population (millions)	16	Population growth (%)	2.0
Surface area (1,000 sq. km)	475	National poverty rate (% pop.)	40
GNI ($ billions)	10	GNI per capita ($)	630

	1990	2002	2003
People			
Life expectancy at birth (years)	54	48	48
Fertility rate (births per woman)	6.0	4.6	4.6
Infant mortality rate (per 1,000 live births)	85	95	95
Under-five mortality rate (per 1,000)	139	166	166
Births attended by skilled health staff (% of total)	58	60	..
Child malnutrition, underweight (% of under age 5)	15	22	..
Child immunization, measles (% of ages 12–23 mon.)	56	53	61
HIV prevalence rate (% of ages 15–49)	..	7.0	6.9
Adult literacy, male (% of ages 15 and older)	69	77	..
Adult literacy, female (% of ages 15 and older)	48	60	..
Primary completion rate, total (% of age group)	56	60	70
Primary completion rate, female (% of age group)	52	55	64
Net primary enrollment (% of age group)	74	..	..
Net secondary enrollment (% of age group)	..	..	..
Environment			
Forests (1,000 sq. km)	261	239	..
Deforestation (average annual %, 1990–2000)		0.9	
Freshwater use (% of internal resources)			0
Carbon dioxide emissions (metric tons per capita)	0.1	0.4	..
Access to improved water source (% of total pop.)	50	63	..
Access to improved sanitation (% of urban pop.)	43	63	..
Energy use per capita (kg oil equivalent)	431	417	..
Electricity use per capita (kilowatt-hours)	201	161	..
Economy			
GDP ($ billions)	11	10	12
GDP growth (annual %)	–6.1	4.2	4.7
GDP implicit price deflator (annual % growth)	1.6	4.3	0.9
Value added in agriculture (% of GDP)	25	44	44
Value added in industry (% of GDP)	29	17	17
Value added in services (% of GDP)	46	39	39
Exports of goods and services (% of GDP)	20	27	26
Imports of goods and services (% of GDP)	17	29	25
Gross capital formation (% of GDP)	18	18	17
Central government revenue (% of GDP)	15.4	..	..
Cash surplus/deficit (% of GDP)	–5.7	..	..
Technology and infrastructure			
Fixed-line and mobile subscribers (per 1,000 people)	3	50	..
Cost of 3-minute local call ($)	..	0.06	..
Personal computers (per 1,000 people)	..	5.7	..
Internet users (per 1,000 people)	..	4	..
Paved roads (% of total)	10.5	12.5	..
Aircraft departures (thousands)	7	10	10
Trade and finance			
Trade in goods (% of GDP)	30.5	37.2	36.6
Trade growth less GDP growth (avg. %, 1990–2003)			2.2
High-technology exports (% of manufactured exports)	3	1	2
Net barter terms of trade (2000 = 100)	81	100	..
Foreign direct investment ($ millions)	–113	86	215
Present value of debt ($ millions)			5,078
Total debt service (% of goods and services exports)	20.5	..	..
Short-term debt ($ millions)	960	778	345
Aid per capita ($)	38	39	55

Canada

High income

Population (milliions)	32	Population growth (%)	0.9
Surface area (1,000 sq. km)	9,971	National poverty rate (% pop.)	..
GNI ($ billions)	774	GNI per capita ($)	24,470

	1990	2002	2003
People			
Life expectancy at birth (years)	77	79	79
Fertility rate (births per woman)	1.8	1.5	1.5
Infant mortality rate (per 1,000 live births)	7	5	..
Under-five mortality rate (per 1,000)	8	7	..
Births attended by skilled health staff (% of total)	..	..	..
Child malnutrition, underweight (% of under age 5)	..	..	..
Child immunization, measles (% of ages 12–23 mon.)	89	95	95
HIV prevalence rate (% of ages 15–49)	..	0.3	0.3
Adult literacy, male (% of ages 15 and older)	..	..	..
Adult literacy, female (% of ages 15 and older)	..	..	..
Primary completion rate, total (% of age group)	..	..	..
Primary completion rate, female (% of age group)	..	..	..
Net primary enrollment (% of age group)	98	100	..
Net secondary enrollment (% of age group)	89	98	..
Environment			
Forests (1,000 sq. km)	2,446	2,446	..
Deforestation (average annual %, 1990–2000)		0.0	
Freshwater use (% of internal resources)			2
Carbon dioxide emissions (metric tons per capita)	15.4	14.2	..
Access to improved water source (% of total pop.)	100	100	..
Access to improved sanitation (% of urban pop.)	100	100	..
Energy use per capita (kg oil equivalent)	7,524	7,973	..
Electricity use per capita (kilowatt-hours)	15,042	15,613	..
Economy			
GDP ($ billions)	574	725	857
GDP growth (annual %)	0.2	3.3	2.0
GDP implicit price deflator (annual % growth)	3.2	0.9	..
Value added in agriculture (% of GDP)	3	2	..
Value added in industry (% of GDP)	32	34	..
Value added in services (% of GDP)	65	64	..
Exports of goods and services (% of GDP)	26	42	..
Imports of goods and services (% of GDP)	26	37	..
Gross capital formation (% of GDP)	21	20	..
Central government revenue (% of GDP)	21.5	20.1	20.0
Cash surplus/deficit (% of GDP)	–4.6	0.9	1.4
Technology and infrastructure			
Fixed-line and mobile subscribers (per 1,000 people)	587	1,013	1,046
Cost of 3-minute local call ($)	0.00	0.00	..
Personal computers (per 1,000 people)	107.1	487.0	..
Internet users (per 1,000 people)	4	513	..
Paved roads (% of total)	35.0	..	..
Aircraft departures (thousands)	347	1,092	1,036
Trade and finance			
Trade in goods (% of GDP)	43.7	66.2	60.4
Trade growth less GDP growth (avg. %, 1990–2003)			3.7
High-technology exports (% of manufactured exports)	14	14	14
Net barter terms of trade (2000 = 100)	97	97	104
Foreign direct investment ($ billions)	8	21	6
Present value of debt ($ millions)			..
Total debt service (% of goods and services exports)	..	..	..
Short-term debt ($ millions)	..	..	..
Aid per capita ($)	..	..	..

Cape Verde

Sub-Saharan Africa   **Lower middle income**

Population (thousands)	470	Population growth (%)	2.5
Surface area (1,000 sq. km)	4	National poverty rate (% pop.)	..
GNI ($ millions)	675	GNI per capita ($)	1,440

	1990	2002	2003
People			
Life expectancy at birth (years)	65	69	69
Fertility rate (births per woman)	5.5	3.5	3.5
Infant mortality rate (per 1,000 live births)	45	30	26
Under-five mortality rate (per 1,000)	60	40	35
Births attended by skilled health staff (% of total)	..	89	..
Child malnutrition, underweight (% of under age 5)	..	..	..
Child immunization, measles (% of ages 12–23 mon.)	79	85	68
HIV prevalence rate (% of ages 15–49)	..	..	..
Adult literacy, male (% of ages 15 and older)	76	85	..
Adult literacy, female (% of ages 15 and older)	54	68	..
Primary completion rate, total (% of age group)	54	96	..
Primary completion rate, female (% of age group)	51	105	..
Net primary enrollment (% of age group)	94	99	..
Net secondary enrollment (% of age group)	..	58	..
Environment			
Forests (1,000 sq. km)	0	1	..
Deforestation (average annual %, 1990–2000)		–9.3	
Freshwater use (% of internal resources)			..
Carbon dioxide emissions (metric tons per capita)	0.2	0.3	..
Access to improved water source (% of total pop.)	..	80	..
Access to improved sanitation (% of urban pop.)	..	61	..
Energy use per capita (kg oil equivalent)	..	..	..
Electricity use per capita (kilowatt-hours)	..	..	..
Economy			
GDP ($ millions)	339	616	797
GDP growth (annual %)	0.7	4.6	5.0
GDP implicit price deflator (annual % growth)	2.3	1.8	2.8
Value added in agriculture (% of GDP)	14	11	7
Value added in industry (% of GDP)	21	17	20
Value added in services (% of GDP)	64	72	73
Exports of goods and services (% of GDP)	13	31	32
Imports of goods and services (% of GDP)	44	68	68
Gross capital formation (% of GDP)	23	21	20
Central government revenue (% of GDP)	..	..	..
Cash surplus/deficit (% of GDP)	..	..	..
Technology and infrastructure			
Fixed-line and mobile subscribers (per 1,000 people)	24	258	273
Cost of 3-minute local call ($)	0.06	0.04	..
Personal computers (per 1,000 people)	..	79.7	..
Internet users (per 1,000 people)	..	36	44
Paved roads (% of total)	78.0	78.0	..
Aircraft departures (thousands)	7	9	9
Trade and finance			
Trade in goods (% of GDP)	41.9	46.4	39.8
Trade growth less GDP growth (avg. %, 1990–2003)			4.4
High-technology exports (% of manufactured exports)	..	1	..
Net barter terms of trade (2000 = 100)	100	100	..
Foreign direct investment ($ millions)	0	15	15
Present value of debt ($ millions)			329
Total debt service (% of goods and services exports)	4.8	7.6	5.7
Short-term debt ($ millions)	5	25	38
Aid per capita ($)	316	201	306

Cayman Islands

High income

Population (thousands)	42	Population growth (%)		..
Surface area (sq. km)	260	National poverty rate (% pop.)		..
GNI ($ millions)	..	GNI per capita ($)		..

	1990	2002	2003
People			
Life expectancy at birth (years)	..	..	..
Fertility rate (births per woman)	..	..	..
Infant mortality rate (per 1,000 live births)	..	..	..
Under-five mortality rate (per 1,000)	..	..	..
Births attended by skilled health staff (% of total)	..	..	..
Child malnutrition, underweight (% of under age 5)	..	..	..
Child immunization, measles (% of ages 12–23 mon.)	..	..	..
HIV prevalence rate (% of ages 15–49)	..	..	..
Adult literacy, male (% of ages 15 and older)	..	..	..
Adult literacy, female (% of ages 15 and older)	..	..	..
Primary completion rate, total (% of age group)	..	..	..
Primary completion rate, female (% of age group)	..	..	..
Net primary enrollment (% of age group)	..	..	..
Net secondary enrollment (% of age group)	..	..	..
Environment			
Forests (1,000 sq. km)	0	0	..
Deforestation (average annual %, 1990–2000)		0.0	
Freshwater use (% of internal resources)			..
Carbon dioxide emissions (metric tons per capita)	..	..	..
Access to improved water source (% of total pop.)	..	..	..
Access to improved sanitation (% of urban pop.)	..	..	..
Energy use per capita (kg oil equivalent)	..	..	..
Electricity use per capita (kilowatt-hours)	..	..	..
Economy			
GDP ($ millions)	..	..	..
GDP growth (annual %)	..	..	..
GDP implicit price deflator (annual % growth)	..	..	..
Value added in agriculture (% of GDP)	..	..	..
Value added in industry (% of GDP)	..	..	..
Value added in services (% of GDP)	..	..	..
Exports of goods and services (% of GDP)	..	..	..
Imports of goods and services (% of GDP)	..	..	..
Gross capital formation (% of GDP)	..	..	..
Central government revenue (% of GDP)	..	..	..
Cash surplus/deficit (% of GDP)	..	..	..
Technology and infrastructure			
Fixed-line and mobile subscribers (per 1,000 people)	456	1,229	..
Cost of 3-minute local call ($)	..	0.11	..
Personal computers (per 1,000 people)	..	..	..
Internet users (per 1,000 people)	..	..	..
Paved roads (% of total)	..	..	..
Aircraft departures (thousands)	..	..	..
Trade and finance			
Trade in goods (% of GDP)	..	..	..
Trade growth less GDP growth (avg. %, 1990–2003)			..
High-technology exports (% of manufactured exports)	..	..	..
Net barter terms of trade (2000 = 100)	..	..	..
Foreign direct investment ($ millions)	..	..	..
Present value of debt ($ millions)			..
Total debt service (% of goods and services exports)	..	..	..
Short-term debt ($ millions)	..	..	..
Aid per capita ($)	..	..	..

Central African Republic

Sub-Saharan Africa			Low income

Population (millions)	4	Population growth (%)	1.6
Surface area (1,000 sq. km)	623	National poverty rate (% pop.)	..
GNI ($ millions)	1,019	GNI per capita ($)	260

	1990	2002	2003
People			
Life expectancy at birth (years)	48	42	42
Fertility rate (births per woman)	5.5	4.6	4.6
Infant mortality rate (per 1,000 live births)	115	115	115
Under-five mortality rate (per 1,000)	180	180	180
Births attended by skilled health staff (% of total)	..	44	..
Child malnutrition, underweight (% of under age 5)	..	..	..
Child immunization, measles (% of ages 12–23 mon.)	83	35	35
HIV prevalence rate (% of ages 15–49)	..	13.5	13.5
Adult literacy, male (% of ages 15 and older)	47	65	..
Adult literacy, female (% of ages 15 and older)	21	33	..
Primary completion rate, total (% of age group)	27	..	..
Primary completion rate, female (% of age group)	19	..	..
Net primary enrollment (% of age group)	53	..	..
Net secondary enrollment (% of age group)	..	..	..
Environment			
Forests (1,000 sq. km)	232	229	..
Deforestation (average annual %, 1990–2000)		0.1	
Freshwater use (% of internal resources)			0
Carbon dioxide emissions (metric tons per capita)	0.1	0.1	..
Access to improved water source (% of total pop.)	48	75	..
Access to improved sanitation (% of urban pop.)	32	47	..
Energy use per capita (kg oil equivalent)	..	..	..
Electricity use per capita (kilowatt-hours)	..	..	..
Economy			
GDP ($ millions)	1,488	1,046	1,198
GDP growth (annual %)	–2.1	–0.8	–7.3
GDP implicit price deflator (annual % growth)	2.3	3.6	3.1
Value added in agriculture (% of GDP)	48	57	61
Value added in industry (% of GDP)	20	22	25
Value added in services (% of GDP)	33	21	14
Exports of goods and services (% of GDP)	15	12	24
Imports of goods and services (% of GDP)	28	17	31
Gross capital formation (% of GDP)	12	15	18
Central government revenue (% of GDP)	..	..	..
Cash surplus/deficit (% of GDP)	..	..	..
Technology and infrastructure			
Fixed-line and mobile subscribers (per 1,000 people)	2	5	..
Cost of 3-minute local call ($)	1.13	0.43	..
Personal computers (per 1,000 people)	..	2.0	..
Internet users (per 1,000 people)	..	1	1
Paved roads (% of total)	..	2.7	..
Aircraft departures (thousands)	4	1	..
Trade and finance			
Trade in goods (% of GDP)	18.4	25.5	20.4
Trade growth less GDP growth (avg. %, 1990–2003)			..
High-technology exports (% of manufactured exports)	..	0	0
Net barter terms of trade (2000 = 100)	238	106	..
Foreign direct investment ($ millions)	1	6	4
Present value of debt ($ millions)			1,651
Total debt service (% of goods and services exports)	13.2	..	..
Short-term debt ($ millions)	38	52	374
Aid per capita ($)	85	16	13

Chad

Sub-Saharan Africa | **Low income**

Population (millions)	9	Population growth (%)		2.8
Surface area (1,000 sq. km)	1,284	National poverty rate (% pop.)		..
GNI ($ millions)	2,073	GNI per capita ($)		240

	1990	2002	2003
People			
Life expectancy at birth (years)	46	48	48
Fertility rate (births per woman)	7.1	6.2	6.2
Infant mortality rate (per 1,000 live births)	117	117	117
Under-five mortality rate (per 1,000)	203	200	200
Births attended by skilled health staff (% of total)	..	16	..
Child malnutrition, underweight (% of under age 5)	..	28	..
Child immunization, measles (% of ages 12–23 mon.)	32	55	61
HIV prevalence rate (% of ages 15–49)	..	4.9	4.8
Adult literacy, male (% of ages 15 and older)	37	55	..
Adult literacy, female (% of ages 15 and older)	19	38	..
Primary completion rate, total (% of age group)	19	25	..
Primary completion rate, female (% of age group)	7	16	..
Net primary enrollment (% of age group)	36	63	..
Net secondary enrollment (% of age group)	..	10	..
Environment			
Forests (1,000 sq. km)	135	127	..
Deforestation (average annual %, 1990–2000)		0.6	
Freshwater use (% of internal resources)			1
Carbon dioxide emissions (metric tons per capita)	0.0	0.0	..
Access to improved water source (% of total pop.)	20	34	..
Access to improved sanitation (% of urban pop.)	27	30	..
Energy use per capita (kg oil equivalent)	..	..	..
Electricity use per capita (kilowatt-hours)	..	..	..
Economy			
GDP ($ millions)	1,739	2,008	2,608
GDP growth (annual %)	–4.2	9.9	11.3
GDP implicit price deflator (annual % growth)	8.0	3.9	–0.5
Value added in agriculture (% of GDP)	29	39	46
Value added in industry (% of GDP)	18	15	13
Value added in services (% of GDP)	53	46	41
Exports of goods and services (% of GDP)	13	12	21
Imports of goods and services (% of GDP)	28	64	53
Gross capital formation (% of GDP)	16	62	53
Central government revenue (% of GDP)	..	..	..
Cash surplus/deficit (% of GDP)	..	..	..
Technology and infrastructure			
Fixed-line and mobile subscribers (per 1,000 people)	1	6	..
Cost of 3-minute local call ($)	0.37	0.11	..
Personal computers (per 1,000 people)	..	1.7	..
Internet users (per 1,000 people)	..	2	..
Paved roads (% of total)	0.8	0.8	..
Aircraft departures (thousands)	1	1	..
Trade and finance			
Trade in goods (% of GDP)	27.2	58.9	42.6
Trade growth less GDP growth (avg. %, 1990–2003)			3.8
High-technology exports (% of manufactured exports)	..	..	..
Net barter terms of trade (2000 = 100)	112	165	..
Foreign direct investment ($ millions)	9	1,030	837
Present value of debt ($ millions)			892
Total debt service (% of goods and services exports)	4.4	..	23
Short-term debt ($ millions)	30	26	23
Aid per capita ($)	54	27	29

Channel Islands

		High income
Population (thousands)	149	Population growth (%)	0.0
Surface area (sq. km)	200	National poverty rate (% pop.)	..
GNI ($ millions)	..	GNI per capita ($)	..

	1990	2002	2003
People			
Life expectancy at birth (years)	77	79	79
Fertility rate (births per woman)	1.7	1.8	1.8
Infant mortality rate (per 1,000 live births)	..	..	..
Under-five mortality rate (per 1,000)	..	..	..
Births attended by skilled health staff (% of total)	..	..	..
Child malnutrition, underweight (% of under age 5)	..	..	..
Child immunization, measles (% of ages 12–23 mon.)	..	..	..
HIV prevalence rate (% of ages 15–49)	..	..	..
Adult literacy, male (% of ages 15 and older)	..	..	..
Adult literacy, female (% of ages 15 and older)	..	..	..
Primary completion rate, total (% of age group)	..	..	..
Primary completion rate, female (% of age group)	..	..	..
Net primary enrollment (% of age group)	..	..	..
Net secondary enrollment (% of age group)	..	..	..
Environment			
Forests (1,000 sq. km)	..	..	..
Deforestation (average annual %, 1990–2000)		..	
Freshwater use (% of internal resources)			..
Carbon dioxide emissions (metric tons per capita)	..	..	..
Access to improved water source (% of total pop.)	..	..	..
Access to improved sanitation (% of urban pop.)	..	..	..
Energy use per capita (kg oil equivalent)	..	..	..
Electricity use per capita (kilowatt-hours)	..	..	..
Economy			
GDP ($ millions)	..	..	..
GDP growth (annual %)	..	..	..
GDP implicit price deflator (annual % growth)	..	..	..
Value added in agriculture (% of GDP)	..	..	..
Value added in industry (% of GDP)	..	..	..
Value added in services (% of GDP)	..	..	..
Exports of goods and services (% of GDP)	..	..	..
Imports of goods and services (% of GDP)	..	..	..
Gross capital formation (% of GDP)	..	..	..
Central government revenue (% of GDP)	..	..	..
Cash surplus/deficit (% of GDP)	..	..	..
Technology and infrastructure			
Fixed-line and mobile subscribers (per 1,000 people)	..	..	..
Cost of 3-minute local call ($)	..	..	..
Personal computers (per 1,000 people)	..	..	..
Internet users (per 1,000 people)	..	..	..
Paved roads (% of total)	..	..	..
Aircraft departures (thousands)	..	..	..
Trade and finance			
Trade in goods (% of GDP)	..	..	..
Trade growth less GDP growth (avg. %, 1990–2003)			..
High-technology exports (% of manufactured exports)	..	..	..
Net barter terms of trade (2000 = 100)	..	..	..
Foreign direct investment ($ millions)	..	..	..
Present value of debt ($ millions)			..
Total debt service (% of goods and services exports)	..	..	..
Short-term debt ($ millions)	..	..	..
Aid per capita ($)	..	..	..

Chile

Latin America & Caribbean **Upper middle income**

Population (millions)	16	Population growth (%)		1.2
Surface area (1,000 sq. km)	757	National poverty rate (% pop.)		17
GNI ($ billions)	69	GNI per capita ($)		4,360

	1990	2002	2003
People			
Life expectancy at birth (years)	74	76	76
Fertility rate (births per woman)	2.6	2.2	2.2
Infant mortality rate (per 1,000 live births)	17	11	8
Under-five mortality rate (per 1,000)	19	12	9
Births attended by skilled health staff (% of total)	..	100	..
Child malnutrition, underweight (% of under age 5)	..	1	..
Child immunization, measles (% of ages 12–23 mon.)	82	99	99
HIV prevalence rate (% of ages 15–49)	..	0.3	0.3
Adult literacy, male (% of ages 15 and older)	94	96	..
Adult literacy, female (% of ages 15 and older)	94	96	..
Primary completion rate, total (% of age group)	..	104	..
Primary completion rate, female (% of age group)	..	103	..
Net primary enrollment (% of age group)	88	86	..
Net secondary enrollment (% of age group)	55	79	..
Environment			
Forests (1,000 sq. km)	157	155	..
Deforestation (average annual %, 1990–2000)		0.1	
Freshwater use (% of internal resources)			2
Carbon dioxide emissions (metric tons per capita)	2.7	3.9	..
Access to improved water source (% of total pop.)	90	95	..
Access to improved sanitation (% of urban pop.)	91	96	..
Energy use per capita (kg oil equivalent)	1,040	1,585	..
Electricity use per capita (kilowatt-hours)	1,178	2,617	..
Economy			
GDP ($ billions)	30	67	72
GDP growth (annual %)	3.7	2.2	3.3
GDP implicit price deflator (annual % growth)	21.2	7.6	4.4
Value added in agriculture (% of GDP)	9	9	9
Value added in industry (% of GDP)	41	34	34
Value added in services (% of GDP)	50	57	57
Exports of goods and services (% of GDP)	35	33	36
Imports of goods and services (% of GDP)	31	31	33
Gross capital formation (% of GDP)	25	22	24
Central government revenue (% of GDP)	..	..	21.2
Cash surplus/deficit (% of GDP)	..	..	–0.5
Technology and infrastructure			
Fixed-line and mobile subscribers (per 1,000 people)	67	659	732
Cost of 3-minute local call ($)	..	0.10	0.10
Personal computers (per 1,000 people)	9.4	119.3	..
Internet users (per 1,000 people)	0	238	272
Paved roads (% of total)	13.8	20.2	..
Aircraft departures (thousands)	40	78	83
Trade and finance			
Trade in goods (% of GDP)	53.1	52.5	55.9
Trade growth less GDP growth (avg. %, 1990–2003)			2.8
High-technology exports (% of manufactured exports)	5	4	3
Net barter terms of trade (2000 = 100)	114	93	..
Foreign direct investment ($ millions)	661	1,888	2,982
Present value of debt ($ billions)			44
Total debt service (% of goods and services exports)	25.9	32.8	31.3
Short-term debt ($ millions)	3,382	5,823	7,504
Aid per capita ($)	8	–1	5

China

East Asia & Pacific		Lower middle income	
Population (millions)	1,288	Population growth (%)	0.6
Surface area (1,000 sq. km)	9,598	National poverty rate (% pop.)	5
GNI ($ billions)	1,417	GNI per capita ($)	1,100

	1990	2002	2003
People			
Life expectancy at birth (years)	69	71	71
Fertility rate (births per woman)	2.1	1.9	1.9
Infant mortality rate (per 1,000 live births)	38	32	30
Under-five mortality rate (per 1,000)	49	40	37
Births attended by skilled health staff (% of total)	50	97	..
Child malnutrition, underweight (% of under age 5)	17	10	..
Child immunization, measles (% of ages 12–23 mon.)	98	84	84
HIV prevalence rate (% of ages 15–49)	..	0.1	0.1
Adult literacy, male (% of ages 15 and older)	87	95	..
Adult literacy, female (% of ages 15 and older)	69	87	..
Primary completion rate, total (% of age group)	105	105	98
Primary completion rate, female (% of age group)	..	102	95
Net primary enrollment (% of age group)	97	95	..
Net secondary enrollment (% of age group)	..	..	..
Environment			
Forests (1,000 sq. km)	1,454	1,635	..
Deforestation (average annual %, 1990–2000)		–1.2	
Freshwater use (% of internal resources)			19
Carbon dioxide emissions (metric tons per capita)	2.1	2.2	..
Access to improved water source (% of total pop.)	70	77	..
Access to improved sanitation (% of urban pop.)	64	69	..
Energy use per capita (kg oil equivalent)	775	960	..
Electricity use per capita (kilowatt-hours)	424	987	..
Economy			
GDP ($ billions)	355	1,271	1,417
GDP growth (annual %)	3.8	8.3	9.3
GDP implicit price deflator (annual % growth)	5.7	–0.6	2.2
Value added in agriculture (% of GDP)	27	15	15
Value added in industry (% of GDP)	42	51	52
Value added in services (% of GDP)	31	34	33
Exports of goods and services (% of GDP)	18	29	34
Imports of goods and services (% of GDP)	14	26	32
Gross capital formation (% of GDP)	35	40	44
Central government revenue (% of GDP)	6.3	8.9	..
Cash surplus/deficit (% of GDP)	..	..	..
Technology and infrastructure			
Fixed-line and mobile subscribers (per 1,000 people)	6	328	424
Cost of 3-minute local call ($)	..	0.03	0.03
Personal computers (per 1,000 people)	0.4	27.6	..
Internet users (per 1,000 people)	..	46	63
Paved roads (% of total)	..	..	..
Aircraft departures (thousands)	196	932	946
Trade and finance			
Trade in goods (% of GDP)	32.5	48.8	60.1
Trade growth less GDP growth (avg. %, 1990–2003)			..
High-technology exports (% of manufactured exports)	6	23	27
Net barter terms of trade (2000 = 100)	102	102	..
Foreign direct investment ($ billions)	3	49	54
Present value of debt ($ billions)			189
Total debt service (% of goods and services exports)	11.7	8.2	7.3
Short-term debt ($ billions)	9	48	73
Aid per capita ($)	2	1	1

Colombia

Latin America & Caribbean   **Lower middle income**

Population (millions)	45	Population growth (%)		1.7
Surface area (1,000 sq. km)	1,139	National poverty rate (% pop.)		64
GNI ($ billions)	81	GNI per capita ($)		1,810

	1990	2002	2003
People			
Life expectancy at birth (years)	68	72	72
Fertility rate (births per woman)	3.1	2.5	2.5
Infant mortality rate (per 1,000 live births)	30	20	18
Under-five mortality rate (per 1,000)	36	24	21
Births attended by skilled health staff (% of total)	82	86	..
Child malnutrition, underweight (% of under age 5)	10	7	..
Child immunization, measles (% of ages 12–23 mon.)	82	89	92
HIV prevalence rate (% of ages 15–49)	..	0.5	0.7
Adult literacy, male (% of ages 15 and older)	89	92	..
Adult literacy, female (% of ages 15 and older)	88	92	..
Primary completion rate, total (% of age group)	71	88	..
Primary completion rate, female (% of age group)	82	90	..
Net primary enrollment (% of age group)	68	87	..
Net secondary enrollment (% of age group)	..	54	..
Environment			
Forests (1,000 sq. km)	515	496	..
Deforestation (average annual %, 1990–2000)		0.4	
Freshwater use (% of internal resources)			0
Carbon dioxide emissions (metric tons per capita)	1.6	1.4	..
Access to improved water source (% of total pop.)	92	92	..
Access to improved sanitation (% of urban pop.)	95	96	..
Energy use per capita (kg oil equivalent)	716	625	..
Electricity use per capita (kilowatt-hours)	768	817	..
Economy			
GDP ($ billions)	40	80	79
GDP growth (annual %)	6.0	1.9	3.9
GDP implicit price deflator (annual % growth)	26.1	5.1	8.2
Value added in agriculture (% of GDP)	17	14	12
Value added in industry (% of GDP)	38	30	29
Value added in services (% of GDP)	45	56	58
Exports of goods and services (% of GDP)	21	20	21
Imports of goods and services (% of GDP)	15	21	22
Gross capital formation (% of GDP)	19	15	15
Central government revenue (% of GDP)	..	17.1	18.8
Cash surplus/deficit (% of GDP)	..	–9.7	–4.6
Technology and infrastructure			
Fixed-line and mobile subscribers (per 1,000 people)	69	286	321
Cost of 3-minute local call ($)	0.01	0.03	0.03
Personal computers (per 1,000 people)	8.8	49.3	..
Internet users (per 1,000 people)	..	46	53
Paved roads (% of total)	11.9	14.4	..
Aircraft departures (thousands)	117	180	172
Trade and finance			
Trade in goods (% of GDP)	30.7	30.7	33.8
Trade growth less GDP growth (avg. %, 1990–2003)			2.9
High-technology exports (% of manufactured exports)	5	7	7
Net barter terms of trade (2000 = 100)	81	93	..
Foreign direct investment ($ millions)	500	2,115	1,746
Present value of debt ($ billions)			36
Total debt service (% of goods and services exports)	40.9	39.5	43.9
Short-term debt ($ millions)	1,438	3,659	3,556
Aid per capita ($)	3	10	18

Comoros

Sub-Saharan Africa **Low income**

Population (thousands)	600	Population growth (%)		2.4
Surface area (1,000 sq. km)	2	National poverty rate (% pop.)		..
GNI ($ millions)	269	GNI per capita ($)		450

	1990	2002	2003
People			
Life expectancy at birth (years)	56	61	62
Fertility rate (births per woman)	5.8	4.1	4.0
Infant mortality rate (per 1,000 live births)	88	61	54
Under-five mortality rate (per 1,000)	120	82	73
Births attended by skilled health staff (% of total)	..	62	..
Child malnutrition, underweight (% of under age 5)	19	25	..
Child immunization, measles (% of ages 12–23 mon.)	87	71	63
HIV prevalence rate (% of ages 15–49)	..	..	..
Adult literacy, male (% of ages 15 and older)	61	63	..
Adult literacy, female (% of ages 15 and older)	46	49	..
Primary completion rate, total (% of age group)	39	54	58
Primary completion rate, female (% of age group)	36	51	51
Net primary enrollment (% of age group)	57	55	..
Net secondary enrollment (% of age group)	..	..	..
Environment			
Forests (1,000 sq. km)	0	0	..
Deforestation (average annual %, 1990–2000)		4.0	
Freshwater use (% of internal resources)			..
Carbon dioxide emissions (metric tons per capita)	0.2	0.1	..
Access to improved water source (% of total pop.)	89	94	..
Access to improved sanitation (% of urban pop.)	41	38	..
Energy use per capita (kg oil equivalent)	..	..	..
Electricity use per capita (kilowatt-hours)	..	..	..
Economy			
GDP ($ millions)	263	247	323
GDP growth (annual %)	5.1	2.5	2.5
GDP implicit price deflator (annual % growth)	7.3	4.5	6.2
Value added in agriculture (% of GDP)	39	41	41
Value added in industry (% of GDP)	8	12	12
Value added in services (% of GDP)	53	47	47
Exports of goods and services (% of GDP)	14	16	13
Imports of goods and services (% of GDP)	35	28	25
Gross capital formation (% of GDP)	19	13	13
Central government revenue (% of GDP)	..	..	..
Cash surplus/deficit (% of GDP)	..	..	..
Technology and infrastructure			
Fixed-line and mobile subscribers (per 1,000 people)	8	13	19
Cost of 3-minute local call ($)	0.27	0.14	0.17
Personal computers (per 1,000 people)	0.1	5.5	5.8
Internet users (per 1,000 people)	..	4	6
Paved roads (% of total)	69.3	76.5	..
Aircraft departures (thousands)	1	..	..
Trade and finance			
Trade in goods (% of GDP)	26.7	43.3	43.4
Trade growth less GDP growth (avg. %, 1990–2003)			1.2
High-technology exports (% of manufactured exports)	..	1	..
Net barter terms of trade (2000 = 100)	86	140	..
Foreign direct investment ($ millions)	0	0	1
Present value of debt ($ millions)			210
Total debt service (% of goods and services exports)	2.3	..	..
Short-term debt ($ millions)	12	30	28
Aid per capita ($)	105	55	41

Congo, Dem. Rep.

Sub-Saharan Africa   **Low income**

Population (millions)	53	Population growth (%)	3.0
Surface area (1,000 sq. km)	2,345	National poverty rate (% pop.)	..
GNI ($ millions)	5,425	GNI per capita ($)	100

	1990	2002	2003
People			
Life expectancy at birth (years)	52	45	45
Fertility rate (births per woman)	6.7	6.7	6.7
Infant mortality rate (per 1,000 live births)	129	129	129
Under-five mortality rate (per 1,000)	205	205	205
Births attended by skilled health staff (% of total)	..	61	..
Child malnutrition, underweight (% of under age 5)	..	31	..
Child immunization, measles (% of ages 12–23 mon.)	38	45	54
HIV prevalence rate (% of ages 15–49)	..	4.2	4.2
Adult literacy, male (% of ages 15 and older)	..	..	..
Adult literacy, female (% of ages 15 and older)	..	..	..
Primary completion rate, total (% of age group)	47	32	..
Primary completion rate, female (% of age group)	35	30	..
Net primary enrollment (% of age group)	54	35	..
Net secondary enrollment (% of age group)	..	..	..
Environment			
Forests (1,000 sq. km)	1,405	1,352	..
Deforestation (average annual %, 1990–2000)		0.4	
Freshwater use (% of internal resources)			0
Carbon dioxide emissions (metric tons per capita)	0.1	0.1	..
Access to improved water source (% of total pop.)	43	46	..
Access to improved sanitation (% of urban pop.)	56	43	..
Energy use per capita (kg oil equivalent)	319	299	..
Electricity use per capita (kilowatt-hours)	55	43	..
Economy			
GDP ($ millions)	9,348	5,547	5,671
GDP growth (annual %)	–6.6	3.5	5.6
GDP implicit price deflator (annual % growth)	109.0	26.8	13.3
Value added in agriculture (% of GDP)	30	58	..
Value added in industry (% of GDP)	28	19	..
Value added in services (% of GDP)	42	23	..
Exports of goods and services (% of GDP)	30	19	..
Imports of goods and services (% of GDP)	29	22	..
Gross capital formation (% of GDP)	9	7	14
Central government revenue (% of GDP)	10.1	7.9	–0.0
Cash surplus/deficit (% of GDP)	–6.5	–0.1	..
Technology and infrastructure			
Fixed-line and mobile subscribers (per 1,000 people)	1	11	..
Cost of 3-minute local call ($)	..	..	..
Personal computers (per 1,000 people)	..	..	..
Internet users (per 1,000 people)	..	0	..
Paved roads (% of total)	..	..	..
Aircraft departures (thousands)	5	5	..
Trade and finance			
Trade in goods (% of GDP)	43.5	46.7	45.2
Trade growth less GDP growth (avg. %, 1990–2003)			6.5
High-technology exports (% of manufactured exports)	..	..	..
Net barter terms of trade (2000 = 100)	86	110	..
Foreign direct investment ($ millions)	–15	117	158
Present value of debt ($ millions)			7,560
Total debt service (% of goods and services exports)	..	..	..
Short-term debt ($ millions)	744	643	390
Aid per capita ($)	24	23	101

Congo, Rep.

Sub-Saharan Africa		Low income

Population (millions)	4	Population growth (%)	2.7
Surface area (1,000 sq. km)	342	National poverty rate (% pop.)	..
GNI ($ millions)	2,443	GNI per capita ($)	650

	1990	2002	2003
People			
Life expectancy at birth (years)	51	52	52
Fertility rate (births per woman)	6.3	6.3	6.3
Infant mortality rate (per 1,000 live births)	83	*81*	81
Under-five mortality rate (per 1,000)	110	*108*	108
Births attended by skilled health staff (% of total)	..	..	..
Child malnutrition, underweight (% of under age 5)	..	..	..
Child immunization, measles (% of ages 12–23 mon.)	75	37	50
HIV prevalence rate (% of ages 15–49)	..	5.3	4.9
Adult literacy, male (% of ages 15 and older)	77	89	..
Adult literacy, female (% of ages 15 and older)	58	77	..
Primary completion rate, total (% of age group)	54	47	59
Primary completion rate, female (% of age group)	48	45	56
Net primary enrollment (% of age group)	79	54	..
Net secondary enrollment (% of age group)	..	..	..
Environment			
Forests (1,000 sq. km)	222	*221*	..
Deforestation (average annual %, 1990–2000)		*0.1*	
Freshwater use (% of internal resources)			0
Carbon dioxide emissions (metric tons per capita)	0.8	*0.5*	..
Access to improved water source (% of total pop.)	..	46	..
Access to improved sanitation (% of urban pop.)	..	14	..
Energy use per capita (kg oil equivalent)	423	252	..
Electricity use per capita (kilowatt-hours)	139	82	..
Economy			
GDP ($ millions)	2,799	3,017	3,564
GDP growth (annual %)	1.0	3.5	2.7
GDP implicit price deflator (annual % growth)	–1.0	–0.6	–4.0
Value added in agriculture (% of GDP)	13	6	6
Value added in industry (% of GDP)	41	63	60
Value added in services (% of GDP)	46	30	34
Exports of goods and services (% of GDP)	54	81	78
Imports of goods and services (% of GDP)	46	54	53
Gross capital formation (% of GDP)	16	23	23
Central government revenue (% of GDP)	*22.5*	31.9	..
Cash surplus/deficit (% of GDP)	*–13.1*	–5.2	..
Technology and infrastructure			
Fixed-line and mobile subscribers (per 1,000 people)	7	74	96
Cost of 3-minute local call ($)	0.26	..	..
Personal computers (per 1,000 people)	..	3.9	4.3
Internet users (per 1,000 people)	..	0	4
Paved roads (% of total)	9.7	*9.7*	..
Aircraft departures (thousands)	4	5	5
Trade and finance			
Trade in goods (% of GDP)	57.2	111.8	119.4
Trade growth less GDP growth (avg. %, 1990–2003)			2.7
High-technology exports (% of manufactured exports)	..	..	..
Net barter terms of trade (2000 = 100)	63	95	..
Foreign direct investment ($ millions)	23	331	201
Present value of debt ($ millions)			8,385
Total debt service (% of goods and services exports)	35.3	1.0	4.0
Short-term debt ($ millions)	736	1,145	1,062
Aid per capita ($)	87	16	19

Costa Rica

Latin America & Caribbean **Upper middle income**

Population (millions)	4	Population growth (%)	1.6
Surface area (1,000 sq. km)	51	National poverty rate (% pop.)	..
GNI ($ billions)	17	GNI per capita ($)	4,300

	1990	2002	2003
People			
Life expectancy at birth (years)	77	79	79
Fertility rate (births per woman)	3.2	2.3	2.3
Infant mortality rate (per 1,000 live births)	15	10	8
Under-five mortality rate (per 1,000)	17	12	10
Births attended by skilled health staff (% of total)	98	98	..
Child malnutrition, underweight (% of under age 5)	3	..	..
Child immunization, measles (% of ages 12–23 mon.)	90	94	89
HIV prevalence rate (% of ages 15–49)	..	0.6	0.6
Adult literacy, male (% of ages 15 and older)	94	96	..
Adult literacy, female (% of ages 15 and older)	94	96	..
Primary completion rate, total (% of age group)	72	94	94
Primary completion rate, female (% of age group)	78	95	..
Net primary enrollment (% of age group)	87	90	..
Net secondary enrollment (% of age group)	37	50	..
Environment			
Forests (1,000 sq. km)	21	20	..
Deforestation (average annual %, 1990–2000)		0.8	
Freshwater use (% of internal resources)			5
Carbon dioxide emissions (metric tons per capita)	1.0	1.4	..
Access to improved water source (% of total pop.)	..	97	..
Access to improved sanitation (% of urban pop.)	..	89	..
Energy use per capita (kg oil equivalent)	664	904	..
Electricity use per capita (kilowatt-hours)	1,091	1,611	..
Economy			
GDP ($ billions)	6	17	17
GDP growth (annual %)	3.6	2.9	6.5
GDP implicit price deflator (annual % growth)	18.6	9.1	7.8
Value added in agriculture (% of GDP)	18	9	9
Value added in industry (% of GDP)	29	29	29
Value added in services (% of GDP)	53	62	62
Exports of goods and services (% of GDP)	35	42	47
Imports of goods and services (% of GDP)	41	48	49
Gross capital formation (% of GDP)	27	22	20
Central government revenue (% of GDP)	23.1	22.6	22.7
Cash surplus/deficit (% of GDP)	–2.5	–3.4	–1.6
Technology and infrastructure			
Fixed-line and mobile subscribers (per 1,000 people)	101	362	..
Cost of 3-minute local call ($)	0.07	0.03	0.02
Personal computers (per 1,000 people)	..	197.2	..
Internet users (per 1,000 people)	0	193	..
Paved roads (% of total)	15.3	12.0	..
Aircraft departures (thousands)	13	33	35
Trade and finance			
Trade in goods (% of GDP)	60.2	74.0	78.9
Trade growth less GDP growth (avg. %, 1990–2003)			3.4
High-technology exports (% of manufactured exports)	..	37	45
Net barter terms of trade (2000 = 100)	75	97	..
Foreign direct investment ($ millions)	163	662	577
Present value of debt ($ millions)			5,833
Total debt service (% of goods and services exports)	23.9	8.7	9.7
Short-term debt ($ millions)	377	1,498	1,626
Aid per capita ($)	75	1	7

Côte d'Ivoire

Sub-Saharan Africa		Low income

Population (millions)	17	Population growth (%)	1.9
Surface area (1,000 sq. km)	322	National poverty rate (% pop.)	..
GNI ($ billions)	11	GNI per capita ($)	660

	1990	2002	2003
People			
Life expectancy at birth (years)	50	45	45
Fertility rate (births per woman)	6.2	4.6	4.5
Infant mortality rate (per 1,000 live births)	103	115	117
Under-five mortality rate (per 1,000)	157	188	192
Births attended by skilled health staff (% of total)	..	63	..
Child malnutrition, underweight (% of under age 5)	..	21	..
Child immunization, measles (% of ages 12–23 mon.)	56	56	56
HIV prevalence rate (% of ages 15–49)	..	6.7	7.0
Adult literacy, male (% of ages 15 and older)	51	59	..
Adult literacy, female (% of ages 15 and older)	26	36	..
Primary completion rate, total (% of age group)	46	51	..
Primary completion rate, female (% of age group)	34	40	..
Net primary enrollment (% of age group)	46	61	..
Net secondary enrollment (% of age group)	..	21	..
Environment			
Forests (1,000 sq. km)	98	71	..
Deforestation (average annual %, 1990–2000)		3.1	
Freshwater use (% of internal resources)			1
Carbon dioxide emissions (metric tons per capita)	1.0	0.7	..
Access to improved water source (% of total pop.)	69	84	..
Access to improved sanitation (% of urban pop.)	52	61	..
Energy use per capita (kg oil equivalent)	374	397	..
Electricity use per capita (kilowatt-hours)	..	..	..
Economy			
GDP ($ billions)	11	12	14
GDP growth (annual %)	–1.1	–1.6	–3.8
GDP implicit price deflator (annual % growth)	–4.5	5.2	1.8
Value added in agriculture (% of GDP)	32	26	26
Value added in industry (% of GDP)	23	20	19
Value added in services (% of GDP)	44	54	55
Exports of goods and services (% of GDP)	32	49	47
Imports of goods and services (% of GDP)	27	33	34
Gross capital formation (% of GDP)	7	10	10
Central government revenue (% of GDP)	..	17.0	..
Cash surplus/deficit (% of GDP)	..	..	..
Technology and infrastructure			
Fixed-line and mobile subscribers (per 1,000 people)	6	83	91
Cost of 3-minute local call ($)	0.12	0.22	0.09
Personal computers (per 1,000 people)	..	9.3	..
Internet users (per 1,000 people)	..	3	14
Paved roads (% of total)	8.7	9.7	..
Aircraft departures (thousands)	5	1	..
Trade and finance			
Trade in goods (% of GDP)	47.9	77.5	75.3
Trade growth less GDP growth (avg. %, 1990–2003)			0.1
High-technology exports (% of manufactured exports)	..	3	8
Net barter terms of trade (2000 = 100)	143	118	..
Foreign direct investment ($ millions)	48	213	180
Present value of debt ($ billions)			10
Total debt service (% of goods and services exports)	35.4	13.9	8.5
Short-term debt ($ millions)	3,597	932	917
Aid per capita ($)	58	65	15

Croatia

Europe & Central Asia	Upper middle income

Population (millions)	4	Population growth (%)	0.1
Surface area (1,000 sq. km)	57	National poverty rate (% pop.)	..
GNI ($ billions)	24	GNI per capita ($)	5,370

	1990	2002	2003
People			
Life expectancy at birth (years)	72	74	74
Fertility rate (births per woman)	1.6	1.5	1.4
Infant mortality rate (per 1,000 live births)	12	7	6
Under-five mortality rate (per 1,000)	13	8	7
Births attended by skilled health staff (% of total)	..	100	..
Child malnutrition, underweight (% of under age 5)	..	..	..
Child immunization, measles (% of ages 12–23 mon.)	90	95	95
HIV prevalence rate (% of ages 15–49)	..	..	0.1
Adult literacy, male (% of ages 15 and older)	99	99	..
Adult literacy, female (% of ages 15 and older)	95	97	..
Primary completion rate, total (% of age group)	..	94	96
Primary completion rate, female (% of age group)	..	94	96
Net primary enrollment (% of age group)	74	89	..
Net secondary enrollment (% of age group)	57	87	..
Environment			
Forests (1,000 sq. km)	18	18	..
Deforestation (average annual %, 1990–2000)		–0.1	
Freshwater use (% of internal resources)			2
Carbon dioxide emissions (metric tons per capita)	3.8	4.5	..
Access to improved water source (% of total pop.)	..	..	..
Access to improved sanitation (% of urban pop.)	..	..	..
Energy use per capita (kg oil equivalent)	1,502	1,852	..
Electricity use per capita (kilowatt-hours)	2,112	2,855	..
Economy			
GDP ($ billions)	25	23	29
GDP growth (annual %)	–21.1	5.2	4.3
GDP implicit price deflator (annual % growth)	99.3	2.9	3.2
Value added in agriculture (% of GDP)	10	9	8
Value added in industry (% of GDP)	34	30	30
Value added in services (% of GDP)	56	61	62
Exports of goods and services (% of GDP)	78	45	47
Imports of goods and services (% of GDP)	86	55	57
Gross capital formation (% of GDP)	14	28	30
Central government revenue (% of GDP)	33.0	39.5	..
Cash surplus/deficit (% of GDP)	–4.6	–4.8	..
Technology and infrastructure			
Fixed-line and mobile subscribers (per 1,000 people)	172	952	..
Cost of 3-minute local call ($)	0.03	0.09	0.10
Personal computers (per 1,000 people)	14.6	173.8	..
Internet users (per 1,000 people)	..	180	232
Paved roads (% of total)	..	84.6	..
Aircraft departures (thousands)	2	19	20
Trade and finance			
Trade in goods (% of GDP)	88.8	68.5	70.5
Trade growth less GDP growth (avg. %, 1990–2003)			4.2
High-technology exports (% of manufactured exports)	5	12	12
Net barter terms of trade (2000 = 100)	..	..	..
Foreign direct investment ($ millions)	0	1,124	1,998
Present value of debt ($ billions)			23
Total debt service (% of goods and services exports)	..	26.2	20.9
Short-term debt ($ billions)	..	2	4
Aid per capita ($)	0	30	27

Cuba

Latin America & Caribbean | **Lower middle income**

Population (millions)	11	Population growth (%)	0.7
Surface area (1,000 sq. km)	111	National poverty rate (% pop.)	..
GNI ($ millions)	..	GNI per capita ($)	..

	1990	2002	2003
People			
Life expectancy at birth (years)	75	77	77
Fertility rate (births per woman)	1.7	1.6	1.6
Infant mortality rate (per 1,000 live births)	11	7	..
Under-five mortality rate (per 1,000)	13	8	..
Births attended by skilled health staff (% of total)	..	100	..
Child malnutrition, underweight (% of under age 5)	..	4	..
Child immunization, measles (% of ages 12–23 mon.)	94	98	99
HIV prevalence rate (% of ages 15–49)	..	0.1	0.1
Adult literacy, male (% of ages 15 and older)	95	97	..
Adult literacy, female (% of ages 15 and older)	95	97	..
Primary completion rate, total (% of age group)	94	94	..
Primary completion rate, female (% of age group)	..	94	..
Net primary enrollment (% of age group)	92	93	..
Net secondary enrollment (% of age group)	69	86	..
Environment			
Forests (1,000 sq. km)	21	23	..
Deforestation (average annual %, 1990–2000)		–1.3	
Freshwater use (% of internal resources)			14
Carbon dioxide emissions (metric tons per capita)	3.0	2.8	..
Access to improved water source (% of total pop.)	..	91	..
Access to improved sanitation (% of urban pop.)	99	99	..
Energy use per capita (kg oil equivalent)	1,555	1,262	..
Electricity use per capita (kilowatt-hours)	1,125	1,094	..
Economy			
GDP ($ millions)	..	..	..
GDP growth (annual %)	..	..	..
GDP implicit price deflator (annual % growth)	..	2.6	..
Value added in agriculture (% of GDP)	..	7	..
Value added in industry (% of GDP)	..	46	..
Value added in services (% of GDP)	..	47	..
Exports of goods and services (% of GDP)	..	16	..
Imports of goods and services (% of GDP)	..	18	..
Gross capital formation (% of GDP)	..	10	..
Central government revenue (% of GDP)	..	..	..
Cash surplus/deficit (% of GDP)	..	..	..
Technology and infrastructure			
Fixed-line and mobile subscribers (per 1,000 people)	31	52	..
Cost of 3-minute local call ($)	0.00	0.09	..
Personal computers (per 1,000 people)	..	31.8	..
Internet users (per 1,000 people)	..	11	..
Paved roads (% of total)	50.5	49.0	..
Aircraft departures (thousands)	19	10	9
Trade and finance			
Trade in goods (% of GDP)	..	..	..
Trade growth less GDP growth (avg. %, 1990–2003)			..
High-technology exports (% of manufactured exports)	..	29	..
Net barter terms of trade (2000 = 100)	..	..	..
Foreign direct investment ($ millions)	..	..	..
Present value of debt ($ millions)			..
Total debt service (% of goods and services exports)	..	..	..
Short-term debt ($ millions)	..	..	..
Aid per capita ($)	5	5	6

Cyprus

High income

Population (thousands)	770	Population growth (%)	0.6
Surface area (1,000 sq. km)	9	National poverty rate (% pop.)	..
GNI ($ millions)	..	GNI per capita ($)	..

	1990	2002	2003
People			
Life expectancy at birth (years)	77	78	78
Fertility rate (births per woman)	2.4	1.9	1.9
Infant mortality rate (per 1,000 live births)	10	6	4
Under-five mortality rate (per 1,000)	12	7	5
Births attended by skilled health staff (% of total)	..	..	..
Child malnutrition, underweight (% of under age 5)	..	..	..
Child immunization, measles (% of ages 12–23 mon.)	77	86	86
HIV prevalence rate (% of ages 15–49)	..	..	..
Adult literacy, male (% of ages 15 and older)	98	99	..
Adult literacy, female (% of ages 15 and older)	91	95	..
Primary completion rate, total (% of age group)	90	87	..
Primary completion rate, female (% of age group)	90	88	..
Net primary enrollment (% of age group)	87	96	..
Net secondary enrollment (% of age group)	69	92	..
Environment			
Forests (1,000 sq. km)	1	2	..
Deforestation (average annual %, 1990–2000)		–3.8	
Freshwater use (% of internal resources)			..
Carbon dioxide emissions (metric tons per capita)	6.8	8.5	..
Access to improved water source (% of total pop.)	100	100	..
Access to improved sanitation (% of urban pop.)	100	100	..
Energy use per capita (kg oil equivalent)	2,256	3,225	..
Electricity use per capita (kilowatt-hours)	2,630	4,425	..
Economy			
GDP ($ millions)	5,592	10,106	11,385
GDP growth (annual %)	7.4	2.0	4.0
GDP implicit price deflator (annual % growth)	5.4	3.0	4.5
Value added in agriculture (% of GDP)	7	..	..
Value added in industry (% of GDP)	26	..	..
Value added in services (% of GDP)	67	..	..
Exports of goods and services (% of GDP)	52	45	..
Imports of goods and services (% of GDP)	57	48	..
Gross capital formation (% of GDP)	27	19	..
Central government revenue (% of GDP)	27.6	31.4	..
Cash surplus/deficit (% of GDP)	–4.9	–5.5	..
Technology and infrastructure			
Fixed-line and mobile subscribers (per 1,000 people)	424	1,272	1,316
Cost of 3-minute local call ($)	0.03	0.03	0.08
Personal computers (per 1,000 people)	8.5	269.9	..
Internet users (per 1,000 people)	1	294	337
Paved roads (% of total)	59.6	62.2	..
Aircraft departures (thousands)	8	15	17
Trade and finance			
Trade in goods (% of GDP)	62.9	48.8	47.3
Trade growth less GDP growth (avg. %, 1990–2003)			..
High-technology exports (% of manufactured exports)	6	3	5
Net barter terms of trade (2000 = 100)	..	..	..
Foreign direct investment ($ millions)	127	1,086	1,025
Present value of debt ($ millions)			..
Total debt service (% of goods and services exports)	..	..	..
Short-term debt ($ millions)	..	..	..
Aid per capita ($)	57	45	24

Czech Republic

Europe & Central Asia		Upper middle income
Population (millions)	10	Population growth (%)	0.0
Surface area (1,000 sq. km)	79	National poverty rate (% pop.)	..
GNI ($ billions)	73	GNI per capita ($)	7,150

	1990	2002	2003
People			
Life expectancy at birth (years)	71	75	75
Fertility rate (births per woman)	1.9	1.2	1.2
Infant mortality rate (per 1,000 live births)	11	4	4
Under-five mortality rate (per 1,000)	13	5	..
Births attended by skilled health staff (% of total)	..	..	..
Child malnutrition, underweight (% of under age 5)	1	..	..
Child immunization, measles (% of ages 12–23 mon.)	..	99	99
HIV prevalence rate (% of ages 15–49)	..	0.1	0.1
Adult literacy, male (% of ages 15 and older)	..	..	..
Adult literacy, female (% of ages 15 and older)	..	..	..
Primary completion rate, total (% of age group)	..	106	..
Primary completion rate, female (% of age group)	..	106	..
Net primary enrollment (% of age group)	87	88	..
Net secondary enrollment (% of age group)	..	89	..
Environment			
Forests (1,000 sq. km)	26	26	..
Deforestation (average annual %, 1990–2000)		0.0	
Freshwater use (% of internal resources)			21
Carbon dioxide emissions (metric tons per capita)	13.4	11.6	..
Access to improved water source (% of total pop.)	..	..	..
Access to improved sanitation (% of urban pop.)	..	..	..
Energy use per capita (kg oil equivalent)	4,572	4,090	..
Electricity use per capita (kilowatt-hours)	4,649	4,982	..
Economy			
GDP ($ billions)	35	74	90
GDP growth (annual %)	–11.6	1.5	3.1
GDP implicit price deflator (annual % growth)	36.2	2.8	1.7
Value added in agriculture (% of GDP)	6	4	3
Value added in industry (% of GDP)	49	40	39
Value added in services (% of GDP)	45	57	57
Exports of goods and services (% of GDP)	45	62	63
Imports of goods and services (% of GDP)	43	64	65
Gross capital formation (% of GDP)	25	28	28
Central government revenue (% of GDP)	..	32.4	33.2
Cash surplus/deficit (% of GDP)	..	–6.1	–5.0
Technology and infrastructure			
Fixed-line and mobile subscribers (per 1,000 people)	158	1,211	1,325
Cost of 3-minute local call ($)	0.06	0.13	0.15
Personal computers (per 1,000 people)	11.6	177.4	..
Internet users (per 1,000 people)	..	256	308
Paved roads (% of total)	100.0	100.0	..
Aircraft departures (thousands)	22	47	52
Trade and finance			
Trade in goods (% of GDP)	83.6	107.1	111.3
Trade growth less GDP growth (avg. %, 1990–2003)			8.7
High-technology exports (% of manufactured exports)	..	13	13
Net barter terms of trade (2000 = 100)	..	..	..
Foreign direct investment ($ millions)	0	8,497	2,514
Present value of debt ($ billions)			34
Total debt service (% of goods and services exports)	..	9.3	9.3
Short-term debt ($ billions)	..	11	14
Aid per capita ($)	1	16	26

Denmark

High income

Population (millions)	5	Population growth (%)	0.2
Surface area (1,000 sq. km)	43	National poverty rate (% pop.)	..
GNI ($ billions)	181	GNI per capita ($)	33,570

	1990	2002	2003
People			
Life expectancy at birth (years)	75	77	77
Fertility rate (births per woman)	1.7	1.7	1.8
Infant mortality rate (per 1,000 live births)	8	4	4
Under-five mortality rate (per 1,000)	9	6	..
Births attended by skilled health staff (% of total)	..	..	..
Child malnutrition, underweight (% of under age 5)	..	..	..
Child immunization, measles (% of ages 12–23 mon.)	84	99	96
HIV prevalence rate (% of ages 15–49)	..	0.2	0.2
Adult literacy, male (% of ages 15 and older)	..	..	..
Adult literacy, female (% of ages 15 and older)	..	..	..
Primary completion rate, total (% of age group)	98	107	..
Primary completion rate, female (% of age group)	97	107	..
Net primary enrollment (% of age group)	98	100	..
Net secondary enrollment (% of age group)	87	93	..
Environment			
Forests (1,000 sq. km)	4	5	..
Deforestation (average annual %, 1990–2000)		–0.2	
Freshwater use (% of internal resources)			20
Carbon dioxide emissions (metric tons per capita)	9.9	8.4	..
Access to improved water source (% of total pop.)	100	100	..
Access to improved sanitation (% of urban pop.)	..	..	..
Energy use per capita (kg oil equivalent)	3,420	3,675	..
Electricity use per capita (kilowatt-hours)	5,518	6,024	..
Economy			
GDP ($ billions)	133	172	212
GDP growth (annual %)	1.0	1.0	0.4
GDP implicit price deflator (annual % growth)	3.7	1.6	2.1
Value added in agriculture (% of GDP)	4	2	2
Value added in industry (% of GDP)	27	26	26
Value added in services (% of GDP)	69	71	71
Exports of goods and services (% of GDP)	36	44	43
Imports of goods and services (% of GDP)	31	39	37
Gross capital formation (% of GDP)	20	21	20
Central government revenue (% of GDP)	..	37.7	37.6
Cash surplus/deficit (% of GDP)	..	2.0	2.0
Technology and infrastructure			
Fixed-line and mobile subscribers (per 1,000 people)	596	1,522	1,553
Cost of 3-minute local call ($)	0.13	0.08	0.11
Personal computers (per 1,000 people)	114.9	576.8	..
Internet users (per 1,000 people)	1	513	..
Paved roads (% of total)	100.0	100.0	..
Aircraft departures (thousands)	91	98	91
Trade and finance			
Trade in goods (% of GDP)	52.6	62.6	59.1
Trade growth less GDP growth (avg. %, 1990–2003)			3.4
High-technology exports (% of manufactured exports)	15	22	20
Net barter terms of trade (2000 = 100)	102	101	103
Foreign direct investment ($ millions)	1,132	4,431	1,185
Present value of debt ($ millions)			..
Total debt service (% of goods and services exports)	..	..	..
Short-term debt ($ millions)	..	..	..
Aid per capita ($)	..	..	..

Djibouti

Middle East & North Africa			Lower middle income

Population (thousands)	705	Population growth (%)	1.7
Surface area (1,000 sq. km)	23	National poverty rate (% pop.)	..
GNI ($ millions)	643	GNI per capita ($)	910

	1990	2002	2003
People			
Life expectancy at birth (years)	48	44	43
Fertility rate (births per woman)	6.0	5.2	5.2
Infant mortality rate (per 1,000 live births)	119	*102*	97
Under-five mortality rate (per 1,000)	175	*146*	138
Births attended by skilled health staff (% of total)	..	..	61
Child malnutrition, underweight (% of under age 5)	23	..	..
Child immunization, measles (% of ages 12–23 mon.)	85	62	66
HIV prevalence rate (% of ages 15–49)	..	*2.8*	2.9
Adult literacy, male (% of ages 15 and older)	..	..	..
Adult literacy, female (% of ages 15 and older)	..	..	..
Primary completion rate, total (% of age group)	32	35	35
Primary completion rate, female (% of age group)	..	32	32
Net primary enrollment (% of age group)	31	*34*	..
Net secondary enrollment (% of age group)	..	17	..
Environment			
Forests (1,000 sq. km)	0	*0*	..
Deforestation (average annual %, 1990–2000)		*0.0*	
Freshwater use (% of internal resources)			..
Carbon dioxide emissions (metric tons per capita)	0.7	*0.6*	..
Access to improved water source (% of total pop.)	78	80	..
Access to improved sanitation (% of urban pop.)	55	55	..
Energy use per capita (kg oil equivalent)	..	..	..
Electricity use per capita (kilowatt-hours)	..	..	..
Economy			
GDP ($ millions)	418	592	625
GDP growth (annual %)	–1.9	2.6	3.5
GDP implicit price deflator (annual % growth)	4.0	0.6	2.0
Value added in agriculture (% of GDP)	3	*4*	..
Value added in industry (% of GDP)	20	*14*	..
Value added in services (% of GDP)	77	*82*	..
Exports of goods and services (% of GDP)	..	*45*	..
Imports of goods and services (% of GDP)	..	*63*	..
Gross capital formation (% of GDP)	..	*13*	..
Central government revenue (% of GDP)	..	..	..
Cash surplus/deficit (% of GDP)	..	..	..
Technology and infrastructure			
Fixed-line and mobile subscribers (per 1,000 people)	11	38	50
Cost of 3-minute local call ($)	0.20	0.20	0.08
Personal computers (per 1,000 people)	1.9	15.2	21.7
Internet users (per 1,000 people)	..	7	10
Paved roads (% of total)	12.6	*12.6*	..
Aircraft departures (thousands)	4	..	..
Trade and finance			
Trade in goods (% of GDP)	57.5	59.6	62.4
Trade growth less GDP growth (avg. %, 1990–2003)			..
High-technology exports (% of manufactured exports)	..	..	..
Net barter terms of trade (2000 = 100)	..	..	..
Foreign direct investment ($ millions)	0	4	11
Present value of debt ($ millions)			267
Total debt service (% of goods and services exports)	*5.2*	..	..
Short-term debt ($ millions)	50	10	9
Aid per capita ($)	395	112	110

Dominica

Latin America & Caribbean   **Upper middle income**

Population (thousands)	71	Population growth (%)	0.2
Surface area (sq. km)	750	National poverty rate (% pop.)	..
GNI ($ millions)	237	GNI per capita ($)	3,330

	1990	2002	2003
People			
Life expectancy at birth (years)	73	77	77
Fertility rate (births per woman)	2.7	1.9	1.9
Infant mortality rate (per 1,000 live births)	19	14	12
Under-five mortality rate (per 1,000)	23	16	14
Births attended by skilled health staff (% of total)	..	100	..
Child malnutrition, underweight (% of under age 5)	..	..	..
Child immunization, measles (% of ages 12–23 mon.)	88	98	99
HIV prevalence rate (% of ages 15–49)	..	..	..
Adult literacy, male (% of ages 15 and older)	..	..	..
Adult literacy, female (% of ages 15 and older)	..	..	..
Primary completion rate, total (% of age group)	..	91	..
Primary completion rate, female (% of age group)	..	90	..
Net primary enrollment (% of age group)	..	81	..
Net secondary enrollment (% of age group)	..	91	..
Environment			
Forests (1,000 sq. km)	1	0	..
Deforestation (average annual %, 1990–2000)		0.8	
Freshwater use (% of internal resources)			..
Carbon dioxide emissions (metric tons per capita)	0.8	1.4	..
Access to improved water source (% of total pop.)	..	97	..
Access to improved sanitation (% of urban pop.)	..	86	..
Energy use per capita (kg oil equivalent)	..	..	..
Electricity use per capita (kilowatt-hours)	..	..	..
Economy			
GDP ($ millions)	166	252	259
GDP growth (annual %)	5.3	–5.2	–0.6
GDP implicit price deflator (annual % growth)	3.0	0.8	1.8
Value added in agriculture (% of GDP)	25	19	..
Value added in industry (% of GDP)	19	21	..
Value added in services (% of GDP)	56	60	..
Exports of goods and services (% of GDP)	55	54	54
Imports of goods and services (% of GDP)	81	62	62
Gross capital formation (% of GDP)	41	11	..
Central government revenue (% of GDP)	..	..	..
Cash surplus/deficit (% of GDP)	..	..	..
Technology and infrastructure			
Fixed-line and mobile subscribers (per 1,000 people)	164	424	..
Cost of 3-minute local call ($)	0.10	0.10	..
Personal computers (per 1,000 people)	..	89.7	..
Internet users (per 1,000 people)	..	160	..
Paved roads (% of total)	45.6	50.4	..
Aircraft departures (thousands)	..	..	..
Trade and finance			
Trade in goods (% of GDP)	104.0	62.3	63.7
Trade growth less GDP growth (avg. %, 1990–2003)			–0.5
High-technology exports (% of manufactured exports)	..	8	7
Net barter terms of trade (2000 = 100)	..	..	..
Foreign direct investment ($ millions)	13	11	0
Present value of debt ($ millions)			284
Total debt service (% of goods and services exports)	5.6	9.7	14.6
Short-term debt ($ millions)	2	26	73
Aid per capita ($)	273	421	153

Dominican Republic

Latin America & Caribbean		Lower middle income	
Population (millions)	9	Population growth (%)	1.4
Surface area (1,000 sq. km)	49	National poverty rate (% pop.)	29
GNI ($ billions)	19	GNI per capita ($)	2,130

	1990	2002	2003
People			
Life expectancy at birth (years)	66	67	67
Fertility rate (births per woman)	3.4	2.6	2.6
Infant mortality rate (per 1,000 live births)	50	*33*	29
Under-five mortality rate (per 1,000)	65	*40*	35
Births attended by skilled health staff (% of total)	*93*	98	..
Child malnutrition, underweight (% of under age 5)	*10*	5	..
Child immunization, measles (% of ages 12–23 mon.)	96	82	79
HIV prevalence rate (% of ages 15–49)	..	*1.8*	1.7
Adult literacy, male (% of ages 15 and older)	80	84	..
Adult literacy, female (% of ages 15 and older)	79	84	..
Primary completion rate, total (% of age group)	..	94	93
Primary completion rate, female (% of age group)	..	99	97
Net primary enrollment (% of age group)	58	92	..
Net secondary enrollment (% of age group)	..	36	..
Environment			
Forests (1,000 sq. km)	14	*14*	..
Deforestation (average annual %, 1990–2000)		*0.0*	
Freshwater use (% of internal resources)			40
Carbon dioxide emissions (metric tons per capita)	1.3	*3.0*	..
Access to improved water source (% of total pop.)	86	93	..
Access to improved sanitation (% of urban pop.)	60	67	..
Energy use per capita (kg oil equivalent)	586	948	..
Electricity use per capita (kilowatt-hours)	440	853	..
Economy			
GDP ($ billions)	7	22	17
GDP growth (annual %)	–5.8	4.1	–0.4
GDP implicit price deflator (annual % growth)	51.1	5.4	27.4
Value added in agriculture (% of GDP)	13	12	11
Value added in industry (% of GDP)	31	32	31
Value added in services (% of GDP)	55	56	58
Exports of goods and services (% of GDP)	34	38	52
Imports of goods and services (% of GDP)	44	47	54
Gross capital formation (% of GDP)	25	23	23
Central government revenue (% of GDP)	12.0	17.3	..
Cash surplus/deficit (% of GDP)	0.6	–0.2	..
Technology and infrastructure			
Fixed-line and mobile subscribers (per 1,000 people)	48	317	387
Cost of 3-minute local call ($)	*0.00*	0.06	..
Personal computers (per 1,000 people)	..	..	..
Internet users (per 1,000 people)	..	*19*	64
Paved roads (% of total)	44.7	49.4	..
Aircraft departures (thousands)	10	*0*	..
Trade and finance			
Trade in goods (% of GDP)	73.2	64.8	80.5
Trade growth less GDP growth (avg. %, 1990–2003)			3.9
High-technology exports (% of manufactured exports)	..	*1*	..
Net barter terms of trade (2000 = 100)	96	101	..
Foreign direct investment ($ millions)	133	917	310
Present value of debt ($ millions)			6,244
Total debt service (% of goods and services exports)	10.4	6.4	8.2
Short-term debt ($ millions)	782	2,023	1,084
Aid per capita ($)	14	17	8

Ecuador

Latin America & Caribbean		Lower middle income

Population (millions)	13	Population growth (%)	1.6
Surface area (1,000 sq. km)	284	National poverty rate (% pop.)	..
GNI ($ billions)	24	GNI per capita ($)	1,830

	1990	2002	2003
People			
Life expectancy at birth (years)	68	71	71
Fertility rate (births per woman)	3.7	2.8	2.7
Infant mortality rate (per 1,000 live births)	43	27	24
Under-five mortality rate (per 1,000)	57	32	27
Births attended by skilled health staff (% of total)	..	91	..
Child malnutrition, underweight (% of under age 5)	..	14	..
Child immunization, measles (% of ages 12–23 mon.)	60	80	99
HIV prevalence rate (% of ages 15–49)	..	0.3	0.3
Adult literacy, male (% of ages 15 and older)	90	92	..
Adult literacy, female (% of ages 15 and older)	85	90	..
Primary completion rate, total (% of age group)	..	100	..
Primary completion rate, female (% of age group)	..	100	..
Net primary enrollment (% of age group)	98	100	..
Net secondary enrollment (% of age group)	..	50	..
Environment			
Forests (1,000 sq. km)	119	106	..
Deforestation (average annual %, 1990–2000)		1.2	
Freshwater use (% of internal resources)			4
Carbon dioxide emissions (metric tons per capita)	1.6	2.0	..
Access to improved water source (% of total pop.)	69	86	..
Access to improved sanitation (% of urban pop.)	73	80	..
Energy use per capita (kg oil equivalent)	597	706	..
Electricity use per capita (kilowatt-hours)	467	665	..
Economy			
GDP ($ billions)	10	24	27
GDP growth (annual %)	2.7	3.4	2.7
GDP implicit price deflator (annual % growth)	5.9	11.8	9.0
Value added in agriculture (% of GDP)	13	9	8
Value added in industry (% of GDP)	38	28	29
Value added in services (% of GDP)	49	63	64
Exports of goods and services (% of GDP)	33	24	24
Imports of goods and services (% of GDP)	32	31	29
Gross capital formation (% of GDP)	21	28	28
Central government revenue (% of GDP)	..	..	..
Cash surplus/deficit (% of GDP)	..	..	..
Technology and infrastructure			
Fixed-line and mobile subscribers (per 1,000 people)	48	231	312
Cost of 3-minute local call ($)	0.00	0.03	0.03
Personal computers (per 1,000 people)	1.9	31.1	..
Internet users (per 1,000 people)	0	43	46
Paved roads (% of total)	13.4	18.9	..
Aircraft departures (thousands)	28	15	13
Trade and finance			
Trade in goods (% of GDP)	44.2	47.2	46.2
Trade growth less GDP growth (avg. %, 1990–2003)			1.9
High-technology exports (% of manufactured exports)	0	7	6
Net barter terms of trade (2000 = 100)	114	95	..
Foreign direct investment ($ millions)	126	1,275	1,555
Present value of debt ($ billions)			19
Total debt service (% of goods and services exports)	32.5	28.9	27.9
Short-term debt ($ millions)	1,814	2,314	1,772
Aid per capita ($)	16	17	14

Egypt, Arab Rep.

Middle East & North Africa			Lower middle income

Population (millions)	68	Population growth (%)	1.8
Surface area (1,000 sq. km)	1,001	National poverty rate (% pop.)	17
GNI ($ billions)	94	GNI per capita ($)	1,390

	1990	2002	2003
People			
Life expectancy at birth (years)	63	69	69
Fertility rate (births per woman)	4.0	3.2	3.1
Infant mortality rate (per 1,000 live births)	76	40	33
Under-five mortality rate (per 1,000)	104	49	39
Births attended by skilled health staff (% of total)	37	61	69
Child malnutrition, underweight (% of under age 5)	10	4	9
Child immunization, measles (% of ages 12–23 mon.)	86	97	98
HIV prevalence rate (% of ages 15–49)	..	0.1	0.1
Adult literacy, male (% of ages 15 and older)	60	..	..
Adult literacy, female (% of ages 15 and older)	34	..	..
Primary completion rate, total (% of age group)	..	89	91
Primary completion rate, female (% of age group)	..	88	90
Net primary enrollment (% of age group)	84	90	..
Net secondary enrollment (% of age group)	..	81	..
Environment			
Forests (1,000 sq. km)	1	1	..
Deforestation (average annual %, 1990–2000)		–3.3	
Freshwater use (% of internal resources)			3,300
Carbon dioxide emissions (metric tons per capita)	1.4	2.2	..
Access to improved water source (% of total pop.)	94	98	..
Access to improved sanitation (% of urban pop.)	70	84	..
Energy use per capita (kg oil equivalent)	608	789	..
Electricity use per capita (kilowatt-hours)	690	1,073	..
Economy			
GDP ($ billions)	43	90	82
GDP growth (annual %)	5.7	3.2	3.2
GDP implicit price deflator (annual % growth)	18.4	3.8	3.8
Value added in agriculture (% of GDP)	19	17	16
Value added in industry (% of GDP)	29	33	34
Value added in services (% of GDP)	52	50	50
Exports of goods and services (% of GDP)	20	16	22
Imports of goods and services (% of GDP)	33	23	24
Gross capital formation (% of GDP)	29	17	17
Central government revenue (% of GDP)	23.0	26.9	..
Cash surplus/deficit (% of GDP)	–2.0	–1.7	..
Technology and infrastructure			
Fixed-line and mobile subscribers (per 1,000 people)	30	177	212
Cost of 3-minute local call ($)	0.02	0.02	0.02
Personal computers (per 1,000 people)	..	16.6	21.9
Internet users (per 1,000 people)	..	7	39
Paved roads (% of total)	72.0	78.1	..
Aircraft departures (thousands)	20	42	42
Trade and finance			
Trade in goods (% of GDP)	36.8	19.2	20.7
Trade growth less GDP growth (avg. %, 1990–2003)			–2.4
High-technology exports (% of manufactured exports)	..	1	0
Net barter terms of trade (2000 = 100)	101	98	..
Foreign direct investment ($ millions)	734	647	237
Present value of debt ($ billions)			28
Total debt service (% of goods and services exports)	20.4	10.3	11.7
Short-term debt ($ millions)	4,453	3,468	3,801
Aid per capita ($)	104	19	13

El Salvador

Latin America & Caribbean | **Lower middle income**

Population (millions)	7	Population growth (%)	1.8
Surface area (1,000 sq. km)	21	National poverty rate (% pop.)	..
GNI ($ billions)	15	GNI per capita ($)	2.340

	1990	2002	2003
People			
Life expectancy at birth (years)	66	70	70
Fertility rate (births per woman)	3.8	2.9	2.8
Infant mortality rate (per 1,000 live births)	46	34	32
Under-five mortality rate (per 1,000)	60	40	36
Births attended by skilled health staff (% of total)	52	..	69
Child malnutrition, underweight (% of under age 5)	15	12	10
Child immunization, measles (% of age 12–23 mon.)	98	93	99
HIV prevalence rate (% of ages 15–49)	..	0.6	0.7
Adult literacy, male (% of ages 15 and older)	76	82	..
Adult literacy, female (% of ages 15 and older)	69	77	..
Primary completion rate, total (% of age group)	62	86	89
Primary completion rate, female (% of age group)	63	86	..
Net primary enrollment (% of age group)	73	90	..
Net secondary enrollment (% of age group)	..	49	..
Environment			
Forests (1,000 sq. km)	2	1	..
Deforestation (average annual %, 1990–2000)		4.6	
Freshwater use (% of internal resources)			4
Carbon dioxide emissions (metric tons per capita)	0.5	1.1	..
Access to improved water source (% of total pop.)	67	82	..
Access to improved sanitation (% of urban pop.)	70	78	..
Energy use per capita (kg oil equivalent)	496	670	..
Electricity use per capita (kilowatt-hours)	358	595	..
Economy			
GDP ($ billions)	5	14	15
GDP growth (annual %)	4.8	2.2	1.8
GDP implicit price deflator (annual % growth)	22.5	1.4	2.1
Value added in agriculture (% of GDP)	17	9	9
Value added in industry (% of GDP)	27	30	32
Value added in services (% of GDP)	56	61	59
Exports of goods and services (% of GDP)	19	26	27
Imports of goods and services (% of GDP)	31	41	43
Gross capital formation (% of GDP)	14	16	16
Central government revenue (% of GDP)	..	16.0	15.4
Cash surplus/deficit (% of GDP)	..	−4.7	−2.5
Technology and infrastructure			
Fixed-line and mobile subscribers (per 1,000 people)	24	241	292
Cost of 3-minute local call ($)	0.00	0.07	..
Personal computers (per 1,000 people)	..	25.2	..
Internet users (per 1,000 people)	..	46	84
Paved roads (% of total)	14.4	19.8	..
Aircraft departures (thousands)	11	19	25
Trade and finance			
Trade in goods (% of GDP)	38.4	57.2	59.8
Trade growth less GDP growth (avg. %, 1990–2003)			6.5
High-technology exports (% of manufactured exports)	..	6	5
Net barter terms of trade (2000 = 100)	84	96	..
Foreign direct investment ($ millions)	2	470	89
Present value of debt ($ millions)			7,812
Total debt service (% of goods and services exports)	15.3	7.7	8.8
Short-term debt ($ millions)	210	1,164	1,759
Aid per capita ($)	68	36	29

Equatorial Guinea

Sub-Saharan Africa		Low income

Population (thousands)	494	Population growth (%)		2.5
Surface area (1,000 sq. km)	28	National poverty rate (% pop.)		..
GNI ($ millions)	..	GNI per capita ($)		..

	1990	2002	2003
People			
Life expectancy at birth (years)	47	52	52
Fertility rate (births per woman)	5.9	5.5	5.4
Infant mortality rate (per 1,000 live births)	122	103	97
Under-five mortality rate (per 1,000)	206	156	146
Births attended by skilled health staff (% of total)	..	65	..
Child malnutrition, underweight (% of under age 5)	..	..	..
Child immunization, measles (% of ages 12–23 mon.)	88	51	51
HIV prevalence rate (% of ages 15–49)	..	..	..
Adult literacy, male (% of ages 15 and older)	..	..	..
Adult literacy, female (% of ages 15 and older)	..	..	..
Primary completion rate, total (% of age group)	..	45	..
Primary completion rate, female (% of age group)	..	48	..
Net primary enrollment (% of age group)	91	85	..
Net secondary enrollment (% of age group)	..	37	..
Environment			
Forests (1,000 sq. km)	19	18	..
Deforestation (average annual %, 1990–2000)		0.6	
Freshwater use (% of internal resources)			0
Carbon dioxide emissions (metric tons per capita)	0.3	0.4	..
Access to improved water source (% of total pop.)	..	44	..
Access to improved sanitation (% of urban pop.)	..	60	..
Energy use per capita (kg oil equivalent)	..	..	..
Electricity use per capita (kilowatt-hours)	..	..	..
Economy			
GDP ($ millions)	132	2,118	2,915
GDP growth (annual %)	3.3	17.6	14.7
GDP implicit price deflator (annual % growth)	–2.5	0.6	0.1
Value added in agriculture (% of GDP)	62	9	7
Value added in industry (% of GDP)	11	86	89
Value added in services (% of GDP)	28	5	4
Exports of goods and services (% of GDP)	32	102	..
Imports of goods and services (% of GDP)	70	173	..
Gross capital formation (% of GDP)	17	92	..
Central government revenue (% of GDP)	..	..	..
Cash surplus/deficit (% of GDP)	..	..	..
Technology and infrastructure			
Fixed-line and mobile subscribers (per 1,000 people)	4	81	94
Cost of 3-minute local call ($)	..	0.05	..
Personal computers (per 1,000 people)	..	6.9	..
Internet users (per 1,000 people)	..	2	..
Paved roads (% of total)	..	..	..
Aircraft departures (thousands)	0	1	..
Trade and finance			
Trade in goods (% of GDP)	95.4	125.6	125.6
Trade growth less GDP growth (avg. %, 1990–2003)			..
High-technology exports (% of manufactured exports)	..	..	..
Net barter terms of trade (2000 = 100)	38	37	..
Foreign direct investment ($ millions)	11	323	1,431
Present value of debt ($ millions)			272
Total debt service (% of goods and services exports)	12.1	..	..
Short-term debt ($ millions)	26	50	91
Aid per capita ($)	173	42	43

Eritrea

Sub-Saharan Africa			Low income

Population (millions)	4	Population growth (%)	2.2
Surface area (1,000 sq. km)	118	National poverty rate (% pop.)	..
GNI ($ millions)	851	GNI per capita ($)	190

	1990	2002	2003
People			
Life expectancy at birth (years)	49	51	51
Fertility rate (births per woman)	6.5	4.8	4.8
Infant mortality rate (per 1,000 live births)	85	53	45
Under-five mortality rate (per 1,000)	147	97	85
Births attended by skilled health staff (% of total)	..	28	..
Child malnutrition, underweight (% of under age 5)	..	40	..
Child immunization, measles (% of ages 12–23 mon.)	..	84	84
HIV prevalence rate (% of ages 15–49)	..	2.8	2.7
Adult literacy, male (% of ages 15 and older)	..	..	..
Adult literacy, female (% of ages 15 and older)	..	..	..
Primary completion rate, total (% of age group)	..	36	40
Primary completion rate, female (% of age group)	..	30	33
Net primary enrollment (% of age group)	16	45	..
Net secondary enrollment (% of age group)	..	22	..
Environment			
Forests (1,000 sq. km)	16	16	..
Deforestation (average annual %, 1990–2000)		0.3	
Freshwater use (% of internal resources)			..
Carbon dioxide emissions (metric tons per capita)	..	0.1	..
Access to improved water source (% of total pop.)	40	57	..
Access to improved sanitation (% of urban pop.)	46	34	..
Energy use per capita (kg oil equivalent)	..	..	..
Electricity use per capita (kilowatt-hours)	..	..	..
Economy			
GDP ($ millions)	477	631	751
GDP growth (annual %)	..	0.7	3.0
GDP implicit price deflator (annual % growth)	..	15.2	14.8
Value added in agriculture (% of GDP)	31	13	14
Value added in industry (% of GDP)	12	25	25
Value added in services (% of GDP)	57	62	61
Exports of goods and services (% of GDP)	11	20	14
Imports of goods and services (% of GDP)	45	80	99
Gross capital formation (% of GDP)	8	27	22
Central government revenue (% of GDP)	..	..	..
Cash surplus/deficit (% of GDP)	..	..	..
Technology and infrastructure			
Fixed-line and mobile subscribers (per 1,000 people)	4	9	..
Cost of 3-minute local call ($)	0.03	0.03	..
Personal computers (per 1,000 people)	..	2.5	2.9
Internet users (per 1,000 people)	..	2	7
Paved roads (% of total)	19.4	21.8	..
Aircraft departures (thousands)	..	..	..
Trade and finance			
Trade in goods (% of GDP)	76.9	93.5	96.7
Trade growth less GDP growth (avg. %, 1990–2003)			−1.1
High-technology exports (% of manufactured exports)	..	..	..
Net barter terms of trade (2000 = 100)	99	99	..
Foreign direct investment ($ millions)	0	21	22
Present value of debt ($ millions)			389
Total debt service (% of goods and services exports)	..	7.3	14.1
Short-term debt ($ billions)	..	0	0
Aid per capita ($)	..	54	70

Estonia

Europe & Central Asia		Upper middle income	

Population (millions)	1	Population growth (%)	−0.4
Surface area (1,000 sq. km)	45	National poverty rate (% pop.)	..
GNI ($ millions)	7,276	GNI per capita ($)	5,380

	1990	2002	2003
People			
Life expectancy at birth (years)	69	71	71
Fertility rate (births per woman)	2.0	1.4	1.4
Infant mortality rate (per 1,000 live births)	12	8	8
Under-five mortality rate (per 1,000)	17	11	9
Births attended by skilled health staff (% of total)	..	..	..
Child malnutrition, underweight (% of under age 5)	..	..	..
Child immunization, measles (% of ages 12–23 mon.)	..	95	95
HIV prevalence rate (% of ages 15–49)	..	0.7	1.1
Adult literacy, male (% of ages 15 and older)	100	100	..
Adult literacy, female (% of ages 15 and older)	100	100	..
Primary completion rate, total (% of age group)	95	104	..
Primary completion rate, female (% of age group)	95	103	..
Net primary enrollment (% of age group)	99	96	..
Net secondary enrollment (% of age group)	..	87	..
Environment			
Forests (1,000 sq. km)	19	21	..
Deforestation (average annual %, 1990–2000)		−0.6	
Freshwater use (% of internal resources)			2
Carbon dioxide emissions (metric tons per capita)	16.2	11.7	..
Access to improved water source (% of total pop.)	..	..	..
Access to improved sanitation (% of urban pop.)	..	93	..
Energy use per capita (kg oil equivalent)	4,091	3,324	..
Electricity use per capita (kilowatt-hours)	3,747	3,882	..
Economy			
GDP ($ millions)	5,010	7,040	9,082
GDP growth (annual %)	−7.1	7.2	5.1
GDP implicit price deflator (annual % growth)	33.7	4.4	2.4
Value added in agriculture (% of GDP)	17	5	4
Value added in industry (% of GDP)	50	28	28
Value added in services (% of GDP)	34	67	67
Exports of goods and services (% of GDP)	60	74	75
Imports of goods and services (% of GDP)	54	81	83
Gross capital formation (% of GDP)	30	32	31
Central government revenue (% of GDP)	26.2	28.1	..
Cash surplus/deficit (% of GDP)	3.4	0.9	..
Technology and infrastructure			
Fixed-line and mobile subscribers (per 1,000 people)	204	1,001	1,119
Cost of 3-minute local call ($)	0.01	0.09	0.11
Personal computers (per 1,000 people)	..	210.3	440.4
Internet users (per 1,000 people)	1	328	444
Paved roads (% of total)	51.8	24.8	..
Aircraft departures (thousands)	6	8	8
Trade and finance			
Trade in goods (% of GDP)	..	144.9	148.9
Trade growth less GDP growth (avg. %, 1990–2003)			8.1
High-technology exports (% of manufactured exports)	..	12	13
Net barter terms of trade (2000 = 100)	..	..	..
Foreign direct investment ($ millions)	0	285	891
Present value of debt ($ millions)			7,039
Total debt service (% of goods and services exports)	0.6	14.4	17.2
Short-term debt ($ millions)	0	1,590	2,442
Aid per capita ($)	10	40	62

Ethiopia

Sub-Saharan Africa | **Low income**

Population (millions)	69	Population growth (%)	2.1
Surface area (1,000 sq. km)	1,104	National poverty rate (% pop.)	44
GNI ($ millions)	6,355	GNI per capita ($)	90

	1990	2002	2003
People			
Life expectancy at birth (years)	45	42	42
Fertility rate (births per woman)	6.9	5.6	5.6
Infant mortality rate (per 1,000 live births)	131	*116*	112
Under-five mortality rate (per 1,000)	204	*176*	169
Births attended by skilled health staff (% of total)	..	6	..
Child malnutrition, underweight (% of under age 5)	*48*	47	..
Child immunization, measles (% of ages 12–23 mon.)	38	52	52
HIV prevalence rate (% of ages 15–49)	..	*4.1*	4.4
Adult literacy, male (% of ages 15 and older)	37	49	..
Adult literacy, female (% of ages 15 and older)	20	34	..
Primary completion rate, total (% of age group)	*22*	37	39
Primary completion rate, female (% of age group)	*17*	26	29
Net primary enrollment (% of age group)	23	47	..
Net secondary enrollment (% of age group)	..	15	..
Environment			
Forests (1,000 sq. km)	50	*46*	..
Deforestation (average annual %, 1990–2000)		0.8	
Freshwater use (% of internal resources)			2
Carbon dioxide emissions (metric tons per capita)	0.1	*0.1*	..
Access to improved water source (% of total pop.)	25	22	..
Access to improved sanitation (% of urban pop.)	14	19	..
Energy use per capita (kg oil equivalent)	296	297	..
Electricity use per capita (kilowatt-hours)	18	25	..
Economy			
GDP ($ millions)	8,609	6,059	6,652
GDP growth (annual %)	2.6	2.7	–3.7
GDP implicit price deflator (annual % growth)	3.4	–7.0	14.5
Value added in agriculture (% of GDP)	49	42	42
Value added in industry (% of GDP)	13	11	11
Value added in services (% of GDP)	38	47	47
Exports of goods and services (% of GDP)	8	16	17
Imports of goods and services (% of GDP)	12	34	37
Gross capital formation (% of GDP)	12	21	20
Central government revenue (% of GDP)	17.3	*19.0*	..
Cash surplus/deficit (% of GDP)	–9.3	*–5.0*	..
Technology and infrastructure			
Fixed-line and mobile subscribers (per 1,000 people)	3	6	8
Cost of 3-minute local call ($)	0.10	0.02	..
Personal computers (per 1,000 people)	..	1.5	2.2
Internet users (per 1,000 people)	..	1	1
Paved roads (% of total)	15.0	12.0	..
Aircraft departures (thousands)	21	28	27
Trade and finance			
Trade in goods (% of GDP)	16.0	35.4	38.3
Trade growth less GDP growth (avg. %, 1990–2003)			2.9
High-technology exports (% of manufactured exports)	..	0	0
Net barter terms of trade (2000 = 100)	121	84	..
Foreign direct investment ($ millions)	12	75	60
Present value of debt ($ millions)			1,551
Total debt service (% of goods and services exports)	39.0	7.6	6.8
Short-term debt ($ millions)	145	64	87
Aid per capita ($)	20	19	22

Faeroe Islands

High income

Population (thousands)	47	Population growth (%)	..
Surface area (1,000 sq. km)	1	National poverty rate (% pop.)	..
GNI ($ millions)	..	GNI per capita ($)	..

	1990	2002	2003
People			
Life expectancy at birth (years)	..	..	..
Fertility rate (births per woman)	..	..	..
Infant mortality rate (per 1,000 live births)	..	..	..
Under-five mortality rate (per 1,000)	..	..	..
Births attended by skilled health staff (% of total)	..	..	..
Child malnutrition, underweight (% of under age 5)	..	..	..
Child immunization, measles (% of ages 12–23 mon.)	..	..	..
HIV prevalence rate (% of ages 15–49)	..	..	..
Adult literacy, male (% of ages 15 and older)	..	..	..
Adult literacy, female (% of ages 15 and older)	..	..	..
Primary completion rate, total (% of age group)	..	..	..
Primary completion rate, female (% of age group)	..	..	..
Net primary enrollment (% of age group)	..	..	..
Net secondary enrollment (% of age group)	..	..	..
Environment			
Forests (1,000 sq. km)	..	..	..
Deforestation (average annual %, 1990–2000)		..	
Freshwater use (% of internal resources)			..
Carbon dioxide emissions (metric tons per capita)	..	..	..
Access to improved water source (% of total pop.)	..	..	..
Access to improved sanitation (% of urban pop.)	..	..	..
Energy use per capita (kg oil equivalent)	..	..	..
Electricity use per capita (kilowatt-hours)	..	..	..
Economy			
GDP ($ millions)	..	..	..
GDP growth (annual %)	..	..	..
GDP implicit price deflator (annual % growth)	..	..	..
Value added in agriculture (% of GDP)	..	..	..
Value added in industry (% of GDP)	..	..	..
Value added in services (% of GDP)	..	..	..
Exports of goods and services (% of GDP)	..	..	..
Imports of goods and services (% of GDP)	..	..	..
Gross capital formation (% of GDP)	..	..	..
Central government revenue (% of GDP)	..	..	..
Cash surplus/deficit (% of GDP)	..	..	..
Technology and infrastructure			
Fixed-line and mobile subscribers (per 1,000 people)	538	1,126	..
Cost of 3-minute local call ($)	0.37	0.40	..
Personal computers (per 1,000 people)	..	..	..
Internet users (per 1,000 people)	..	333	..
Paved roads (% of total)	..	..	..
Aircraft departures (thousands)	..	..	..
Trade and finance			
Trade in goods (% of GDP)	..	..	..
Trade growth less GDP growth (avg. %, 1990–2003)			..
High-technology exports (% of manufactured exports)	0	0	0
Net barter terms of trade (2000 = 100)	..	..	..
Foreign direct investment ($ millions)	..	..	..
Present value of debt ($ millions)			..
Total debt service (% of goods and services exports)	..	..	..
Short-term debt ($ millions)	..	..	..
Aid per capita ($)	..	..	..

East Asia & Pacific | **Lower middle income**

Population (thousands)	835	Population growth (%)	1.4
Surface area (1,000 sq. km)	18	National poverty rate (% pop.)	..
GNI ($ millions)	1,871	GNI per capita ($)	2,240

	1990	2002	2003
People			
Life expectancy at birth (years)	67	70	70
Fertility rate (births per woman)	3.1	2.6	2.6
Infant mortality rate (per 1,000 live births)	25	18	16
Under-five mortality rate (per 1,000)	31	22	20
Births attended by skilled health staff (% of total)	..	100	..
Child malnutrition, underweight (% of under age 5)	..	..	..
Child immunization, measles (% of ages 12–23 mon.)	84	88	91
HIV prevalence rate (% of ages 15–49)	..	0.1	0.1
Adult literacy, male (% of ages 15 and older)	92	..	..
Adult literacy, female (% of ages 15 and older)	85	..	..
Primary completion rate, total (% of age group)	..	101	..
Primary completion rate, female (% of age group)	..	104	..
Net primary enrollment (% of age group)	100	100	..
Net secondary enrollment (% of age group)	..	76	..
Environment			
Forests (1,000 sq. km)	8	8	..
Deforestation (average annual %, 1990–2000)		0.2	
Freshwater use (% of internal resources)			0
Carbon dioxide emissions (metric tons per capita)	1.1	0.9	..
Access to improved water source (% of total pop.)	..	..	..
Access to improved sanitation (% of urban pop.)	99	99	..
Energy use per capita (kg oil equivalent)	..	..	..
Electricity use per capita (kilowatt-hours)	..	..	..
Economy			
GDP ($ millions)	1,358	1,742	2,036
GDP growth (annual %)	3.6	4.3	4.8
GDP implicit price deflator (annual % growth)	8.1	1.3	2.4
Value added in agriculture (% of GDP)	20	16	..
Value added in industry (% of GDP)	24	27	..
Value added in services (% of GDP)	56	57	..
Exports of goods and services (% of GDP)	62	73	..
Imports of goods and services (% of GDP)	67	66	..
Gross capital formation (% of GDP)	14	14	..
Central government revenue (% of GDP)	26.8	..	..
Cash surplus/deficit (% of GDP)	0.9	..	..
Technology and infrastructure			
Fixed-line and mobile subscribers (per 1,000 people)	58	229	257
Cost of 3-minute local call ($)	0.07	0.05	0.06
Personal computers (per 1,000 people)	..	48.8	..
Internet users (per 1,000 people)	..	61	67
Paved roads (% of total)	44.5	49.2	..
Aircraft departures (thousands)	24	38	39
Trade and finance			
Trade in goods (% of GDP)	92.1	83.1	82.2
Trade growth less GDP growth (avg. %, 1990–2003)			..
High-technology exports (% of manufactured exports)	12	1	1
Net barter terms of trade (2000 = 100)	..	..	..
Foreign direct investment ($ millions)	92	26	20
Present value of debt ($ millions)			257
Total debt service (% of goods and services exports)	12.0	3.4	..
Short-term debt ($ millions)	12	37	86
Aid per capita ($)	69	41	61

Finland

High income

Population (millions)	5	Population growth (%)	0.2
Surface area (1,000 sq. km)	338	National poverty rate (% pop.)	..
GNI ($ billions)	141	GNI per capita ($)	27,060

	1990	2002	2003
People			
Life expectancy at birth (years)	75	78	78
Fertility rate (births per woman)	1.8	1.7	1.8
Infant mortality rate (per 1,000 live births)	6	3	3
Under-five mortality rate (per 1,000)	7	4	..
Births attended by skilled health staff (% of total)	..	..	..
Child malnutrition, underweight (% of under age 5)	..	..	..
Child immunization, measles (% of ages 12–23 mon.)	97	96	97
HIV prevalence rate (% of ages 15–49)	..	0.1	0.1
Adult literacy, male (% of ages 15 and older)	..	..	..
Adult literacy, female (% of ages 15 and older)	..	..	..
Primary completion rate, total (% of age group)	97	101	..
Primary completion rate, female (% of age group)	97	101	..
Net primary enrollment (% of age group)	98	100	..
Net secondary enrollment (% of age group)	93	94	..
Environment			
Forests (1,000 sq. km)	219	219	..
Deforestation (average annual %, 1990–2000)		0.0	
Freshwater use (% of internal resources)			2
Carbon dioxide emissions (metric tons per capita)	10.6	10.3	..
Access to improved water source (% of total pop.)	100	100	..
Access to improved sanitation (% of urban pop.)	100	100	..
Energy use per capita (kg oil equivalent)	5,851	6,852	..
Electricity use per capita (kilowatt-hours)	11,822	15,326	..
Economy			
GDP ($ billions)	137	132	162
GDP growth (annual %)	–0.3	2.3	1.9
GDP implicit price deflator (annual % growth)	6.4	0.9	0.7
Value added in agriculture (% of GDP)	7	4	3
Value added in industry (% of GDP)	34	32	31
Value added in services (% of GDP)	59	65	66
Exports of goods and services (% of GDP)	23	39	37
Imports of goods and services (% of GDP)	24	30	30
Gross capital formation (% of GDP)	29	19	18
Central government revenue (% of GDP)	..	40.1	39.0
Cash surplus/deficit (% of GDP)	..	4.7	2.9
Technology and infrastructure			
Fixed-line and mobile subscribers (per 1,000 people)	586	1,391	1,402
Cost of 3-minute local call ($)	0.17	0.13	0.16
Personal computers (per 1,000 people)	100.0	441.7	..
Internet users (per 1,000 people)	4	510	534
Paved roads (% of total)	61.0	64.0	..
Aircraft departures (thousands)	93	109	107
Trade and finance			
Trade in goods (% of GDP)	39.1	60.3	58.7
Trade growth less GDP growth (avg. %, 1990–2003)			4.8
High-technology exports (% of manufactured exports)	8	24	24
Net barter terms of trade (2000 = 100)	111	96	92
Foreign direct investment ($ millions)	812	8,156	3,436
Present value of debt ($ millions)			..
Total debt service (% of goods and services exports)	..	..	..
Short-term debt ($ millions)	..	..	..
Aid per capita ($)	..	..	..

France

High income

Population (millions)	60	Population growth (%)	0.5
Surface area (1,000 sq. km)	552	National poverty rate (% pop.)	..
GNI ($ billions)	1,522	GNI per capita ($)	24,730

	1990	2002	2003
People			
Life expectancy at birth (years)	77	79	79
Fertility rate (births per woman)	1.8	1.9	1.9
Infant mortality rate (per 1,000 live births)	7	4	..
Under-five mortality rate (per 1,000)	9	6	..
Births attended by skilled health staff (% of total)	..	..	..
Child malnutrition, underweight (% of under age 5)	..	..	..
Child immunization, measles (% of ages 12–23 mon.)	71	86	86
HIV prevalence rate (% of ages 15–49)	..	0.4	0.4
Adult literacy, male (% of ages 15 and older)	..	..	..
Adult literacy, female (% of ages 15 and older)	..	..	..
Primary completion rate, total (% of age group)	104	98	..
Primary completion rate, female (% of age group)	..	98	..
Net primary enrollment (% of age group)	100	100	..
Net secondary enrollment (% of age group)	..	93	..
Environment			
Forests (1,000 sq. km)	147	153	..
Deforestation (average annual %, 1990–2000)		−0.4	
Freshwater use (% of internal resources)			18
Carbon dioxide emissions (metric tons per capita)	6.3	6.2	..
Access to improved water source (% of total pop.)	..	..	..
Access to improved sanitation (% of urban pop.)	..	..	..
Energy use per capita (kg oil equivalent)	4,006	4,470	..
Electricity use per capita (kilowatt-hours)	5,321	6,606	..
Economy			
GDP ($ billions)	1,216	1,437	1,758
GDP growth (annual %)	2.6	1.2	0.5
GDP implicit price deflator (annual % growth)	2.9	2.3	1.5
Value added in agriculture (% of GDP)	4	3	3
Value added in industry (% of GDP)	30	25	24
Value added in services (% of GDP)	66	72	73
Exports of goods and services (% of GDP)	21	27	26
Imports of goods and services (% of GDP)	22	25	25
Gross capital formation (% of GDP)	23	19	..
Central government revenue (% of GDP)	..	43.9	43.9
Cash surplus/deficit (% of GDP)	..	−3.4	−4.3
Technology and infrastructure			
Fixed-line and mobile subscribers (per 1,000 people)	500	1,216	1,262
Cost of 3-minute local call ($)	0.13	0.12	0.15
Personal computers (per 1,000 people)	70.5	347.1	..
Internet users (per 1,000 people)	1	314	366
Paved roads (% of total)	..	100.0	..
Aircraft departures (thousands)	442	735	696
Trade and finance			
Trade in goods (% of GDP)	37.1	46.0	44.2
Trade growth less GDP growth (avg. %, 1990–2003)			3.8
High-technology exports (% of manufactured exports)	16	21	19
Net barter terms of trade (2000 = 100)	103	110	110
Foreign direct investment ($ billions)	13	49	48
Present value of debt ($ millions)			..
Total debt service (% of goods and services exports)	..	..	..
Short-term debt ($ millions)	..	..	..
Aid per capita ($)	..	..	..

French Polynesia

High income

Population (thousands)	243	Population growth (%)		1.3
Surface area (1,000 sq. km)	4	National poverty rate (% pop.)		..
GNI ($ millions)	..	GNI per capita ($)		..

	1990	2002	2003
People			
Life expectancy at birth (years)	70	74	74
Fertility rate (births per woman)	3.3	2.5	2.5
Infant mortality rate (per 1,000 live births)	..	..	..
Under-five mortality rate (per 1,000)	..	..	..
Births attended by skilled health staff (% of total)	..	..	..
Child malnutrition, underweight (% of under age 5)	..	..	..
Child immunization, measles (% of ages 12–23 mon.)	..	..	..
HIV prevalence rate (% of ages 15–49)	..	..	..
Adult literacy, male (% of ages 15 and older)	..	..	..
Adult literacy, female (% of ages 15 and older)	..	..	..
Primary completion rate, total (% of age group)	..	..	..
Primary completion rate, female (% of age group)	..	..	..
Net primary enrollment (% of age group)	..	..	..
Net secondary enrollment (% of age group)	..	..	..
Environment			
Forests (1,000 sq. km)	1	*1*	..
Deforestation (average annual %, 1990–2000)		*0.0*	
Freshwater use (% of internal resources)			..
Carbon dioxide emissions (metric tons per capita)	3.1	*2.3*	..
Access to improved water source (% of total pop.)	100	100	..
Access to improved sanitation (% of urban pop.)	99	99	..
Energy use per capita (kg oil equivalent)	..	..	..
Electricity use per capita (kilowatt-hours)	..	..	..
Economy			
GDP ($ millions)	3,181	*3,448*	..
GDP growth (annual %)	2.2	*4.0*	..
GDP implicit price deflator (annual % growth)	0.8	*1.0*	..
Value added in agriculture (% of GDP)	1	5	..
Value added in industry (% of GDP)	..	..	..
Value added in services (% of GDP)	..	..	..
Exports of goods and services (% of GDP)	*1*	5	..
Imports of goods and services (% of GDP)	*28*	24	..
Gross capital formation (% of GDP)	..	..	..
Central government revenue (% of GDP)	..	..	..
Cash surplus/deficit (% of GDP)	..	..	..
Technology and infrastructure			
Fixed-line and mobile subscribers (per 1,000 people)	194	580	..
Cost of 3-minute local call ($)	*0.30*	0.30	0.32
Personal computers (per 1,000 people)	..	285.1	..
Internet users (per 1,000 people)	..	81	140
Paved roads (% of total)	..	..	..
Aircraft departures (thousands)	..	..	..
Trade and finance			
Trade in goods (% of GDP)	32.7	*34.6*	..
Trade growth less GDP growth (avg. %, 1990–2003)			..
High-technology exports (% of manufactured exports)	..	2	3
Net barter terms of trade (2000 = 100)	..	..	..
Foreign direct investment ($ millions)	..	..	..
Present value of debt ($ millions)			..
Total debt service (% of goods and services exports)	..	..	..
Short-term debt ($ millions)	..	..	..
Aid per capita ($)	1,318	1,745	2,134

Gabon

Sub-Saharan Africa | **Upper middle income**

Population (millions)	1	Population growth (%)	2.2
Surface area (1,000 sq. km)	268	National poverty rate (% pop.)	..
GNI ($ millions)	4,489	GNI per capita ($)	3,340

	1990	2002	2003
People			
Life expectancy at birth (years)	52	53	53
Fertility rate (births per woman)	5.1	4.1	4.0
Infant mortality rate (per 1,000 live births)	60	60	60
Under-five mortality rate (per 1,000)	92	91	91
Births attended by skilled health staff (% of total)	..	86	..
Child malnutrition, underweight (% of under age 5)	..	12	..
Child immunization, measles (% of ages 12–23 mon.)	76	55	55
HIV prevalence rate (% of ages 15–49)	..	6.9	8.1
Adult literacy, male (% of ages 15 and older)	..	..	..
Adult literacy, female (% of ages 15 and older)	..	..	..
Primary completion rate, total (% of age group)	67	74	..
Primary completion rate, female (% of age group)	71	76	..
Net primary enrollment (% of age group)	86	78	..
Net secondary enrollment (% of age group)	..	..	..
Environment			
Forests (1,000 sq. km)	219	218	..
Deforestation (average annual %, 1990–2000)		0.0	
Freshwater use (% of internal resources)			0
Carbon dioxide emissions (metric tons per capita)	7.0	2.8	..
Access to improved water source (% of total pop.)	..	87	..
Access to improved sanitation (% of urban pop.)	..	37	..
Energy use per capita (kg oil equivalent)	1,303	1,209	..
Electricity use per capita (kilowatt-hours)	812	804	..
Economy			
GDP ($ millions)	5,952	4,971	6,057
GDP growth (annual %)	5.2	–0.0	2.8
GDP implicit price deflator (annual % growth)	15.4	9.1	–1.2
Value added in agriculture (% of GDP)	7	8	8
Value added in industry (% of GDP)	43	46	62
Value added in services (% of GDP)	50	46	30
Exports of goods and services (% of GDP)	46	59	62
Imports of goods and services (% of GDP)	31	39	41
Gross capital formation (% of GDP)	22	28	24
Central government revenue (% of GDP)	..	..	..
Cash surplus/deficit (% of GDP)	..	..	..
Technology and infrastructure			
Fixed-line and mobile subscribers (per 1,000 people)	22	240	253
Cost of 3-minute local call ($)	0.24	0.22	0.26
Personal computers (per 1,000 people)	..	19.2	22.4
Internet users (per 1,000 people)	..	19	26
Paved roads (% of total)	8.2	9.9	..
Aircraft departures (thousands)	10	8	8
Trade and finance			
Trade in goods (% of GDP)	52.5	61.2	59.7
Trade growth less GDP growth (avg. %, 1990–2003)			–1.6
High-technology exports (% of manufactured exports)	..	7	..
Net barter terms of trade (2000 = 100)	157	142	..
Foreign direct investment ($ millions)	74	123	53
Present value of debt ($ millions)			3,884
Total debt service (% of goods and services exports)	6.4	18.7	..
Short-term debt ($ millions)	693	238	339
Aid per capita ($)	139	55	–8

Gambia, The

Sub-Saharan Africa   **Low income**

Population (millions)	1	Population growth (%)	2.3
Surface area (1,000 sq. km)	11	National poverty rate (% pop.)	58
GNI ($ millions)	387	GNI per capita ($)	270

	1990	2002	2003
People			
Life expectancy at birth (years)	49	53	53
Fertility rate (births per woman)	5.9	4.8	4.8
Infant mortality rate (per 1,000 live births)	103	*92*	90
Under-five mortality rate (per 1,000)	154	*128*	123
Births attended by skilled health staff (% of total)	44	55	..
Child malnutrition, underweight (% of under age 5)	..	17	..
Child immunization, measles (% of ages 12–23 mon.)	86	90	90
HIV prevalence rate (% of ages 15–49)	..	*1.2*	1.2
Adult literacy, male (% of ages 15 and older)	..	..	..
Adult literacy, female (% of ages 15 and older)	..	..	..
Primary completion rate, total (% of age group)	*45*	*68*	..
Primary completion rate, female (% of age group)	*34*	*60*	..
Net primary enrollment (% of age group)	48	79	..
Net secondary enrollment (% of age group)	..	33	..
Environment			
Forests (1,000 sq. km)	4	*5*	..
Deforestation (average annual %, 1990–2000)		*–1.0*	
Freshwater use (% of internal resources)			0
Carbon dioxide emissions (metric tons per capita)	0.2	*0.2*	..
Access to improved water source (% of total pop.)	..	82	..
Access to improved sanitation (% of urban pop.)	..	72	..
Energy use per capita (kg oil equivalent)	..	..	..
Electricity use per capita (kilowatt-hours)	..	..	..
Economy			
GDP ($ millions)	317	370	395
GDP growth (annual %)	3.6	–3.2	6.7
GDP implicit price deflator (annual % growth)	12.0	16.0	30.8
Value added in agriculture (% of GDP)	29	27	30
Value added in industry (% of GDP)	13	15	15
Value added in services (% of GDP)	58	58	55
Exports of goods and services (% of GDP)	60	52	41
Imports of goods and services (% of GDP)	72	58	45
Gross capital formation (% of GDP)	22	21	19
Central government revenue (% of GDP)	19.4	..	..
Cash surplus/deficit (% of GDP)	2.1	..	..
Technology and infrastructure			
Fixed-line and mobile subscribers (per 1,000 people)	7	101	..
Cost of 3-minute local call ($)	0.06	0.03	..
Personal computers (per 1,000 people)	..	13.8	..
Internet users (per 1,000 people)		9	..
Paved roads (% of total)	32.0	*35.4*	..
Aircraft departures (thousands)	..	..	..
Trade and finance			
Trade in goods (% of GDP)	69.1	43.5	50.1
Trade growth less GDP growth (avg. %, 1990–2003)			–2.8
High-technology exports (% of manufactured exports)	..	3	..
Net barter terms of trade (2000 = 100)	100	100	..
Foreign direct investment ($ millions)	0	43	60
Present value of debt ($ millions)			335
Total debt service (% of goods and services exports)	22.2	*11.5*	..
Short-term debt ($ millions)	16	37	33
Aid per capita ($)	107	44	42

Georgia

Europe & Central Asia   **Lower middle income**

Population (millions)	5	Population growth (%)	−1.0
Surface area (1,000 sq. km)	70	National poverty rate (% pop.)	11
GNI ($ millions)	3,934	GNI per capita ($)	770

	1990	2002	2003
People			
Life expectancy at birth (years)	72	73	73
Fertility rate (births per woman)	2.2	1.1	1.1
Infant mortality rate (per 1,000 live births)	43	41	41
Under-five mortality rate (per 1,000)	47	45	45
Births attended by skilled health staff (% of total)	..	96	..
Child malnutrition, underweight (% of under age 5)	..	3	..
Child immunization, measles (% of ages 12–23 mon.)	16	73	73
HIV prevalence rate (% of ages 15–49)	..	0.1	0.1
Adult literacy, male (% of ages 15 and older)	..	..	..
Adult literacy, female (% of ages 15 and older)	..	..	..
Primary completion rate, total (% of age group)	..	85	82
Primary completion rate, female (% of age group)	..	85	82
Net primary enrollment (% of age group)	97	89	..
Net secondary enrollment (% of age group)	..	61	..
Environment			
Forests (1,000 sq. km)	30	30	..
Deforestation (average annual %, 1990–2000)		0.0	
Freshwater use (% of internal resources)			6
Carbon dioxide emissions (metric tons per capita)	2.8	1.2	..
Access to improved water source (% of total pop.)	..	76	..
Access to improved sanitation (% of urban pop.)	96	96	..
Energy use per capita (kg oil equivalent)	1,611	494	..
Electricity use per capita (kilowatt-hours)	1,787	1,032	..
Economy			
GDP ($ millions)	7,738	3,396	3,988
GDP growth (annual %)	−14.8	5.5	11.1
GDP implicit price deflator (annual % growth)	22.4	6.3	3.5
Value added in agriculture (% of GDP)	32	21	20
Value added in industry (% of GDP)	33	24	25
Value added in services (% of GDP)	35	55	54
Exports of goods and services (% of GDP)	40	29	32
Imports of goods and services (% of GDP)	46	41	46
Gross capital formation (% of GDP)	31	22	24
Central government revenue (% of GDP)	..	10.5	10.3
Cash surplus/deficit (% of GDP)	..	−1.8	−0.9
Technology and infrastructure			
Fixed-line and mobile subscribers (per 1,000 people)	99	234	240
Cost of 3-minute local call ($)	0.00	0.03	..
Personal computers (per 1,000 people)	..	31.6	..
Internet users (per 1,000 people)	..	15	31
Paved roads (% of total)	93.8	93.5	..
Aircraft departures (thousands)	..	2	2
Trade and finance			
Trade in goods (% of GDP)	..	31.8	37.7
Trade growth less GDP growth (avg. %, 1990–2003)			11.8
High-technology exports (% of manufactured exports)	..	38	24
Net barter terms of trade (2000 = 100)	..	..	..
Foreign direct investment ($ millions)	0	167	338
Present value of debt ($ millions)			1,519
Total debt service (% of goods and services exports)	..	10.4	11.9
Short-term debt ($ millions)	0	33	38
Aid per capita ($)	0	60	43

Germany

High income

Population (millions)	83	Population growth (%)	0.0
Surface area (1,000 sq. km)	357	National poverty rate (% pop.)	..
GNI ($ billions)	2,085	GNI per capita ($)	25,270

	1990	2002	2003
People			
Life expectancy at birth (years)	75	78	78
Fertility rate (births per woman)	1.5	1.3	1.3
Infant mortality rate (per 1,000 live births)	7	4	4
Under-five mortality rate (per 1,000)	9	5	..
Births attended by skilled health staff (% of total)	..	..	..
Child malnutrition, underweight (% of under age 5)	..	..	..
Child immunization, measles (% of ages 12–23 mon.)	75	92	92
HIV prevalence rate (% of ages 15–49)	..	0.1	0.1
Adult literacy, male (% of ages 15 and older)	..	..	..
Adult literacy, female (% of ages 15 and older)	..	..	..
Primary completion rate, total (% of age group)	101	101	..
Primary completion rate, female (% of age group)	101	101	..
Net primary enrollment (% of age group)	84	..	..
Net secondary enrollment (% of age group)	..	88	..
Environment			
Forests (1,000 sq. km)	107	107	..
Deforestation (average annual %, 1990–2000)		0.0	
Freshwater use (% of internal resources)			43
Carbon dioxide emissions (metric tons per capita)	11.1	9.6	..
Access to improved water source (% of total pop.)	100	100	..
Access to improved sanitation (% of urban pop.)	..	..	..
Energy use per capita (kg oil equivalent)	4,485	4,198	..
Electricity use per capita (kilowatt-hours)	5,729	6,046	..
Economy			
GDP ($ billions)	1,671	1,986	2,403
GDP growth (annual %)	5.7	0.2	–0.1
GDP implicit price deflator (annual % growth)	3.2	1.6	1.0
Value added in agriculture (% of GDP)	2	1	1
Value added in industry (% of GDP)	39	30	29
Value added in services (% of GDP)	59	69	69
Exports of goods and services (% of GDP)	25	36	36
Imports of goods and services (% of GDP)	25	32	32
Gross capital formation (% of GDP)	24	18	18
Central government revenue (% of GDP)	..	30.0	30.2
Cash surplus/deficit (% of GDP)	..	–1.9	–2.1
Technology and infrastructure			
Fixed-line and mobile subscribers (per 1,000 people)	445	1,378	1,442
Cost of 3-minute local call ($)	0.14	0.09	0.11
Personal computers (per 1,000 people)	89.9	431.3	484.7
Internet users (per 1,000 people)	1	436	473
Paved roads (% of total)	99.0	..	..
Aircraft departures (thousands)	344	796	845
Trade and finance			
Trade in goods (% of GDP)	46.5	55.7	56.2
Trade growth less GDP growth (avg. %, 1990–2003)			4.0
High-technology exports (% of manufactured exports)	11	17	16
Net barter terms of trade (2000 = 100)	110	104	107
Foreign direct investment ($ billions)	3	36	11
Present value of debt ($ millions)			..
Total debt service (% of goods and services exports)	..	..	..
Short-term debt ($ millions)	..	..	..
Aid per capita ($)	..	..	..

Ghana

Sub-Saharan Africa   **Low income**

Population (millions)	21	Population growth (%)	1.8
Surface area (1,000 sq. km)	239	National poverty rate (% pop.)	40
GNI ($ millions)	6,548	GNI per capita ($)	320

	1990	2002	2003
People			
Life expectancy at birth (years)	57	55	54
Fertility rate (births per woman)	5.5	4.4	4.4
Infant mortality rate (per 1,000 live births)	78	*62*	59
Under-five mortality rate (per 1,000)	125	*100*	95
Births attended by skilled health staff (% of total)	*40*	44	..
Child malnutrition, underweight (% of under age 5)	*30*	25	22
Child immunization, measles (% of ages 12–23 mon.)	61	81	80
HIV prevalence rate (% of ages 15–49)	..	*3.1*	3.1
Adult literacy, male (% of ages 15 and older)	70	82	..
Adult literacy, female (% of ages 15 and older)	47	66	..
Primary completion rate, total (% of age group)	61	61	62
Primary completion rate, female (% of age group)	53	63	60
Net primary enrollment (% of age group)	52	63	..
Net secondary enrollment (% of age group)	..	33	..
Environment			
Forests (1,000 sq. km)	75	63	..
Deforestation (average annual %, 1990–2000)		*1.7*	
Freshwater use (% of internal resources)			1
Carbon dioxide emissions (metric tons per capita)	0.2	*0.3*	..
Access to improved water source (% of total pop.)	54	79	..
Access to improved sanitation (% of urban pop.)	54	74	..
Energy use per capita (kg oil equivalent)	349	411	..
Electricity use per capita (kilowatt-hours)	293	297	..
Economy			
GDP ($ millions)	5,886	6,160	7,624
GDP growth (annual %)	3.3	4.5	5.2
GDP implicit price deflator (annual % growth)	31.2	22.8	28.7
Value added in agriculture (% of GDP)	45	36	36
Value added in industry (% of GDP)	17	24	25
Value added in services (% of GDP)	38	40	39
Exports of goods and services (% of GDP)	17	42	40
Imports of goods and services (% of GDP)	26	54	52
Gross capital formation (% of GDP)	14	20	23
Central government revenue (% of GDP)	12.5	..	..
Cash surplus/deficit (% of GDP)	..	..	..
Technology and infrastructure			
Fixed-line and mobile subscribers (per 1,000 people)	3	33	49
Cost of 3-minute local call ($)	0.06	0.03	..
Personal computers (per 1,000 people)	0.0	3.8	..
Internet users (per 1,000 people)	..	8	..
Paved roads (% of total)	19.6	*18.4*	..
Aircraft departures (thousands)	13	4	3
Trade and finance			
Trade in goods (% of GDP)	35.7	76.1	75.4
Trade growth less GDP growth (avg. %, 1990–2003)			3.7
High-technology exports (% of manufactured exports)	2	3	..
Net barter terms of trade (2000 = 100)	100	112	..
Foreign direct investment ($ millions)	15	59	137
Present value of debt ($ millions)			2,370
Total debt service (% of goods and services exports)	38.4	7.3	14.7
Short-term debt ($ millions)	320	593	700
Aid per capita ($)	37	32	44

Greece

High income

Population (millions)	11	Population growth (%)	0.3
Surface area (1,000 sq. km)	132	National poverty rate (% pop.)	..
GNI ($ billions)	146	GNI per capita ($)	13,230

	1990	2002	2003
People			
Life expectancy at birth (years)	77	78	78
Fertility rate (births per woman)	1.4	1.3	1.3
Infant mortality rate (per 1,000 live births)	10	5	4
Under-five mortality rate (per 1,000)	11	6	5
Births attended by skilled health staff (% of total)	..	..	..
Child malnutrition, underweight (% of under age 5)	..	..	..
Child immunization, measles (% of ages 12–23 mon.)	76	88	88
HIV prevalence rate (% of ages 15–49)	..	0.2	0.2
Adult literacy, male (% of ages 15 and older)	98	99	..
Adult literacy, female (% of ages 15 and older)	92	96	..
Primary completion rate, total (% of age group)	100	..	..
Primary completion rate, female (% of age group)	100	..	..
Net primary enrollment (% of age group)	95	97	..
Net secondary enrollment (% of age group)	83	85	..
Environment			
Forests (1,000 sq. km)	33	36	..
Deforestation (average annual %, 1990–2000)		–0.9	
Freshwater use (% of internal resources)			15
Carbon dioxide emissions (metric tons per capita)	7.1	8.2	..
Access to improved water source (% of total pop.)	..	..	..
Access to improved sanitation (% of urban pop.)	..	..	..
Energy use per capita (kg oil equivalent)	2,183	2,637	..
Electricity use per capita (kilowatt-hours)	2,802	4,231	..
Economy			
GDP ($ billions)	84	133	172
GDP growth (annual %)	0.0	3.9	4.3
GDP implicit price deflator (annual % growth)	20.7	3.9	3.5
Value added in agriculture (% of GDP)	11	7	7
Value added in industry (% of GDP)	28	23	24
Value added in services (% of GDP)	61	70	69
Exports of goods and services (% of GDP)	18	21	20
Imports of goods and services (% of GDP)	28	28	28
Gross capital formation (% of GDP)	23	24	26
Central government revenue (% of GDP)	..	46.5	..
Cash surplus/deficit (% of GDP)	..	–1.1	..
Technology and infrastructure			
Fixed-line and mobile subscribers (per 1,000 people)	389	1,337	1,356
Cost of 3-minute local call ($)	0.00	0.07	0.09
Personal computers (per 1,000 people)	17.2	81.7	..
Internet users (per 1,000 people)	0	135	150
Paved roads (% of total)	91.7	91.8	..
Aircraft departures (thousands)	80	113	114
Trade and finance			
Trade in goods (% of GDP)	33.2	31.3	33.0
Trade growth less GDP growth (avg. %, 1990–2003)			3.8
High-technology exports (% of manufactured exports)	2	12	12
Net barter terms of trade (2000 = 100)	100	100	99
Foreign direct investment ($ millions)	1,005	53	717
Present value of debt ($ millions)			..
Total debt service (% of goods and services exports)	..	..	..
Short-term debt ($ millions)	..	..	..
Aid per capita ($)	..	..	..

Greenland

High income

Population (thousands)	56	Population growth (%)	−0.4
Surface area (1,000 sq. km)	410	National poverty rate (% pop.)	..
GNI ($ millions)	..	GNI per capita ($)	..

	1990	2002	2003
People			
Life expectancy at birth (years)	65	69	..
Fertility rate (births per woman)	2.4	2.4	..
Infant mortality rate (per 1,000 live births)	33	..	..
Under-five mortality rate (per 1,000)	..	..	..
Births attended by skilled health staff (% of total)	..	..	..
Child malnutrition, underweight (% of under age 5)	..	..	..
Child immunization, measles (% of ages 12–23 mon.)	..	..	..
HIV prevalence rate (% of ages 15–49)	..	..	..
Adult literacy, male (% of ages 15 and older)	..	..	..
Adult literacy, female (% of ages 15 and older)	..	..	..
Primary completion rate, total (% of age group)	..	..	..
Primary completion rate, female (% of age group)	..	..	..
Net primary enrollment (% of age group)	..	..	..
Net secondary enrollment (% of age group)	..	..	..
Environment			
Forests (1,000 sq. km)	..	..	
Deforestation (average annual %, 1990–2000)		..	
Freshwater use (% of internal resources)			..
Carbon dioxide emissions (metric tons per capita)	10.0	9.9	..
Access to improved water source (% of total pop.)	..	..	..
Access to improved sanitation (% of urban pop.)	..	..	..
Energy use per capita (kg oil equivalent)	..	..	..
Electricity use per capita (kilowatt-hours)	..	..	..
Economy			
GDP ($ millions)	..	..	..
GDP growth (annual %)	..	..	..
GDP implicit price deflator (annual % growth)	..	..	..
Value added in agriculture (% of GDP)	..	..	..
Value added in industry (% of GDP)	..	..	..
Value added in services (% of GDP)	..	..	..
Exports of goods and services (% of GDP)	..	..	..
Imports of goods and services (% of GDP)	..	..	..
Gross capital formation (% of GDP)	..	..	..
Central government revenue (% of GDP)	..	..	..
Cash surplus/deficit (% of GDP)	..	..	..
Technology and infrastructure			
Fixed-line and mobile subscribers (per 1,000 people)	299	798	..
Cost of 3-minute local call ($)	0.48	0.27	..
Personal computers (per 1,000 people)	..	..	..
Internet users (per 1,000 people)	..	441	..
Paved roads (% of total)	..	..	..
Aircraft departures (thousands)	..	..	..
Trade and finance			
Trade in goods (% of GDP)	..	..	..
Trade growth less GDP growth (avg. %, 1990–2003)			..
High-technology exports (% of manufactured exports)	10	53	..
Net barter terms of trade (2000 = 100)	..	..	..
Foreign direct investment ($ millions)	..	..	..
Present value of debt ($ millions)			..
Total debt service (% of goods and services exports)	..	..	..
Short-term debt ($ millions)	..	..	..
Aid per capita ($)	..	..	..

Grenada

Latin America & Caribbean		Upper middle income	
Population (thousands)	105	Population growth (%)	1.1
Surface area (sq. km)	340	National poverty rate (% pop.)	..
GNI ($ millions)	388	GNI per capita ($)	3,710

	1990	2002	2003
People			
Life expectancy at birth (years)	..	73	73
Fertility rate (births per woman)	..	3.0	3.0
Infant mortality rate (per 1,000 live births)	30	21	18
Under-five mortality rate (per 1,000)	37	26	23
Births attended by skilled health staff (% of total)	..	99	..
Child malnutrition, underweight (% of under age 5)	..	..	..
Child immunization, measles (% of ages 12–23 mon.)	85	96	99
HIV prevalence rate (% of ages 15–49)	..	..	..
Adult literacy, male (% of ages 15 and older)	..	..	..
Adult literacy, female (% of ages 15 and older)	..	..	..
Primary completion rate, total (% of age group)	..	80	..
Primary completion rate, female (% of age group)	..	77	..
Net primary enrollment (% of age group)	..	84	..
Net secondary enrollment (% of age group)	..	..	..
Environment			
Forests (1,000 sq. km)	0	0	..
Deforestation (average annual %, 1990–2000)		0.0	
Freshwater use (% of internal resources)			..
Carbon dioxide emissions (metric tons per capita)	1.3	2.1	..
Access to improved water source (% of total pop.)	..	95	..
Access to improved sanitation (% of urban pop.)	96	96	..
Energy use per capita (kg oil equivalent)	..	..	..
Electricity use per capita (kilowatt-hours)	..	..	..
Economy			
GDP ($ millions)	221	414	439
GDP growth (annual %)	5.2	–1.1	5.8
GDP implicit price deflator (annual % growth)	–1.4	2.8	3.5
Value added in agriculture (% of GDP)	13	8	..
Value added in industry (% of GDP)	18	23	..
Value added in services (% of GDP)	69	70	..
Exports of goods and services (% of GDP)	42	47	..
Imports of goods and services (% of GDP)	63	57	..
Gross capital formation (% of GDP)	38	38	..
Central government revenue (% of GDP)	–3.5	..	..
Cash surplus/deficit (% of GDP)	..	..	..
Technology and infrastructure			
Fixed-line and mobile subscribers (per 1,000 people)	178	388	667
Cost of 3-minute local call ($)	0.00	0.09	0.09
Personal computers (per 1,000 people)	..	132.1	..
Internet users (per 1,000 people)	0	142	169
Paved roads (% of total)	55.4	61.3	..
Aircraft departures (thousands)	..	..	..
Trade and finance			
Trade in goods (% of GDP)	59.7	57.2	64.2
Trade growth less GDP growth (avg. %, 1990–2003)			1.2
High-technology exports (% of manufactured exports)	..	8	1
Net barter terms of trade (2000 = 100)	..	..	..
Foreign direct investment ($ millions)	13	58	0
Present value of debt ($ millions)			349
Total debt service (% of goods and services exports)	3.1	15.9	18.0
Short-term debt ($ millions)	13	72	73
Aid per capita ($)	148	94	112

Guam

High income

Population (thousands)	162	Population growth (%)	1.4
Surface area (sq. km)	550	National poverty rate (% pop.)	..
GNI ($ millions)	..	GNI per capita ($)	..

	1990	2002	2003
People			
Life expectancy at birth (years)	74	78	78
Fertility rate (births per woman)	3.3	3.8	3.7
Infant mortality rate (per 1,000 live births)	9	6	..
Under-five mortality rate (per 1,000)	..	..	..
Births attended by skilled health staff (% of total)	..	..	..
Child malnutrition, underweight (% of under age 5)	..	..	..
Child immunization, measles (% of ages 12–23 mon.)	..	..	..
HIV prevalence rate (% of ages 15–49)	..	..	..
Adult literacy, male (% of ages 15 and older)	..	..	..
Adult literacy, female (% of ages 15 and older)	..	..	..
Primary completion rate, total (% of age group)	..	..	..
Primary completion rate, female (% of age group)	..	..	..
Net primary enrollment (% of age group)	..	..	..
Net secondary enrollment (% of age group)	..	..	..
Environment			
Forests (1,000 sq. km)	0	0	..
Deforestation (average annual %, 1990–2000)		0.0	
Freshwater use (% of internal resources)			..
Carbon dioxide emissions (metric tons per capita)	16.9	26.3	..
Access to improved water source (% of total pop.)	100	100	..
Access to improved sanitation (% of urban pop.)	99	99	..
Energy use per capita (kg oil equivalent)	..	..	..
Electricity use per capita (kilowatt-hours)	..	..	..
Economy			
GDP ($ millions)	..	..	..
GDP growth (annual %)	..	..	..
GDP implicit price deflator (annual % growth)	..	..	..
Value added in agriculture (% of GDP)	..	..	..
Value added in industry (% of GDP)	..	..	..
Value added in services (% of GDP)	..	..	..
Exports of goods and services (% of GDP)	..	..	..
Imports of goods and services (% of GDP)	..	..	..
Gross capital formation (% of GDP)	..	..	..
Central government revenue (% of GDP)	..	..	..
Cash surplus/deficit (% of GDP)	..	..	..
Technology and infrastructure			
Fixed-line and mobile subscribers (per 1,000 people)	293	716	..
Cost of 3-minute local call ($)	0.00	0.00	..
Personal computers (per 1,000 people)	..	..	..
Internet users (per 1,000 people)	..	313	..
Paved roads (% of total)	..	..	..
Aircraft departures (thousands)	..	..	..
Trade and finance			
Trade in goods (% of GDP)	..	..	..
Trade growth less GDP growth (avg. %, 1990–2003)			..
High-technology exports (% of manufactured exports)	..	..	..
Net barter terms of trade (2000 = 100)	..	..	..
Foreign direct investment ($ millions)	..	..	..
Present value of debt ($ millions)			..
Total debt service (% of goods and services exports)	..	..	..
Short-term debt ($ millions)	..	..	..
Aid per capita ($)	..	..	..

Guatemala

Latin America & Caribbean		Lower middle income		

Population (millions)	12	Population growth (%)		2.6
Surface area (1,000 sq. km)	109	National poverty rate (% pop.)		56
GNI ($ billions)	23	GNI per capita ($)		1,910

	1990	2002	2003
People			
Life expectancy at birth (years)	61	66	66
Fertility rate (births per woman)	5.3	4.3	4.3
Infant mortality rate (per 1,000 live births)	60	*39*	35
Under-five mortality rate (per 1,000)	82	*53*	47
Births attended by skilled health staff (% of total)	..	41	..
Child malnutrition, underweight (% of under age 5)	..	23	..
Child immunization, measles (% of ages 12–23 mon.)	68	75	75
HIV prevalence rate (% of ages 15–49)	..	*1.1*	1.1
Adult literacy, male (% of ages 15 and older)	69	77	..
Adult literacy, female (% of ages 15 and older)	53	62	..
Primary completion rate, total (% of age group)	..	63	66
Primary completion rate, female (% of age group)	..	59	63
Net primary enrollment (% of age group)	64	87	..
Net secondary enrollment (% of age group)	..	30	..
Environment			
Forests (1,000 sq. km)	34	29	..
Deforestation (average annual %, 1990–2000)		*1.7*	
Freshwater use (% of internal resources)			1
Carbon dioxide emissions (metric tons per capita)	0.6	*0.9*	..
Access to improved water source (% of total pop.)	77	95	..
Access to improved sanitation (% of urban pop.)	71	72	..
Energy use per capita (kg oil equivalent)	512	616	..
Electricity use per capita (kilowatt-hours)	226	361	..
Economy			
GDP ($ billions)	8	23	25
GDP growth (annual %)	3.1	2.2	2.1
GDP implicit price deflator (annual % growth)	40.5	8.0	5.8
Value added in agriculture (% of GDP)	26	22	22
Value added in industry (% of GDP)	20	19	19
Value added in services (% of GDP)	54	58	58
Exports of goods and services (% of GDP)	21	16	16
Imports of goods and services (% of GDP)	25	28	28
Gross capital formation (% of GDP)	14	19	17
Central government revenue (% of GDP)	7.9	11.2	10.9
Cash surplus/deficit (% of GDP)	–1.9	–0.9	–2.3
Technology and infrastructure			
Fixed-line and mobile subscribers (per 1,000 people)	21	202	..
Cost of 3-minute local call ($)	0.04	*0.08*	..
Personal computers (per 1,000 people)	..	14.4	..
Internet users (per 1,000 people)	..	33	..
Paved roads (% of total)	24.9	*34.5*	..
Aircraft departures (thousands)	3	7	..
Trade and finance			
Trade in goods (% of GDP)	36.8	37.7	37.8
Trade growth less GDP growth (avg. %, 1990–2003)			2.9
High-technology exports (% of manufactured exports)	..	8	7
Net barter terms of trade (2000 = 100)	115	97	..
Foreign direct investment ($ millions)	48	111	116
Present value of debt ($ millions)			4,862
Total debt service (% of goods and services exports)	12.6	7.1	7.4
Short-term debt ($ millions)	409	932	1,257
Aid per capita ($)	23	21	20

Guinea

Sub-Saharan Africa			**Low income**
Population (millions)	8	Population growth (%)	2.1
Surface area (1,000 sq. km)	246	National poverty rate (% pop.)	..
GNI ($ millions)	3,384	GNI per capita ($)	430

	1990	2002	2003
People			
Life expectancy at birth (years)	44	46	46
Fertility rate (births per woman)	5.9	5.0	5.0
Infant mortality rate (per 1,000 live births)	145	112	104
Under-five mortality rate (per 1,000)	240	175	160
Births attended by skilled health staff (% of total)	31	35	..
Child malnutrition, underweight (% of under age 5)	..	23	..
Child immunization, measles (% of ages 12–23 mon.)	35	54	52
HIV prevalence rate (% of ages 15–49)	..	2.8	3.2
Adult literacy, male (% of ages 15 and older)	..	..	..
Adult literacy, female (% of ages 15 and older)	..	..	..
Primary completion rate, total (% of age group)	17	41	..
Primary completion rate, female (% of age group)	9	31	..
Net primary enrollment (% of age group)	25	65	..
Net secondary enrollment (% of age group)	..	21	..
Environment			
Forests (1,000 sq. km)	73	69	..
Deforestation (average annual %, 1990–2000)		0.5	
Freshwater use (% of internal resources)			0
Carbon dioxide emissions (metric tons per capita)	0.2	0.2	..
Access to improved water source (% of total pop.)	42	51	..
Access to improved sanitation (% of urban pop.)	27	25	..
Energy use per capita (kg oil equivalent)	..	..	..
Electricity use per capita (kilowatt-hours)	..	..	..
Economy			
GDP ($ millions)	2,818	3,208	3,630
GDP growth (annual %)	4.4	4.2	1.2
GDP implicit price deflator (annual % growth)	23.9	2.7	12.4
Value added in agriculture (% of GDP)	24	24	25
Value added in industry (% of GDP)	33	37	36
Value added in services (% of GDP)	43	39	39
Exports of goods and services (% of GDP)	31	24	22
Imports of goods and services (% of GDP)	31	28	25
Gross capital formation (% of GDP)	18	13	10
Central government revenue (% of GDP)	16.0	..	..
Cash surplus/deficit (% of GDP)	–3.3	..	..
Technology and infrastructure			
Fixed-line and mobile subscribers (per 1,000 people)	2	15	18
Cost of 3-minute local call ($)	0.09	0.08	..
Personal computers (per 1,000 people)	..	5.5	5.5
Internet users (per 1,000 people)	..	5	5
Paved roads (% of total)	15.2	16.5	..
Aircraft departures (thousands)	1	1	..
Trade and finance			
Trade in goods (% of GDP)	49.5	49.9	45.3
Trade growth less GDP growth (avg. %, 1990–2003)			–1.2
High-technology exports (% of manufactured exports)	..	0	..
Net barter terms of trade (2000 = 100)	122	100	..
Foreign direct investment ($ millions)	18	30	79
Present value of debt ($ millions)			1,906
Total debt service (% of goods and services exports)	20.0	15.2	15.1
Short-term debt ($ millions)	172	289	166
Aid per capita ($)	51	32	30

Guinea-Bissau

Sub-Saharan Africa			Low income

Population (millions)	1	Population growth (%)	2.9
Surface area (1,000 sq. km)	36	National poverty rate (% pop.)	..
GNI ($ millions)	202	GNI per capita ($)	140

	1990	2002	2003
People			
Life expectancy at birth (years)	42	45	46
Fertility rate (births per woman)	7.1	6.6	6.6
Infant mortality rate (per 1,000 live births)	153	132	126
Under-five mortality rate (per 1,000)	253	215	204
Births attended by skilled health staff (% of total)	..	35	..
Child malnutrition, underweight (% of under age 5)	..	25	..
Child immunization, measles (% of ages 12–23 mon.)	53	47	61
HIV prevalence rate (% of ages 15–49)	..	..	..
Adult literacy, male (% of ages 15 and older)	..	..	..
Adult literacy, female (% of ages 15 and older)	..	..	..
Primary completion rate, total (% of age group)	..	28	..
Primary completion rate, female (% of age group)	..	20	..
Net primary enrollment (% of age group)	38	45	..
Net secondary enrollment (% of age group)	..	9	..
Environment			
Forests (1,000 sq. km)	24	22	..
Deforestation (average annual %, 1990–2000)		0.9	
Freshwater use (% of internal resources)			0
Carbon dioxide emissions (metric tons per capita)	0.8	0.2	..
Access to improved water source (% of total pop.)	..	59	..
Access to improved sanitation (% of urban pop.)	..	57	..
Energy use per capita (kg oil equivalent)	..	..	..
Electricity use per capita (kilowatt-hours)	..	..	..
Economy			
GDP ($ millions)	244	204	239
GDP growth (annual %)	6.1	–7.2	0.6
GDP implicit price deflator (annual % growth)	30.2	4.8	–2.8
Value added in agriculture (% of GDP)	61	62	69
Value added in industry (% of GDP)	19	13	13
Value added in services (% of GDP)	21	25	18
Exports of goods and services (% of GDP)	10	30	30
Imports of goods and services (% of GDP)	37	51	44
Gross capital formation (% of GDP)	30	10	13
Central government revenue (% of GDP)	..	..	..
Cash surplus/deficit (% of GDP)	..	..	..
Technology and infrastructure			
Fixed-line and mobile subscribers (per 1,000 people)	6	9	9
Cost of 3-minute local call ($)	0.08	0.15	..
Personal computers (per 1,000 people)	..	..	..
Internet users (per 1,000 people)	..	11	15
Paved roads (% of total)	8.3	10.3	..
Aircraft departures (thousands)	1	1	..
Trade and finance			
Trade in goods (% of GDP)	43.0	77.6	87.6
Trade growth less GDP growth (avg. %, 1990–2003)			4.0
High-technology exports (% of manufactured exports)	..	..	..
Net barter terms of trade (2000 = 100)	146	105	..
Foreign direct investment ($ millions)	2	1	2
Present value of debt ($ millions)			497
Total debt service (% of goods and services exports)	31.0	13.8	16.2
Short-term debt ($ millions)	57	14	12
Aid per capita ($)	127	41	98

Guyana

Latin America & Caribbean   **Lower middle income**

Population (thousands)	769	Population growth (%)	0.4
Surface area (1,000 sq. km)	215	National poverty rate (% pop.)	..
GNI ($ millions)	689	GNI per capita ($)	900

	1990	2002	2003
People			
Life expectancy at birth (years)	64	62	62
Fertility rate (births per woman)	2.6	2.3	2.3
Infant mortality rate (per 1,000 live births)	65	55	52
Under-five mortality rate (per 1,000)	90	74	69
Births attended by skilled health staff (% of total)	..	86	..
Child malnutrition, underweight (% of under age 5)	..	14	..
Child immunization, measles (% of ages 12–23 mon.)	73	93	89
HIV prevalence rate (% of ages 15–49)	..	2.5	2.5
Adult literacy, male (% of ages 15 and older)	..	..	..
Adult literacy, female (% of ages 15 and older)	..	..	..
Primary completion rate, total (% of age group)	90	99	..
Primary completion rate, female (% of age group)	92	..	..
Net primary enrollment (% of age group)	89	98	..
Net secondary enrollment (% of age group)	67	77	..
Environment			
Forests (1,000 sq. km)	174	169	..
Deforestation (average annual %, 1990–2000)		0.3	
Freshwater use (% of internal resources)			1
Carbon dioxide emissions (metric tons per capita)	1.5	2.1	..
Access to improved water source (% of total pop.)	..	83	..
Access to improved sanitation (% of urban pop.)	..	86	..
Energy use per capita (kg oil equivalent)	..	..	..
Electricity use per capita (kilowatt-hours)	..	..	..
Economy			
GDP ($ millions)	397	722	742
GDP growth (annual %)	–3.0	–1.1	–0.6
GDP implicit price deflator (annual % growth)	56.4	4.4	5.1
Value added in agriculture (% of GDP)	38	31	..
Value added in industry (% of GDP)	25	29	..
Value added in services (% of GDP)	37	41	..
Exports of goods and services (% of GDP)	63	93	..
Imports of goods and services (% of GDP)	80	106	..
Gross capital formation (% of GDP)	31	20	..
Central government revenue (% of GDP)	..	..	..
Cash surplus/deficit (% of GDP)	..	..	..
Technology and infrastructure			
Fixed-line and mobile subscribers (per 1,000 people)	20	191	..
Cost of 3-minute local call ($)	0.01	0.00	0.00
Personal computers (per 1,000 people)	..	27.3	..
Internet users (per 1,000 people)	..	142	..
Paved roads (% of total)	6.6	7.4	..
Aircraft departures (thousands)	4	0	..
Trade and finance			
Trade in goods (% of GDP)	143.2	146.2	146.9
Trade growth less GDP growth (avg. %, 1990–2003)			0.0
High-technology exports (% of manufactured exports)	..	7	1
Net barter terms of trade (2000 = 100)	..	..	..
Foreign direct investment ($ millions)	8	44	26
Present value of debt ($ millions)			568
Total debt service (% of goods and services exports)	20.7	8.8	7.5
Short-term debt ($ millions)	75	132	126
Aid per capita ($)	231	85	113

Haiti

Latin America & Caribbean		Low income	
Population (millions)	8	Population growth (%)	1.8
Surface area (1,000 sq. km)	28	National poverty rate (% pop.)	..
GNI ($ millions)	3,342	GNI per capita ($)	400

	1990	2002	2003
People			
Life expectancy at birth (years)	53	52	52
Fertility rate (births per woman)	5.4	4.2	4.2
Infant mortality rate (per 1,000 live births)	102	*81*	76
Under-five mortality rate (per 1,000)	150	*125*	118
Births attended by skilled health staff (% of total)	23	24	..
Child malnutrition, underweight (% of under age 5)	27	*17*	..
Child immunization, measles (% of ages 12–23 mon.)	31	53	53
HIV prevalence rate (% of ages 15–49)	..	5.5	5.6
Adult literacy, male (% of ages 15 and older)	43	54	..
Adult literacy, female (% of ages 15 and older)	37	50	..
Primary completion rate, total (% of age group)	29	..	..
Primary completion rate, female (% of age group)	28	..	..
Net primary enrollment (% of age group)	22	..	..
Net secondary enrollment (% of age group)	..	..	..
Environment			
Forests (1,000 sq. km)	2	*1*	..
Deforestation (average annual %, 1990–2000)		*5.7*	
Freshwater use (% of internal resources)			8
Carbon dioxide emissions (metric tons per capita)	0.2	*0.2*	..
Access to improved water source (% of total pop.)	53	71	..
Access to improved sanitation (% of urban pop.)	27	52	..
Energy use per capita (kg oil equivalent)	245	251	..
Electricity use per capita (kilowatt-hours)	61	36	..
Economy			
GDP ($ millions)	2,864	3,465	2,921
GDP growth (annual %)	–0.1	–0.5	0.4
GDP implicit price deflator (annual % growth)	14.1	10.0	25.4
Value added in agriculture (% of GDP)	..	28	..
Value added in industry (% of GDP)	..	17	..
Value added in services (% of GDP)	..	55	..
Exports of goods and services (% of GDP)	18	13	..
Imports of goods and services (% of GDP)	20	37	..
Gross capital formation (% of GDP)	13	25	31
Central government revenue (% of GDP)	..	..	..
Cash surplus/deficit (% of GDP)	..	..	..
Technology and infrastructure			
Fixed-line and mobile subscribers (per 1,000 people)	7	33	55
Cost of 3-minute local call ($)	..	..	..
Personal computers (per 1,000 people)	..	..	..
Internet users (per 1,000 people)	..	10	18
Paved roads (% of total)	21.9	*24.3*	..
Aircraft departures (thousands)	1	..	..
Trade and finance			
Trade in goods (% of GDP)	17.2	40.7	52.5
Trade growth less GDP growth (avg. %, 1990–2003)			–1.3
High-technology exports (% of manufactured exports)	14	4	..
Net barter terms of trade (2000 = 100)	132	100	..
Foreign direct investment ($ millions)	0	6	8
Present value of debt ($ millions)			952
Total debt service (% of goods and services exports)	11.0	2.5	4.1
Short-term debt ($ millions)	101	154	117
Aid per capita ($)	26	19	24

Honduras

Latin America & Caribbean　　　　**Lower middle income**

Population (millions)	7	Population growth (%)		2.5
Surface area (1,000 sq. km)	112	National poverty rate (% pop.)		..
GNI ($ millions)	6,760	GNI per capita ($)		970

	1990	2002	2003
People			
Life expectancy at birth (years)	65	66	66
Fertility rate (births per woman)	5.2	4.0	4.0
Infant mortality rate (per 1,000 live births)	44	33	32
Under-five mortality rate (per 1,000)	59	43	41
Births attended by skilled health staff (% of total)	45	56	..
Child malnutrition, underweight (% of under age 5)	18	17	..
Child immunization, measles (% of ages 12–23 mon.)	90	97	95
HIV prevalence rate (% of ages 15–49)	..	1.6	1.8
Adult literacy, male (% of ages 15 and older)	69	80	..
Adult literacy, female (% of ages 15 and older)	67	80	..
Primary completion rate, total (% of age group)	65	..	79
Primary completion rate, female (% of age group)	62	..	..
Net primary enrollment (% of age group)	90	87	..
Net secondary enrollment (% of age group)	..	..	..
Environment			
Forests (1,000 sq. km)	60	54	..
Deforestation (average annual %, 1990–2000)		1.0	
Freshwater use (% of internal resources)			2
Carbon dioxide emissions (metric tons per capita)	0.5	0.7	..
Access to improved water source (% of total pop.)	83	90	..
Access to improved sanitation (% of urban pop.)	77	89	..
Energy use per capita (kg oil equivalent)	496	504	..
Electricity use per capita (kilowatt-hours)	370	537	..
Economy			
GDP ($ millions)	3,049	6,594	6,978
GDP growth (annual %)	0.1	2.0	3.0
GDP implicit price deflator (annual % growth)	21.2	7.3	8.6
Value added in agriculture (% of GDP)	22	13	13
Value added in industry (% of GDP)	26	31	31
Value added in services (% of GDP)	51	56	56
Exports of goods and services (% of GDP)	36	37	36
Imports of goods and services (% of GDP)	40	53	54
Gross capital formation (% of GDP)	23	28	29
Central government revenue (% of GDP)	..	..	..
Cash surplus/deficit (% of GDP)	..	..	..
Technology and infrastructure			
Fixed-line and mobile subscribers (per 1,000 people)	17	97	..
Cost of 3-minute local call ($)	0.02	0.06	..
Personal computers (per 1,000 people)	..	13.6	..
Internet users (per 1,000 people)	..	25	..
Paved roads (% of total)	21.1	20.4	..
Aircraft departures (thousands)	17	..	..
Trade and finance			
Trade in goods (% of GDP)	57.9	65.2	66.0
Trade growth less GDP growth (avg. %, 1990–2003)			–0.3
High-technology exports (% of manufactured exports)	..	0	..
Net barter terms of trade (2000 = 100)	78	95	..
Foreign direct investment ($ millions)	44	176	198
Present value of debt ($ millions)			3,490
Total debt service (% of goods and services exports)	35.3	12.1	11.6
Short-term debt ($ millions)	199	524	464
Aid per capita ($)	92	64	56

Hong Kong, China

High income

Population (millions)	7	Population growth (%)	0.4
Surface area (1,000 sq. km)	1	National poverty rate (% pop.)	..
GNI ($ billions)	176	GNI per capita ($)	25,860

	1990	2002	2003
People			
Life expectancy at birth (years)	78	80	80
Fertility rate (births per woman)	1.3	1.0	1.0
Infant mortality rate (per 1,000 live births)	6	3	..
Under-five mortality rate (per 1,000)	..	..	..
Births attended by skilled health staff (% of total)	..	..	..
Child malnutrition, underweight (% of under age 5)	..	..	..
Child immunization, measles (% of ages 12–23 mon.)	..	..	..
HIV prevalence rate (% of ages 15–49)	..	0.1	0.1
Adult literacy, male (% of ages 15 and older)	..	..	..
Adult literacy, female (% of ages 15 and older)	..	..	..
Primary completion rate, total (% of age group)	102	101	..
Primary completion rate, female (% of age group)	..	..	..
Net primary enrollment (% of age group)	..	98	..
Net secondary enrollment (% of age group)	..	72	..
Environment			
Forests (1,000 sq. km)	..	..	
Deforestation (average annual %, 1990–2000)		..	
Freshwater use (% of internal resources)			..
Carbon dioxide emissions (metric tons per capita)	4.6	5.0	..
Access to improved water source (% of total pop.)	..	..	
Access to improved sanitation (% of urban pop.)	..	..	
Energy use per capita (kg oil equivalent)	1,869	2,413	..
Electricity use per capita (kilowatt-hours)	4,178	5,612	..
Economy			
GDP ($ billions)	75	160	157
GDP growth (annual %)	1.9	1.9	3.2
GDP implicit price deflator (annual % growth)	9.4	–3.0	–5.1
Value added in agriculture (% of GDP)	0	0	..
Value added in industry (% of GDP)	25	12	..
Value added in services (% of GDP)	74	88	..
Exports of goods and services (% of GDP)	132	151	170
Imports of goods and services (% of GDP)	124	142	161
Gross capital formation (% of GDP)	28	23	23
Central government revenue (% of GDP)	..	15.3	..
Cash surplus/deficit (% of GDP)	..	–7.0	..
Technology and infrastructure			
Fixed-line and mobile subscribers (per 1,000 people)	475	1,507	1,638
Cost of 3-minute local call ($)	0.00	0.00	0.00
Personal computers (per 1,000 people)	47.3	422.0	..
Internet users (per 1,000 people)	1	278	472
Paved roads (% of total)	100.0	100.0	..
Aircraft departures (thousands)	125	91	87
Trade and finance			
Trade in goods (% of GDP)	221.5	256.3	294.8
Trade growth less GDP growth (avg. %, 1990–2003)			3.5
High-technology exports (% of manufactured exports)	17	17	13
Net barter terms of trade (2000 = 100)	100	102	..
Foreign direct investment ($ billions)	..	10	14
Present value of debt ($ millions)			..
Total debt service (% of goods and services exports)	..	..	..
Short-term debt ($ millions)	..	..	..
Aid per capita ($)	7	1	1

Hungary

Europe & Central Asia   **Upper middle income**

Population (millions)	10	Population growth (%)	–0.3
Surface area (1,000 sq. km)	93	National poverty rate (% pop.)	17
GNI ($ billions)	64	GNI per capita ($)	6,350

	1990	2002	2003
People			
Life expectancy at birth (years)	69	72	73
Fertility rate (births per woman)	1.8	1.3	1.3
Infant mortality rate (per 1,000 live births)	15	7	8
Under-five mortality rate (per 1,000)	17	7	7
Births attended by skilled health staff (% of total)	..	..	..
Child malnutrition, underweight (% of under age 5)	2	..	..
Child immunization, measles (% of ages 12–23 mon.)	99	99	99
HIV prevalence rate (% of ages 15–49)	..	..	0.1
Adult literacy, male (% of ages 15 and older)	99	99	..
Adult literacy, female (% of ages 15 and older)	99	99	..
Primary completion rate, total (% of age group)	82	102	..
Primary completion rate, female (% of age group)	91	101	..
Net primary enrollment (% of age group)	91	91	..
Net secondary enrollment (% of age group)	75	92	..
Environment			
Forests (1,000 sq. km)	18	18	..
Deforestation (average annual %, 1990–2000)		–0.4	
Freshwater use (% of internal resources)			113
Carbon dioxide emissions (metric tons per capita)	5.6	5.4	..
Access to improved water source (% of total pop.)	99	99	..
Access to improved sanitation (% of urban pop.)	100	100	..
Energy use per capita (kg oil equivalent)	2,755	2,505	..
Electricity use per capita (kilowatt-hours)	3,048	3,099	..
Economy			
GDP ($ billions)	33	65	83
GDP growth (annual %)	–3.5	3.5	3.0
GDP implicit price deflator (annual % growth)	25.7	8.9	7.8
Value added in agriculture (% of GDP)	15	4	..
Value added in industry (% of GDP)	39	31	..
Value added in services (% of GDP)	46	65	..
Exports of goods and services (% of GDP)	31	65	..
Imports of goods and services (% of GDP)	29	68	..
Gross capital formation (% of GDP)	25	24	..
Central government revenue (% of GDP)	..	37.7	37.3
Cash surplus/deficit (% of GDP)	..	–8.6	–6.2
Technology and infrastructure			
Fixed-line and mobile subscribers (per 1,000 people)	96	1,037	1,117
Cost of 3-minute local call ($)	0.08	0.13	0.16
Personal computers (per 1,000 people)	9.6	108.4	..
Internet users (per 1,000 people)	0	158	232
Paved roads (% of total)	50.4	43.9	..
Aircraft departures (thousands)	19	33	35
Trade and finance			
Trade in goods (% of GDP)	61.5	111.4	108.9
Trade growth less GDP growth (avg. %, 1990–2003)			8.8
High-technology exports (% of manufactured exports)	4	25	26
Net barter terms of trade (2000 = 100)	111	100	100
Foreign direct investment ($ millions)	311	2,863	2,506
Present value of debt ($ billions)			44
Total debt service (% of goods and services exports)	34.3	34.4	28.9
Short-term debt ($ millions)	2,940	5,668	9,016
Aid per capita ($)	6	16	25

Iceland

High income

Population (thousands)	289	Population growth (%)	0.3
Surface area (1,000 sq. km)	103	National poverty rate (% pop.)	..
GNI ($ millions)	8,932	GNI per capita ($)	30,910

	1990	2002	2003
People			
Life expectancy at birth (years)	78	80	80
Fertility rate (births per woman)	2.3	1.9	2.0
Infant mortality rate (per 1,000 live births)	5	3	3
Under-five mortality rate (per 1,000)	5	4	4
Births attended by skilled health staff (% of total)	..	..	..
Child malnutrition, underweight (% of under age 5)	..	..	..
Child immunization, measles (% of ages 12–23 mon.)	99	91	93
HIV prevalence rate (% of ages 15–49)	..	0.2	0.2
Adult literacy, male (% of ages 15 and older)	..	..	..
Adult literacy, female (% of ages 15 and older)	..	..	..
Primary completion rate, total (% of age group)	..	105	..
Primary completion rate, female (% of age group)	..	108	..
Net primary enrollment (% of age group)	100	100	..
Net secondary enrollment (% of age group)	..	85	..
Environment			
Forests (1,000 sq. km)	0	0	..
Deforestation (average annual %, 1990–2000)		–2.2	
Freshwater use (% of internal resources)			0
Carbon dioxide emissions (metric tons per capita)	7.9	7.7	..
Access to improved water source (% of total pop.)	100	100	..
Access to improved sanitation (% of urban pop.)	..	..	..
Energy use per capita (kg oil equivalent)	8,524	11,819	..
Electricity use per capita (kilowatt-hours)	15,345	26,247	..
Economy			
GDP ($ millions)	6,238	8,493	10,513
GDP growth (annual %)	1.2	–0.5	4.0
GDP implicit price deflator (annual % growth)	16.9	5.3	–0.4
Value added in agriculture (% of GDP)	12	10	..
Value added in industry (% of GDP)	29	28	..
Value added in services (% of GDP)	59	63	..
Exports of goods and services (% of GDP)	34	40	35
Imports of goods and services (% of GDP)	33	38	39
Gross capital formation (% of GDP)	20	19	21
Central government revenue (% of GDP)	..	33.3	..
Cash surplus/deficit (% of GDP)	..	–0.4	..
Technology and infrastructure			
Fixed-line and mobile subscribers (per 1,000 people)	549	1,559	1,626
Cost of 3-minute local call ($)	0.05	0.09	..
Personal computers (per 1,000 people)	39.1	451.4	..
Internet users (per 1,000 people)	5	648	675
Paved roads (% of total)	19.9	31.5	..
Aircraft departures (thousands)	18	10	10
Trade and finance			
Trade in goods (% of GDP)	52.5	53.0	49.2
Trade growth less GDP growth (avg. %, 1990–2003)			1.6
High-technology exports (% of manufactured exports)	10	6	6
Net barter terms of trade (2000 = 100)	..	..	..
Foreign direct investment ($ millions)	22	124	345
Present value of debt ($ millions)			..
Total debt service (% of goods and services exports)	..	..	..
Short-term debt ($ millions)	..	..	..
Aid per capita ($)	..	..	..

India

South Asia | **Low income**

Population (millions)	1,064	Population growth (%)	1.5
Surface area (1,000 sq. km)	3,287	National poverty rate (% pop.)	29
GNI ($ billions)	571	GNI per capita ($)	540

	1990	2002	2003
People			
Life expectancy at birth (years)	59	63	63
Fertility rate (births per woman)	3.8	2.9	2.9
Infant mortality rate (per 1,000 live births)	84	68	63
Under-five mortality rate (per 1,000)	123	94	87
Births attended by skilled health staff (% of total)	..	43	..
Child malnutrition, underweight (% of under age 5)	64	47	..
Child immunization, measles (% of ages 12–23 mon.)	56	67	67
HIV prevalence rate (% of ages 15–49)	..	0.8	0.9
Adult literacy, male (% of ages 15 and older)	62	68	..
Adult literacy, female (% of ages 15 and older)	36	45	..
Primary completion rate, total (% of age group)	..	81	..
Primary completion rate, female (% of age group)	..	77	..
Net primary enrollment (% of age group)	..	83	..
Net secondary enrollment (% of age group)	..	..	..
Environment			
Forests (1,000 sq. km)	637	641	..
Deforestation (average annual %, 1990–2000)		–0.1	
Freshwater use (% of internal resources)			40
Carbon dioxide emissions (metric tons per capita)	0.8	1.1	..
Access to improved water source (% of total pop.)	68	86	..
Access to improved sanitation (% of urban pop.)	43	58	..
Energy use per capita (kg oil equivalent)	430	513	..
Electricity use per capita (kilowatt-hours)	249	380	..
Economy			
GDP ($ billions)	317	510	601
GDP growth (annual %)	5.8	4.1	8.6
GDP implicit price deflator (annual % growth)	10.5	3.5	3.2
Value added in agriculture (% of GDP)	31	23	22
Value added in industry (% of GDP)	28	27	27
Value added in services (% of GDP)	41	51	51
Exports of goods and services (% of GDP)	7	15	14
Imports of goods and services (% of GDP)	9	16	16
Gross capital formation (% of GDP)	24	23	24
Central government revenue (% of GDP)	12.6	11.9	11.6
Cash surplus/deficit (% of GDP)	–3.4	–4.6	–4.3
Technology and infrastructure			
Fixed-line and mobile subscribers (per 1,000 people)	6	52	71
Cost of 3-minute local call ($)	0.05	0.02	0.02
Personal computers (per 1,000 people)	0.3	7.2	..
Internet users (per 1,000 people)	0	16	17
Paved roads (% of total)	47.3	57.3	..
Aircraft departures (thousands)	126	231	264
Trade and finance			
Trade in goods (% of GDP)	13.1	20.7	21.1
Trade growth less GDP growth (avg. %, 1990–2003)			6.9
High-technology exports (% of manufactured exports)	2	5	5
Net barter terms of trade (2000 = 100)	86	88	..
Foreign direct investment ($ millions)	237	3,700	4,269
Present value of debt ($ billions)			100
Total debt service (% of goods and services exports)	31.9	14.1	18.1
Short-term debt ($ millions)	8,544	4,569	4,736
Aid per capita ($)	2	1	1

Indonesia

East Asia & Pacific		Lower middle income

Population (milliions)	215	Population growth (%)	1.3
Surface area (1,000 sq. km)	1,905	National poverty rate (% pop.)	27
GNI ($ billions)	174	GNI per capita ($)	810

	1990	2002	2003
People			
Life expectancy at birth (years)	62	67	67
Fertility rate (births per woman)	3.1	2.5	2.4
Infant mortality rate (per 1,000 live births)	60	35	31
Under-five mortality rate (per 1,000)	91	48	41
Births attended by skilled health staff (% of total)	32	68	..
Child malnutrition, underweight (% of under age 5)	..	27	..
Child immunization, measles (% of ages 12–23 mon.)	58	72	72
HIV prevalence rate (% of ages 15–49)	..	0.1	0.1
Adult literacy, male (% of ages 15 and older)	87	92	..
Adult literacy, female (% of ages 15 and older)	73	83	..
Primary completion rate, total (% of age group)	93	95	95
Primary completion rate, female (% of age group)	..	107	..
Net primary enrollment (% of age group)	97	92	..
Net secondary enrollment (% of age group)	39	48	..
Environment			
Forests (1,000 sq. km)	1,181	1,050	..
Deforestation (average annual %, 1990–2000)		1.2	
Freshwater use (% of internal resources)			3
Carbon dioxide emissions (metric tons per capita)	0.9	1.3	..
Access to improved water source (% of total pop.)	71	78	..
Access to improved sanitation (% of urban pop.)	66	71	..
Energy use per capita (kg oil equivalent)	532	737	..
Electricity use per capita (kilowatt-hours)	152	411	..
Economy			
GDP ($ billions)	114	173	208
GDP growth (annual %)	9.0	3.7	4.1
GDP implicit price deflator (annual % growth)	7.7	7.2	6.5
Value added in agriculture (% of GDP)	19	17	17
Value added in industry (% of GDP)	39	44	44
Value added in services (% of GDP)	41	39	40
Exports of goods and services (% of GDP)	25	36	31
Imports of goods and services (% of GDP)	24	29	26
Gross capital formation (% of GDP)	31	16	16
Central government revenue (% of GDP)	18.8	21.0	..
Cash surplus/deficit (% of GDP)	0.4	−2.5	..
Technology and infrastructure			
Fixed-line and mobile subscribers (per 1,000 people)	6	92	127
Cost of 3-minute local call ($)	0.05	0.03	0.03
Personal computers (per 1,000 people)	1.1	11.9	..
Internet users (per 1,000 people)	..	21	38
Paved roads (% of total)	45.1	58.0	..
Aircraft departures (thousands)	205	152	156
Trade and finance			
Trade in goods (% of GDP)	41.5	51.1	44.9
Trade growth less GDP growth (avg. %, 1990–2003)			0.6
High-technology exports (% of manufactured exports)	1	16	14
Net barter terms of trade (2000 = 100)	95	100	..
Foreign direct investment ($ millions)	1,093	−1,513	−597
Present value of debt ($ billions)			137
Total debt service (% of goods and services exports)	33.3	24.8	26.0
Short-term debt ($ billions)	11	23	23
Aid per capita ($)	10	6	8

Iran, Islamic Rep.

Middle East & North Africa   **Lower middle income**

Population (millions)	66	Population growth (%)	1.3
Surface area (1,000 sq. km)	1,648	National poverty rate (% pop.)	..
GNI ($ billions)	133	GNI per capita ($)	2,010

	1990	2002	2003
People			
Life expectancy at birth (years)	65	69	69
Fertility rate (births per woman)	4.7	2.0	2.0
Infant mortality rate (per 1,000 live births)	54	36	33
Under-five mortality rate (per 1,000)	72	44	39
Births attended by skilled health staff (% of total)	..	90	..
Child malnutrition, underweight (% of under age 5)	..	11	..
Child immunization, measles (% of ages 12–23 mon.)	85	99	99
HIV prevalence rate (% of ages 15–49)	..	0.1	0.1
Adult literacy, male (% of ages 15 and older)	72	84	..
Adult literacy, female (% of ages 15 and older)	54	70	..
Primary completion rate, total (% of age group)	101	107	..
Primary completion rate, female (% of age group)	93	104	..
Net primary enrollment (% of age group)	92	87	..
Net secondary enrollment (% of age group)	..	..	..
Environment			
Forests (1,000 sq. km)	73	73	..
Deforestation (average annual %, 1990–2000)		0.0	
Freshwater use (% of internal resources)			54
Carbon dioxide emissions (metric tons per capita)	3.9	4.9	..
Access to improved water source (% of total pop.)	91	93	..
Access to improved sanitation (% of urban pop.)	86	86	..
Energy use per capita (kg oil equivalent)	1,264	2,044	..
Electricity use per capita (kilowatt-hours)	906	1,677	..
Economy			
GDP ($ billions)	120	114	137
GDP growth (annual %)	11.2	7.4	6.6
GDP implicit price deflator (annual % growth)	18.6	23.4	16.5
Value added in agriculture (% of GDP)	24	12	11
Value added in industry (% of GDP)	29	41	41
Value added in services (% of GDP)	48	48	48
Exports of goods and services (% of GDP)	22	27	25
Imports of goods and services (% of GDP)	24	25	23
Gross capital formation (% of GDP)	29	39	41
Central government revenue (% of GDP)	18.1	27.1	29.7
Cash surplus/deficit (% of GDP)	–1.8	0.7	1.6
Technology and infrastructure			
Fixed-line and mobile subscribers (per 1,000 people)	40	220	271
Cost of 3-minute local call ($)	0.01	0.01	0.01
Personal computers (per 1,000 people)	..	75.0	90.5
Internet users (per 1,000 people)	..	10	72
Paved roads (% of total)	..	56.3	..
Aircraft departures (thousands)	40	93	85
Trade and finance			
Trade in goods (% of GDP)	32.9	44.4	45.0
Trade growth less GDP growth (avg. %, 1990–2003)			–8.4
High-technology exports (% of manufactured exports)	..	3	2
Net barter terms of trade (2000 = 100)	..	..	..
Foreign direct investment ($ millions)	–362	276	120
Present value of debt ($ billions)			10
Total debt service (% of goods and services exports)	3.2	4.3	3.8
Short-term debt ($ millions)	7,224	2,357	3,204
Aid per capita ($)	2	2	2

Iraq

Middle East & North Africa   **Lower middle income**

Population (millions)	25	Population growth (%)	2.2
Surface area (1,000 sq. km)	438	National poverty rate (% pop.)	..
GNI ($ millions)	..	GNI per capita ($)	..

	1990	2002	2003
People			
Life expectancy at birth (years)	61	63	63
Fertility rate (births per woman)	5.9	4.1	4.0
Infant mortality rate (per 1,000 live births)	40	*102*	102
Under-five mortality rate (per 1,000)	50	*125*	125
Births attended by skilled health staff (% of total)	*54*	*72*	..
Child malnutrition, underweight (% of under age 5)	*12*	*16*	..
Child immunization, measles (% of ages 12–23 mon.)	80	90	90
HIV prevalence rate (% of ages 15–49)	..	..	0.1
Adult literacy, male (% of ages 15 and older)	..	..	..
Adult literacy, female (% of ages 15 and older)	..	..	..
Primary completion rate, total (% of age group)	*61*	*56*	..
Primary completion rate, female (% of age group)	56	50	..
Net primary enrollment (% of age group)	100	*91*	..
Net secondary enrollment (% of age group)	..	*33*	..

	1990	2002	2003
Environment			
Forests (1,000 sq. km)	8	*8*	..
Deforestation (average annual %, 1990–2000)		*0.0*	
Freshwater use (% of internal resources)			122
Carbon dioxide emissions (metric tons per capita)	2.7	*3.3*	..
Access to improved water source (% of total pop.)	83	81	..
Access to improved sanitation (% of urban pop.)	95	95	..
Energy use per capita (kg oil equivalent)	1,153	1,199	..
Electricity use per capita (kilowatt-hours)	1,261	1,213	..

	1990	2002	2003
Economy			
GDP ($ millions)	48,657	..	..
GDP growth (annual %)	..	..	..
GDP implicit price deflator (annual % growth)	45.0	..	..
Value added in agriculture (% of GDP)	..	..	..
Value added in industry (% of GDP)	..	..	..
Value added in services (% of GDP)	..	..	..
Exports of goods and services (% of GDP)	..	..	..
Imports of goods and services (% of GDP)	..	..	..
Gross capital formation (% of GDP)	..	..	..
Central government revenue (% of GDP)	..	..	..
Cash surplus/deficit (% of GDP)	..	..	..

	1990	2002	2003
Technology and infrastructure			
Fixed-line and mobile subscribers (per 1,000 people)	39	29	..
Cost of 3-minute local call ($)	..	..	..
Personal computers (per 1,000 people)	..	8.3	..
Internet users (per 1,000 people)	..	1	..
Paved roads (% of total)	77.9	*84.3*	..
Aircraft departures (thousands)	8	..	..

	1990	2002	2003
Trade and finance			
Trade in goods (% of GDP)	41.2	..	..
Trade growth less GDP growth (avg. %, 1990–2003)			..
High-technology exports (% of manufactured exports)	..	..	..
Net barter terms of trade (2000 = 100)	..	..	..
Foreign direct investment ($ millions)	..	..	..
Present value of debt ($ millions)			..
Total debt service (% of goods and services exports)	..	..	..
Short-term debt ($ millions)	..	..	..
Aid per capita ($)	4	5	92

Ireland

High income

Population (millions)	4	Population growth (%)	1.6
Surface area (1,000 sq. km)	70	National poverty rate (% pop.)	..
GNI ($ billions)	108	GNI per capita ($)	27,010

	1990	2002	2003
People			
Life expectancy at birth (years)	75	78	78
Fertility rate (births per woman)	2.1	2.0	2.0
Infant mortality rate (per 1,000 live births)	8	5	5
Under-five mortality rate (per 1,000)	9	7	..
Births attended by skilled health staff (% of total)	..	..	..
Child malnutrition, underweight (% of under age 5)	..	..	..
Child immunization, measles (% of ages 12–23 mon.)	78	76	78
HIV prevalence rate (% of ages 15–49)	..	0.1	0.1
Adult literacy, male (% of ages 15 and older)	..	..	..
Adult literacy, female (% of ages 15 and older)	..	..	..
Primary completion rate, total (% of age group)	..	..	..
Primary completion rate, female (% of age group)	..	..	..
Net primary enrollment (% of age group)	90	95	..
Net secondary enrollment (% of age group)	80	82	..
Environment			
Forests (1,000 sq. km)	5	7	..
Deforestation (average annual %, 1990–2000)		–3.0	
Freshwater use (% of internal resources)			2
Carbon dioxide emissions (metric tons per capita)	8.5	11.1	..
Access to improved water source (% of total pop.)	..	..	..
Access to improved sanitation (% of urban pop.)	..	..	..
Energy use per capita (kg oil equivalent)	3,016	3,894	..
Electricity use per capita (kilowatt-hours)	3,385	5,555	..
Economy			
GDP ($ billions)	47	122	154
GDP growth (annual %)	8.5	6.9	3.7
GDP implicit price deflator (annual % growth)	–0.7	5.4	..
Value added in agriculture (% of GDP)	9	3	..
Value added in industry (% of GDP)	35	42	..
Value added in services (% of GDP)	56	55	..
Exports of goods and services (% of GDP)	57	94	..
Imports of goods and services (% of GDP)	52	75	..
Gross capital formation (% of GDP)	21	22	..
Central government revenue (% of GDP)	27.8	25.1	..
Cash surplus/deficit (% of GDP)	–1.9	0.5	..
Technology and infrastructure			
Fixed-line and mobile subscribers (per 1,000 people)	288	1,266	1,371
Cost of 3-minute local call ($)	0.18	0.14	0.17
Personal computers (per 1,000 people)	85.6	420.8	..
Internet users (per 1,000 people)	1	280	317
Paved roads (% of total)	94.0	100.0	..
Aircraft departures (thousands)	80	177	231
Trade and finance			
Trade in goods (% of GDP)	93.9	115.6	95.0
Trade growth less GDP growth (avg. %, 1990–2003)			6.8
High-technology exports (% of manufactured exports)	41	41	34
Net barter terms of trade (2000 = 100)	106	102	103
Foreign direct investment ($ billions)	1	29	27
Present value of debt ($ millions)			..
Total debt service (% of goods and services exports)	..	..	..
Short-term debt ($ millions)	..	..	..
Aid per capita ($)	..	..	..

Isle of Man

High income

Population (thousands)	74	Population growth (%)		..
Surface area (sq. km)	572	National poverty rate (% pop.)		..
GNI ($ millions)	..	GNI per capita ($)		..

	1990	2002	2003
People			
Life expectancy at birth (years)	..	..	..
Fertility rate (births per woman)	..	..	..
Infant mortality rate (per 1,000 live births)	..	..	..
Under-five mortality rate (per 1,000)	..	..	..
Births attended by skilled health staff (% of total)	..	..	..
Child malnutrition, underweight (% of under age 5)	..	..	..
Child immunization, measles (% of ages 12–23 mon.)	..	..	..
HIV prevalence rate (% of ages 15–49)	..	..	..
Adult literacy, male (% of ages 15 and older)	..	..	..
Adult literacy, female (% of ages 15 and older)	..	..	..
Primary completion rate, total (% of age group)	..	..	..
Primary completion rate, female (% of age group)	..	..	..
Net primary enrollment (% of age group)	..	..	..
Net secondary enrollment (% of age group)	..	..	..
Environment			
Forests (1,000 sq. km)	..	..	..
Deforestation (average annual %, 1990–2000)		..	
Freshwater use (% of internal resources)			..
Carbon dioxide emissions (metric tons per capita)	..	..	
Access to improved water source (% of total pop.)	..	..	..
Access to improved sanitation (% of urban pop.)	..	..	..
Energy use per capita (kg oil equivalent)	..	..	..
Electricity use per capita (kilowatt-hours)	..	..	..
Economy			
GDP ($ millions)	..	..	..
GDP growth (annual %)	..	..	..
GDP implicit price deflator (annual % growth)	..	..	..
Value added in agriculture (% of GDP)	..	..	..
Value added in industry (% of GDP)	..	..	..
Value added in services (% of GDP)	..	..	..
Exports of goods and services (% of GDP)	..	..	..
Imports of goods and services (% of GDP)	..	..	..
Gross capital formation (% of GDP)	..	..	..
Central government revenue (% of GDP)	..	..	..
Cash surplus/deficit (% of GDP)	..	..	..
Technology and infrastructure			
Fixed-line and mobile subscribers (per 1,000 people)	..	..	..
Cost of 3-minute local call ($)	..	..	..
Personal computers (per 1,000 people)	..	..	..
Internet users (per 1,000 people)	..	..	..
Paved roads (% of total)	..	..	..
Aircraft departures (thousands)	..	..	..
Trade and finance			
Trade in goods (% of GDP)	..	..	..
Trade growth less GDP growth (avg. %, 1990–2003)			..
High-technology exports (% of manufactured exports)	..	..	..
Net barter terms of trade (2000 = 100)	..	..	..
Foreign direct investment ($ millions)	..	..	..
Present value of debt ($ millions)			..
Total debt service (% of goods and services exports)	..	..	..
Short-term debt ($ millions)	..	..	..
Aid per capita ($)	..	..	..

Israel

High income

Population (millions)	7	Population growth (%)		1.8
Surface area (1,000 sq. km)	22	National poverty rate (% pop.)		..
GNI ($ billions)	109	GNI per capita ($)		16,240

	1990	2002	2003
People			
Life expectancy at birth (years)	76	79	79
Fertility rate (births per woman)	2.8	2.7	..
Infant mortality rate (per 1,000 live births)	10	6	5
Under-five mortality rate (per 1,000)	12	6	6
Births attended by skilled health staff (% of total)	..	..	..
Child malnutrition, underweight (% of under age 5)	..	..	..
Child immunization, measles (% of ages 12–23 mon.)	91	95	95
HIV prevalence rate (% of ages 15–49)	..	..	0.1
Adult literacy, male (% of ages 15 and older)	95	97	..
Adult literacy, female (% of ages 15 and older)	88	93	..
Primary completion rate, total (% of age group)	..	..	..
Primary completion rate, female (% of age group)	..	..	..
Net primary enrollment (% of age group)	92	100	..
Net secondary enrollment (% of age group)	..	89	..
Environment			
Forests (1,000 sq. km)	1	1	..
Deforestation (average annual %, 1990–2000)		–4.9	
Freshwater use (% of internal resources)			160
Carbon dioxide emissions (metric tons per capita)	7.4	10.0	..
Access to improved water source (% of total pop.)	100	100	..
Access to improved sanitation (% of urban pop.)	100	100	..
Energy use per capita (kg oil equivalent)	2,599	3,191	..
Electricity use per capita (kilowatt-hours)	3,902	5,857	..
Economy			
GDP ($ billions)	52	104	110
GDP growth (annual %)	6.8	–0.7	1.3
GDP implicit price deflator (annual % growth)	15.9	4.5	0.1
Value added in agriculture (% of GDP)	..	..	..
Value added in industry (% of GDP)	..	..	..
Value added in services (% of GDP)	..	..	..
Exports of goods and services (% of GDP)	35	37	37
Imports of goods and services (% of GDP)	45	46	44
Gross capital formation (% of GDP)	25	18	16
Central government revenue (% of GDP)	..	44.4	..
Cash surplus/deficit (% of GDP)	..	–4.1	..
Technology and infrastructure			
Fixed-line and mobile subscribers (per 1,000 people)	346	1,422	1,419
Cost of 3-minute local call ($)	0.08	0.02	..
Personal computers (per 1,000 people)	63.3	242.6	..
Internet users (per 1,000 people)	1	301	..
Paved roads (% of total)	100.0	100.0	..
Aircraft departures (thousands)	30	40	36
Trade and finance			
Trade in goods (% of GDP)	55.0	62.2	61.6
Trade growth less GDP growth (avg. %, 1990–2003)			0.9
High-technology exports (% of manufactured exports)	10	20	18
Net barter terms of trade (2000 = 100)	89	98	96
Foreign direct investment ($ millions)	151	1,723	3,672
Present value of debt ($ millions)			..
Total debt service (% of goods and services exports)	..	..	..
Short-term debt ($ millions)	..	..	..
Aid per capita ($)	294	115	66

Italy

High income

Population (millions)	58	Population growth (%)		–0.1
Surface area (1,000 sq. km)	301	National poverty rate (% pop.)		..
GNI ($ billions)	1,243	GNI per capita ($)		21,570

	1990	2002	2003
People			
Life expectancy at birth (years)	77	80	80
Fertility rate (births per woman)	1.3	1.3	1.3
Infant mortality rate (per 1,000 live births)	8	5	4
Under-five mortality rate (per 1,000)	9	6	..
Births attended by skilled health staff (% of total)	..	..	..
Child malnutrition, underweight (% of under age 5)	..	..	..
Child immunization, measles (% of ages 12–23 mon.)	43	80	83
HIV prevalence rate (% of ages 15–49)	..	0.5	0.5
Adult literacy, male (% of ages 15 and older)	98	99	..
Adult literacy, female (% of ages 15 and older)	97	98	..
Primary completion rate, total (% of age group)	104	101	..
Primary completion rate, female (% of age group)	104	101	..
Net primary enrollment (% of age group)	100	99	..
Net secondary enrollment (% of age group)	..	91	..
Environment			
Forests (1,000 sq. km)	97	100	..
Deforestation (average annual %, 1990–2000)		–0.3	
Freshwater use (% of internal resources)			23
Carbon dioxide emissions (metric tons per capita)	7.0	7.4	..
Access to improved water source (% of total pop.)	..	..	..
Access to improved sanitation (% of urban pop.)	..	..	..
Energy use per capita (kg oil equivalent)	2,690	2,994	..
Electricity use per capita (kilowatt-hours)	3,784	4,901	..
Economy			
GDP ($ billions)	1,102	1,186	1,468
GDP growth (annual %)	2.0	0.4	0.3
GDP implicit price deflator (annual % growth)	8.2	3.1	2.9
Value added in agriculture (% of GDP)	4	3	3
Value added in industry (% of GDP)	34	28	28
Value added in services (% of GDP)	63	69	70
Exports of goods and services (% of GDP)	20	27	25
Imports of goods and services (% of GDP)	20	26	25
Gross capital formation (% of GDP)	22	20	20
Central government revenue (% of GDP)	..	38.1	..
Cash surplus/deficit (% of GDP)	..	–0.5	..
Technology and infrastructure			
Fixed-line and mobile subscribers (per 1,000 people)	392	1,419	1,502
Cost of 3-minute local call ($)	0.11	0.11	..
Personal computers (per 1,000 people)	36.4	230.7	..
Internet users (per 1,000 people)	0	352	337
Paved roads (% of total)	100.0	100.0	..
Aircraft departures (thousands)	229	351	328
Trade and finance			
Trade in goods (% of GDP)	32.0	42.3	39.7
Trade growth less GDP growth (avg. %, 1990–2003)			3.0
High-technology exports (% of manufactured exports)	8	9	8
Net barter terms of trade (2000 = 100)	94	103	104
Foreign direct investment ($ billions)	6	15	17
Present value of debt ($ millions)			..
Total debt service (% of goods and services exports)	..	..	..
Short-term debt ($ millions)	..	..	..
Aid per capita ($)	..	..	..

Jamaica

Latin America & Caribbean **Lower middle income**

Population (millions)	3	Population growth (%)	0.8
Surface area (1,000 sq. km)	11	National poverty rate (% pop.)	19
GNI ($ millions)	7,882	GNI per capita ($)	2,980

	1990	2002	2003
People			
Life expectancy at birth (years)	73	76	76
Fertility rate (births per woman)	2.9	2.3	2.3
Infant mortality rate (per 1,000 live births)	17	17	17
Under-five mortality rate (per 1,000)	20	20	20
Births attended by skilled health staff (% of total)	79	95	..
Child malnutrition, underweight (% of under age 5)	5	4	..
Child immunization, measles (% of ages 12–23 mon.)	74	86	78
HIV prevalence rate (% of ages 15–49)	..	0.8	1.2
Adult literacy, male (% of ages 15 and older)	78	84	..
Adult literacy, female (% of ages 15 and older)	86	91	..
Primary completion rate, total (% of age group)	89	89	85
Primary completion rate, female (% of age group)	93	90	85
Net primary enrollment (% of age group)	96	95	..
Net secondary enrollment (% of age group)	64	75	..
Environment			
Forests (1,000 sq. km)	4	3	..
Deforestation (average annual %, 1990–2000)		1.5	
Freshwater use (% of internal resources)			10
Carbon dioxide emissions (metric tons per capita)	3.3	4.2	..
Access to improved water source (% of total pop.)	92	93	..
Access to improved sanitation (% of urban pop.)	85	90	..
Energy use per capita (kg oil equivalent)	1,231	1,493	..
Electricity use per capita (kilowatt-hours)	690	2,406	..
Economy			
GDP ($ millions)	4,592	8,443	8,147
GDP growth (annual %)	6.3	1.1	2.3
GDP implicit price deflator (annual % growth)	22.7	8.4	12.5
Value added in agriculture (% of GDP)	7	6	5
Value added in industry (% of GDP)	40	29	30
Value added in services (% of GDP)	52	65	65
Exports of goods and services (% of GDP)	48	36	41
Imports of goods and services (% of GDP)	52	56	59
Gross capital formation (% of GDP)	26	32	30
Central government revenue (% of GDP)	–0.6	32.1	32.5
Cash surplus/deficit (% of GDP)	..	–7.4	–9.8
Technology and infrastructure			
Fixed-line and mobile subscribers (per 1,000 people)	45	704	..
Cost of 3-minute local call ($)	0.01	0.07	0.02
Personal computers (per 1,000 people)	..	53.9	..
Internet users (per 1,000 people)	..	228	..
Paved roads (% of total)	64.0	70.1	..
Aircraft departures (thousands)	21	23	24
Trade and finance			
Trade in goods (% of GDP)	67.2	55.0	59.2
Trade growth less GDP growth (avg. %, 1990–2003)			–1.6
High-technology exports (% of manufactured exports)	0	0	..
Net barter terms of trade (2000 = 100)	..	..	..
Foreign direct investment ($ millions)	138	481	721
Present value of debt ($ millions)			6,144
Total debt service (% of goods and services exports)	26.9	18.6	16.5
Short-term debt ($ millions)	346	775	982
Aid per capita ($)	113	9	1

Japan

High income

Population (millions)	128	Population growth (%)	0.1
Surface area (1,000 sq. km)	378	National poverty rate (% pop.)	..
GNI ($ billions)	4,361	GNI per capita ($)	34,180

	1990	2002	2003
People			
Life expectancy at birth (years)	79	82	82
Fertility rate (births per woman)	1.5	1.3	1.3
Infant mortality rate (per 1,000 live births)	5	3	..
Under-five mortality rate (per 1,000)	6	5	..
Births attended by skilled health staff (% of total)	100	..	..
Child malnutrition, underweight (% of under age 5)	..	..	..
Child immunization, measles (% of ages 12–23 mon.)	73	99	99
HIV prevalence rate (% of ages 15–49)	..	0.1	0.1
Adult literacy, male (% of ages 15 and older)	..	..	..
Adult literacy, female (% of ages 15 and older)	..	..	..
Primary completion rate, total (% of age group)	101	..	..
Primary completion rate, female (% of age group)	102	..	..
Net primary enrollment (% of age group)	100	100	..
Net secondary enrollment (% of age group)	97	100	..
Environment			
Forests (1,000 sq. km)	240	241	..
Deforestation (average annual %, 1990–2000)		0.0	
Freshwater use (% of internal resources)			21
Carbon dioxide emissions (metric tons per capita)	8.7	9.3	..
Access to improved water source (% of total pop.)	100	100	..
Access to improved sanitation (% of urban pop.)	100	100	..
Energy use per capita (kg oil equivalent)	3,610	4,058	..
Electricity use per capita (kilowatt-hours)	6,200	7,718	..
Economy			
GDP ($ billions)	3,040	3,972	4,301
GDP growth (annual %)	5.2	–0.4	2.7
GDP implicit price deflator (annual % growth)	2.4	–1.2	–2.5
Value added in agriculture (% of GDP)	2	1	..
Value added in industry (% of GDP)	39	30	..
Value added in services (% of GDP)	58	68	..
Exports of goods and services (% of GDP)	10	11	12
Imports of goods and services (% of GDP)	9	10	10
Gross capital formation (% of GDP)	33	24	24
Central government revenue (% of GDP)	14.1	..	..
Cash surplus/deficit (% of GDP)	–1.2	..	..
Technology and infrastructure			
Fixed-line and mobile subscribers (per 1,000 people)	448	1,195	1,151
Cost of 3-minute local call ($)	0.07	0.07	0.07
Personal computers (per 1,000 people)	59.9	382.2	..
Internet users (per 1,000 people)	0	449	483
Paved roads (% of total)	69.2	77.1	..
Aircraft departures (thousands)	476	644	639
Trade and finance			
Trade in goods (% of GDP)	17.2	19.0	19.9
Trade growth less GDP growth (avg. %, 1990–2003)			2.7
High-technology exports (% of manufactured exports)	24	24	24
Net barter terms of trade (2000 = 100)	105	101	98
Foreign direct investment ($ millions)	1,777	9,087	6,238
Present value of debt ($ millions)			..
Total debt service (% of goods and services exports)	..	..	..
Short-term debt ($ millions)	..	..	..
Aid per capita ($)	..	..	..

Jordan

Middle East & North Africa		Lower middle income

Population (millions)	5	Population growth (%)		2.6
Surface area (1,000 sq. km)	89	National poverty rate (% pop.)		12
GNI ($ billions)	10	GNI per capita ($)		1,850

	1990	2002	2003
People			
Life expectancy at birth (years)	68	72	72
Fertility rate (births per woman)	5.4	3.5	3.5
Infant mortality rate (per 1,000 live births)	33	25	23
Under-five mortality rate (per 1,000)	40	30	28
Births attended by skilled health staff (% of total)	87	100	..
Child malnutrition, underweight (% of under age 5)	6	4	..
Child immunization, measles (% of ages 12–23 mon.)	87	95	96
HIV prevalence rate (% of ages 15–49)	..	0.1	0.1
Adult literacy, male (% of ages 15 and older)	90	96	..
Adult literacy, female (% of ages 15 and older)	72	86	..
Primary completion rate, total (% of age group)	104	98	..
Primary completion rate, female (% of age group)	104	99	..
Net primary enrollment (% of age group)	94	91	..
Net secondary enrollment (% of age group)	..	81	..
Environment			
Forests (1,000 sq. km)	1	1	..
Deforestation (average annual %, 1990–2000)		0.0	
Freshwater use (% of internal resources)			100
Carbon dioxide emissions (metric tons per capita)	3.2	3.2	..
Access to improved water source (% of total pop.)	98	91	..
Access to improved sanitation (% of urban pop.)	97	94	..
Energy use per capita (kg oil equivalent)	1,104	1,036	..
Electricity use per capita (kilowatt-hours)	959	1,317	..
Economy			
GDP ($ billions)	4	9	10
GDP growth (annual %)	1.0	5.0	3.2
GDP implicit price deflator (annual % growth)	11.4	1.2	1.9
Value added in agriculture (% of GDP)	8	2	2
Value added in industry (% of GDP)	28	26	26
Value added in services (% of GDP)	64	72	72
Exports of goods and services (% of GDP)	62	46	45
Imports of goods and services (% of GDP)	93	66	70
Gross capital formation (% of GDP)	32	23	23
Central government revenue (% of GDP)	26.1	25.2	24.0
Cash surplus/deficit (% of GDP)	–3.5	–3.2	–0.3
Technology and infrastructure			
Fixed-line and mobile subscribers (per 1,000 people)	72	355	356
Cost of 3-minute local call ($)	0.02	0.04	0.05
Personal computers (per 1,000 people)	..	37.5	44.7
Internet users (per 1,000 people)	..	58	81
Paved roads (% of total)	100.0	100.0	..
Aircraft departures (thousands)	14	16	15
Trade and finance			
Trade in goods (% of GDP)	91.1	83.0	88.6
Trade growth less GDP growth (avg. %, 1990–2003)			–2.2
High-technology exports (% of manufactured exports)	1	3	2
Net barter terms of trade (2000 = 100)	94	97	..
Foreign direct investment ($ millions)	38	31	376
Present value of debt ($ millions)			7,817
Total debt service (% of goods and services exports)	20.4	8.8	16.4
Short-term debt ($ millions)	1,037	554	743
Aid per capita ($)	280	101	233

Kazakhstan

Europe & Central Asia		Lower middle income	

Population (millions)	15	Population growth (%)	0.0
Surface area (1,000 sq. km)	2,725	National poverty rate (% pop.)	..
GNI ($ billions)	27	GNI per capita ($)	1,780

	1990	2002	2003
People			
Life expectancy at birth (years)	68	62	61
Fertility rate (births per woman)	2.7	1.8	1.8
Infant mortality rate (per 1,000 live births)	53	63	63
Under-five mortality rate (per 1,000)	63	73	73
Births attended by skilled health staff (% of total)	..	99	..
Child malnutrition, underweight (% of under age 5)	..	4	..
Child immunization, measles (% of ages 12–23 mon.)	89	95	99
HIV prevalence rate (% of ages 15–49)	..	0.1	0.2
Adult literacy, male (% of ages 15 and older)	99	100	..
Adult literacy, female (% of ages 15 and older)	98	99	..
Primary completion rate, total (% of age group)	..	102	110
Primary completion rate, female (% of age group)	..	102	110
Net primary enrollment (% of age group)	88	91	..
Net secondary enrollment (% of age group)	..	87	..
Environment			
Forests (1,000 sq. km)	98	121	..
Deforestation (average annual %, 1990–2000)		−2.2	
Freshwater use (% of internal resources)			45
Carbon dioxide emissions (metric tons per capita)	15.3	8.1	..
Access to improved water source (% of total pop.)	86	86	..
Access to improved sanitation (% of urban pop.)	87	87	..
Energy use per capita (kg oil equivalent)	4,823	3,123	..
Electricity use per capita (kilowatt-hours)	5,329	2,911	..
Economy			
GDP ($ billions)	27	25	30
GDP growth (annual %)	−11.0	9.8	9.2
GDP implicit price deflator (annual % growth)	96.4	5.8	7.9
Value added in agriculture (% of GDP)	27	9	8
Value added in industry (% of GDP)	45	39	38
Value added in services (% of GDP)	29	53	54
Exports of goods and services (% of GDP)	74	47	50
Imports of goods and services (% of GDP)	75	46	44
Gross capital formation (% of GDP)	32	27	27
Central government revenue (% of GDP)	..	13.2	14.4
Cash surplus/deficit (% of GDP)	..	0.3	−0.6
Technology and infrastructure			
Fixed-line and mobile subscribers (per 1,000 people)	80	195	..
Cost of 3-minute local call ($)	0.00	0.00	..
Personal computers (per 1,000 people)	..	..	..
Internet users (per 1,000 people)	..	16	..
Paved roads (% of total)	55.1	93.9	..
Aircraft departures (thousands)	..	15	20
Trade and finance			
Trade in goods (% of GDP)	..	66.1	71.4
Trade growth less GDP growth (avg. %, 1990–2003)			−2.8
High-technology exports (% of manufactured exports)	..	10	9
Net barter terms of trade (2000 = 100)	..	..	..
Foreign direct investment ($ millions)	0	2,583	2,088
Present value of debt ($ billions)			23
Total debt service (% of goods and services exports)	..	34.4	34.5
Short-term debt ($ millions)	9	1,842	2,833
Aid per capita ($)	7	13	18

Kenya

Sub-Saharan Africa   **Low income**

Population (millions)	32	Population growth (%)	1.8
Surface area (1,000 sq. km)	580	National poverty rate (% pop.)	52
GNI ($ billions)	13	GNI per capita ($)	400

	1990	2002	2003
People			
Life expectancy at birth (years)	57	46	45
Fertility rate (births per woman)	5.6	4.9	4.8
Infant mortality rate (per 1,000 live births)	63	77	79
Under-five mortality rate (per 1,000)	97	120	123
Births attended by skilled health staff (% of total)	50	44	41
Child malnutrition, underweight (% of under age 5)	..	22	20
Child immunization, measles (% of ages 12–23 mon.)	78	72	72
HIV prevalence rate (% of ages 15–49)	..	8.0	6.7
Adult literacy, male (% of ages 15 and older)	81	90	..
Adult literacy, female (% of ages 15 and older)	61	79	..
Primary completion rate, total (% of age group)	..	73	..
Primary completion rate, female (% of age group)	..	69	..
Net primary enrollment (% of age group)	74	66	..
Net secondary enrollment (% of age group)	..	25	..
Environment			
Forests (1,000 sq. km)	180	171	..
Deforestation (average annual %, 1990–2000)		0.5	
Freshwater use (% of internal resources)			10
Carbon dioxide emissions (metric tons per capita)	0.2	0.3	..
Access to improved water source (% of total pop.)	45	62	..
Access to improved sanitation (% of urban pop.)	49	56	..
Energy use per capita (kg oil equivalent)	534	489	..
Electricity use per capita (kilowatt-hours)	116	120	..
Economy			
GDP ($ billions)	9	12	14
GDP growth (annual %)	4.2	1.1	1.8
GDP implicit price deflator (annual % growth)	9.4	8.4	11.4
Value added in agriculture (% of GDP)	29	17	16
Value added in industry (% of GDP)	19	19	20
Value added in services (% of GDP)	52	64	65
Exports of goods and services (% of GDP)	26	27	25
Imports of goods and services (% of GDP)	31	28	29
Gross capital formation (% of GDP)	20	13	13
Central government revenue (% of GDP)	22.4	24.4	..
Cash surplus/deficit (% of GDP)	..	2.6	..
Technology and infrastructure			
Fixed-line and mobile subscribers (per 1,000 people)	8	52	61
Cost of 3-minute local call ($)	..	0.07	..
Personal computers (per 1,000 people)	0.4	6.4	..
Internet users (per 1,000 people)	..	13	..
Paved roads (% of total)	12.8	12.1	..
Aircraft departures (thousands)	13	26	27
Trade and finance			
Trade in goods (% of GDP)	38.1	43.9	42.7
Trade growth less GDP growth (avg. %, 1990–2003)			1.8
High-technology exports (% of manufactured exports)	4	10	4
Net barter terms of trade (2000 = 100)	70	98	..
Foreign direct investment ($ millions)	57	28	82
Present value of debt ($ millions)			5,340
Total debt service (% of goods and services exports)	35.4	16.6	15.8
Short-term debt ($ millions)	934	753	926
Aid per capita ($)	51	13	15

Kiribati

East Asia & Pacific		Lower middle income	

Population (thousands)	96	Population growth (%)	1.8
Surface area (sq. km)	730	National poverty rate (% pop.)	..
GNI ($ millions)	83	GNI per capita ($)	860

	1990	2002	2003
People			
Life expectancy at birth (years)	57	63	63
Fertility rate (births per woman)	4.0	3.6	3.6
Infant mortality rate (per 1,000 live births)	65	52	49
Under-five mortality rate (per 1,000)	88	70	66
Births attended by skilled health staff (% of total)	..	85	..
Child malnutrition, underweight (% of under age 5)	..	..	..
Child immunization, measles (% of ages 12–23 mon.)	75	88	88
HIV prevalence rate (% of ages 15–49)	..	..	..
Adult literacy, male (% of ages 15 and older)	..	..	..
Adult literacy, female (% of ages 15 and older)	..	..	..
Primary completion rate, total (% of age group)	..	..	..
Primary completion rate, female (% of age group)	..	..	..
Net primary enrollment (% of age group)	..	..	..
Net secondary enrollment (% of age group)	..	..	..
Environment			
Forests (1,000 sq. km)	0	0	..
Deforestation (average annual %, 1990–2000)		0.0	
Freshwater use (% of internal resources)			..
Carbon dioxide emissions (metric tons per capita)	0.3	0.3	..
Access to improved water source (% of total pop.)	48	64	..
Access to improved sanitation (% of urban pop.)	33	59	..
Energy use per capita (kg oil equivalent)	..	..	..
Electricity use per capita (kilowatt-hours)	..	..	..
Economy			
GDP ($ millions)	28	50	55
GDP growth (annual %)	2.1	1.0	2.5
GDP implicit price deflator (annual % growth)	–4.7	6.0	–9.7
Value added in agriculture (% of GDP)	19	14	..
Value added in industry (% of GDP)	8	11	..
Value added in services (% of GDP)	74	75	..
Exports of goods and services (% of GDP)	12	27	..
Imports of goods and services (% of GDP)	147	67	..
Gross capital formation (% of GDP)	93	..	..
Central government revenue (% of GDP)	..	..	..
Cash surplus/deficit (% of GDP)	..	..	..
Technology and infrastructure			
Fixed-line and mobile subscribers (per 1,000 people)	17	57	..
Cost of 3-minute local call ($)	..	0.09	0.12
Personal computers (per 1,000 people)	..	11.4	..
Internet users (per 1,000 people)	..	23	..
Paved roads (% of total)	..	..	..
Aircraft departures (thousands)	3	3	..
Trade and finance			
Trade in goods (% of GDP)	105.5	91.9	78.7
Trade growth less GDP growth (avg. %, 1990–2003)			..
High-technology exports (% of manufactured exports)	..	..	..
Net barter terms of trade (2000 = 100)	..	..	..
Foreign direct investment ($ millions)	..	..	..
Present value of debt ($ millions)			..
Total debt service (% of goods and services exports)	..	..	..
Short-term debt ($ millions)	..	..	..
Aid per capita ($)	280	220	191

Korea, Dem. Rep.

East Asia & Pacific			**Low income**

Population (millions)	23	Population growth (%)	0.5
Surface area (1,000 sq. km)	121	National poverty rate (% pop.)	..
GNI ($ millions)	..	GNI per capita ($)	..

	1990	2002	2003
People			
Life expectancy at birth (years)	66	62	63
Fertility rate (births per woman)	2.4	2.1	2.1
Infant mortality rate (per 1,000 live births)	42	42	42
Under-five mortality rate (per 1,000)	55	55	55
Births attended by skilled health staff (% of total)	..	97	..
Child malnutrition, underweight (% of under age 5)	..	28	..
Child immunization, measles (% of ages 12–23 mon.)	98	98	95
HIV prevalence rate (% of ages 15–49)	..	..	..
Adult literacy, male (% of ages 15 and older)	..	..	..
Adult literacy, female (% of ages 15 and older)	..	..	..
Primary completion rate, total (% of age group)	..	..	..
Primary completion rate, female (% of age group)	..	..	..
Net primary enrollment (% of age group)	..	..	..
Net secondary enrollment (% of age group)	..	..	..
Environment			
Forests (1,000 sq. km)	82	82	..
Deforestation (average annual %, 1990–2000)		0.0	
Freshwater use (% of internal resources)			21
Carbon dioxide emissions (metric tons per capita)	12.3	8.5	..
Access to improved water source (% of total pop.)	100	100	..
Access to improved sanitation (% of urban pop.)	..	58	..
Energy use per capita (kg oil equivalent)	1,647	869	..
Electricity use per capita (kilowatt-hours)	..	..	..
Economy			
GDP ($ millions)	..	..	..
GDP growth (annual %)	..	..	..
GDP implicit price deflator (annual % growth)	..	..	..
Value added in agriculture (% of GDP)	..	..	..
Value added in industry (% of GDP)	..	..	..
Value added in services (% of GDP)	..	..	..
Exports of goods and services (% of GDP)	..	..	..
Imports of goods and services (% of GDP)	..	..	..
Gross capital formation (% of GDP)	..	..	..
Central government revenue (% of GDP)	..	..	..
Cash surplus/deficit (% of GDP)	..	..	..
Technology and infrastructure			
Fixed-line and mobile subscribers (per 1,000 people)	25	21	..
Cost of 3-minute local call ($)	..	..	..
Personal computers (per 1,000 people)	..	..	..
Internet users (per 1,000 people)	..	..	..
Paved roads (% of total)	5.7	6.4	..
Aircraft departures (thousands)	6	1	1
Trade and finance			
Trade in goods (% of GDP)	..	..	..
Trade growth less GDP growth (avg. %, 1990–2003)			..
High-technology exports (% of manufactured exports)	..	..	..
Net barter terms of trade (2000 = 100)	..	..	..
Foreign direct investment ($ millions)	..	..	..
Present value of debt ($ millions)			..
Total debt service (% of goods and services exports)	..	..	..
Short-term debt ($ millions)	..	..	..
Aid per capita ($)	0	12	7

Korea, Rep.

High income

Population (millions)	48	Population growth (%)		0.6
Surface area (1,000 sq. km)	99	National poverty rate (% pop.)		..
GNI ($ billions)	576	GNI per capita ($)		12,030

	1990	2002	2003
People			
Life expectancy at birth (years)	70	74	74
Fertility rate (births per woman)	1.8	1.5	1.5
Infant mortality rate (per 1,000 live births)	8	5	5
Under-five mortality rate (per 1,000)	9	5	5
Births attended by skilled health staff (% of total)	98	100	..
Child malnutrition, underweight (% of under age 5)	..	..	..
Child immunization, measles (% of ages 12–23 mon.)	93	97	96
HIV prevalence rate (% of ages 15–49)	..	0.1	0.1
Adult literacy, male (% of ages 15 and older)	..	..	..
Adult literacy, female (% of ages 15 and older)	..	..	..
Primary completion rate, total (% of age group)	98	97	..
Primary completion rate, female (% of age group)	98	97	..
Net primary enrollment (% of age group)	100	100	..
Net secondary enrollment (% of age group)	86	87	..
Environment			
Forests (1,000 sq. km)	63	62	..
Deforestation (average annual %, 1990–2000)		0.1	
Freshwater use (% of internal resources)			36
Carbon dioxide emissions (metric tons per capita)	5.6	9.1	..
Access to improved water source (% of total pop.)	..	92	..
Access to improved sanitation (% of urban pop.)	..	..	..
Energy use per capita (kg oil equivalent)	2,161	4,272	..
Electricity use per capita (kilowatt-hours)	2,202	6,171	..
Economy			
GDP ($ billions)	264	547	605
GDP growth (annual %)	9.2	7.0	3.1
GDP implicit price deflator (annual % growth)	10.7	2.8	2.3
Value added in agriculture (% of GDP)	..	4	3
Value added in industry (% of GDP)	..	34	35
Value added in services (% of GDP)	..	63	62
Exports of goods and services (% of GDP)	28	35	38
Imports of goods and services (% of GDP)	29	34	36
Gross capital formation (% of GDP)	36	29	29
Central government revenue (% of GDP)	16.8	22.8	..
Cash surplus/deficit (% of GDP)	1.7	2.9	..
Technology and infrastructure			
Fixed-line and mobile subscribers (per 1,000 people)	308	1,168	1,239
Cost of 3-minute local call ($)	0.04	0.03	0.03
Personal computers (per 1,000 people)	36.8	555.8	558.0
Internet users (per 1,000 people)	0	414	610
Paved roads (% of total)	71.5	76.7	..
Aircraft departures (thousands)	120	239	240
Trade and finance			
Trade in goods (% of GDP)	51.1	57.5	61.6
Trade growth less GDP growth (avg. %, 1990–2003)			6.2
High-technology exports (% of manufactured exports)	18	31	32
Net barter terms of trade (2000 = 100)	134	95	..
Foreign direct investment ($ millions)	788	2,392	3,222
Present value of debt ($ millions)			..
Total debt service (% of goods and services exports)	..	..	..
Short-term debt ($ millions)	..	..	..
Aid per capita ($)	1	–2	–10

Kuwait

High income

Population (millions)	2	Population growth (%)	2.6
Surface area (1,000 sq. km)	18	National poverty rate (% pop.)	..
GNI ($ billions)	43	GNI per capita ($)	17,960

	1990	2002	2003
People			
Life expectancy at birth (years)	75	77	77
Fertility rate (births per woman)	3.4	2.5	2.5
Infant mortality rate (per 1,000 live births)	14	9	8
Under-five mortality rate (per 1,000)	16	10	9
Births attended by skilled health staff (% of total)	..	..	..
Child malnutrition, underweight (% of under age 5)	..	2	..
Child immunization, measles (% of ages 12–23 mon.)	66	98	97
HIV prevalence rate (% of ages 15–49)	..	..	..
Adult literacy, male (% of ages 15 and older)	79	85	..
Adult literacy, female (% of ages 15 and older)	73	81	..
Primary completion rate, total (% of age group)	53	96	..
Primary completion rate, female (% of age group)	52	96	..
Net primary enrollment (% of age group)	49	83	..
Net secondary enrollment (% of age group)	..	77	
Environment			
Forests (1,000 sq. km)	0	0	..
Deforestation (average annual %, 1990–2000)		–5.2	
Freshwater use (% of internal resources)			..
Carbon dioxide emissions (metric tons per capita)	19.9	21.9	..
Access to improved water source (% of total pop.)	..	..	
Access to improved sanitation (% of urban pop.)	..	..	
Energy use per capita (kg oil equivalent)	3,567	9,503	..
Electricity use per capita (kilowatt-hours)	4,518	10,888	..
Economy			
GDP ($ billions)	18	35	42
GDP growth (annual %)	25.9	–0.4	9.9
GDP implicit price deflator (annual % growth)	–1.7	3.4	..
Value added in agriculture (% of GDP)	1	..	..
Value added in industry (% of GDP)	52	..	..
Value added in services (% of GDP)	47	..	..
Exports of goods and services (% of GDP)	45	48	..
Imports of goods and services (% of GDP)	58	40	..
Gross capital formation (% of GDP)	18	9	..
Central government revenue (% of GDP)	58.7	34.5	..
Cash surplus/deficit (% of GDP)	3.7	–9.7	..
Technology and infrastructure			
Fixed-line and mobile subscribers (per 1,000 people)	200	723	776
Cost of 3-minute local call ($)	0.00	0.00	0.00
Personal computers (per 1,000 people)	5.1	120.6	162.8
Internet users (per 1,000 people)	..	106	228
Paved roads (% of total)	72.9	80.6	..
Aircraft departures (thousands)	10	19	18
Trade and finance			
Trade in goods (% of GDP)	59.8	69.3	72.3
Trade growth less GDP growth (avg. %, 1990–2003)			..
High-technology exports (% of manufactured exports)	3	1	..
Net barter terms of trade (2000 = 100)	..	..	..
Foreign direct investment ($ millions)	0	7	–67
Present value of debt ($ millions)			..
Total debt service (% of goods and services exports)	..	..	..
Short-term debt ($ millions)	..	..	..
Aid per capita ($)	3	2	2

Kyrgyz Republic

Europe & Central Asia			Low income
Population (millions)	5	Population growth (%)	1.0
Surface area (1,000 sq. km)	200	National poverty rate (% pop.)	48
GNI ($ millions)	1,717	GNI per capita ($)	340

	1990	2002	2003
People			
Life expectancy at birth (years)	68	65	65
Fertility rate (births per woman)	3.7	2.4	2.4
Infant mortality rate (per 1,000 live births)	68	60	59
Under-five mortality rate (per 1,000)	80	70	68
Births attended by skilled health staff (% of total)	..	98	..
Child malnutrition, underweight (% of under age 5)	..	6	..
Child immunization, measles (% of ages 12–23 mon.)	94	98	99
HIV prevalence rate (% of ages 15–49)	..	0.1	0.1
Adult literacy, male (% of ages 15 and older)	..	..	..
Adult literacy, female (% of ages 15 and older)	..	..	..
Primary completion rate, total (% of age group)	..	93	..
Primary completion rate, female (% of age group)	..	91	..
Net primary enrollment (% of age group)	..	89	..
Net secondary enrollment (% of age group)	..	..	..
Environment			
Forests (1,000 sq. km)	8	10	..
Deforestation (average annual %, 1990–2000)		–2.6	
Freshwater use (% of internal resources)			22
Carbon dioxide emissions (metric tons per capita)	2.4	0.9	..
Access to improved water source (% of total pop.)	..	76	..
Access to improved sanitation (% of urban pop.)	..	75	..
Energy use per capita (kg oil equivalent)	1,114	507	..
Electricity use per capita (kilowatt-hours)	1,795	1,269	..
Economy			
GDP ($ millions)	2,674	1,606	1,909
GDP growth (annual %)	5.7	–0.0	6.7
GDP implicit price deflator (annual % growth)	7.9	2.0	3.8
Value added in agriculture (% of GDP)	34	38	39
Value added in industry (% of GDP)	36	23	23
Value added in services (% of GDP)	30	39	38
Exports of goods and services (% of GDP)	29	40	38
Imports of goods and services (% of GDP)	50	43	42
Gross capital formation (% of GDP)	24	18	16
Central government revenue (% of GDP)	..	16.1	..
Cash surplus/deficit (% of GDP)	..	–0.8	..
Technology and infrastructure			
Fixed-line and mobile subscribers (per 1,000 people)	72	88	103
Cost of 3-minute local call ($)	0.00	0.09	..
Personal computers (per 1,000 people)	..	12.7	..
Internet users (per 1,000 people)	..	11	38
Paved roads (% of total)	90.0	91.1	..
Aircraft departures (thousands)	..	4	5
Trade and finance			
Trade in goods (% of GDP)	..	66.8	68.1
Trade growth less GDP growth (avg. %, 1990–2003)			–2.3
High-technology exports (% of manufactured exports)	..	6	2
Net barter terms of trade (2000 = 100)	..	..	..
Foreign direct investment ($ millions)	0	5	46
Present value of debt ($ millions)			1,584
Total debt service (% of goods and services exports)	..	24.5	16.0
Short-term debt ($ millions)	0	19	39
Aid per capita ($)	5	37	39

Lao PDR

East Asia & Pacific   **Low income**

Population (millions)	6	Population growth (%)	2.3
Surface area (1,000 sq. km)	237	National poverty rate (% pop.)	39
GNI ($ millions)	1,945	GNI per capita ($)	340

	1990	2002	2003
People			
Life expectancy at birth (years)	50	55	55
Fertility rate (births per woman)	6.0	4.8	4.8
Infant mortality rate (per 1,000 live births)	120	*90*	82
Under-five mortality rate (per 1,000)	163	*105*	91
Births attended by skilled health staff (% of total)	..	19	..
Child malnutrition, underweight (% of under age 5)	..	40	..
Child immunization, measles (% of ages 12–23 mon.)	32	55	42
HIV prevalence rate (% of ages 15–49)	..	*0.1*	0.1
Adult literacy, male (% of ages 15 and older)	70	77	..
Adult literacy, female (% of ages 15 and older)	43	55	..
Primary completion rate, total (% of age group)	*43*	73	74
Primary completion rate, female (% of age group)	*37*	69	69
Net primary enrollment (% of age group)	63	85	..
Net secondary enrollment (% of age group)	..	35	..
Environment			
Forests (1,000 sq. km)	131	*126*	..
Deforestation (average annual %, 1990–2000)		*0.4*	
Freshwater use (% of internal resources)			1
Carbon dioxide emissions (metric tons per capita)	0.1	*0.1*	..
Access to improved water source (% of total pop.)	..	43	..
Access to improved sanitation (% of urban pop.)	..	61	..
Energy use per capita (kg oil equivalent)	..	..	..
Electricity use per capita (kilowatt-hours)	..	..	..
Economy			
GDP ($ millions)	866	1,719	2,122
GDP growth (annual %)	6.7	5.0	5.0
GDP implicit price deflator (annual % growth)	38.0	11.8	16.7
Value added in agriculture (% of GDP)	61	50	49
Value added in industry (% of GDP)	15	25	26
Value added in services (% of GDP)	24	25	25
Exports of goods and services (% of GDP)	11	27	25
Imports of goods and services (% of GDP)	25	27	25
Gross capital formation (% of GDP)	*14*	20	20
Central government revenue (% of GDP)	..	..	..
Cash surplus/deficit (% of GDP)	..	..	..
Technology and infrastructure			
Fixed-line and mobile subscribers (per 1,000 people)	2	21	32
Cost of 3-minute local call ($)	*0.28*	*0.02*	0.06
Personal computers (per 1,000 people)	..	3.3	3.5
Internet users (per 1,000 people)	..	*1*	..
Paved roads (% of total)	24.0	*44.5*	..
Aircraft departures (thousands)	3	7	7
Trade and finance			
Trade in goods (% of GDP)	30.5	42.4	42.5
Trade growth less GDP growth (avg. %, 1990–2003)			..
High-technology exports (% of manufactured exports)	..	..	..
Net barter terms of trade (2000 = 100)	..	..	..
Foreign direct investment ($ millions)	6	25	19
Present value of debt ($ millions)			1,659
Total debt service (% of goods and services exports)	8.7	10.3	10.3
Short-term debt ($ millions)	2	1	1
Aid per capita ($)	36	50	53

Latvia

Europe & Central Asia	Upper middle income

Population (millions)	2	Population growth (%)	−0.7
Surface area (1,000 sq. km)	65	National poverty rate (% pop.)	..
GNI ($ billions)	10	GNI per capita ($)	4,400

	1990	2002	2003
People			
Life expectancy at birth (years)	69	70	71
Fertility rate (births per woman)	2.0	1.2	1.3
Infant mortality rate (per 1,000 live births)	14	10	10
Under-five mortality rate (per 1,000)	18	13	12
Births attended by skilled health staff (% of total)	..	..	..
Child malnutrition, underweight (% of under age 5)	..	..	..
Child immunization, measles (% of ages 12–23 mon.)	95	98	99
HIV prevalence rate (% of ages 15–49)	..	0.5	0.6
Adult literacy, male (% of ages 15 and older)	100	100	..
Adult literacy, female (% of ages 15 and older)	100	100	..
Primary completion rate, total (% of age group)	..	101	..
Primary completion rate, female (% of age group)	..	100	..
Net primary enrollment (% of age group)	92	88	..
Net secondary enrollment (% of age group)	..	88	..
Environment			
Forests (1,000 sq. km)	28	29	..
Deforestation (average annual %, 1990–2000)		−0.4	
Freshwater use (% of internal resources)			2
Carbon dioxide emissions (metric tons per capita)	4.8	2.5	..
Access to improved water source (% of total pop.)	..	..	..
Access to improved sanitation (% of urban pop.)	..	..	..
Energy use per capita (kg oil equivalent)	2,272	1,825	..
Electricity use per capita (kilowatt-hours)	2,530	2,088	..
Economy			
GDP ($ billions)	7	9	11
GDP growth (annual %)	−7.9	6.4	7.5
GDP implicit price deflator (annual % growth)	15.7	1.8	−1.1
Value added in agriculture (% of GDP)	22	5	5
Value added in industry (% of GDP)	46	25	24
Value added in services (% of GDP)	32	71	71
Exports of goods and services (% of GDP)	48	45	47
Imports of goods and services (% of GDP)	49	56	57
Gross capital formation (% of GDP)	40	27	31
Central government revenue (% of GDP)	..	26.4	26.3
Cash surplus/deficit (% of GDP)	..	−1.8	−1.3
Technology and infrastructure			
Fixed-line and mobile subscribers (per 1,000 people)	234	695	811
Cost of 3-minute local call ($)	0.00	0.11	0.12
Personal computers (per 1,000 people)	..	171.7	188.0
Internet users (per 1,000 people)		133	404
Paved roads (% of total)	13.4	94.6	..
Aircraft departures (thousands)	1	9	10
Trade and finance			
Trade in goods (% of GDP)	..	68.8	73.5
Trade growth less GDP growth (avg. %, 1990–2003)			5.5
High-technology exports (% of manufactured exports)	..	4	4
Net barter terms of trade (2000 = 100)	..	..	..
Foreign direct investment ($ millions)	0	254	300
Present value of debt ($ millions)			8,729
Total debt service (% of goods and services exports)	0.0	15.9	18.5
Short-term debt ($ millions)	0	4,163	5,632
Aid per capita ($)	1	33	49

Lebanon

Middle East & North Africa		**Upper middle income**

Population (millions)	4	Population growth (%) 1.3
Surface area (1,000 sq. km)	10	National poverty rate (% pop.) ..
GNI ($ billions)	18	GNI per capita ($) 4,040

	1990	2002	2003
People			
Life expectancy at birth (years)	68	71	71
Fertility rate (births per woman)	3.2	2.2	2.2
Infant mortality rate (per 1,000 live births)	32	*28*	27
Under-five mortality rate (per 1,000)	37	*32*	31
Births attended by skilled health staff (% of total)	..	..	..
Child malnutrition, underweight (% of under age 5)	..	..	..
Child immunization, measles (% of ages 12–23 mon.)	61	96	96
HIV prevalence rate (% of ages 15–49)	..	*0.1*	0.1
Adult literacy, male (% of ages 15 and older)	..	..	..
Adult literacy, female (% of ages 15 and older)	..	..	..
Primary completion rate, total (% of age group)	..	69	68
Primary completion rate, female (% of age group)	..	72	..
Net primary enrollment (% of age group)	78	91	..
Net secondary enrollment (% of age group)	..	..	..
Environment			
Forests (1,000 sq. km)	0	*0*	..
Deforestation (average annual %, 1990–2000)		*0.3*	
Freshwater use (% of internal resources)			26
Carbon dioxide emissions (metric tons per capita)	2.5	*3.5*	..
Access to improved water source (% of total pop.)	100	100	..
Access to improved sanitation (% of urban pop.)	100	100	..
Energy use per capita (kg oil equivalent)	635	1,209	..
Electricity use per capita (kilowatt-hours)	369	1,951	..
Economy			
GDP ($ billions)	3	18	19
GDP growth (annual %)	26.5	2.2	2.7
GDP implicit price deflator (annual % growth)	15.5	1.8	1.3
Value added in agriculture (% of GDP)	..	12	12
Value added in industry (% of GDP)	..	21	20
Value added in services (% of GDP)	..	67	68
Exports of goods and services (% of GDP)	18	13	13
Imports of goods and services (% of GDP)	100	39	39
Gross capital formation (% of GDP)	18	17	17
Central government revenue (% of GDP)	..	19.6	..
Cash surplus/deficit (% of GDP)	..	–13.3	..
Technology and infrastructure			
Fixed-line and mobile subscribers (per 1,000 people)	155	426	..
Cost of 3-minute local call ($)	*0.03*	*0.07*	0.10
Personal computers (per 1,000 people)	..	80.5	..
Internet users (per 1,000 people)	..	117	..
Paved roads (% of total)	95.0	*84.9*	..
Aircraft departures (thousands)	10	11	11
Trade and finance			
Trade in goods (% of GDP)	106.5	41.0	45.8
Trade growth less GDP growth (avg. %, 1990–2003)			–2.2
High-technology exports (% of manufactured exports)	..	2	2
Net barter terms of trade (2000 = 100)	..	..	..
Foreign direct investment ($ millions)	6	257	358
Present value of debt ($ billions)			20
Total debt service (% of goods and services exports)	3.3	57.5	66.1
Short-term debt ($ millions)	1,421	2,547	3,124
Aid per capita ($)	69	102	51

Lesotho

Sub-Saharan Africa		Low income

Population (millions)	2	Population growth (%)	0.9
Surface area (1,000 sq. km)	30	National poverty rate (% pop.)	..
GNI ($ millions)	1,089	GNI per capita ($)	610

	1990	2002	2003
People			
Life expectancy at birth (years)	58	38	37
Fertility rate (births per woman)	5.1	4.3	4.3
Infant mortality rate (per 1,000 live births)	74	75	79
Under-five mortality rate (per 1,000)	104	105	110
Births attended by skilled health staff (% of total)	..	60	..
Child malnutrition, underweight (% of under age 5)	16	18	..
Child immunization, measles (% of ages 12–23 mon.)	80	70	70
HIV prevalence rate (% of ages 15–49)	..	29.6	28.9
Adult literacy, male (% of ages 15 and older)	65	74	..
Adult literacy, female (% of ages 15 and older)	89	90	..
Primary completion rate, total (% of age group)	67	67	..
Primary completion rate, female (% of age group)	87	77	..
Net primary enrollment (% of age group)	73	86	..
Net secondary enrollment (% of age group)	..	22	..
Environment			
Forests (1,000 sq. km)	0	0	..
Deforestation (average annual %, 1990–2000)		0.0	
Freshwater use (% of internal resources)			2
Carbon dioxide emissions (metric tons per capita)	..	..	..
Access to improved water source (% of total pop.)	..	76	..
Access to improved sanitation (% of urban pop.)	61	61	..
Energy use per capita (kg oil equivalent)	..	..	..
Electricity use per capita (kilowatt-hours)	..	..	..
Economy			
GDP ($ millions)	615	737	1,139
GDP growth (annual %)	6.4	3.8	3.3
GDP implicit price deflator (annual % growth)	8.6	13.3	7.3
Value added in agriculture (% of GDP)	24	17	17
Value added in industry (% of GDP)	33	43	44
Value added in services (% of GDP)	43	40	40
Exports of goods and services (% of GDP)	17	44	41
Imports of goods and services (% of GDP)	122	103	95
Gross capital formation (% of GDP)	53	33	30
Central government revenue (% of GDP)	39.4	39.0	39.9
Cash surplus/deficit (% of GDP)	−0.5	−4.6	0.6
Technology and infrastructure			
Fixed-line and mobile subscribers (per 1,000 people)	7	56	..
Cost of 3-minute local call ($)	0.03	0.11	..
Personal computers (per 1,000 people)	..	..	..
Internet users (per 1,000 people)	..	10	..
Paved roads (% of total)	18.0	18.3	..
Aircraft departures (thousands)	5	0	..
Trade and finance			
Trade in goods (% of GDP)	119.3	155.9	131.5
Trade growth less GDP growth (avg. %, 1990–2003)			−0.6
High-technology exports (% of manufactured exports)	..	..	..
Net barter terms of trade (2000 = 100)	100	100	..
Foreign direct investment ($ millions)	17	81	42
Present value of debt ($ millions)			508
Total debt service (% of goods and services exports)	4.2	11.7	8.8
Short-term debt ($ millions)	3	4	4
Aid per capita ($)	90	43	44

Liberia

Sub-Saharan Africa   **Low income**

Population (millions)	3	Population growth (%)	2.4
Surface area (1,000 sq. km)	111	National poverty rate (% pop.)	..
GNI ($ millions)	355	GNI per capita ($)	110

	1990	2002	2003
People			
Life expectancy at birth (years)	45	47	47
Fertility rate (births per woman)	6.8	5.8	5.8
Infant mortality rate (per 1,000 live births)	157	157	157
Under-five mortality rate (per 1,000)	235	235	235
Births attended by skilled health staff (% of total)	..	51	..
Child malnutrition, underweight (% of under age 5)	..	27	..
Child immunization, measles (% of ages 12–23 mon.)	..	57	53
HIV prevalence rate (% of ages 15–49)	..	5.1	5.9
Adult literacy, male (% of ages 15 and older)	55	72	..
Adult literacy, female (% of ages 15 and older)	23	39	..
Primary completion rate, total (% of age group)	..	21	..
Primary completion rate, female (% of age group)	..	10	..
Net primary enrollment (% of age group)	..	70	..
Net secondary enrollment (% of age group)	..	18	..
Environment			
Forests (1,000 sq. km)	42	35	..
Deforestation (average annual %, 1990–2000)		2.0	
Freshwater use (% of internal resources)			0
Carbon dioxide emissions (metric tons per capita)	0.2	0.1	..
Access to improved water source (% of total pop.)	56	62	..
Access to improved sanitation (% of urban pop.)	59	49	..
Energy use per capita (kg oil equivalent)	..	..	..
Electricity use per capita (kilowatt-hours)	..	..	..
Economy			
GDP ($ millions)	384	562	442
GDP growth (annual %)	–51.0	3.3	–29.5
GDP implicit price deflator (annual % growth)	–0.2	29.4	–18.8
Value added in agriculture (% of GDP)	..	..	..
Value added in industry (% of GDP)	..	..	..
Value added in services (% of GDP)	..	..	..
Exports of goods and services (% of GDP)	..	..	..
Imports of goods and services (% of GDP)	..	..	..
Gross capital formation (% of GDP)	..	..	..
Central government revenue (% of GDP)	..	..	..
Cash surplus/deficit (% of GDP)	..	..	..
Technology and infrastructure			
Fixed-line and mobile subscribers (per 1,000 people)	4	3	..
Cost of 3-minute local call ($)	..	..	..
Personal computers (per 1,000 people)	..	..	..
Internet users (per 1,000 people)	..	0	..
Paved roads (% of total)	5.5	6.2	..
Aircraft departures (thousands)	2	..	..
Trade and finance			
Trade in goods (% of GDP)	374.1	145.6	178.7
Trade growth less GDP growth (avg. %, 1990–2003)			..
High-technology exports (% of manufactured exports)	..	..	..
Net barter terms of trade (2000 = 100)	..	..	..
Foreign direct investment ($ millions)	0	3	0
Present value of debt ($ millions)			2,750
Total debt service (% of goods and services exports)	..	0.4	0.1
Short-term debt ($ millions)	411	956	1,108
Aid per capita ($)	47	16	32

Libya

Middle East & North Africa   **Upper middle income**

Population (millions)	6	Population growth (%)	2.0
Surface area (1,000 sq. km)	1,760	National poverty rate (% pop.)	..
GNI ($ millions)	..	GNI per capita ($)	..

	1990	2002	2003
People			
Life expectancy at birth (years)	68	72	73
Fertility rate (births per woman)	4.7	3.3	3.3
Infant mortality rate (per 1,000 live births)	34	17	13
Under-five mortality rate (per 1,000)	42	20	16
Births attended by skilled health staff (% of total)	..	..	..
Child malnutrition, underweight (% of under age 5)	..	..	..
Child immunization, measles (% of ages 12–23 mon.)	89	91	91
HIV prevalence rate (% of ages 15–49)	..	..	0.3
Adult literacy, male (% of ages 15 and older)	83	92	..
Adult literacy, female (% of ages 15 and older)	51	71	..
Primary completion rate, total (% of age group)	..	..	..
Primary completion rate, female (% of age group)	..	..	..
Net primary enrollment (% of age group)	96	..	..
Net secondary enrollment (% of age group)	..	..	..
Environment			
Forests (1,000 sq. km)	3	4	..
Deforestation (average annual %, 1990–2000)		–1.4	
Freshwater use (% of internal resources)			450
Carbon dioxide emissions (metric tons per capita)	8.8	10.9	..
Access to improved water source (% of total pop.)	71	72	..
Access to improved sanitation (% of urban pop.)	97	97	..
Energy use per capita (kg oil equivalent)	2,680	3,433	..
Electricity use per capita (kilowatt-hours)	1,677	2,250	..
Economy			
GDP ($ millions)	28,905	19,131	..
GDP growth (annual %)	..	..	..
GDP implicit price deflator (annual % growth)	..	..	..
Value added in agriculture (% of GDP)	..	..	..
Value added in industry (% of GDP)	..	..	..
Value added in services (% of GDP)	..	..	..
Exports of goods and services (% of GDP)	40	48	..
Imports of goods and services (% of GDP)	31	36	..
Gross capital formation (% of GDP)	19	14	..
Central government revenue (% of GDP)	..	..	..
Cash surplus/deficit (% of GDP)	..	..	..
Technology and infrastructure			
Fixed-line and mobile subscribers (per 1,000 people)	48	127	159
Cost of 3-minute local call ($)	0.05	..	..
Personal computers (per 1,000 people)	..	23.4	..
Internet users (per 1,000 people)	..	23	29
Paved roads (% of total)	51.7	57.2	..
Aircraft departures (thousands)	18	6	6
Trade and finance			
Trade in goods (% of GDP)	64.2	85.2	..
Trade growth less GDP growth (avg. %, 1990–2003)			..
High-technology exports (% of manufactured exports)	..	..	..
Net barter terms of trade (2000 = 100)	..	..	..
Foreign direct investment ($ millions)	..	..	..
Present value of debt ($ millions)			..
Total debt service (% of goods and services exports)	..	..	..
Short-term debt ($ millions)	..	..	..
Aid per capita ($)	5	2	2

Liechtenstein

High income

Population (thousands)	33	Population growth (%)		..
Surface area (sq. km)	160	National poverty rate (% pop.)		..
GNI ($ millions)	..	GNI per capita ($)		..

	1990	2002	2003
People			
Life expectancy at birth (years)	..	..	..
Fertility rate (births per woman)	..	..	..
Infant mortality rate (per 1,000 live births)	..	10	10
Under-five mortality rate (per 1,000)	..	11	11
Births attended by skilled health staff (% of total)	..	..	..
Child malnutrition, underweight (% of under age 5)	..	..	..
Child immunization, measles (% of ages 12–23 mon.)	..	..	..
HIV prevalence rate (% of ages 15–49)	..	..	..
Adult literacy, male (% of ages 15 and older)	..	..	..
Adult literacy, female (% of ages 15 and older)	..	..	..
Primary completion rate, total (% of age group)	..	..	..
Primary completion rate, female (% of age group)	..	..	..
Net primary enrollment (% of age group)	..	..	..
Net secondary enrollment (% of age group)	..	..	..
Environment			
Forests (1,000 sq. km)	0	0	..
Deforestation (average annual %, 1990–2000)		–1.6	
Freshwater use (% of internal resources)			..
Carbon dioxide emissions (metric tons per capita)	..	..	..
Access to improved water source (% of total pop.)	..	..	..
Access to improved sanitation (% of urban pop.)	..	..	..
Energy use per capita (kg oil equivalent)	..	..	..
Electricity use per capita (kilowatt-hours)	..	..	..
Economy			
GDP ($ millions)	..	..	..
GDP growth (annual %)	..	..	..
GDP implicit price deflator (annual % growth)	..	..	..
Value added in agriculture (% of GDP)	..	..	..
Value added in industry (% of GDP)	..	..	..
Value added in services (% of GDP)	..	..	..
Exports of goods and services (% of GDP)	..	..	..
Imports of goods and services (% of GDP)	..	..	..
Gross capital formation (% of GDP)	..	..	..
Central government revenue (% of GDP)	..	..	..
Cash surplus/deficit (% of GDP)	..	..	..
Technology and infrastructure			
Fixed-line and mobile subscribers (per 1,000 people)	..	916	..
Cost of 3-minute local call ($)	..	0.11	..
Personal computers (per 1,000 people)	..	..	..
Internet users (per 1,000 people)	..	591	..
Paved roads (% of total)	..	..	..
Aircraft departures (thousands)	..	..	..
Trade and finance			
Trade in goods (% of GDP)	..	..	..
Trade growth less GDP growth (avg. %, 1990–2003)			..
High-technology exports (% of manufactured exports)	..	..	..
Net barter terms of trade (2000 = 100)	..	..	..
Foreign direct investment ($ millions)	..	..	..
Present value of debt ($ millions)			..
Total debt service (% of goods and services exports)	..	..	..
Short-term debt ($ millions)	..	..	..
Aid per capita ($)	..	..	..

Lithuania

Europe & Central Asia   **Upper middle income**

Population (millions)	3	Population growth (%)	–0.4
Surface area (1,000 sq. km)	65	National poverty rate (% pop.)	..
GNI ($ billions)	16	GNI per capita ($)	4,500

	1990	2002	2003
People			
Life expectancy at birth (years)	71	72	72
Fertility rate (births per woman)	2.0	1.2	1.3
Infant mortality rate (per 1,000 live births)	12	9	8
Under-five mortality rate (per 1,000)	14	12	11
Births attended by skilled health staff (% of total)	..	..	..
Child malnutrition, underweight (% of under age 5)	..	..	..
Child immunization, measles (% of ages 12–23 mon.)	89	98	98
HIV prevalence rate (% of ages 15–49)	..	0.1	0.1
Adult literacy, male (% of ages 15 and older)	100	100	..
Adult literacy, female (% of ages 15 and older)	99	100	..
Primary completion rate, total (% of age group)	..	108	102
Primary completion rate, female (% of age group)	..	108	101
Net primary enrollment (% of age group)	..	94	..
Net secondary enrollment (% of age group)	..	93	..
Environment			
Forests (1,000 sq. km)	19	20	..
Deforestation (average annual %, 1990–2000)		–0.2	
Freshwater use (% of internal resources)			2
Carbon dioxide emissions (metric tons per capita)	5.8	3.4	..
Access to improved water source (% of total pop.)	..	..	..
Access to improved sanitation (% of urban pop.)	..	..	..
Energy use per capita (kg oil equivalent)	2,996	2,476	..
Electricity use per capita (kilowatt-hours)	2,479	1,938	..
Economy			
GDP ($ billions)	11	14	18
GDP growth (annual %)	–5.7	6.8	9.0
GDP implicit price deflator (annual % growth)	228.3	–0.0	1.3
Value added in agriculture (% of GDP)	27	7	7
Value added in industry (% of GDP)	31	31	34
Value added in services (% of GDP)	42	62	59
Exports of goods and services (% of GDP)	52	53	54
Imports of goods and services (% of GDP)	61	59	60
Gross capital formation (% of GDP)	33	22	21
Central government revenue (% of GDP)	..	28.1	28.1
Cash surplus/deficit (% of GDP)	..	–1.5	–2.0
Technology and infrastructure			
Fixed-line and mobile subscribers (per 1,000 people)	212	746	869
Cost of 3-minute local call ($)	..	0.14	0.16
Personal computers (per 1,000 people)	..	109.7	..
Internet users (per 1,000 people)	..	144	202
Paved roads (% of total)	81.8	89.7	..
Aircraft departures (thousands)	5	10	10
Trade and finance			
Trade in goods (% of GDP)	..	95.3	93.8
Trade growth less GDP growth (avg. %, 1990–2003)			8.5
High-technology exports (% of manufactured exports)	..	4	5
Net barter terms of trade (2000 = 100)	..	..	..
Foreign direct investment ($ millions)	0	712	179
Present value of debt ($ millions)			8,390
Total debt service (% of goods and services exports)	..	56.7	67.7
Short-term debt ($ millions)	5	2,123	3,504
Aid per capita ($)	1	38	108

Luxembourg

High income

Population (thousands)	448	Population growth (%)	1.0
Surface area (1,000 sq. km)	3	National poverty rate (% pop.)	..
GNI ($ billions)	20	GNI per capita ($)	45,740

	1990	2002	2003
People			
Life expectancy at birth (years)	75	78	78
Fertility rate (births per woman)	1.6	1.6	1.6
Infant mortality rate (per 1,000 live births)	7	5	5
Under-five mortality rate (per 1,000)	9	6	..
Births attended by skilled health staff (% of total)	..	..	..
Child malnutrition, underweight (% of under age 5)	..	..	..
Child immunization, measles (% of ages 12–23 mon.)	80	91	91
HIV prevalence rate (% of ages 15–49)	..	0.2	0.2
Adult literacy, male (% of ages 15 and older)	..	..	..
Adult literacy, female (% of ages 15 and older)	..	..	..
Primary completion rate, total (% of age group)	..	86	..
Primary completion rate, female (% of age group)	..	90	..
Net primary enrollment (% of age group)	..	96	..
Net secondary enrollment (% of age group)	..	80	..
Environment			
Forests (1,000 sq. km)	..	..	..
Deforestation (average annual %, 1990–2000)		..	
Freshwater use (% of internal resources)			..
Carbon dioxide emissions (metric tons per capita)	25.9	19.4	..
Access to improved water source (% of total pop.)	100	100	..
Access to improved sanitation (% of urban pop.)	..	..	..
Energy use per capita (kg oil equivalent)	9,351	9,112	..
Electricity use per capita (kilowatt-hours)	10,806	12,791	..
Economy			
GDP ($ billions)	11	21	26
GDP growth (annual %)	5.3	1.7	2.1
GDP implicit price deflator (annual % growth)	2.5	0.7	2.1
Value added in agriculture (% of GDP)	2	1	1
Value added in industry (% of GDP)	32	20	20
Value added in services (% of GDP)	66	79	79
Exports of goods and services (% of GDP)	104	146	140
Imports of goods and services (% of GDP)	100	128	123
Gross capital formation (% of GDP)	26	21	21
Central government revenue (% of GDP)	..	42.8	42.7
Cash surplus/deficit (% of GDP)	..	2.5	–0.0
Technology and infrastructure			
Fixed-line and mobile subscribers (per 1,000 people)	483	1,857	1,991
Cost of 3-minute local call ($)	0.15	0.80	1.04
Personal computers (per 1,000 people)	..	594.2	..
Internet users (per 1,000 people)	2	370	377
Paved roads (% of total)	99.1	100.0	..
Aircraft departures (thousands)	12	25	41
Trade and finance			
Trade in goods (% of GDP)	..	..	..
Trade growth less GDP growth (avg. %, 1990–2003)			3.6
High-technology exports (% of manufactured exports)	..	15	12
Net barter terms of trade (2000 = 100)	..	..	..
Foreign direct investment ($ billions)	..	130	93
Present value of debt ($ millions)			..
Total debt service (% of goods and services exports)	..	..	..
Short-term debt ($ millions)	..	..	..
Aid per capita ($)	..	..	..

Macao, China

				High income
Population (thousands)	444	Population growth (%)		1.1
Surface area (sq. km)	21	National poverty rate (% pop.)		..
GNI ($ millions)	..	GNI per capita ($)		..

	1990	2002	2003
People			
Life expectancy at birth (years)	77	79	79
Fertility rate (births per woman)	1.8	1.1	1.1
Infant mortality rate (per 1,000 live births)	..	*3*	..
Under-five mortality rate (per 1,000)	..	..	..
Births attended by skilled health staff (% of total)	..	..	..
Child malnutrition, underweight (% of under age 5)	..	..	..
Child immunization, measles (% of ages 12–23 mon.)	..	..	..
HIV prevalence rate (% of ages 15–49)	..	..	..
Adult literacy, male (% of ages 15 and older)	95	*95*	..
Adult literacy, female (% of ages 15 and older)	87	*88*	..
Primary completion rate, total (% of age group)	*93*	102	..
Primary completion rate, female (% of age group)	*97*	97	..
Net primary enrollment (% of age group)	81	87	..
Net secondary enrollment (% of age group)	..	74	..
Environment			
Forests (1,000 sq. km)	..	..	..
Deforestation (average annual %, 1990–2000)		..	
Freshwater use (% of internal resources)			..
Carbon dioxide emissions (metric tons per capita)	2.8	*3.8*	..
Access to improved water source (% of total pop.)	..	..	..
Access to improved sanitation (% of urban pop.)	..	..	..
Energy use per capita (kg oil equivalent)	..	..	..
Electricity use per capita (kilowatt-hours)	..	..	..
Economy			
GDP ($ millions)	3,263	6,765	..
GDP growth (annual %)	9.8	10.1	..
GDP implicit price deflator (annual % growth)	8.1	–1.0	..
Value added in agriculture (% of GDP)	..	..	..
Value added in industry (% of GDP)	..	*11*	..
Value added in services (% of GDP)	..	*72*	..
Exports of goods and services (% of GDP)	97	100	..
Imports of goods and services (% of GDP)	67	61	..
Gross capital formation (% of GDP)	25	11	..
Central government revenue (% of GDP)	..	21.9	..
Cash surplus/deficit (% of GDP)	..	2.9	..
Technology and infrastructure			
Fixed-line and mobile subscribers (per 1,000 people)	261	1,024	1,201
Cost of 3-minute local call ($)	0.00	0.00	0.00
Personal computers (per 1,000 people)	..	208.3	260.9
Internet users (per 1,000 people)	..	*136*	268
Paved roads (% of total)	100.0	*100.0*	..
Aircraft departures (thousands)	..	15	14
Trade and finance			
Trade in goods (% of GDP)	99.3	72.2	..
Trade growth less GDP growth (avg. %, 1990–2003)			1.2
High-technology exports (% of manufactured exports)	2	1	1
Net barter terms of trade (2000 = 100)	..	..	..
Foreign direct investment ($ millions)	..	..	..
Present value of debt ($ millions)			..
Total debt service (% of goods and services exports)	..	..	..
Short-term debt ($ millions)	..	..	..
Aid per capita ($)	1	2	75

Macedonia, FYR

Europe & Central Asia   **Lower middle income**

Population (millions)	2	Population growth (%)	0.5
Surface area (1,000 sq. km)	26	National poverty rate (% pop.)	..
GNI ($ millions)	4,052	GNI per capita ($)	1,980

	1990	2002	2003
People			
Life expectancy at birth (years)	72	73	74
Fertility rate (births per woman)	2.1	1.8	..
Infant mortality rate (per 1,000 live births)	32	12	10
Under-five mortality rate (per 1,000)	33	14	11
Births attended by skilled health staff (% of total)	..	98	..
Child malnutrition, underweight (% of under age 5)	..	6	..
Child immunization, measles (% of ages 12–23 mon.)	..	98	96
HIV prevalence rate (% of ages 15–49)	..	0.1	0.1
Adult literacy, male (% of ages 15 and older)	..	..	..
Adult literacy, female (% of ages 15 and older)	..	..	..
Primary completion rate, total (% of age group)	99	100	..
Primary completion rate, female (% of age group)	..	102	..
Net primary enrollment (% of age group)	94	92	..
Net secondary enrollment (% of age group)	..	81	..
Environment			
Forests (1,000 sq. km)	9	9	..
Deforestation (average annual %, 1990–2000)		0.0	
Freshwater use (% of internal resources)			38
Carbon dioxide emissions (metric tons per capita)	5.5	5.5	..
Access to improved water source (% of total pop.)	..	..	..
Access to improved sanitation (% of urban pop.)	..	..	..
Energy use per capita (kg oil equivalent)	..	..	..
Electricity use per capita (kilowatt-hours)	..	..	..
Economy			
GDP ($ millions)	4,478	3,791	4,666
GDP growth (annual %)	–6.2	0.9	3.2
GDP implicit price deflator (annual % growth)	79.0	3.4	1.8
Value added in agriculture (% of GDP)	9	12	12
Value added in industry (% of GDP)	46	30	30
Value added in services (% of GDP)	45	57	57
Exports of goods and services (% of GDP)	26	38	35
Imports of goods and services (% of GDP)	36	57	53
Gross capital formation (% of GDP)	19	20	22
Central government revenue (% of GDP)	..	..	..
Cash surplus/deficit (% of GDP)	..	..	..
Technology and infrastructure			
Fixed-line and mobile subscribers (per 1,000 people)	148	448	..
Cost of 3-minute local call ($)	..	0.01	..
Personal computers (per 1,000 people)	..	..	..
Internet users (per 1,000 people)	..	25	..
Paved roads (% of total)	58.9	63.8	..
Aircraft departures (thousands)	..	2	2
Trade and finance			
Trade in goods (% of GDP)	103.8	80.2	77.0
Trade growth less GDP growth (avg. %, 1990–2003)			5.1
High-technology exports (% of manufactured exports)	..	1	1
Net barter terms of trade (2000 = 100)	..	..	..
Foreign direct investment ($ millions)	0	78	95
Present value of debt ($ millions)			1,591
Total debt service (% of goods and services exports)	..	15.8	12.9
Short-term debt ($ billions)	..	0	0
Aid per capita ($)	..	135	114

Madagascar

Sub-Saharan Africa		Low income

Population (millions)	17	Population growth (%)	2.7
Surface area (1,000 sq. km)	587	National poverty rate (% pop.)	71
GNI ($ millions)	4,857	GNI per capita ($)	290

	1990	2002	2003
People			
Life expectancy at birth (years)	53	55	56
Fertility rate (births per woman)	6.2	5.2	5.2
Infant mortality rate (per 1,000 live births)	103	84	78
Under-five mortality rate (per 1,000)	168	137	126
Births attended by skilled health staff (% of total)	57	46	..
Child malnutrition, underweight (% of under age 5)	41	33	..
Child immunization, measles (% of ages 12–23 mon.)	47	55	55
HIV prevalence rate (% of ages 15–49)	..	1.3	1.7
Adult literacy, male (% of ages 15 and older)	..	..	..
Adult literacy, female (% of ages 15 and older)	..	..	..
Primary completion rate, total (% of age group)	35	40	47
Primary completion rate, female (% of age group)	35	41	48
Net primary enrollment (% of age group)	65	79	..
Net secondary enrollment (% of age group)	..	11	..
Environment			
Forests (1,000 sq. km)	129	117	..
Deforestation (average annual %, 1990–2000)		0.9	
Freshwater use (% of internal resources)			5
Carbon dioxide emissions (metric tons per capita)	0.1	0.1	..
Access to improved water source (% of total pop.)	40	45	..
Access to improved sanitation (% of urban pop.)	25	49	..
Energy use per capita (kg oil equivalent)	..	..	..
Electricity use per capita (kilowatt-hours)	..	..	..
Economy			
GDP ($ millions)	3,081	4,397	5,474
GDP growth (annual %)	3.1	–12.7	9.8
GDP implicit price deflator (annual % growth)	11.5	15.3	2.8
Value added in agriculture (% of GDP)	29	32	29
Value added in industry (% of GDP)	13	14	15
Value added in services (% of GDP)	59	54	55
Exports of goods and services (% of GDP)	17	16	21
Imports of goods and services (% of GDP)	28	23	32
Gross capital formation (% of GDP)	17	14	18
Central government revenue (% of GDP)	..	8.0	..
Cash surplus/deficit (% of GDP)	..	–4.4	..
Technology and infrastructure			
Fixed-line and mobile subscribers (per 1,000 people)	3	14	21
Cost of 3-minute local call ($)	0.08	0.07	..
Personal computers (per 1,000 people)	..	4.4	4.9
Internet users (per 1,000 people)	..	3	4
Paved roads (% of total)	15.4	11.6	..
Aircraft departures (thousands)	17	9	9
Trade and finance			
Trade in goods (% of GDP)	31.5	24.8	33.7
Trade growth less GDP growth (avg. %, 1990–2003)			2.8
High-technology exports (% of manufactured exports)	8	1	0
Net barter terms of trade (2000 = 100)	81	114	..
Foreign direct investment ($ millions)	22	8	13
Present value of debt ($ millions)			1,467
Total debt service (% of goods and services exports)	45.5	8.7	6.1
Short-term debt ($ millions)	226	231	164
Aid per capita ($)	34	23	32

Malawi

Sub-Saharan Africa   **Low income**

Population (millions)	11	Population growth (%)		2.0
Surface area (1,000 sq. km)	118	National poverty rate (% pop.)		65
GNI ($ millions)	1,808	GNI per capita ($)		160

	1990	2002	2003
People			
Life expectancy at birth (years)	45	38	38
Fertility rate (births per woman)	7.0	6.1	6.0
Infant mortality rate (per 1,000 live births)	146	117	112
Under-five mortality rate (per 1,000)	241	188	178
Births attended by skilled health staff (% of total)	55	61	..
Child malnutrition, underweight (% of under age 5)	28	25	..
Child immunization, measles (% of ages 12–23 mon.)	81	69	77
HIV prevalence rate (% of ages 15–49)	..	14.3	14.2
Adult literacy, male (% of ages 15 and older)	69	76	..
Adult literacy, female (% of ages 15 and older)	36	49	..
Primary completion rate, total (% of age group)	36	69	71
Primary completion rate, female (% of age group)	31	68	69
Net primary enrollment (% of age group)	50	..	..
Net secondary enrollment (% of age group)	..	29	..
Environment			
Forests (1,000 sq. km)	33	26	..
Deforestation (average annual %, 1990–2000)		2.4	
Freshwater use (% of internal resources)			6
Carbon dioxide emissions (metric tons per capita)	0.1	0.1	..
Access to improved water source (% of total pop.)	41	67	..
Access to improved sanitation (% of urban pop.)	52	66	..
Energy use per capita (kg oil equivalent)	..	..	..
Electricity use per capita (kilowatt-hours)	..	..	..
Economy			
GDP ($ millions)	1,881	1,880	1,714
GDP growth (annual %)	5.7	1.8	4.4
GDP implicit price deflator (annual % growth)	10.7	15.1	11.2
Value added in agriculture (% of GDP)	45	37	38
Value added in industry (% of GDP)	29	15	15
Value added in services (% of GDP)	26	48	47
Exports of goods and services (% of GDP)	24	25	27
Imports of goods and services (% of GDP)	33	44	41
Gross capital formation (% of GDP)	23	13	8
Central government revenue (% of GDP)	..	..	..
Cash surplus/deficit (% of GDP)	..	..	..
Technology and infrastructure			
Fixed-line and mobile subscribers (per 1,000 people)	3	15	21
Cost of 3-minute local call ($)	0.04	0.06	..
Personal computers (per 1,000 people)	..	1.3	1.5
Internet users (per 1,000 people)	..	3	3
Paved roads (% of total)	22.0	18.5	..
Aircraft departures (thousands)	4	5	5
Trade and finance			
Trade in goods (% of GDP)	52.7	57.2	68.0
Trade growth less GDP growth (avg. %, 1990–2003)			–2.2
High-technology exports (% of manufactured exports)	0	0	1
Net barter terms of trade (2000 = 100)	148	99	..
Foreign direct investment ($ millions)	23	6	23
Present value of debt ($ millions)			1,868
Total debt service (% of goods and services exports)	29.3	6.3	7.7
Short-term debt ($ millions)	58	130	72
Aid per capita ($)	59	35	45

Malaysia

East Asia & Pacific   **Upper middle income**

Population (millions)	25	Population growth (%)	1.9
Surface area (1,000 sq. km)	330	National poverty rate (% pop.)	..
GNI ($ billions)	96	GNI per capita ($)	3,880

	1990	2002	2003
People			
Life expectancy at birth (years)	71	73	73
Fertility rate (births per woman)	3.8	2.8	2.8
Infant mortality rate (per 1,000 live births)	16	8	7
Under-five mortality rate (per 1,000)	21	9	7
Births attended by skilled health staff (% of total)	..	97	..
Child malnutrition, underweight (% of under age 5)	25	19	..
Child immunization, measles (% of ages 12–23 mon.)	70	92	92
HIV prevalence rate (% of ages 15–49)	..	0.4	0.4
Adult literacy, male (% of ages 15 and older)	87	92	..
Adult literacy, female (% of ages 15 and older)	74	85	..
Primary completion rate, total (% of age group)	88	92	92
Primary completion rate, female (% of age group)	88	92	92
Net primary enrollment (% of age group)	94	95	..
Net secondary enrollment (% of age group)	..	69	..
Environment			
Forests (1,000 sq. km)	217	193	..
Deforestation (average annual %, 1990–2000)		1.2	
Freshwater use (% of internal resources)			2
Carbon dioxide emissions (metric tons per capita)	3.0	6.2	..
Access to improved water source (% of total pop.)	..	95	..
Access to improved sanitation (% of urban pop.)	94	..	..
Energy use per capita (kg oil equivalent)	1,234	2,129	..
Electricity use per capita (kilowatt-hours)	1,095	2,832	..
Economy			
GDP ($ billions)	44	95	104
GDP growth (annual %)	9.0	4.1	5.3
GDP implicit price deflator (annual % growth)	3.8	3.8	3.5
Value added in agriculture (% of GDP)	15	9	10
Value added in industry (% of GDP)	42	47	49
Value added in services (% of GDP)	43	43	42
Exports of goods and services (% of GDP)	75	115	114
Imports of goods and services (% of GDP)	72	96	93
Gross capital formation (% of GDP)	32	24	21
Central government revenue (% of GDP)	26.4	24.4	23.7
Cash surplus/deficit (% of GDP)	−2.9	−6.3	−4.3
Technology and infrastructure			
Fixed-line and mobile subscribers (per 1,000 people)	94	567	624
Cost of 3-minute local call ($)	0.05	0.03	0.02
Personal computers (per 1,000 people)	8.4	146.8	166.9
Internet users (per 1,000 people)	0	320	344
Paved roads (% of total)	70.0	77.9	..
Aircraft departures (thousands)	131	189	152
Trade and finance			
Trade in goods (% of GDP)	133.4	181.9	174.8
Trade growth less GDP growth (avg. %, 1990–2003)			3.0
High-technology exports (% of manufactured exports)	38	58	58
Net barter terms of trade (2000 = 100)	103	98	..
Foreign direct investment ($ millions)	2,332	3,203	2,473
Present value of debt ($ billions)			50
Total debt service (% of goods and services exports)	12.6	7.1	7.8
Short-term debt ($ millions)	1,906	8,369	8,825
Aid per capita ($)	26	4	4

Maldives

South Asia	Lower middle income

Population (thousands)	293	Population growth (%)	2.2
Surface area (sq. km)	300	National poverty rate (% pop.)	..
GNI ($ millions)	690	GNI per capita ($)	2,350

	1990	2002	2003
People			
Life expectancy at birth (years)	62	69	69
Fertility rate (births per woman)	5.7	4.0	4.0
Infant mortality rate (per 1,000 live births)	80	59	55
Under-five mortality rate (per 1,000)	115	80	72
Births attended by skilled health staff (% of total)	..	70	..
Child malnutrition, underweight (% of under age 5)	..	30	..
Child immunization, measles (% of ages 12–23 mon.)	96	99	96
HIV prevalence rate (% of ages 15–49)	..	..	..
Adult literacy, male (% of ages 15 and older)	95	97	..
Adult literacy, female (% of ages 15 and older)	95	97	..
Primary completion rate, total (% of age group)	..	..	..
Primary completion rate, female (% of age group)	..	..	..
Net primary enrollment (% of age group)	87	92	..
Net secondary enrollment (% of age group)	..	51	..
Environment			
Forests (1,000 sq. km)	0	0	..
Deforestation (average annual %, 1990–2000)		0.0	
Freshwater use (% of internal resources)			..
Carbon dioxide emissions (metric tons per capita)	0.7	1.8	..
Access to improved water source (% of total pop.)	99	84	..
Access to improved sanitation (% of urban pop.)	100	100	..
Energy use per capita (kg oil equivalent)	..	..	..
Electricity use per capita (kilowatt-hours)	..	..	..
Economy			
GDP ($ millions)	215	641	715
GDP growth (annual %)	..	6.1	9.2
GDP implicit price deflator (annual % growth)	..	1.0	2.3
Value added in agriculture (% of GDP)	..	..	..
Value added in industry (% of GDP)	..	..	..
Value added in services (% of GDP)	..	..	..
Exports of goods and services (% of GDP)	24	86	85
Imports of goods and services (% of GDP)	64	66	66
Gross capital formation (% of GDP)	..	26	32
Central government revenue (% of GDP)	22.1	31.3	30.9
Cash surplus/deficit (% of GDP)	–7.5	–7.5	–9.2
Technology and infrastructure			
Fixed-line and mobile subscribers (per 1,000 people)	29	251	..
Cost of 3-minute local call ($)	0.05	0.06	0.06
Personal computers (per 1,000 people)	..	71.2	..
Internet users (per 1,000 people)	0	53	..
Paved roads (% of total)	..	..	..
Aircraft departures (thousands)	1	3	4
Trade and finance			
Trade in goods (% of GDP)	88.4	75.2	81.6
Trade growth less GDP growth (avg. %, 1990–2003)			–0.2
High-technology exports (% of manufactured exports)	..	..	..
Net barter terms of trade (2000 = 100)	..	..	..
Foreign direct investment ($ millions)	6	12	14
Present value of debt ($ millions)			216
Total debt service (% of goods and services exports)	4.8	4.4	3.6
Short-term debt ($ millions)	14	49	26
Aid per capita ($)	99	96	61

Mali

Sub-Saharan Africa		Low income
Population (millions)	12	Population growth (%)	2.4
Surface area (1,000 sq. km)	1,240	National poverty rate (% pop.)	64
GNI ($ millions)	3,428	GNI per capita ($)	290

	1990	2002	2003
People			
Life expectancy at birth (years)	45	41	41
Fertility rate (births per woman)	*6.9*	6.4	6.4
Infant mortality rate (per 1,000 live births)	140	*124*	122
Under-five mortality rate (per 1,000)	250	224	220
Births attended by skilled health staff (% of total)	..	*41*	..
Child malnutrition, underweight (% of under age 5)	..	*33*	..
Child immunization, measles (% of ages 12–23 mon.)	43	64	68
HIV prevalence rate (% of ages 15–49)	..	*1.7*	1.9
Adult literacy, male (% of ages 15 and older)	28	27	..
Adult literacy, female (% of ages 15 and older)	10	*12*	..
Primary completion rate, total (% of age group)	12	39	40
Primary completion rate, female (% of age group)	9	30	32
Net primary enrollment (% of age group)	20	44	..
Net secondary enrollment (% of age group)	5	..	..
Environment			
Forests (1,000 sq. km)	142	*132*	..
Deforestation (average annual %, 1990–2000)		*0.7*	
Freshwater use (% of internal resources)			2
Carbon dioxide emissions (metric tons per capita)	0.0	*0.1*	..
Access to improved water source (% of total pop.)	34	48	..
Access to improved sanitation (% of urban pop.)	50	59	..
Energy use per capita (kg oil equivalent)	..	..	..
Electricity use per capita (kilowatt-hours)	..	..	..
Economy			
GDP ($ millions)	2,421	3,343	4,326
GDP growth (annual %)	-1.9	4.4	6.0
GDP implicit price deflator (annual % growth)	4.9	15.8	1.8
Value added in agriculture (% of GDP)	46	34	38
Value added in industry (% of GDP)	16	30	26
Value added in services (% of GDP)	39	36	36
Exports of goods and services (% of GDP)	17	32	26
Imports of goods and services (% of GDP)	34	32	31
Gross capital formation (% of GDP)	23	19	23
Central government revenue (% of GDP)	..	..	..
Cash surplus/deficit (% of GDP)	..	..	..
Technology and infrastructure			
Fixed-line and mobile subscribers (per 1,000 people)	1	10	..
Cost of 3-minute local call ($)	0.26	*0.07*	..
Personal computers (per 1,000 people)	..	1.4	..
Internet users (per 1,000 people)	..	2	..
Paved roads (% of total)	10.9	*12.1*	..
Aircraft departures (thousands)	1	*1*	..
Trade and finance			
Trade in goods (% of GDP)	39.7	52.5	50.4
Trade growth less GDP growth (avg. %, 1990–2003)			2.2
High-technology exports (% of manufactured exports)	..	8	..
Net barter terms of trade (2000 = 100)	135	100	..
Foreign direct investment ($ millions)	6	244	129
Present value of debt ($ millions)			1,374
Total debt service (% of goods and services exports)	12.3	6.9	..
Short-term debt ($ millions)	62	151	50
Aid per capita ($)	57	41	45

Malta

High income

Population (thousands)	399	Population growth (%)	0.5
Surface area (sq. km)	320	National poverty rate (% pop.)	..
GNI ($ millions)	4,302	GNI per capita ($)	10,780

	1990	2002	2003
People			
Life expectancy at birth (years)	75	78	79
Fertility rate (births per woman)	2.0	1.5	1.4
Infant mortality rate (per 1,000 live births)	11	6	5
Under-five mortality rate (per 1,000)	14	8	6
Births attended by skilled health staff (% of total)	..	..	..
Child malnutrition, underweight (% of under age 5)	..	..	..
Child immunization, measles (% of ages 12–23 mon.)	80	65	90
HIV prevalence rate (% of ages 15–49)	..	0.1	0.2
Adult literacy, male (% of ages 15 and older)	88	92	..
Adult literacy, female (% of ages 15 and older)	89	93	..
Primary completion rate, total (% of age group)	100	108	..
Primary completion rate, female (% of age group)	101	109	..
Net primary enrollment (% of age group)	97	97	..
Net secondary enrollment (% of age group)	78	82	..
Environment			
Forests (1,000 sq. km)	..	0	..
Deforestation (average annual %, 1990–2000)		..	
Freshwater use (% of internal resources)			..
Carbon dioxide emissions (metric tons per capita)	4.6	7.2	..
Access to improved water source (% of total pop.)	100	100	..
Access to improved sanitation (% of urban pop.)	100	100	..
Energy use per capita (kg oil equivalent)	2,150	2,247	..
Electricity use per capita (kilowatt-hours)	2,528	4,174	..
Economy			
GDP ($ millions)	2,312	4,055	4,851
GDP growth (annual %)	6.3	2.3	−1.7
GDP implicit price deflator (annual % growth)	3.2	1.1	..
Value added in agriculture (% of GDP)	3	..	..
Value added in industry (% of GDP)	39	..	..
Value added in services (% of GDP)	58	..	..
Exports of goods and services (% of GDP)	85	88	..
Imports of goods and services (% of GDP)	99	89	..
Gross capital formation (% of GDP)	33	16	..
Central government revenue (% of GDP)	38.1	31.1	..
Cash surplus/deficit (% of GDP)	−5.3	−5.3	..
Technology and infrastructure			
Fixed-line and mobile subscribers (per 1,000 people)	360	1,223	1,246
Cost of 3-minute local call ($)	0.03	0.12	..
Personal computers (per 1,000 people)	14.0	255.1	..
Internet users (per 1,000 people)	..	303	..
Paved roads (% of total)	..	90.0	..
Aircraft departures (thousands)	7	15	14
Trade and finance			
Trade in goods (% of GDP)	133.9	124.9	120.8
Trade growth less GDP growth (avg. %, 1990–2003)			..
High-technology exports (% of manufactured exports)	45	62	..
Net barter terms of trade (2000 = 100)	..	..	..
Foreign direct investment ($ millions)	..	..	..
Present value of debt ($ millions)			..
Total debt service (% of goods and services exports)	..	..	..
Short-term debt ($ millions)	..	..	..
Aid per capita ($)	15	28	25

Marshall Islands

East Asia & Pacific		Lower middle income

Population (thousands)	53	Population growth (%)	0.0
Surface area (sq. km)	181	National poverty rate (% pop.)	..
GNI ($ millions)	142	GNI per capita ($)	2,710

	1990	2002	2003
People			
Life expectancy at birth (years)	..	65	..
Fertility rate (births per woman)	..	..	..
Infant mortality rate (per 1,000 live births)	63	55	53
Under-five mortality rate (per 1,000)	92	68	61
Births attended by skilled health staff (% of total)	..	95	..
Child malnutrition, underweight (% of under age 5)	..	..	..
Child immunization, measles (% of ages 12–23 mon.)	52	80	90
HIV prevalence rate (% of ages 15–49)	..	..	..
Adult literacy, male (% of ages 15 and older)	..	..	..
Adult literacy, female (% of ages 15 and older)	..	..	..
Primary completion rate, total (% of age group)	..	..	..
Primary completion rate, female (% of age group)	..	..	..
Net primary enrollment (% of age group)	..	96	..
Net secondary enrollment (% of age group)	..	..	..
Environment			
Forests (1,000 sq. km)	..	..	..
Deforestation (average annual %, 1990–2000)		..	
Freshwater use (% of internal resources)			..
Carbon dioxide emissions (metric tons per capita)	..	..	..
Access to improved water source (% of total pop.)	96	85	..
Access to improved sanitation (% of urban pop.)	88	93	..
Energy use per capita (kg oil equivalent)	..	..	..
Electricity use per capita (kilowatt-hours)	..	..	..
Economy			
GDP ($ millions)	69	106	106
GDP growth (annual %)	7.0	4.0	2.0
GDP implicit price deflator (annual % growth)	0.7	0.2	–1.9
Value added in agriculture (% of GDP)	14	14	..
Value added in industry (% of GDP)	13	16	..
Value added in services (% of GDP)	73	70	..
Exports of goods and services (% of GDP)	..	..	..
Imports of goods and services (% of GDP)	..	..	..
Gross capital formation (% of GDP)	..	..	..
Central government revenue (% of GDP)	..	..	..
Cash surplus/deficit (% of GDP)	..	..	..
Technology and infrastructure			
Fixed-line and mobile subscribers (per 1,000 people)	11	87	94
Cost of 3-minute local call ($)	0.00	0.00	0.00
Personal computers (per 1,000 people)	0.1	53.0	..
Internet users (per 1,000 people)	0	24	26
Paved roads (% of total)	..	..	..
Aircraft departures (thousands)	3	4	4
Trade and finance			
Trade in goods (% of GDP)	..	54.8	62.3
Trade growth less GDP growth (avg. %, 1990–2003)			..
High-technology exports (% of manufactured exports)	..	..	..
Net barter terms of trade (2000 = 100)	..	..	..
Foreign direct investment ($ millions)	..	..	..
Present value of debt ($ millions)			..
Total debt service (% of goods and services exports)	..	..	..
Short-term debt ($ millions)	..	..	..
Aid per capita ($)	..	1,189	1,076

Mauritania

Sub-Saharan Africa		Low income	

Population (millions)	3	Population growth (%)	2.2
Surface area (1,000 sq. km)	1,026	National poverty rate (% pop.)	46
GNI ($ millions)	1,142	GNI per capita ($)	400

	1990	2002	2003
People			
Life expectancy at birth (years)	49	51	51
Fertility rate (births per woman)	6.0	4.6	4.6
Infant mortality rate (per 1,000 live births)	112	84	77
Under-five mortality rate (per 1,000)	162	119	107
Births attended by skilled health staff (% of total)	40	57	..
Child malnutrition, underweight (% of under age 5)	48	32	..
Child immunization, measles (% of ages 12–23 mon.)	38	81	71
HIV prevalence rate (% of ages 15–49)	..	0.5	0.6
Adult literacy, male (% of ages 15 and older)	46	51	..
Adult literacy, female (% of ages 15 and older)	24	31	..
Primary completion rate, total (% of age group)	33	46	43
Primary completion rate, female (% of age group)	26	44	41
Net primary enrollment (% of age group)	35	68	..
Net secondary enrollment (% of age group)	..	16	..

	1990	2002	2003
Environment			
Forests (1,000 sq. km)	4	3	..
Deforestation (average annual %, 1990–2000)		2.7	
Freshwater use (% of internal resources)			..
Carbon dioxide emissions (metric tons per capita)	1.3	1.2	..
Access to improved water source (% of total pop.)	41	56	..
Access to improved sanitation (% of urban pop.)	31	64	..
Energy use per capita (kg oil equivalent)	..	..	..
Electricity use per capita (kilowatt-hours)	..	..	..

	1990	2002	2003
Economy			
GDP ($ millions)	1,020	991	1,093
GDP growth (annual %)	–1.8	3.3	4.9
GDP implicit price deflator (annual % growth)	2.6	6.0	1.8
Value added in agriculture (% of GDP)	30	21	19
Value added in industry (% of GDP)	29	29	30
Value added in services (% of GDP)	42	50	51
Exports of goods and services (% of GDP)	46	39	34
Imports of goods and services (% of GDP)	61	66	75
Gross capital formation (% of GDP)	20	33	45
Central government revenue (% of GDP)	..	..	..
Cash surplus/deficit (% of GDP)	..	..	..

	1990	2002	2003
Technology and infrastructure			
Fixed-line and mobile subscribers (per 1,000 people)	3	104	141
Cost of 3-minute local call ($)	0.16	0.13	0.11
Personal computers (per 1,000 people)	..	10.8	..
Internet users (per 1,000 people)	..	4	4
Paved roads (% of total)	11.0	11.3	..
Aircraft departures (thousands)	4	2	2

	1990	2002	2003
Trade and finance			
Trade in goods (% of GDP)	84.1	83.8	84.1
Trade growth less GDP growth (avg. %, 1990–2003)			–4.1
High-technology exports (% of manufactured exports)	..	..	
Net barter terms of trade (2000 = 100)	97	88	..
Foreign direct investment ($ millions)	7	118	214
Present value of debt ($ millions)			785
Total debt service (% of goods and services exports)	29.8	27.7	..
Short-term debt ($ millions)	238	212	172
Aid per capita ($)	117	124	85

Mauritius

Sub-Saharan Africa		Upper middle income

Population (millions)	1	Population growth (%)	1.0
Surface area (1,000 sq. km)	2	National poverty rate (% pop.)	..
GNI ($ millions)	5,009	GNI per capita ($)	4,100

	1990	2002	2003
People			
Life expectancy at birth (years)	69	72	72
Fertility rate (births per woman)	2.3	2.0	2.0
Infant mortality rate (per 1,000 live births)	21	17	16
Under-five mortality rate (per 1,000)	25	20	18
Births attended by skilled health staff (% of total)	..	99	..
Child malnutrition, underweight (% of under age 5)	..	..	..
Child immunization, measles (% of ages 12–23 mon.)	76	84	94
HIV prevalence rate (% of ages 15–49)	..	..	
Adult literacy, male (% of ages 15 and older)	85	88	..
Adult literacy, female (% of ages 15 and older)	75	81	..
Primary completion rate, total (% of age group)	102	105	105
Primary completion rate, female (% of age group)	102	104	105
Net primary enrollment (% of age group)	95	90	..
Net secondary enrollment (% of age group)	..	71	..
Environment			
Forests (1,000 sq. km)	0	0	..
Deforestation (average annual %, 1990–2000)		0.6	
Freshwater use (% of internal resources)			..
Carbon dioxide emissions (metric tons per capita)	1.1	2.4	..
Access to improved water source (% of total pop.)	100	100	..
Access to improved sanitation (% of urban pop.)	100	100	..
Energy use per capita (kg oil equivalent)	..	..	..
Electricity use per capita (kilowatt-hours)	..	..	..
Economy			
GDP ($ millions)	2,383	4,542	5,224
GDP growth (annual %)	5.8	4.4	3.2
GDP implicit price deflator (annual % growth)	10.6	5.0	5.6
Value added in agriculture (% of GDP)	13	7	6
Value added in industry (% of GDP)	33	31	31
Value added in services (% of GDP)	54	62	63
Exports of goods and services (% of GDP)	64	61	60
Imports of goods and services (% of GDP)	71	57	57
Gross capital formation (% of GDP)	31	21	23
Central government revenue (% of GDP)	24.3	20.1	21.8
Cash surplus/deficit (% of GDP)	0.3	–3.7	–3.4
Technology and infrastructure			
Fixed-line and mobile subscribers (per 1,000 people)	55	559	552
Cost of 3-minute local call ($)	0.06	0.04	..
Personal computers (per 1,000 people)	3.8	116.5	..
Internet users (per 1,000 people)	..	103	123
Paved roads (% of total)	93.0	98.0	..
Aircraft departures (thousands)	8	13	15
Trade and finance			
Trade in goods (% of GDP)	118.0	87.4	82.7
Trade growth less GDP growth (avg. %, 1990–2003)			–0.2
High-technology exports (% of manufactured exports)	1	2	5
Net barter terms of trade (2000 = 100)	93	98	..
Foreign direct investment ($ millions)	41	32	63
Present value of debt ($ millions)			2,492
Total debt service (% of goods and services exports)	8.8	8.3	7.2
Short-term debt ($ millions)	52	892	1,550
Aid per capita ($)	84	20	–12

Mayotte

Population (thousands)	166	Population growth (%)	..
Surface area (sq. km)	374	National poverty rate (% pop.)	..
GNI ($ millions)	..	GNI per capita ($)	..

	1990	2002	2003
People			
Life expectancy at birth (years)	..	..	..
Fertility rate (births per woman)	..	..	..
Infant mortality rate (per 1,000 live births)	..	..	..
Under-five mortality rate (per 1,000)	..	..	..
Births attended by skilled health staff (% of total)	..	..	..
Child malnutrition, underweight (% of under age 5)	..	..	..
Child immunization, measles (% of ages 12–23 mon.)	..	..	..
HIV prevalence rate (% of ages 15–49)	..	..	..
Adult literacy, male (% of ages 15 and older)	..	..	..
Adult literacy, female (% of ages 15 and older)	..	..	..
Primary completion rate, total (% of age group)	..	..	..
Primary completion rate, female (% of age group)	..	..	..
Net primary enrollment (% of age group)	..	..	..
Net secondary enrollment (% of age group)	..	..	..
Environment			
Forests (1,000 sq. km)	..	..	..
Deforestation (average annual %, 1990–2000)		..	
Freshwater use (% of internal resources)			..
Carbon dioxide emissions (metric tons per capita)	..	..	..
Access to improved water source (% of total pop.)	..	..	..
Access to improved sanitation (% of urban pop.)	..	..	..
Energy use per capita (kg oil equivalent)	..	..	..
Electricity use per capita (kilowatt-hours)	..	..	..
Economy			
GDP ($ millions)	..	..	..
GDP growth (annual %)	..	..	..
GDP implicit price deflator (annual % growth)	..	..	..
Value added in agriculture (% of GDP)	..	..	..
Value added in industry (% of GDP)	..	..	..
Value added in services (% of GDP)	..	..	..
Exports of goods and services (% of GDP)	..	..	..
Imports of goods and services (% of GDP)	..	..	..
Gross capital formation (% of GDP)	..	..	..
Central government revenue (% of GDP)	..	..	..
Cash surplus/deficit (% of GDP)	..	..	..
Technology and infrastructure			
Fixed-line and mobile subscribers (per 1,000 people)	31	*70*	..
Cost of 3-minute local call ($)	..	*0.11*	..
Personal computers (per 1,000 people)	..	..	..
Internet users (per 1,000 people)	..	..	..
Paved roads (% of total)	..	..	..
Aircraft departures (thousands)	..	..	..
Trade and finance			
Trade in goods (% of GDP)	..	..	..
Trade growth less GDP growth (avg. %, 1990–2003)			..
High-technology exports (% of manufactured exports)	..	..	..
Net barter terms of trade (2000 = 100)	..	..	..
Foreign direct investment ($ millions)	..	..	..
Present value of debt ($ millions)			..
Total debt service (% of goods and services exports)	..	..	..
Short-term debt ($ millions)	..	..	..
Aid per capita ($)	..	..	..

Mexico

Latin America & Caribbean		Upper middle income	

Population (millions)	102	Population growth (%)	1.4
Surface area (1,000 sq. km)	1,958	National poverty rate (% pop.)	..
GNI ($ billions)	637	GNI per capita ($)	6,230

	1990	2002	2003
People			
Life expectancy at birth (years)	71	73	74
Fertility rate (births per woman)	3.3	2.3	2.2
Infant mortality rate (per 1,000 live births)	37	25	23
Under-five mortality rate (per 1,000)	46	30	28
Births attended by skilled health staff (% of total)	..	86	..
Child malnutrition, underweight (% of under age 5)	17	8	..
Child immunization, measles (% of ages 12–23 mon.)	75	96	96
HIV prevalence rate (% of ages 15–49)	..	0.3	0.3
Adult literacy, male (% of ages 15 and older)	91	93	..
Adult literacy, female (% of ages 15 and older)	84	89	..
Primary completion rate, total (% of age group)	88	98	99
Primary completion rate, female (% of age group)	92	98	100
Net primary enrollment (% of age group)	99	99	..
Net secondary enrollment (% of age group)	45	60	..
Environment			
Forests (1,000 sq. km)	615	552	..
Deforestation (average annual %, 1990–2000)		1.1	
Freshwater use (% of internal resources)			19
Carbon dioxide emissions (metric tons per capita)	3.7	4.3	..
Access to improved water source (% of total pop.)	80	91	..
Access to improved sanitation (% of urban pop.)	84	90	..
Energy use per capita (kg oil equivalent)	1,491	1,560	..
Electricity use per capita (kilowatt-hours)	1,204	1,660	..
Economy			
GDP ($ billions)	263	648	626
GDP growth (annual %)	5.1	0.7	1.3
GDP implicit price deflator (annual % growth)	28.1	6.9	6.5
Value added in agriculture (% of GDP)	8	4	4
Value added in industry (% of GDP)	28	26	26
Value added in services (% of GDP)	64	70	70
Exports of goods and services (% of GDP)	19	27	28
Imports of goods and services (% of GDP)	20	29	30
Gross capital formation (% of GDP)	23	21	20
Central government revenue (% of GDP)	15.3	14.7	..
Cash surplus/deficit (% of GDP)	–2.5	–1.2	..
Technology and infrastructure			
Fixed-line and mobile subscribers (per 1,000 people)	66	401	449
Cost of 3-minute local call ($)	0.11	0.16	..
Personal computers (per 1,000 people)	8.2	82.0	..
Internet users (per 1,000 people)	0	98	118
Paved roads (% of total)	35.1	32.8	..
Aircraft departures (thousands)	177	279	287
Trade and finance			
Trade in goods (% of GDP)	32.1	52.0	54.9
Trade growth less GDP growth (avg. %, 1990–2003)			8.6
High-technology exports (% of manufactured exports)	8	21	21
Net barter terms of trade (2000 = 100)	102	100	..
Foreign direct investment ($ billions)	3	15	11
Present value of debt ($ billions)			157
Total debt service (% of goods and services exports)	20.7	22.7	20.9
Short-term debt ($ billions)	16	10	9
Aid per capita ($)	2	1	1

Micronesia, Fed. Sts.

East Asia & Pacific   **Lower middle income**

Population (thousands)	125	Population growth (%)	1.8
Surface area (sq. km)	702	National poverty rate (% pop.)	..
GNI ($ millions)	258	GNI per capita ($)	2,070

	1990	2002	2003
People			
Life expectancy at birth (years)	63	69	69
Fertility rate (births per woman)	4.8	3.5	3.4
Infant mortality rate (per 1,000 live births)	26	20	19
Under-five mortality rate (per 1,000)	31	24	23
Births attended by skilled health staff (% of total)	..	93	..
Child malnutrition, underweight (% of under age 5)	..	..	..
Child immunization, measles (% of ages 12–23 mon.)	81	86	91
HIV prevalence rate (% of ages 15–49)	..	..	..
Adult literacy, male (% of ages 15 and older)	..	..	..
Adult literacy, female (% of ages 15 and older)	..	..	..
Primary completion rate, total (% of age group)	..	..	..
Primary completion rate, female (% of age group)	..	..	..
Net primary enrollment (% of age group)	..	..	..
Net secondary enrollment (% of age group)	..	..	..
Environment			
Forests (1,000 sq. km)	..	..	
Deforestation (average annual %, 1990–2000)		..	
Freshwater use (% of internal resources)			..
Carbon dioxide emissions (metric tons per capita)	..	..	
Access to improved water source (% of total pop.)	87	94	..
Access to improved sanitation (% of urban pop.)	53	61	..
Energy use per capita (kg oil equivalent)	..	..	..
Electricity use per capita (kilowatt-hours)	..	..	..
Economy			
GDP ($ millions)	147	228	243
GDP growth (annual %)	3.7	0.8	2.4
GDP implicit price deflator (annual % growth)	4.9	0.0	1.5
Value added in agriculture (% of GDP)	..	..	..
Value added in industry (% of GDP)	..	..	..
Value added in services (% of GDP)	..	..	..
Exports of goods and services (% of GDP)	..	..	..
Imports of goods and services (% of GDP)	..	..	..
Gross capital formation (% of GDP)	..	..	..
Central government revenue (% of GDP)	..	..	..
Cash surplus/deficit (% of GDP)	..	..	..
Technology and infrastructure			
Fixed-line and mobile subscribers (per 1,000 people)	25	87	158
Cost of 3-minute local call ($)	0.00	0.00	0.00
Personal computers (per 1,000 people)	..	..	..
Internet users (per 1,000 people)	..	35	93
Paved roads (% of total)	15.9	17.5	..
Aircraft departures (thousands)	..	..	..
Trade and finance			
Trade in goods (% of GDP)	..	47.9	39.1
Trade growth less GDP growth (avg. %, 1990–2003)			..
High-technology exports (% of manufactured exports)	..	..	..
Net barter terms of trade (2000 = 100)	..	..	..
Foreign direct investment ($ millions)	..	..	..
Present value of debt ($ millions)			..
Total debt service (% of goods and services exports)	..	..	..
Short-term debt ($ millions)	..	..	..
Aid per capita ($)	5	913	923

Moldova

Europe & Central Asia		Low income

Population (millions)	4	Population growth (%)	–0.4
Surface area (1,000 sq. km)	34	National poverty rate (% pop.)	23
GNI ($ millions)	2,137	GNI per capita ($)	590

	1990	2002	2003
People			
Life expectancy at birth (years)	68	67	67
Fertility rate (births per woman)	2.4	1.4	1.4
Infant mortality rate (per 1,000 live births)	30	27	26
Under-five mortality rate (per 1,000)	37	33	32
Births attended by skilled health staff (% of total)	..	99	..
Child malnutrition, underweight (% of under age 5)	..	..	..
Child immunization, measles (% of ages 12–23 mon.)	92	94	96
HIV prevalence rate (% of ages 15–49)	..	..	0.2
Adult literacy, male (% of ages 15 and older)	99	100	..
Adult literacy, female (% of ages 15 and older)	96	99	..
Primary completion rate, total (% of age group)	..	83	83
Primary completion rate, female (% of age group)	..	83	..
Net primary enrollment (% of age group)	89	79	..
Net secondary enrollment (% of age group)	..	69	..
Environment			
Forests (1,000 sq. km)	3	3	..
Deforestation (average annual %, 1990–2000)		–0.2	
Freshwater use (% of internal resources)			300
Carbon dioxide emissions (metric tons per capita)	4.8	1.5	..
Access to improved water source (% of total pop.)	..	92	..
Access to improved sanitation (% of urban pop.)	..	86	..
Energy use per capita (kg oil equivalent)	1,582	703	..
Electricity use per capita (kilowatt-hours)	1,886	909	..
Economy			
GDP ($ millions)	3,549	1,662	1,964
GDP growth (annual %)	–2.4	7.8	6.3
GDP implicit price deflator (annual % growth)	142.8	10.0	13.9
Value added in agriculture (% of GDP)	43	24	23
Value added in industry (% of GDP)	8	23	25
Value added in services (% of GDP)	5	53	53
Exports of goods and services (% of GDP)	49	52	54
Imports of goods and services (% of GDP)	51	77	88
Gross capital formation (% of GDP)	25	22	22
Central government revenue (% of GDP)	..	24.8	27.0
Cash surplus/deficit (% of GDP)	..	1.0	2.0
Technology and infrastructure			
Fixed-line and mobile subscribers (per 1,000 people)	106	238	351
Cost of 3-minute local call ($)	..	0.02	0.02
Personal computers (per 1,000 people)	..	17.5	..
Internet users (per 1,000 people)	..	41	80
Paved roads (% of total)	87.1	86.3	..
Aircraft departures (thousands)	..	4	4
Trade and finance			
Trade in goods (% of GDP)	..	101.2	111.5
Trade growth less GDP growth (avg. %, 1990–2003)			11.9
High-technology exports (% of manufactured exports)	..	4	3
Net barter terms of trade (2000 = 100)	..	..	..
Foreign direct investment ($ millions)	0	117	58
Present value of debt ($ millions)			1,808
Total debt service (% of goods and services exports)	..	20.5	10.4
Short-term debt ($ millions)	0	489	541
Aid per capita ($)	2	33	28

Monaco

High income

Population (thousands)	33	Population growth (%) ..
Surface area (sq. km)	2	National poverty rate (% pop.) ..
GNI ($ millions)	..	GNI per capita ($) ..

	1990	2002	2003
People			
Life expectancy at birth (years)	..	..	..
Fertility rate (births per woman)	..	..	..
Infant mortality rate (per 1,000 live births)	..	4	4
Under-five mortality rate (per 1,000)	..	5	4
Births attended by skilled health staff (% of total)	..	..	..
Child malnutrition, underweight (% of under age 5)	..	..	..
Child immunization, measles (% of ages 12–23 mon.)	99	99	99
HIV prevalence rate (% of ages 15–49)	..	..	..
Adult literacy, male (% of ages 15 and older)	..	..	..
Adult literacy, female (% of ages 15 and older)	..	..	..
Primary completion rate, total (% of age group)	..	..	..
Primary completion rate, female (% of age group)	..	..	..
Net primary enrollment (% of age group)	..	..	..
Net secondary enrollment (% of age group)	..	..	..
Environment			
Forests (1,000 sq. km)	..	..	..
Deforestation (average annual %, 1990–2000)		..	
Freshwater use (% of internal resources)			..
Carbon dioxide emissions (metric tons per capita)	..	..	
Access to improved water source (% of total pop.)	..	..	
Access to improved sanitation (% of urban pop.)	100	100	..
Energy use per capita (kg oil equivalent)	..	..	..
Electricity use per capita (kilowatt-hours)	..	..	..
Economy			
GDP ($ millions)	..	..	..
GDP growth (annual %)	..	..	..
GDP implicit price deflator (annual % growth)	..	..	..
Value added in agriculture (% of GDP)	..	..	..
Value added in industry (% of GDP)	..	..	..
Value added in services (% of GDP)	..	..	..
Exports of goods and services (% of GDP)	..	..	..
Imports of goods and services (% of GDP)	..	..	..
Gross capital formation (% of GDP)	..	..	..
Central government revenue (% of GDP)	..	..	..
Cash surplus/deficit (% of GDP)	..	..	..
Technology and infrastructure			
Fixed-line and mobile subscribers (per 1,000 people)	815	1,636	..
Cost of 3-minute local call ($)	..	0.11	..
Personal computers (per 1,000 people)	..	..	..
Internet users (per 1,000 people)	..	422	..
Paved roads (% of total)	100.0	100.0	..
Aircraft departures (thousands)	13	15	14
Trade and finance			
Trade in goods (% of GDP)	..	..	..
Trade growth less GDP growth (avg. %, 1990–2003)			..
High-technology exports (% of manufactured exports)	..	..	..
Net barter terms of trade (2000 = 100)	..	..	..
Foreign direct investment ($ millions)	..	..	..
Present value of debt ($ millions)			..
Total debt service (% of goods and services exports)	..	..	..
Short-term debt ($ millions)	..	..	..
Aid per capita ($)	..	..	..

Mongolia

Population (millions)	2	Population growth (%)	1.3
Surface area (1,000 sq. km)	1,567	National poverty rate (% pop.)	36
GNI ($ millions)	1,188	GNI per capita ($)	480

	1990	2002	2003
People			
Life expectancy at birth (years)	63	65	66
Fertility rate (births per woman)	4.0	2.4	2.4
Infant mortality rate (per 1,000 live births)	74	60	56
Under-five mortality rate (per 1,000)	104	75	68
Births attended by skilled health staff (% of total)	..	97	99
Child malnutrition, underweight (% of under age 5)	12	13	..
Child immunization, measles (% of ages 12–23 mon.)	92	98	98
HIV prevalence rate (% of ages 15–49)	..	0.1	0.1
Adult literacy, male (% of ages 15 and older)	98	98	..
Adult literacy, female (% of ages 15 and older)	97	98	..
Primary completion rate, total (% of age group)	..	108	..
Primary completion rate, female (% of age group)	..	111	..
Net primary enrollment (% of age group)	90	79	..
Net secondary enrollment (% of age group)	..	77	..
Environment			
Forests (1,000 sq. km)	112	106	..
Deforestation (average annual %, 1990–2000)		0.5	
Freshwater use (% of internal resources)			1
Carbon dioxide emissions (metric tons per capita)	4.7	3.1	..
Access to improved water source (% of total pop.)	62	62	..
Access to improved sanitation (% of urban pop.)	..	75	..
Energy use per capita (kg oil equivalent)	..	..	..
Electricity use per capita (kilowatt-hours)	..	..	..
Economy			
GDP ($ millions)	..	1,118	1,274
GDP growth (annual %)	-2.5	4.0	5.6
GDP implicit price deflator (annual % growth)	0.0	3.7	4.7
Value added in agriculture (% of GDP)	17	30	28
Value added in industry (% of GDP)	30	16	15
Value added in services (% of GDP)	52	54	57
Exports of goods and services (% of GDP)	24	67	68
Imports of goods and services (% of GDP)	53	81	80
Gross capital formation (% of GDP)	38	31	31
Central government revenue (% of GDP)	..	..	37.9
Cash surplus/deficit (% of GDP)	..	..	–0.5
Technology and infrastructure			
Fixed-line and mobile subscribers (per 1,000 people)	32	142	186
Cost of 3-minute local call ($)	..	0.02	0.02
Personal computers (per 1,000 people)	..	28.4	77.3
Internet users (per 1,000 people)	..	21	58
Paved roads (% of total)	10.2	3.5	..
Aircraft departures (thousands)	10	6	7
Trade and finance			
Trade in goods (% of GDP)	..	102.1	102.2
Trade growth less GDP growth (avg. %, 1990–2003)			..
High-technology exports (% of manufactured exports)	..	0	0
Net barter terms of trade (2000 = 100)	..	..	..
Foreign direct investment ($ millions)	0	78	132
Present value of debt ($ millions)			1,095
Total debt service (% of goods and services exports)	17.3	6.7	32.3
Short-term debt ($ millions)	59	44	285
Aid per capita ($)	6	85	100

Morocco

Middle East & North Africa		Lower middle income	

Population (millions)	30	Population growth (%)	1.6
Surface area (1,000 sq. km)	447	National poverty rate (% pop.)	19
GNI ($ billions)	39	GNI per capita ($)	1,310

	1990	2002	2003
People			
Life expectancy at birth (years)	63	68	69
Fertility rate (births per woman)	4.0	2.8	2.7
Infant mortality rate (per 1,000 live births)	66	*41*	36
Under-five mortality rate (per 1,000)	85	*46*	39
Births attended by skilled health staff (% of total)	*31*	..	..
Child malnutrition, underweight (% of under age 5)	10	9	..
Child immunization, measles (% of ages 12–23 mon.)	80	96	90
HIV prevalence rate (% of ages 15–49)	..	..	0.1
Adult literacy, male (% of ages 15 and older)	53	63	..
Adult literacy, female (% of ages 15 and older)	25	38	..
Primary completion rate, total (% of age group)	47	68	75
Primary completion rate, female (% of age group)	38	63	72
Net primary enrollment (% of age group)	57	90	..
Net secondary enrollment (% of age group)	..	36	..
Environment			
Forests (1,000 sq. km)	30	*30*	..
Deforestation (average annual %, 1990–2000)		*0.0*	
Freshwater use (% of internal resources)			40
Carbon dioxide emissions (metric tons per capita)	1.0	*1.3*	..
Access to improved water source (% of total pop.)	75	80	..
Access to improved sanitation (% of urban pop.)	87	83	..
Energy use per capita (kg oil equivalent)	280	363	..
Electricity use per capita (kilowatt-hours)	340	475	..
Economy			
GDP ($ billions)	26	36	44
GDP growth (annual %)	4.0	3.2	5.2
GDP implicit price deflator (annual % growth)	5.5	0.6	0.0
Value added in agriculture (% of GDP)	18	16	17
Value added in industry (% of GDP)	32	30	30
Value added in services (% of GDP)	50	54	54
Exports of goods and services (% of GDP)	26	34	32
Imports of goods and services (% of GDP)	32	37	36
Gross capital formation (% of GDP)	25	23	24
Central government revenue (% of GDP)	26.4	*29.6*	..
Cash surplus/deficit (% of GDP)	–2.2	–2.7	..
Technology and infrastructure			
Fixed-line and mobile subscribers (per 1,000 people)	16	247	284
Cost of 3-minute local call ($)	*0.09*	0.15	0.17
Personal computers (per 1,000 people)	..	23.6	19.9
Internet users (per 1,000 people)	..	24	33
Paved roads (% of total)	49.1	56.4	..
Aircraft departures (thousands)	27	38	35
Trade and finance			
Trade in goods (% of GDP)	43.3	54.7	52.3
Trade growth less GDP growth (avg. %, 1990–2003)			2.5
High-technology exports (% of manufactured exports)	..	11	11
Net barter terms of trade (2000 = 100)	85	107	..
Foreign direct investment ($ millions)	165	481	2,279
Present value of debt ($ billions)			18
Total debt service (% of goods and services exports)	21.5	24.0	23.5
Short-term debt ($ millions)	407	1,703	1,253
Aid per capita ($)	44	16	17

Mozambique

Sub-Saharan Africa			Low income
Population (millions)	19	Population growth (%)	1.9
Surface area (1,000 sq. km)	802	National poverty rate (% pop.)	69
GNI ($ millions)	3,906	GNI per capita ($)	210

	1990	2002	2003
People			
Life expectancy at birth (years)	43	41	41
Fertility rate (births per woman)	6.3	5.0	5.0
Infant mortality rate (per 1,000 live births)	146	110	101
Under-five mortality rate (per 1,000)	242	167	147
Births attended by skilled health staff (% of total)	..	44	48
Child malnutrition, underweight (% of under age 5)	..	26	..
Child immunization, measles (% of ages 12–23 mon.)	59	77	77
HIV prevalence rate (% of ages 15–49)	..	12.1	12.2
Adult literacy, male (% of ages 15 and older)	49	62	..
Adult literacy, female (% of ages 15 and older)	18	31	..
Primary completion rate, total (% of age group)	28	48	52
Primary completion rate, female (% of age group)	22	38	45
Net primary enrollment (% of age group)	45	55	..
Net secondary enrollment (% of age group)	..	12	..
Environment			
Forests (1,000 sq. km)	312	306	..
Deforestation (average annual %, 1990–2000)		0.2	
Freshwater use (% of internal resources)			1
Carbon dioxide emissions (metric tons per capita)	0.1	0.1	..
Access to improved water source (% of total pop.)	..	42	..
Access to improved sanitation (% of urban pop.)	..	51	..
Energy use per capita (kg oil equivalent)	509	436	..
Electricity use per capita (kilowatt-hours)	35	341	..
Economy			
GDP ($ millions)	2,463	3,599	4,321
GDP growth (annual %)	1.0	7.4	7.1
GDP implicit price deflator (annual % growth)	34.1	11.5	12.6
Value added in agriculture (% of GDP)	37	27	26
Value added in industry (% of GDP)	18	29	31
Value added in services (% of GDP)	44	45	43
Exports of goods and services (% of GDP)	8	24	23
Imports of goods and services (% of GDP)	36	38	39
Gross capital formation (% of GDP)	22	30	28
Central government revenue (% of GDP)	..	..	..
Cash surplus/deficit (% of GDP)	..	..	..
Technology and infrastructure			
Fixed-line and mobile subscribers (per 1,000 people)	3	19	..
Cost of 3-minute local call ($)	0.06	0.08	..
Personal computers (per 1,000 people)	..	4.5	..
Internet users (per 1,000 people)		3	..
Paved roads (% of total)	16.8	18.7	..
Aircraft departures (thousands)	6	8	8
Trade and finance			
Trade in goods (% of GDP)	40.8	56.5	52.0
Trade growth less GDP growth (avg. %, 1990–2003)			0.0
High-technology exports (% of manufactured exports)	..	3	..
Net barter terms of trade (2000 = 100)	175	101	..
Foreign direct investment ($ millions)	9	348	337
Present value of debt ($ millions)			1,352
Total debt service (% of goods and services exports)	26.2	6.9	6.9
Short-term debt ($ millions)	345	371	340
Aid per capita ($)	71	111	55

Myanmar

East Asia & Pacific **Low income**

Population (millions)	49	Population growth (%)	1.2
Surface area (1,000 sq. km)	677	National poverty rate (% pop.)	..
GNI ($ millions)	..	GNI per capita ($)	..

	1990	2002	2003
People			
Life expectancy at birth (years)	55	57	57
Fertility rate (births per woman)	3.8	2.8	2.8
Infant mortality rate (per 1,000 live births)	91	*78*	76
Under-five mortality rate (per 1,000)	130	*110*	107
Births attended by skilled health staff (% of total)	..	56	..
Child malnutrition, underweight (% of under age 5)	32	*28*	..
Child immunization, measles (% of ages 12–23 mon.)	90	75	75
HIV prevalence rate (% of ages 15–49)	..	*1.0*	1.2
Adult literacy, male (% of ages 15 and older)	87	89	..
Adult literacy, female (% of ages 15 and older)	74	81	..
Primary completion rate, total (% of age group)	..	73	..
Primary completion rate, female (% of age group)	..	73	..
Net primary enrollment (% of age group)	98	84	..
Net secondary enrollment (% of age group)	..	35	..
Environment			
Forests (1,000 sq. km)	396	*344*	..
Deforestation (average annual %, 1990–2000)		*1.4*	
Freshwater use (% of internal resources)			0
Carbon dioxide emissions (metric tons per capita)	0.1	*0.2*	..
Access to improved water source (% of total pop.)	48	80	..
Access to improved sanitation (% of urban pop.)	39	96	..
Energy use per capita (kg oil equivalent)	264	258	..
Electricity use per capita (kilowatt-hours)	43	108	..
Economy			
GDP ($ millions)	..	..	..
GDP growth (annual %)	..	..	..
GDP implicit price deflator (annual % growth)	18.5	*22.6*	..
Value added in agriculture (% of GDP)	57	*57*	..
Value added in industry (% of GDP)	11	*10*	..
Value added in services (% of GDP)	32	*33*	..
Exports of goods and services (% of GDP)	3	*0*	..
Imports of goods and services (% of GDP)	5	*1*	..
Gross capital formation (% of GDP)	13	15	..
Central government revenue (% of GDP)	10.5	*4.7*	..
Cash surplus/deficit (% of GDP)	..	..	..
Technology and infrastructure			
Fixed-line and mobile subscribers (per 1,000 people)	2	8	8
Cost of 3-minute local call ($)	*0.16*	0.05	0.06
Personal computers (per 1,000 people)	..	5.1	5.6
Internet users (per 1,000 people)	..	1	1
Paved roads (% of total)	10.9	..	..
Aircraft departures (thousands)	14	21	21
Trade and finance			
Trade in goods (% of GDP)	..	..	..
Trade growth less GDP growth (avg. %, 1990–2003)			..
High-technology exports (% of manufactured exports)	0	..	..
Net barter terms of trade (2000 = 100)	252	*140*	..
Foreign direct investment ($ millions)	163	191	134
Present value of debt ($ millions)			5,542
Total debt service (% of goods and services exports)	18.4	3.7	4.2
Short-term debt ($ millions)	229	1,192	1,461
Aid per capita ($)	4	2	3

Namibia

Sub-Saharan Africa		Lower middle income	
Population (millions)	2	Population growth (%)	1.5
Surface area (1,000 sq. km)	824	National poverty rate (% pop.)	..
GNI ($ millions)	3,883	GNI per capita ($)	1,930

	1990	2002	2003
People			
Life expectancy at birth (years)	58	42	40
Fertility rate (births per woman)	5.4	4.8	4.8
Infant mortality rate (per 1,000 live births)	60	50	48
Under-five mortality rate (per 1,000)	86	69	65
Births attended by skilled health staff (% of total)	68	78	..
Child malnutrition, underweight (% of under age 5)	26	24	..
Child immunization, measles (% of ages 12–23 mon.)	76	68	70
HIV prevalence rate (% of ages 15–49)	..	21.3	21.3
Adult literacy, male (% of ages 15 and older)	77	84	..
Adult literacy, female (% of ages 15 and older)	72	83	..
Primary completion rate, total (% of age group)	77	92	..
Primary completion rate, female (% of age group)	85	94	..
Net primary enrollment (% of age group)	83	78	..
Net secondary enrollment (% of age group)	..	44	..
Environment			
Forests (1,000 sq. km)	88	80	..
Deforestation (average annual %, 1990–2000)		0.9	
Freshwater use (% of internal resources)			3
Carbon dioxide emissions (metric tons per capita)	0.0	1.0	..
Access to improved water source (% of total pop.)	58	80	..
Access to improved sanitation (% of urban pop.)	68	66	..
Energy use per capita (kg oil equivalent)	445	599	..
Electricity use per capita (kilowatt-hours)	..	..	..
Economy			
GDP ($ millions)	2,350	2,993	4,271
GDP growth (annual %)	2.5	2.5	3.7
GDP implicit price deflator (annual % growth)	4.3	11.2	–1.3
Value added in agriculture (% of GDP)	12	11	11
Value added in industry (% of GDP)	38	30	26
Value added in services (% of GDP)	50	59	64
Exports of goods and services (% of GDP)	52	46	39
Imports of goods and services (% of GDP)	67	50	47
Gross capital formation (% of GDP)	34	17	23
Central government revenue (% of GDP)	31.3	32.7	..
Cash surplus/deficit (% of GDP)	–2.6	–1.0	..
Technology and infrastructure			
Fixed-line and mobile subscribers (per 1,000 people)	39	145	182
Cost of 3-minute local call ($)	0.06	0.03	0.04
Personal computers (per 1,000 people)	..	70.9	99.3
Internet users (per 1,000 people)	..	27	34
Paved roads (% of total)	10.8	12.8	..
Aircraft departures (thousands)	8	5	6
Trade and finance			
Trade in goods (% of GDP)	95.6	86.2	76.4
Trade growth less GDP growth (avg. %, 1990–2003)			0.1
High-technology exports (% of manufactured exports)	..	2	3
Net barter terms of trade (2000 = 100)	93	99	..
Foreign direct investment ($ millions)	..	..	..
Present value of debt ($ millions)			..
Total debt service (% of goods and services exports)	..	..	..
Short-term debt ($ millions)	..	..	..
Aid per capita ($)	86	68	73

Nepal

South Asia		**Low income**

Population (millions)	25	Population growth (%)	2.2
Surface area (1,000 sq. km)	147	National poverty rate (% pop.)	..
GNI ($ millions)	5,868	GNI per capita ($)	240

	1990	2002	2003
People			
Life expectancy at birth (years)	54	60	60
Fertility rate (births per woman)	5.3	4.2	4.1
Infant mortality rate (per 1,000 live births)	100	69	61
Under-five mortality rate (per 1,000)	145	95	82
Births attended by skilled health staff (% of total)	7	11	..
Child malnutrition, underweight (% of under age 5)	..	48	..
Child immunization, measles (% of ages 12–23 mon.)	57	71	75
HIV prevalence rate (% of ages 15–49)	..	0.4	0.5
Adult literacy, male (% of ages 15 and older)	47	62	..
Adult literacy, female (% of ages 15 and older)	14	26	..
Primary completion rate, total (% of age group)	55	78	..
Primary completion rate, female (% of age group)	45	72	..
Net primary enrollment (% of age group)	81	70	..
Net secondary enrollment (% of age group)	..	..	..
Environment			
Forests (1,000 sq. km)	47	39	..
Deforestation (average annual %, 1990–2000)		1.8	
Freshwater use (% of internal resources)			15
Carbon dioxide emissions (metric tons per capita)	0.0	0.1	..
Access to improved water source (% of total pop.)	69	84	..
Access to improved sanitation (% of urban pop.)	62	68	..
Energy use per capita (kg oil equivalent)	320	353	..
Electricity use per capita (kilowatt-hours)	33	64	..
Economy			
GDP ($ millions)	3,628	5,562	5,851
GDP growth (annual %)	4.5	–0.6	3.1
GDP implicit price deflator (annual % growth)	10.7	3.4	4.5
Value added in agriculture (% of GDP)	52	41	41
Value added in industry (% of GDP)	16	22	22
Value added in services (% of GDP)	32	38	38
Exports of goods and services (% of GDP)	11	18	17
Imports of goods and services (% of GDP)	22	29	29
Gross capital formation (% of GDP)	18	24	26
Central government revenue (% of GDP)	8.4	11.4	11.6
Cash surplus/deficit (% of GDP)	..	..	..
Technology and infrastructure			
Fixed-line and mobile subscribers (per 1,000 people)	3	15	18
Cost of 3-minute local call ($)	0.05	0.01	0.01
Personal computers (per 1,000 people)	..	3.7	..
Internet users (per 1,000 people)	0	3	..
Paved roads (% of total)	37.5	30.8	..
Aircraft departures (thousands)	26	13	13
Trade and finance			
Trade in goods (% of GDP)	24.1	35.7	41.3
Trade growth less GDP growth (avg. %, 1990–2003)			..
High-technology exports (% of manufactured exports)	..	0	..
Net barter terms of trade (2000 = 100)	..	..	..
Foreign direct investment ($ millions)	0	–6	15
Present value of debt ($ millions)			2,134
Total debt service (% of goods and services exports)	15.7	6.2	6.0
Short-term debt ($ millions)	24	40	66
Aid per capita ($)	23	15	19

Netherlands

		High income
Population (millions)	16	Population growth (%)	0.5
Surface area (1,000 sq. km)	42	National poverty rate (% pop.)	..
GNI ($ billions)	426	GNI per capita ($)	26,230

	1990	2002	2003
People			
Life expectancy at birth (years)	77	78	78
Fertility rate (births per woman)	1.6	1.7	1.8
Infant mortality rate (per 1,000 live births)	7	5	5
Under-five mortality rate (per 1,000)	9	6	6
Births attended by skilled health staff (% of total)	..	100	..
Child malnutrition, underweight (% of under age 5)	..	..	..
Child immunization, measles (% of ages 12–23 mon.)	94	96	96
HIV prevalence rate (% of ages 15–49)	..	0.2	0.2
Adult literacy, male (% of ages 15 and older)	..	..	..
Adult literacy, female (% of ages 15 and older)	..	..	..
Primary completion rate, total (% of age group)	..	98	..
Primary completion rate, female (% of age group)	..	98	..
Net primary enrollment (% of age group)	95	99	..
Net secondary enrollment (% of age group)	84	90	..
Environment			
Forests (1,000 sq. km)	4	4	..
Deforestation (average annual %, 1990–2000)		–0.3	
Freshwater use (% of internal resources)			71
Carbon dioxide emissions (metric tons per capita)	10.0	8.7	..
Access to improved water source (% of total pop.)	100	100	..
Access to improved sanitation (% of urban pop.)	100	100	..
Energy use per capita (kg oil equivalent)	4,447	4,827	..
Electricity use per capita (kilowatt-hours)	4,917	6,179	..
Economy			
GDP ($ billions)	295	418	512
GDP growth (annual %)	4.1	0.2	–0.9
GDP implicit price deflator (annual % growth)	2.2	3.4	..
Value added in agriculture (% of GDP)	4	3	..
Value added in industry (% of GDP)	31	26	..
Value added in services (% of GDP)	65	72	..
Exports of goods and services (% of GDP)	54	63	..
Imports of goods and services (% of GDP)	51	58	..
Gross capital formation (% of GDP)	23	21	..
Central government revenue (% of GDP)	..	40.8	40.6
Cash surplus/deficit (% of GDP)	..	–1.5	–3.0
Technology and infrastructure			
Fixed-line and mobile subscribers (per 1,000 people)	469	1,362	1,382
Cost of 3-minute local call ($)	0.15	0.11	..
Personal computers (per 1,000 people)	93.6	466.6	..
Internet users (per 1,000 people)	3	506	522
Paved roads (% of total)	88.0	90.0	..
Aircraft departures (thousands)	115	250	248
Trade and finance			
Trade in goods (% of GDP)	87.5	110.7	108.9
Trade growth less GDP growth (avg. %, 1990–2003)			3.7
High-technology exports (% of manufactured exports)	16	28	31
Net barter terms of trade (2000 = 100)	99	96	97
Foreign direct investment ($ billions)	11	29	16
Present value of debt ($ millions)			..
Total debt service (% of goods and services exports)	..	..	..
Short-term debt ($ millions)	..	..	..
Aid per capita ($)	..	..	..

Netherlands Antilles

Population (thousands)	220	Population growth (%)	0.8
Surface area (sq. km)	800	National poverty rate (% pop.)	..
GNI ($ millions)	..	GNI per capita ($)	..

	1990	2002	2003
People			
Life expectancy at birth (years)	74	76	76
Fertility rate (births per woman)	2.3	2.1	2.1
Infant mortality rate (per 1,000 live births)	8	..	..
Under-five mortality rate (per 1,000)	..	..	..
Births attended by skilled health staff (% of total)	..	..	..
Child malnutrition, underweight (% of under age 5)	..	..	..
Child immunization, measles (% of ages 12–23 mon.)	..	..	..
HIV prevalence rate (% of ages 15–49)	..	..	..
Adult literacy, male (% of ages 15 and older)	96	97	..
Adult literacy, female (% of ages 15 and older)	96	97	..
Primary completion rate, total (% of age group)	..	88	..
Primary completion rate, female (% of age group)	..	94	..
Net primary enrollment (% of age group)	..	88	..
Net secondary enrollment (% of age group)	..	63	..
Environment			
Forests (1,000 sq. km)	0	0	..
Deforestation (average annual %, 1990–2000)		0.0	
Freshwater use (% of internal resources)			..
Carbon dioxide emissions (metric tons per capita)	20.5	46.2	..
Access to improved water source (% of total pop.)	..	..	..
Access to improved sanitation (% of urban pop.)	..	..	..
Energy use per capita (kg oil equivalent)	7,879	6,782	..
Electricity use per capita (kilowatt-hours)	3,182	3,817	..
Economy			
GDP ($ millions)	..	..	..
GDP growth (annual %)	..	..	..
GDP implicit price deflator (annual % growth)	..	..	..
Value added in agriculture (% of GDP)	..	..	..
Value added in industry (% of GDP)	..	..	..
Value added in services (% of GDP)	..	..	..
Exports of goods and services (% of GDP)	..	..	..
Imports of goods and services (% of GDP)	..	..	..
Gross capital formation (% of GDP)	..	..	..
Central government revenue (% of GDP)	..	..	..
Cash surplus/deficit (% of GDP)	..	..	..
Technology and infrastructure			
Fixed-line and mobile subscribers (per 1,000 people)	..	442	..
Cost of 3-minute local call ($)	..	..	..
Personal computers (per 1,000 people)	..	..	..
Internet users (per 1,000 people)	..	9	..
Paved roads (% of total)	..	..	..
Aircraft departures (thousands)	..	..	..
Trade and finance			
Trade in goods (% of GDP)	..	..	..
Trade growth less GDP growth (avg. %, 1990–2003)			..
High-technology exports (% of manufactured exports)	..	..	..
Net barter terms of trade (2000 = 100)	..	..	..
Foreign direct investment ($ millions)	8	8	–81
Present value of debt ($ millions)			..
Total debt service (% of goods and services exports)	..	..	..
Short-term debt ($ millions)	..	..	..
Aid per capita ($)	307	424	158

New Caledonia

High income

Population (thousands)	225	Population growth (%)	1.8
Surface area (1,000 sq. km)	19	National poverty rate (% pop.)	..
GNI ($ millions)	..	GNI per capita ($)	..

	1990	2002	2003
People			
Life expectancy at birth (years)	71	74	74
Fertility rate (births per woman)	2.9	2.5	2.5
Infant mortality rate (per 1,000 live births)	..	..	..
Under-five mortality rate (per 1,000)	..	..	..
Births attended by skilled health staff (% of total)	..	..	..
Child malnutrition, underweight (% of under age 5)	..	..	..
Child immunization, measles (% of ages 12–23 mon.)	..	..	..
HIV prevalence rate (% of ages 15–49)	..	..	..
Adult literacy, male (% of ages 15 and older)	..	..	..
Adult literacy, female (% of ages 15 and older)	..	..	..
Primary completion rate, total (% of age group)	..	..	..
Primary completion rate, female (% of age group)	..	..	..
Net primary enrollment (% of age group)	..	..	..
Net secondary enrollment (% of age group)	..	..	..
Environment			
Forests (1,000 sq. km)	4	4	..
Deforestation (average annual %, 1990–2000)		0.0	
Freshwater use (% of internal resources)			..
Carbon dioxide emissions (metric tons per capita)	9.6	7.8	..
Access to improved water source (% of total pop.)	..	..	..
Access to improved sanitation (% of urban pop.)	..	..	..
Energy use per capita (kg oil equivalent)	..	..	..
Electricity use per capita (kilowatt-hours)	..	..	..
Economy			
GDP ($ millions)	2,529	2,682	..
GDP growth (annual %)	3.6	2.1	..
GDP implicit price deflator (annual % growth)	–4.6	–0.6	..
Value added in agriculture (% of GDP)	4	4	..
Value added in industry (% of GDP)	23	20	..
Value added in services (% of GDP)	73	77	..
Exports of goods and services (% of GDP)	18	13	..
Imports of goods and services (% of GDP)	35	33	..
Gross capital formation (% of GDP)	31	..	..
Central government revenue (% of GDP)	..	..	..
Cash surplus/deficit (% of GDP)	..	..	..
Technology and infrastructure			
Fixed-line and mobile subscribers (per 1,000 people)	168	589	651
Cost of 3-minute local call ($)	0.31	0.27	..
Personal computers (per 1,000 people)	..	..	..
Internet users (per 1,000 people)	..	223	262
Paved roads (% of total)	..	..	..
Aircraft departures (thousands)	..	..	..
Trade and finance			
Trade in goods (% of GDP)	52.7	61.6	..
Trade growth less GDP growth (avg. %, 1990–2003)			..
High-technology exports (% of manufactured exports)	..	1	1
Net barter terms of trade (2000 = 100)	..	..	..
Foreign direct investment ($ millions)	..	..	..
Present value of debt ($ millions)			..
Total debt service (% of goods and services exports)	..	..	..
Short-term debt ($ millions)	..	..	..
Aid per capita ($)	1,800	1,469	2,022

New Zealand

High income

Population (millions)	4	Population growth (%)		1.8
Surface area (1,000 sq. km)	271	National poverty rate (% pop.)		..
GNI ($ billions)	62	GNI per capita ($)		15,530

	1990	2002	2003
People			
Life expectancy at birth (years)	75	79	79
Fertility rate (births per woman)	2.2	1.9	1.9
Infant mortality rate (per 1,000 live births)	10	6	5
Under-five mortality rate (per 1,000)	11	6	6
Births attended by skilled health staff (% of total)	..	..	..
Child malnutrition, underweight (% of under age 5)	..	..	..
Child immunization, measles (% of ages 12–23 mon.)	90	85	85
HIV prevalence rate (% of ages 15–49)	..	0.1	0.1
Adult literacy, male (% of ages 15 and older)	..	..	..
Adult literacy, female (% of ages 15 and older)	..	..	..
Primary completion rate, total (% of age group)	98	96	..
Primary completion rate, female (% of age group)	98	95	..
Net primary enrollment (% of age group)	100	100	..
Net secondary enrollment (% of age group)	85	93	..
Environment			
Forests (1,000 sq. km)	76	79	..
Deforestation (average annual %, 1990–2000)		–0.5	
Freshwater use (% of internal resources)			1
Carbon dioxide emissions (metric tons per capita)	6.8	8.3	..
Access to improved water source (% of total pop.)	97	..	..
Access to improved sanitation (% of urban pop.)	..	..	..
Energy use per capita (kg oil equivalent)	4,035	4,573	..
Electricity use per capita (kilowatt-hours)	8,060	8,832	..
Economy			
GDP ($ billions)	44	60	80
GDP growth (annual %)	–0.0	4.4	3.6
GDP implicit price deflator (annual % growth)	2.4	0.3	..
Value added in agriculture (% of GDP)	7	9	..
Value added in industry (% of GDP)	28	25	..
Value added in services (% of GDP)	65	66	..
Exports of goods and services (% of GDP)	27	32	..
Imports of goods and services (% of GDP)	27	31	..
Gross capital formation (% of GDP)	20	21	..
Central government revenue (% of GDP)	..	34.9	36.8
Cash surplus/deficit (% of GDP)	..	1.7	3.1
Technology and infrastructure			
Fixed-line and mobile subscribers (per 1,000 people)	450	1,070	1,097
Cost of 3-minute local call ($)	0.00	0.00	0.00
Personal computers (per 1,000 people)	96.9	413.8	..
Internet users (per 1,000 people)	3	484	526
Paved roads (% of total)	57.0	64.0	..
Aircraft departures (thousands)	128	243	247
Trade and finance			
Trade in goods (% of GDP)	43.3	49.1	44.0
Trade growth less GDP growth (avg. %, 1990–2003)			2.2
High-technology exports (% of manufactured exports)	4	10	10
Net barter terms of trade (2000 = 100)	100	100	100
Foreign direct investment ($ millions)	1,735	738	2,438
Present value of debt ($ millions)			..
Total debt service (% of goods and services exports)	..	..	..
Short-term debt ($ millions)	..	..	..
Aid per capita ($)	..	..	..

Nicaragua

Latin America & Caribbean		Low income
Population (millions)	5	Population growth (%)	2.6
Surface area (1,000 sq. km)	130	National poverty rate (% pop.)	48
GNI ($ millions)	4,082	GNI per capita ($)	740

	1990	2002	2003
People			
Life expectancy at birth (years)	64	69	69
Fertility rate (births per woman)	4.8	3.4	3.4
Infant mortality rate (per 1,000 live births)	52	34	30
Under-five mortality rate (per 1,000)	68	43	38
Births attended by skilled health staff (% of total)	..	67	..
Child malnutrition, underweight (% of under age 5)	..	10	..
Child immunization, measles (% of ages 12–23 mon.)	82	98	93
HIV prevalence rate (% of ages 15–49)	..	0.2	0.2
Adult literacy, male (% of ages 15 and older)	63	77	..
Adult literacy, female (% of ages 15 and older)	63	77	..
Primary completion rate, total (% of age group)	44	75	..
Primary completion rate, female (% of age group)	61	79	..
Net primary enrollment (% of age group)	72	85	..
Net secondary enrollment (% of age group)	..	39	..
Environment			
Forests (1,000 sq. km)	45	33	..
Deforestation (average annual %, 1990–2000)		3.0	
Freshwater use (% of internal resources)			1
Carbon dioxide emissions (metric tons per capita)	0.7	0.7	..
Access to improved water source (% of total pop.)	69	81	..
Access to improved sanitation (% of urban pop.)	64	78	..
Energy use per capita (kg oil equivalent)	554	544	..
Electricity use per capita (kilowatt-hours)	284	279	..
Economy			
GDP ($ millions)	1,009	4,007	4,083
GDP growth (annual %)	–0.1	1.0	2.3
GDP implicit price deflator (annual % growth)	5,018.1	4.7	5.6
Value added in agriculture (% of GDP)	31	18	18
Value added in industry (% of GDP)	21	26	26
Value added in services (% of GDP)	48	56	56
Exports of goods and services (% of GDP)	25	23	24
Imports of goods and services (% of GDP)	46	49	51
Gross capital formation (% of GDP)	19	36	38
Central government revenue (% of GDP)	33.5	19.3	20.9
Cash surplus/deficit (% of GDP)	–35.5	–0.5	–1.1
Technology and infrastructure			
Fixed-line and mobile subscribers (per 1,000 people)	13	70	123
Cost of 3-minute local call ($)	7.14	0.08	0.08
Personal computers (per 1,000 people)	..	27.9	..
Internet users (per 1,000 people)	..	17	..
Paved roads (% of total)	10.5	11.4	..
Aircraft departures (thousands)	4	1	..
Trade and finance			
Trade in goods (% of GDP)	95.9	59.7	61.0
Trade growth less GDP growth (avg. %, 1990–2003)			..
High-technology exports (% of manufactured exports)	..	5	4
Net barter terms of trade (2000 = 100)	155	90	..
Foreign direct investment ($ millions)	0	204	201
Present value of debt ($ millions)			1,553
Total debt service (% of goods and services exports)	3.9	9.9	11.7
Short-term debt ($ millions)	2,432	554	595
Aid per capita ($)	87	97	152

Niger

Sub-Saharan Africa | **Low income**

Population (millions)	12	Population growth (%)	2.9
Surface area (1,000 sq. km)	1,267	National poverty rate (% pop.)	..
GNI ($ millions)	2,382	GNI per capita ($)	200

	1990	2002	2003
People			
Life expectancy at birth (years)	42	46	46
Fertility rate (births per woman)	7.6	7.1	7.1
Infant mortality rate (per 1,000 live births)	191	159	154
Under-five mortality rate (per 1,000)	320	270	262
Births attended by skilled health staff (% of total)	15	16	..
Child malnutrition, underweight (% of under age 5)	43	40	..
Child immunization, measles (% of ages 12–23 mon.)	25	48	64
HIV prevalence rate (% of ages 15–49)	..	1.1	1.2
Adult literacy, male (% of ages 15 and older)	18	25	..
Adult literacy, female (% of ages 15 and older)	5	9	..
Primary completion rate, total (% of age group)	18	21	26
Primary completion rate, female (% of age group)	13	17	20
Net primary enrollment (% of age group)	24	38	..
Net secondary enrollment (% of age group)	6	6	..
Environment			
Forests (1,000 sq. km)	19	13	..
Deforestation (average annual %, 1990–2000)		3.7	
Freshwater use (% of internal resources)			13
Carbon dioxide emissions (metric tons per capita)	0.1	0.1	..
Access to improved water source (% of total pop.)	40	46	..
Access to improved sanitation (% of urban pop.)	35	43	..
Energy use per capita (kg oil equivalent)	..	..	..
Electricity use per capita (kilowatt-hours)	..	..	..
Economy			
GDP ($ millions)	2,481	2,170	2,731
GDP growth (annual %)	–1.3	3.0	5.3
GDP implicit price deflator (annual % growth)	–1.6	3.0	–0.4
Value added in agriculture (% of GDP)	35	40	40
Value added in industry (% of GDP)	16	17	17
Value added in services (% of GDP)	49	43	43
Exports of goods and services (% of GDP)	15	15	16
Imports of goods and services (% of GDP)	22	24	25
Gross capital formation (% of GDP)	8	14	14
Central government revenue (% of GDP)	..	..	..
Cash surplus/deficit (% of GDP)	..	..	..
Technology and infrastructure			
Fixed-line and mobile subscribers (per 1,000 people)	1	3	..
Cost of 3-minute local call ($)	0.24	0.10	..
Personal computers (per 1,000 people)	..	0.6	..
Internet users (per 1,000 people)	..	1	..
Paved roads (% of total)	29.0	7.9	..
Aircraft departures (thousands)	1	1	..
Trade and finance			
Trade in goods (% of GDP)	27.0	31.3	32.6
Trade growth less GDP growth (avg. %, 1990–2003)			..
High-technology exports (% of manufactured exports)	..	3	3
Net barter terms of trade (2000 = 100)	165	100	..
Foreign direct investment ($ millions)	41	8	31
Present value of debt ($ millions)			578
Total debt service (% of goods and services exports)	17.4	..	..
Short-term debt ($ millions)	154	35	40
Aid per capita ($)	52	26	39

Nigeria

Sub-Saharan Africa		**Low income**
Population (millions)	136	Population growth (%)	2.4
Surface area (1,000 sq. km)	924	National poverty rate (% pop.)	..
GNI ($ billions)	48	GNI per capita ($)	350

	1990	2002	2003
People			
Life expectancy at birth (years)	49	45	45
Fertility rate (births per woman)	6.5	5.7	5.6
Infant mortality rate (per 1,000 live births)	115	102	98
Under-five mortality rate (per 1,000)	235	205	198
Births attended by skilled health staff (% of total)	31	42	35
Child malnutrition, underweight (% of under age 5)	35	31	29
Child immunization, measles (% of ages 12–23 mon.)	54	35	35
HIV prevalence rate (% of ages 15–49)	..	5.5	5.4
Adult literacy, male (% of ages 15 and older)	59	74	..
Adult literacy, female (% of ages 15 and older)	38	59	..
Primary completion rate, total (% of age group)	..	82	..
Primary completion rate, female (% of age group)	..	73	..
Net primary enrollment (% of age group)	60	..	..
Net secondary enrollment (% of age group)	..	..	..
Environment			
Forests (1,000 sq. km)	175	135	..
Deforestation (average annual %, 1990–2000)		2.6	
Freshwater use (% of internal resources)			2
Carbon dioxide emissions (metric tons per capita)	0.9	0.3	..
Access to improved water source (% of total pop.)	49	60	..
Access to improved sanitation (% of urban pop.)	50	48	..
Energy use per capita (kg oil equivalent)	737	718	..
Electricity use per capita (kilowatt-hours)	82	68	..
Economy			
GDP ($ billions)	28	47	58
GDP growth (annual %)	8.2	1.5	10.7
GDP implicit price deflator (annual % growth)	7.2	3.9	21.0
Value added in agriculture (% of GDP)	33	31	26
Value added in industry (% of GDP)	41	44	49
Value added in services (% of GDP)	26	25	24
Exports of goods and services (% of GDP)	43	41	50
Imports of goods and services (% of GDP)	29	41	41
Gross capital formation (% of GDP)	15	26	23
Central government revenue (% of GDP)	..	..	..
Cash surplus/deficit (% of GDP)	..	..	..
Technology and infrastructure			
Fixed-line and mobile subscribers (per 1,000 people)	3	19	32
Cost of 3-minute local call ($)	0.11	..	0.10
Personal computers (per 1,000 people)	..	7.1	..
Internet users (per 1,000 people)	..	3	6
Paved roads (% of total)	30.0	30.9	..
Aircraft departures (thousands)	17	11	9
Trade and finance			
Trade in goods (% of GDP)	67.5	48.5	53.3
Trade growth less GDP growth (avg. %, 1990–2003)			1.5
High-technology exports (% of manufactured exports)	..	0	..
Net barter terms of trade (2000 = 100)	89	91	..
Foreign direct investment ($ millions)	588	1,281	1,200
Present value of debt ($ billions)			34
Total debt service (% of goods and services exports)	22.6	6.9	..
Short-term debt ($ millions)	1,504	2,270	3,400
Aid per capita ($)	3	2	2

Northern Mariana Islands

East Asia & Pacific   **Upper middle income**

Population (thousands)	76	Population growth (%)	..
Surface area (sq. km)	477	National poverty rate (% pop.)	..
GNI ($ millions)	..	GNI per capita ($)	..

	1990	2002	2003
People			
Life expectancy at birth (years)	..	..	..
Fertility rate (births per woman)	..	..	..
Infant mortality rate (per 1,000 live births)	..	..	..
Under-five mortality rate (per 1,000)	..	..	..
Births attended by skilled health staff (% of total)	..	..	..
Child malnutrition, underweight (% of under age 5)	..	..	..
Child immunization, measles (% of ages 12–23 mon.)	..	..	..
HIV prevalence rate (% of ages 15–49)	..	..	..
Adult literacy, male (% of ages 15 and older)	..	..	..
Adult literacy, female (% of ages 15 and older)	..	..	..
Primary completion rate, total (% of age group)	..	..	..
Primary completion rate, female (% of age group)	..	..	..
Net primary enrollment (% of age group)	..	..	..
Net secondary enrollment (% of age group)	..	..	..
Environment			
Forests (1,000 sq. km)	0	0	..
Deforestation (average annual %, 1990–2000)		0.0	
Freshwater use (% of internal resources)			..
Carbon dioxide emissions (metric tons per capita)	..	..	..
Access to improved water source (% of total pop.)	98	98	..
Access to improved sanitation (% of urban pop.)	85	94	..
Energy use per capita (kg oil equivalent)	..	..	..
Electricity use per capita (kilowatt-hours)	..	..	..
Economy			
GDP ($ millions)	..	..	..
GDP growth (annual %)	..	..	..
GDP implicit price deflator (annual % growth)	..	..	..
Value added in agriculture (% of GDP)	..	..	..
Value added in industry (% of GDP)	..	..	..
Value added in services (% of GDP)	..	..	..
Exports of goods and services (% of GDP)	..	..	..
Imports of goods and services (% of GDP)	..	..	..
Gross capital formation (% of GDP)	..	..	..
Central government revenue (% of GDP)	..	..	..
Cash surplus/deficit (% of GDP)	..	..	..
Technology and infrastructure			
Fixed-line and mobile subscribers (per 1,000 people)	..	452	..
Cost of 3-minute local call ($)	..	..	..
Personal computers (per 1,000 people)	..	..	..
Internet users (per 1,000 people)	..	..	..
Paved roads (% of total)	..	..	..
Aircraft departures (thousands)	..	..	..
Trade and finance			
Trade in goods (% of GDP)	..	..	..
Trade growth less GDP growth (avg. %, 1990–2003)			..
High-technology exports (% of manufactured exports)	..	..	..
Net barter terms of trade (2000 = 100)	..	..	..
Foreign direct investment ($ millions)	..	..	..
Present value of debt ($ millions)			..
Total debt service (% of goods and services exports)	..	..	..
Short-term debt ($ millions)	..	..	..
Aid per capita ($)	..	..	..

Norway

Population (millions)	5	Population growth (%)	0.5
Surface area (1,000 sq. km)	324	National poverty rate (% pop.)	..
GNI ($ billions)	198	GNI per capita ($)	43,400

	1990	2002	2003
People			
Life expectancy at birth (years)	77	79	79
Fertility rate (births per woman)	1.9	1.8	1.8
Infant mortality rate (per 1,000 live births)	7	4	3
Under-five mortality rate (per 1,000)	9	5	..
Births attended by skilled health staff (% of total)	100	..	..
Child malnutrition, underweight (% of under age 5)	..	..	..
Child immunization, measles (% of ages 12–23 mon.)	87	88	84
HIV prevalence rate (% of ages 15–49)	..	0.1	0.1
Adult literacy, male (% of ages 15 and older)	..	..	..
Adult literacy, female (% of ages 15 and older)	..	..	..
Primary completion rate, total (% of age group)	..	..	..
Primary completion rate, female (% of age group)	..	..	..
Net primary enrollment (% of age group)	100	100	..
Net secondary enrollment (% of age group)	88	95	..
Environment			
Forests (1,000 sq. km)	86	89	..
Deforestation (average annual %, 1990–2000)		–0.4	
Freshwater use (% of internal resources)			1
Carbon dioxide emissions (metric tons per capita)	7.5	11.1	..
Access to improved water source (% of total pop.)	100	100	..
Access to improved sanitation (% of urban pop.)	..	..	..
Energy use per capita (kg oil equivalent)	5,067	5,843	..
Electricity use per capita (kilowatt-hours)	22,824	23,855	..
Economy			
GDP ($ billions)	116	191	221
GDP growth (annual %)	2.0	1.4	0.4
GDP implicit price deflator (annual % growth)	3.8	–1.6	2.3
Value added in agriculture (% of GDP)	4	2	1
Value added in industry (% of GDP)	36	38	38
Value added in services (% of GDP)	61	60	61
Exports of goods and services (% of GDP)	40	41	41
Imports of goods and services (% of GDP)	34	27	28
Gross capital formation (% of GDP)	23	19	18
Central government revenue (% of GDP)	..	48.0	47.6
Cash surplus/deficit (% of GDP)	..	9.0	9.0
Technology and infrastructure			
Fixed-line and mobile subscribers (per 1,000 people)	548	1,578	1,622
Cost of 3-minute local call ($)	0.16	0.15	..
Personal computers (per 1,000 people)	145.1	528.3	..
Internet users (per 1,000 people)	7	307	346
Paved roads (% of total)	69.0	77.5	..
Aircraft departures (thousands)	234	270	249
Trade and finance			
Trade in goods (% of GDP)	52.8	49.6	48.4
Trade growth less GDP growth (avg. %, 1990–2003)			1.4
High-technology exports (% of manufactured exports)	12	22	19
Net barter terms of trade (2000 = 100)	67	91	90
Foreign direct investment ($ millions)	1,003	502	2,055
Present value of debt ($ millions)			..
Total debt service (% of goods and services exports)	..	..	..
Short-term debt ($ millions)	..	..	..
Aid per capita ($)	..	..	..

Oman

Middle East & North Africa   **Upper middle income**

Population (millions)	3	Population growth (%)	2.4
Surface area (1,000 sq. km)	310	National poverty rate (% pop.)	..
GNI ($ millions)	..	GNI per capita ($)	..

	1990	2002	2003
People			
Life expectancy at birth (years)	69	74	74
Fertility rate (births per woman)	7.4	4.0	4.0
Infant mortality rate (per 1,000 live births)	25	12	10
Under-five mortality rate (per 1,000)	30	14	12
Births attended by skilled health staff (% of total)	..	95	..
Child malnutrition, underweight (% of under age 5)	24	18	..
Child immunization, measles (% of ages 12–23 mon.)	98	99	98
HIV prevalence rate (% of ages 15–49)	..	0.1	0.1
Adult literacy, male (% of ages 15 and older)	67	82	..
Adult literacy, female (% of ages 15 and older)	38	65	..
Primary completion rate, total (% of age group)	81	73	..
Primary completion rate, female (% of age group)	76	71	..
Net primary enrollment (% of age group)	69	72	..
Net secondary enrollment (% of age group)	..	69	..
Environment			
Forests (1,000 sq. km)	0	0	..
Deforestation (average annual %, 1990–2000)		0.0	
Freshwater use (% of internal resources)			120
Carbon dioxide emissions (metric tons per capita)	7.1	8.2	..
Access to improved water source (% of total pop.)	77	79	..
Access to improved sanitation (% of urban pop.)	97	97	..
Energy use per capita (kg oil equivalent)	2,804	4,265	..
Electricity use per capita (kilowatt-hours)	2,284	3,177	..
Economy			
GDP ($ millions)	10,535	20,309	..
GDP growth (annual %)	7.5	0.0	..
GDP implicit price deflator (annual % growth)	16.6	1.8	..
Value added in agriculture (% of GDP)	3	..	..
Value added in industry (% of GDP)	58	..	..
Value added in services (% of GDP)	39	..	..
Exports of goods and services (% of GDP)	53	57	..
Imports of goods and services (% of GDP)	31	35	..
Gross capital formation (% of GDP)	13	13	..
Central government revenue (% of GDP)	38.9	27.0	..
Cash surplus/deficit (% of GDP)	–0.4	–2.8	..
Technology and infrastructure			
Fixed-line and mobile subscribers (per 1,000 people)	61	255	..
Cost of 3-minute local call ($)	0.07	0.07	0.07
Personal computers (per 1,000 people)	1.7	35.0	..
Internet users (per 1,000 people)	..	71	..
Paved roads (% of total)	21.0	30.0	..
Aircraft departures (thousands)	12	23	28
Trade and finance			
Trade in goods (% of GDP)	77.7	84.6	..
Trade growth less GDP growth (avg. %, 1990–2003)			..
High-technology exports (% of manufactured exports)	2	2	2
Net barter terms of trade (2000 = 100)	..	..	..
Foreign direct investment ($ millions)	142	24	138
Present value of debt ($ millions)		3,816	
Total debt service (% of goods and services exports)	12.3	14.8	10.3
Short-term debt ($ millions)	335	1,188	1,244
Aid per capita ($)	38	16	17

Pakistan

South Asia — **Low income**

Population (millions)	148	Population growth (%)	2.4
Surface area (1,000 sq. km)	796	National poverty rate (% pop.)	33
GNI ($ billions)	78	GNI per capita ($)	520

	1990	2002	2003
People			
Life expectancy at birth (years)	59	64	64
Fertility rate (births per woman)	5.8	4.5	4.5
Infant mortality rate (per 1,000 live births)	96	*81*	74
Under-five mortality rate (per 1,000)	138	*108*	98
Births attended by skilled health staff (% of total)	19	*23*	..
Child malnutrition, underweight (% of under age 5)	40	*35*	..
Child immunization, measles (% of ages 12–23 mon.)	50	63	61
HIV prevalence rate (% of ages 15–49)	..	*0.1*	0.1
Adult literacy, male (% of ages 15 and older)	49	*53*	..
Adult literacy, female (% of ages 15 and older)	20	*29*	..
Primary completion rate, total (% of age group)	..	..	..
Primary completion rate, female (% of age group)	..	..	..
Net primary enrollment (% of age group)	..	*59*	..
Net secondary enrollment (% of age group)	..	..	..
Environment			
Forests (1,000 sq. km)	28	*24*	..
Deforestation (average annual %, 1990–2000)		*1.5*	
Freshwater use (% of internal resources)			299
Carbon dioxide emissions (metric tons per capita)	0.6	*0.8*	..
Access to improved water source (% of total pop.)	83	90	..
Access to improved sanitation (% of urban pop.)	81	92	..
Energy use per capita (kg oil equivalent)	402	454	..
Electricity use per capita (kilowatt-hours)	267	363	..
Economy			
GDP ($ billions)	40	71	82
GDP growth (annual %)	4.5	3.2	5.1
GDP implicit price deflator (annual % growth)	6.5	3.1	4.6
Value added in agriculture (% of GDP)	26	23	23
Value added in industry (% of GDP)	25	23	23
Value added in services (% of GDP)	49	53	53
Exports of goods and services (% of GDP)	16	19	20
Imports of goods and services (% of GDP)	23	19	20
Gross capital formation (% of GDP)	19	15	15
Central government revenue (% of GDP)	19.1	14.1	14.6
Cash surplus/deficit (% of GDP)	–2.5	–2.9	–2.9
Technology and infrastructure			
Fixed-line and mobile subscribers (per 1,000 people)	8	34	44
Cost of 3-minute local call ($)	0.05	0.02	0.02
Personal computers (per 1,000 people)	1.3	*4.2*	..
Internet users (per 1,000 people)	..	10	..
Paved roads (% of total)	54.0	*59.0*	..
Aircraft departures (thousands)	66	42	45
Trade and finance			
Trade in goods (% of GDP)	32.6	29.6	30.3
Trade growth less GDP growth (avg. %, 1990–2003)			–0.9
High-technology exports (% of manufactured exports)	0	1	1
Net barter terms of trade (2000 = 100)	109	95	..
Foreign direct investment ($ millions)	245	823	534
Present value of debt ($ billions)			30
Total debt service (% of goods and services exports)	21.3	17.9	16.0
Short-term debt ($ millions)	3,185	1,540	1,245
Aid per capita ($)	10	15	7

Palau

East Asia & Pacific   **Upper middle income**

Population (thousands)	20	Population growth (%)		..
Surface area (sq. km)	460	National poverty rate (% pop.)		..
GNI ($ millions)	130	GNI per capita ($)		6,500

	1990	2002	2003
People			
Life expectancy at birth (years)	..	..	..
Fertility rate (births per woman)	..	..	..
Infant mortality rate (per 1,000 live births)	28	24	23
Under-five mortality rate (per 1,000)	34	29	28
Births attended by skilled health staff (% of total)	99	100	..
Child malnutrition, underweight (% of under age 5)	..	..	..
Child immunization, measles (% of ages 12–23 mon.)	98	99	99
HIV prevalence rate (% of ages 15–49)	..	..	..
Adult literacy, male (% of ages 15 and older)	..	..	..
Adult literacy, female (% of ages 15 and older)	..	..	..
Primary completion rate, total (% of age group)	..	99	..
Primary completion rate, female (% of age group)	..	90	..
Net primary enrollment (% of age group)	..	96	..
Net secondary enrollment (% of age group)	..	..	..
Environment			
Forests (1,000 sq. km)	0	0	..
Deforestation (average annual %, 1990–2000)		0.0	
Freshwater use (% of internal resources)			..
Carbon dioxide emissions (metric tons per capita)	..	..	..
Access to improved water source (% of total pop.)	80	84	..
Access to improved sanitation (% of urban pop.)	72	96	..
Energy use per capita (kg oil equivalent)	..	..	..
Electricity use per capita (kilowatt-hours)	..	..	..
Economy			
GDP ($ millions)	77	121	126
GDP growth (annual %)	–6.4	1.1	1.5
GDP implicit price deflator (annual % growth)	5.0	4.9	0.3
Value added in agriculture (% of GDP)	26	4	..
Value added in industry (% of GDP)	13	13	..
Value added in services (% of GDP)	69	83	..
Exports of goods and services (% of GDP)	20	17	..
Imports of goods and services (% of GDP)	39	82	..
Gross capital formation (% of GDP)	..	..	..
Central government revenue (% of GDP)	..	..	..
Cash surplus/deficit (% of GDP)	..	..	..
Technology and infrastructure			
Fixed-line and mobile subscribers (per 1,000 people)	..	..	..
Cost of 3-minute local call ($)	..	..	..
Personal computers (per 1,000 people)	..	..	..
Internet users (per 1,000 people)	..	..	..
Paved roads (% of total)	..	..	..
Aircraft departures (thousands)	..	..	..
Trade and finance			
Trade in goods (% of GDP)	..	..	..
Trade growth less GDP growth (avg. %, 1990–2003)			..
High-technology exports (% of manufactured exports)	..	..	..
Net barter terms of trade (2000 = 100)	..	..	..
Foreign direct investment ($ millions)	..	..	..
Present value of debt ($ millions)			..
Total debt service (% of goods and services exports)	..	..	..
Short-term debt ($ millions)	..	..	..
Aid per capita ($)	..	..	..

Panama

Latin America & Caribbean		Upper middle income	

Population (millions)	3	Population growth (%)	1.5
Surface area (1,000 sq. km)	76	National poverty rate (% pop.)	37
GNI ($ billions)	12	GNI per capita ($)	4,060

	1990	2002	2003
People			
Life expectancy at birth (years)	72	75	75
Fertility rate (births per woman)	3.0	2.4	2.4
Infant mortality rate (per 1,000 live births)	27	20	18
Under-five mortality rate (per 1,000)	34	26	24
Births attended by skilled health staff (% of total)	..	90	..
Child malnutrition, underweight (% of under age 5)	6	8	..
Child immunization, measles (% of ages 12–23 mon.)	73	79	83
HIV prevalence rate (% of ages 15–49)	..	0.7	0.9
Adult literacy, male (% of ages 15 and older)	90	93	..
Adult literacy, female (% of ages 15 and older)	88	92	..
Primary completion rate, total (% of age group)	86	98	98
Primary completion rate, female (% of age group)	87	98	98
Net primary enrollment (% of age group)	92	100	..
Net secondary enrollment (% of age group)	50	63	..
Environment			
Forests (1,000 sq. km)	34	29	..
Deforestation (average annual %, 1990–2000)		1.6	
Freshwater use (% of internal resources)			1
Carbon dioxide emissions (metric tons per capita)	1.3	2.2	..
Access to improved water source (% of total pop.)	..	91	..
Access to improved sanitation (% of urban pop.)	..	89	..
Energy use per capita (kg oil equivalent)	621	1,028	..
Electricity use per capita (kilowatt-hours)	856	1,375	..
Economy			
GDP ($ billions)	5	12	13
GDP growth (annual %)	8.1	2.2	4.1
GDP implicit price deflator (annual % growth)	0.6	1.2	1.4
Value added in agriculture (% of GDP)	9	7	7
Value added in industry (% of GDP)	15	15	16
Value added in services (% of GDP)	76	78	76
Exports of goods and services (% of GDP)	87	62	59
Imports of goods and services (% of GDP)	79	62	58
Gross capital formation (% of GDP)	17	26	26
Central government revenue (% of GDP)	25.6	25.6	..
Cash surplus/deficit (% of GDP)	2.0	0.9	..
Technology and infrastructure			
Fixed-line and mobile subscribers (per 1,000 people)	93	311	390
Cost of 3-minute local call ($)	0.00	0.12	..
Personal computers (per 1,000 people)	..	38.3	..
Internet users (per 1,000 people)	..	62	62
Paved roads (% of total)	32.0	34.6	..
Aircraft departures (thousands)	5	22	26
Trade and finance			
Trade in goods (% of GDP)	35.4	31.3	30.4
Trade growth less GDP growth (avg. %, 1990–2003)			–4.5
High-technology exports (% of manufactured exports)	..	1	1
Net barter terms of trade (2000 = 100)	69	99	..
Foreign direct investment ($ millions)	136	78	792
Present value of debt ($ billions)			11
Total debt service (% of goods and services exports)	6.2	19.4	11.3
Short-term debt ($ millions)	2,379	371	440
Aid per capita ($)	42	8	10

Papua New Guinea

Population (millions)	6	Population growth (%)		2.3
Surface area (1,000 sq. km)	463	National poverty rate (% pop.)		..
GNI ($ millions)	2,753	GNI per capita ($)		500

	1990	2002	2003
People			
Life expectancy at birth (years)	55	57	57
Fertility rate (births per woman)	5.6	4.3	4.3
Infant mortality rate (per 1,000 live births)	74	70	69
Under-five mortality rate (per 1,000)	101	95	93
Births attended by skilled health staff (% of total)	..	..	..
Child malnutrition, underweight (% of under age 5)	..	..	..
Child immunization, measles (% of ages 12–23 mon.)	67	56	49
HIV prevalence rate (% of ages 15–49)	..	0.4	0.6
Adult literacy, male (% of ages 15 and older)	..	..	..
Adult literacy, female (% of ages 15 and older)	..	..	..
Primary completion rate, total (% of age group)	51	53	..
Primary completion rate, female (% of age group)	49	46	..
Net primary enrollment (% of age group)	66	69	..
Net secondary enrollment (% of age group)	..	24	..
Environment			
Forests (1,000 sq. km)	317	306	..
Deforestation (average annual %, 1990–2000)		0.4	
Freshwater use (% of internal resources)			0
Carbon dioxide emissions (metric tons per capita)	0.6	0.5	..
Access to improved water source (% of total pop.)	39	39	..
Access to improved sanitation (% of urban pop.)	67	67	..
Energy use per capita (kg oil equivalent)	..	..	..
Electricity use per capita (kilowatt-hours)	..	..	..
Economy			
GDP ($ millions)	3,221	2,940	3,182
GDP growth (annual %)	–3.0	–0.8	2.7
GDP implicit price deflator (annual % growth)	4.1	12.8	5.8
Value added in agriculture (% of GDP)	29	27	26
Value added in industry (% of GDP)	30	39	39
Value added in services (% of GDP)	41	33	35
Exports of goods and services (% of GDP)	41	47	..
Imports of goods and services (% of GDP)	49	43	..
Gross capital formation (% of GDP)	24	19	..
Central government revenue (% of GDP)	25.2	23.8	..
Cash surplus/deficit (% of GDP)	–2.2	–2.4	..
Technology and infrastructure			
Fixed-line and mobile subscribers (per 1,000 people)	8	14	..
Cost of 3-minute local call ($)	0.17	0.08	0.08
Personal computers (per 1,000 people)	..	58.7	..
Internet users (per 1,000 people)	..	14	..
Paved roads (% of total)	3.2	3.5	..
Aircraft departures (thousands)	62	31	18
Trade and finance			
Trade in goods (% of GDP)	73.6	94.7	109.1
Trade growth less GDP growth (avg. %, 1990–2003)			..
High-technology exports (% of manufactured exports)	..	17	39
Net barter terms of trade (2000 = 100)	..	..	..
Foreign direct investment ($ millions)	155	21	101
Present value of debt ($ millions)			2,264
Total debt service (% of goods and services exports)	37.2	15.0	11.9
Short-term debt ($ millions)	72	64	111
Aid per capita ($)	104	38	40

Paraguay

Latin America & Caribbean   **Lower middle income**

Population (millions)	6	Population growth (%)	2.4
Surface area (1,000 sq. km)	407	National poverty rate (% pop.)	..
GNI ($ millions)	6,273	GNI per capita ($)	1,110

	1990	2002	2003
People			
Life expectancy at birth (years)	68	71	71
Fertility rate (births per woman)	4.6	3.8	3.8
Infant mortality rate (per 1,000 live births)	30	26	25
Under-five mortality rate (per 1,000)	37	31	29
Births attended by skilled health staff (% of total)	67	71	..
Child malnutrition, underweight (% of under age 5)	4	..	..
Child immunization, measles (% of ages 12–23 mon.)	69	82	91
HIV prevalence rate (% of ages 15–49)	..	0.4	0.5
Adult literacy, male (% of ages 15 and older)	92	93	..
Adult literacy, female (% of ages 15 and older)	88	90	..
Primary completion rate, total (% of age group)	66	93	..
Primary completion rate, female (% of age group)	66	93	..
Net primary enrollment (% of age group)	93	92	..
Net secondary enrollment (% of age group)	26	50	..
Environment			
Forests (1,000 sq. km)	246	234	..
Deforestation (average annual %, 1990–2000)		0.5	
Freshwater use (% of internal resources)			0
Carbon dioxide emissions (metric tons per capita)	0.5	0.7	..
Access to improved water source (% of total pop.)	62	83	..
Access to improved sanitation (% of urban pop.)	71	94	..
Energy use per capita (kg oil equivalent)	743	709	..
Electricity use per capita (kilowatt-hours)	477	842	..
Economy			
GDP ($ millions)	5,265	5,539	6,030
GDP growth (annual %)	3.1	–2.3	2.6
GDP implicit price deflator (annual % growth)	36.3	16.4	18.3
Value added in agriculture (% of GDP)	28	24	27
Value added in industry (% of GDP)	25	25	24
Value added in services (% of GDP)	47	51	49
Exports of goods and services (% of GDP)	33	31	32
Imports of goods and services (% of GDP)	39	44	47
Gross capital formation (% of GDP)	23	19	20
Central government revenue (% of GDP)	12.3	15.3	15.2
Cash surplus/deficit (% of GDP)	2.9	–3.0	–0.6
Technology and infrastructure			
Fixed-line and mobile subscribers (per 1,000 people)	27	336	345
Cost of 3-minute local call ($)	0.07	0.09	..
Personal computers (per 1,000 people)	..	34.6	..
Internet users (per 1,000 people)	..	17	20
Paved roads (% of total)	8.5	50.8	..
Aircraft departures (thousands)	6	9	11
Trade and finance			
Trade in goods (% of GDP)	43.9	47.4	55.9
Trade growth less GDP growth (avg. %, 1990–2003)			–2.9
High-technology exports (% of manufactured exports)	0	3	6
Net barter terms of trade (2000 = 100)	103	100	..
Foreign direct investment ($ millions)	77	9	91
Present value of debt ($ millions)			3,107
Total debt service (% of goods and services exports)	12.4	12.4	9.9
Short-term debt ($ millions)	373	486	552
Aid per capita ($)	14	10	9

Peru

Latin America & Caribbean   **Lower middle income**

Population (millions)	27	Population growth (%)	1.5
Surface area (1,000 sq. km)	1,285	National poverty rate (% pop.)	49
GNI ($ millions)	58	GNI per capita ($)	2,140

	1990	2002	2003
People			
Life expectancy at birth (years)	66	70	70
Fertility rate (births per woman)	3.7	2.7	2.7
Infant mortality rate (per 1,000 live births)	60	*32*	26
Under-five mortality rate (per 1,000)	80	*42*	34
Births attended by skilled health staff (% of total)	..	59	..
Child malnutrition, underweight (% of under age 5)	*11*	7	..
Child immunization, measles (% of ages 12–23 mon.)	64	95	95
HIV prevalence rate (% of ages 15–49)	..	*0.4*	0.5
Adult literacy, male (% of ages 15 and older)	92	91	..
Adult literacy, female (% of ages 15 and older)	79	80	..
Primary completion rate, total (% of age group)	..	98	102
Primary completion rate, female (% of age group)	..	98	..
Net primary enrollment (% of age group)	88	*100*	..
Net secondary enrollment (% of age group)	..	*69*	..
Environment			
Forests (1,000 sq. km)	679	*652*	..
Deforestation (average annual %, 1990–2000)		*0.4*	
Freshwater use (% of internal resources)			1
Carbon dioxide emissions (metric tons per capita)	1.0	*1.1*	..
Access to improved water source (% of total pop.)	74	81	..
Access to improved sanitation (% of urban pop.)	68	72	..
Energy use per capita (kg oil equivalent)	461	450	..
Electricity use per capita (kilowatt-hours)	546	723	..
Economy			
GDP ($ billions)	26	56	61
GDP growth (annual %)	–5.1	4.9	3.8
GDP implicit price deflator (annual % growth)	..	..	..
Value added in agriculture (% of GDP)	9	11	10
Value added in industry (% of GDP)	27	29	29
Value added in services (% of GDP)	64	61	60
Exports of goods and services (% of GDP)	16	17	18
Imports of goods and services (% of GDP)	14	17	18
Gross capital formation (% of GDP)	16	19	19
Central government revenue (% of GDP)	12.5	15.6	16.2
Cash surplus/deficit (% of GDP)	–8.1	–2.1	–1.8
Technology and infrastructure			
Fixed-line and mobile subscribers (per 1,000 people)	26	152	173
Cost of 3-minute local call ($)	*0.02*	0.08	..
Personal computers (per 1,000 people)	..	43.0	..
Internet users (per 1,000 people)	..	90	104
Paved roads (% of total)	9.9	*13.4*	..
Aircraft departures (thousands)	22	38	36
Trade and finance			
Trade in goods (% of GDP)	22.3	26.8	28.8
Trade growth less GDP growth (avg. %, 1990–2003)			3.3
High-technology exports (% of manufactured exports)	2	2	2
Net barter terms of trade (2000 = 100)	114	99	..
Foreign direct investment ($ millions)	41	2,156	1,377
Present value of debt ($ billions)			33
Total debt service (% of goods and services exports)	10.8	32.8	21.6
Short-term debt ($ millions)	5,350	2,332	2,525
Aid per capita ($)	19	19	18

Philippines

East Asia & Pacific   **Lower middle income**

Population (millions)	82	Population growth (%)	1.9
Surface area (1,000 sq. km)	300	National poverty rate (% pop.)	37
GNI ($ billions)	88	GNI per capita ($)	1,080

	1990	2002	2003
People			
Life expectancy at birth (years)	66	70	70
Fertility rate (births per woman)	4.1	3.2	3.2
Infant mortality rate (per 1,000 live births)	45	30	27
Under-five mortality rate (per 1,000)	63	40	36
Births attended by skilled health staff (% of total)	..	58	60
Child malnutrition, underweight (% of under age 5)	34	32	..
Child immunization, measles (% of ages 12–23 mon.)	85	80	80
HIV prevalence rate (% of ages 15–49)	..	0.1	0.1
Adult literacy, male (% of ages 15 and older)	92	93	..
Adult literacy, female (% of ages 15 and older)	91	93	..
Primary completion rate, total (% of age group)	87	98	95
Primary completion rate, female (% of age group)	85	102	94
Net primary enrollment (% of age group)	96	93	..
Net secondary enrollment (% of age group)	..	56	..
Environment			
Forests (1,000 sq. km)	67	58	..
Deforestation (average annual %, 1990–2000)		1.4	
Freshwater use (% of internal resources)			12
Carbon dioxide emissions (metric tons per capita)	0.7	1.0	..
Access to improved water source (% of total pop.)	87	85	..
Access to improved sanitation (% of urban pop.)	63	81	..
Energy use per capita (kg oil equivalent)	429	525	..
Electricity use per capita (kilowatt-hours)	342	459	..
Economy			
GDP ($ billions)	44	78	81
GDP growth (annual %)	3.0	4.4	4.5
GDP implicit price deflator (annual % growth)	13.0	4.9	3.7
Value added in agriculture (% of GDP)	22	15	14
Value added in industry (% of GDP)	34	33	32
Value added in services (% of GDP)	44	53	53
Exports of goods and services (% of GDP)	28	49	48
Imports of goods and services (% of GDP)	33	49	51
Gross capital formation (% of GDP)	24	19	19
Central government revenue (% of GDP)	16.2	14.1	14.4
Cash surplus/deficit (% of GDP)	–2.8	–3.9	..
Technology and infrastructure			
Fixed-line and mobile subscribers (per 1,000 people)	10	233	311
Cost of 3-minute local call ($)	0.00	0.00	0.00
Personal computers (per 1,000 people)	3.5	27.7	..
Internet users (per 1,000 people)	..	44	..
Paved roads (% of total)	..	9.5	..
Aircraft departures (thousands)	70	57	56
Trade and finance			
Trade in goods (% of GDP)	47.7	94.5	94.3
Trade growth less GDP growth (avg. %, 1990–2003)			2.7
High-technology exports (% of manufactured exports)	32	74	74
Net barter terms of trade (2000 = 100)	87	104	..
Foreign direct investment ($ millions)	530	1,792	319
Present value of debt ($ billions)			65
Total debt service (% of goods and services exports)	27.0	22.8	22.1
Short-term debt ($ millions)	4,427	5,559	6,179
Aid per capita ($)	21	7	9

Poland

Europe & Central Asia   **Upper middle income**

Population (millions)	38	Population growth (%)		−0.1
Surface area (1,000 sq. km)	313	National poverty rate (% pop.)		..
GNI ($ billions)	202	GNI per capita ($)		5,280

	1990	2002	2003
People			
Life expectancy at birth (years)	71	74	75
Fertility rate (births per woman)	2.0	1.3	1.2
Infant mortality rate (per 1,000 live births)	16	8	6
Under-five mortality rate (per 1,000)	19	9	7
Births attended by skilled health staff (% of total)	..	..	..
Child malnutrition, underweight (% of under age 5)	..	..	..
Child immunization, measles (% of ages 12–23 mon.)	95	98	97
HIV prevalence rate (% of ages 15–49)	..	..	0.1
Adult literacy, male (% of ages 15 and older)	..	..	..
Adult literacy, female (% of ages 15 and older)	..	..	..
Primary completion rate, total (% of age group)	96	97	98
Primary completion rate, female (% of age group)	..	98	99
Net primary enrollment (% of age group)	97	98	..
Net secondary enrollment (% of age group)	76	91	..
Environment			
Forests (1,000 sq. km)	89	90	..
Deforestation (average annual %, 1990–2000)		−0.2	
Freshwater use (% of internal resources)			23
Carbon dioxide emissions (metric tons per capita)	9.1	7.8	..
Access to improved water source (% of total pop.)	..	..	..
Access to improved sanitation (% of urban pop.)	..	..	..
Energy use per capita (kg oil equivalent)	2,619	2,333	..
Electricity use per capita (kilowatt-hours)	2,525	2,514	..
Economy			
GDP ($ billions)	59	191	210
GDP growth (annual %)	−7.0	1.4	3.7
GDP implicit price deflator (annual % growth)	55.2	1.6	0.7
Value added in agriculture (% of GDP)	8	3	3
Value added in industry (% of GDP)	50	30	31
Value added in services (% of GDP)	42	66	66
Exports of goods and services (% of GDP)	29	28	21
Imports of goods and services (% of GDP)	22	31	26
Gross capital formation (% of GDP)	26	19	19
Central government revenue (% of GDP)	..	29.5	..
Cash surplus/deficit (% of GDP)	..	−5.7	..
Technology and infrastructure			
Fixed-line and mobile subscribers (per 1,000 people)	86	554	770
Cost of 3-minute local call ($)	0.02	0.08	0.09
Personal computers (per 1,000 people)	7.9	105.6	142.0
Internet users (per 1,000 people)	0	230	232
Paved roads (% of total)	61.6	68.3	..
Aircraft departures (thousands)	29	70	73
Trade and finance			
Trade in goods (% of GDP)	43.9	50.2	58.0
Trade growth less GDP growth (avg. %, 1990–2003)			7.8
High-technology exports (% of manufactured exports)	4	3	3
Net barter terms of trade (2000 = 100)	92	105	102
Foreign direct investment ($ millions)	89	4,131	4,123
Present value of debt ($ billions)			93
Total debt service (% of goods and services exports)	4.9	22.5	25.1
Short-term debt ($ billions)	10	14	19
Aid per capita ($)	35	23	31

Portugal

High income

Population (millions)	10	Population growth (%)	0.7
Surface area (1,000 sq. km)	92	National poverty rate (% pop.)	..
GNI ($ billions)	123	GNI per capita ($)	11,800

	1990	2002	2003
People			
Life expectancy at birth (years)	74	76	76
Fertility rate (births per woman)	1.4	1.4	1.4
Infant mortality rate (per 1,000 live births)	13	6	4
Under-five mortality rate (per 1,000)	15	6	5
Births attended by skilled health staff (% of total)	98	100	..
Child malnutrition, underweight (% of under age 5)	..	..	..
Child immunization, measles (% of ages 12–23 mon.)	85	93	96
HIV prevalence rate (% of ages 15–49)	..	0.4	0.4
Adult literacy, male (% of ages 15 and older)	91	95	..
Adult literacy, female (% of ages 15 and older)	84	91	..
Primary completion rate, total (% of age group)	98	..	..
Primary completion rate, female (% of age group)	98	..	..
Net primary enrollment (% of age group)	100	100	..
Net secondary enrollment (% of age group)	..	85	..
Environment			
Forests (1,000 sq. km)	31	37	..
Deforestation (average annual %, 1990–2000)		–1.7	
Freshwater use (% of internal resources)			19
Carbon dioxide emissions (metric tons per capita)	4.3	5.8	..
Access to improved water source (% of total pop.)	..	..	..
Access to improved sanitation (% of urban pop.)	..	..	..
Energy use per capita (kg oil equivalent)	1,793	2,546	..
Electricity use per capita (kilowatt-hours)	2,379	4,000	..
Economy			
GDP ($ billions)	71	122	148
GDP growth (annual %)	4.0	0.4	–1.2
GDP implicit price deflator (annual % growth)	13.1	5.1	..
Value added in agriculture (% of GDP)	9	4	..
Value added in industry (% of GDP)	32	29	..
Value added in services (% of GDP)	60	68	..
Exports of goods and services (% of GDP)	33	30	..
Imports of goods and services (% of GDP)	39	38	..
Gross capital formation (% of GDP)	28	25	..
Central government revenue (% of GDP)	..	37.7	..
Cash surplus/deficit (% of GDP)	..	–4.0	..
Technology and infrastructure			
Fixed-line and mobile subscribers (per 1,000 people)	243	1,247	1,310
Cost of 3-minute local call ($)	0.06	0.11	0.13
Personal computers (per 1,000 people)	26.5	134.9	134.4
Internet users (per 1,000 people)	1	194	..
Paved roads (% of total)	..	86.0	..
Aircraft departures (thousands)	45	112	117
Trade and finance			
Trade in goods (% of GDP)	58.3	54.7	51.7
Trade growth less GDP growth (avg. %, 1990–2003)			3.6
High-technology exports (% of manufactured exports)	4	7	9
Net barter terms of trade (2000 = 100)	104	106	102
Foreign direct investment ($ millions)	2,610	1,790	969
Present value of debt ($ millions)			..
Total debt service (% of goods and services exports)	..	..	..
Short-term debt ($ millions)	..	..	..
Aid per capita ($)	..	..	..

Puerto Rico

High income

Population (millions)	4	Population growth (%)	0.8
Surface area (1,000 sq. km)	9	National poverty rate (% pop.)	..
GNI ($ millions)	..	GNI per capita ($)	..

	1990	2002	2003
People			
Life expectancy at birth (years)	75	77	77
Fertility rate (births per woman)	2.2	1.9	1.9
Infant mortality rate (per 1,000 live births)	14	..	..
Under-five mortality rate (per 1,000)	..	..	..
Births attended by skilled health staff (% of total)	..	..	..
Child malnutrition, underweight (% of under age 5)	..	..	..
Child immunization, measles (% of ages 12–23 mon.)	..	..	..
HIV prevalence rate (% of ages 15–49)	..	..	
Adult literacy, male (% of ages 15 and older)	92	94	..
Adult literacy, female (% of ages 15 and older)	91	94	..
Primary completion rate, total (% of age group)	..	..	..
Primary completion rate, female (% of age group)	..	..	..
Net primary enrollment (% of age group)	..	..	..
Net secondary enrollment (% of age group)	..	..	..
Environment			
Forests (1,000 sq. km)	2	2	..
Deforestation (average annual %, 1990–2000)		0.2	
Freshwater use (% of internal resources)			..
Carbon dioxide emissions (metric tons per capita)	3.3	2.3	..
Access to improved water source (% of total pop.)	..	..	..
Access to improved sanitation (% of urban pop.)	..	..	..
Energy use per capita (kg oil equivalent)	..	..	..
Electricity use per capita (kilowatt-hours)	..	..	..
Economy			
GDP ($ millions)	30,604	67,897	..
GDP growth (annual %)	3.8	5.6	..
GDP implicit price deflator (annual % growth)	4.3	5.3	..
Value added in agriculture (% of GDP)	1	1	..
Value added in industry (% of GDP)	42	43	..
Value added in services (% of GDP)	57	56	..
Exports of goods and services (% of GDP)	77	81	..
Imports of goods and services (% of GDP)	101	100	..
Gross capital formation (% of GDP)	17	..	..
Central government revenue (% of GDP)	..	..	..
Cash surplus/deficit (% of GDP)	..	..	..
Technology and infrastructure			
Fixed-line and mobile subscribers (per 1,000 people)	285	662	..
Cost of 3-minute local call ($)	0.13	..	..
Personal computers (per 1,000 people)	..	..	..
Internet users (per 1,000 people)	..	175	..
Paved roads (% of total)	100.0	94.0	..
Aircraft departures (thousands)	..	..	..
Trade and finance			
Trade in goods (% of GDP)	..	..	..
Trade growth less GDP growth (avg. %, 1990–2003)			–0.5
High-technology exports (% of manufactured exports)	..	..	..
Net barter terms of trade (2000 = 100)	..	..	..
Foreign direct investment ($ millions)	..	..	..
Present value of debt ($ millions)			..
Total debt service (% of goods and services exports)	..	..	..
Short-term debt ($ millions)	..	..	..
Aid per capita ($)	..	..	..

Qatar

High income

Population (thousands)	624	Population growth (%)		2.1
Surface area (1,000 sq. km)	11	National poverty rate (% pop.)		..
GNI ($ millions)	..	GNI per capita ($)		..

	1990	2002	2003
People			
Life expectancy at birth (years)	72	75	75
Fertility rate (births per woman)	4.3	2.5	2.5
Infant mortality rate (per 1,000 live births)	19	12	11
Under-five mortality rate (per 1,000)	25	16	15
Births attended by skilled health staff (% of total)	..	..	..
Child malnutrition, underweight (% of under age 5)	..	..	..
Child immunization, measles (% of ages 12–23 mon.)	79	99	93
HIV prevalence rate (% of ages 15–49)	..	..	..
Adult literacy, male (% of ages 15 and older)	77	85	..
Adult literacy, female (% of ages 15 and older)	76	82	..
Primary completion rate, total (% of age group)	67	87	..
Primary completion rate, female (% of age group)	67	84	..
Net primary enrollment (% of age group)	89	94	..
Net secondary enrollment (% of age group)	70	82	..
Environment			
Forests (1,000 sq. km)	..	0	..
Deforestation (average annual %, 1990–2000)		..	
Freshwater use (% of internal resources)			..
Carbon dioxide emissions (metric tons per capita)	28.2	69.6	..
Access to improved water source (% of total pop.)	100	100	..
Access to improved sanitation (% of urban pop.)	100	100	..
Energy use per capita (kg oil equivalent)	13,307	19,915	..
Electricity use per capita (kilowatt-hours)	9,419	15,515	..
Economy			
GDP ($ millions)	7,360	17,466	..
GDP growth (annual %)	..	..	..
GDP implicit price deflator (annual % growth)	..	..	..
Value added in agriculture (% of GDP)	..	..	..
Value added in industry (% of GDP)	..	..	..
Value added in services (% of GDP)	..	..	..
Exports of goods and services (% of GDP)	..	36	..
Imports of goods and services (% of GDP)	..	36	..
Gross capital formation (% of GDP)	..	32	..
Central government revenue (% of GDP)	..	..	..
Cash surplus/deficit (% of GDP)	..	..	..
Technology and infrastructure			
Fixed-line and mobile subscribers (per 1,000 people)	198	727	794
Cost of 3-minute local call ($)	..	0.00	..
Personal computers (per 1,000 people)	..	180.3	..
Internet users (per 1,000 people)	..	113	199
Paved roads (% of total)	85.6	90.0	..
Aircraft departures (thousands)	11	31	24
Trade and finance			
Trade in goods (% of GDP)	75.9	90.6	..
Trade growth less GDP growth (avg. %, 1990–2003)			..
High-technology exports (% of manufactured exports)	0	0	..
Net barter terms of trade (2000 = 100)	..	..	..
Foreign direct investment ($ millions)	..	..	..
Present value of debt ($ millions)			..
Total debt service (% of goods and services exports)	..	..	..
Short-term debt ($ millions)	..	..	..
Aid per capita ($)	3	4	3

Romania

Europe & Central Asia   **Lower middle income**

Population (millions)	22	Population growth (%)		−0.3
Surface area (1,000 sq. km)	238	National poverty rate (% pop.)		..
GNI ($ billions)	49	GNI per capita ($)		2,260

	1990	2002	2003
People			
Life expectancy at birth (years)	70	70	70
Fertility rate (births per woman)	1.8	1.3	1.3
Infant mortality rate (per 1,000 live births)	27	19	18
Under-five mortality rate (per 1,000)	32	22	20
Births attended by skilled health staff (% of total)	..	98	..
Child malnutrition, underweight (% of under age 5)	6	3	..
Child immunization, measles (% of ages 12–23 mon.)	92	98	97
HIV prevalence rate (% of ages 15–49)	..	..	0.1
Adult literacy, male (% of ages 15 and older)	99	98	..
Adult literacy, female (% of ages 15 and older)	96	96	..
Primary completion rate, total (% of age group)	78	89	..
Primary completion rate, female (% of age group)	79	89	..
Net primary enrollment (% of age group)	81	88	..
Net secondary enrollment (% of age group)	..	80	..
Environment			
Forests (1,000 sq. km)	63	64	..
Deforestation (average annual %, 1990–2000)		−0.2	
Freshwater use (% of internal resources)			62
Carbon dioxide emissions (metric tons per capita)	6.7	3.8	..
Access to improved water source (% of total pop.)	..	57	..
Access to improved sanitation (% of urban pop.)	..	86	..
Energy use per capita (kg oil equivalent)	2,689	1,696	..
Electricity use per capita (kilowatt-hours)	2,337	1,632	..
Economy			
GDP ($ billions)	38	46	57
GDP growth (annual %)	−5.6	4.3	4.9
GDP implicit price deflator (annual % growth)	13.6	24.2	23.2
Value added in agriculture (% of GDP)	24	13	12
Value added in industry (% of GDP)	50	38	36
Value added in services (% of GDP)	26	49	52
Exports of goods and services (% of GDP)	17	35	33
Imports of goods and services (% of GDP)	26	41	39
Gross capital formation (% of GDP)	30	23	21
Central government revenue (% of GDP)	34.4	26.7	..
Cash surplus/deficit (% of GDP)	0.9	−3.6	..
Technology and infrastructure			
Fixed-line and mobile subscribers (per 1,000 people)	102	430	524
Cost of 3-minute local call ($)	0.04	0.11	0.12
Personal computers (per 1,000 people)	2.2	69.2	96.6
Internet users (per 1,000 people)	..	101	184
Paved roads (% of total)	51.0	50.4	..
Aircraft departures (thousands)	22	18	27
Trade and finance			
Trade in goods (% of GDP)	32.8	69.4	73.1
Trade growth less GDP growth (avg. %, 1990–2003)			8.7
High-technology exports (% of manufactured exports)	2	3	4
Net barter terms of trade (2000 = 100)	..	..	..
Foreign direct investment ($ millions)	0	1,144	1,844
Present value of debt ($ billions)			22
Total debt service (% of goods and services exports)	0.3	19.1	17.3
Short-term debt ($ millions)	910	492	1,366
Aid per capita ($)	11	19	28

Russian Federation

Europe & Central Asia   **Lower middle income**

Population (millions)	143	Population growth (%)	−0.4
Surface area (1,000 sq. km)	17,075	National poverty rate (% pop.)	..
GNI ($ billions)	375	GNI per capita ($)	2,610

	1990	2002	2003
People			
Life expectancy at birth (years)	69	66	66
Fertility rate (births per woman)	1.9	1.3	1.3
Infant mortality rate (per 1,000 live births)	21	18	16
Under-five mortality rate (per 1,000)	21	21	21
Births attended by skilled health staff (% of total)	..	99	..
Child malnutrition, underweight (% of under age 5)	..	6	..
Child immunization, measles (% of ages 12–23 mon.)	83	98	96
HIV prevalence rate (% of ages 15–49)	..	0.7	1.1
Adult literacy, male (% of ages 15 and older)	100	100	..
Adult literacy, female (% of ages 15 and older)	99	99	..
Primary completion rate, total (% of age group)	..	90	93
Primary completion rate, female (% of age group)	..	..	..
Net primary enrollment (% of age group)	99	..	..
Net secondary enrollment (% of age group)	..	..	..
Environment			
Forests (1,000 sq. km)	8,500	8,514	..
Deforestation (average annual %, 1990–2000)		0.0	
Freshwater use (% of internal resources)			2
Carbon dioxide emissions (metric tons per capita)	13.3	9.9	..
Access to improved water source (% of total pop.)	94	96	..
Access to improved sanitation (% of urban pop.)	93	93	..
Energy use per capita (kg oil equivalent)	5,211	4,288	..
Electricity use per capita (kilowatt-hours)	5,087	4,291	..
Economy			
GDP ($ billions)	517	346	433
GDP growth (annual %)	−3.0	4.7	7.3
GDP implicit price deflator (annual % growth)	15.9	15.7	14.4
Value added in agriculture (% of GDP)	17	6	5
Value added in industry (% of GDP)	48	34	34
Value added in services (% of GDP)	35	60	61
Exports of goods and services (% of GDP)	18	35	32
Imports of goods and services (% of GDP)	18	24	21
Gross capital formation (% of GDP)	30	21	20
Central government revenue (% of GDP)	..	31.7	27.4
Cash surplus/deficit (% of GDP)	..	7.0	2.2
Technology and infrastructure			
Fixed-line and mobile subscribers (per 1,000 people)	140	362	..
Cost of 3-minute local call ($)	0.03	0.02	..
Personal computers (per 1,000 people)	3.4	88.7	..
Internet users (per 1,000 people)	0	20	..
Paved roads (% of total)	74.2	67.4	..
Aircraft departures (thousands)	..	345	351
Trade and finance			
Trade in goods (% of GDP)	..	48.4	48.2
Trade growth less GDP growth (avg. %, 1990–2003)			3.0
High-technology exports (% of manufactured exports)	..	13	19
Net barter terms of trade (2000 = 100)	..	..	..
Foreign direct investment ($ millions)	0	3,461	7,958
Present value of debt ($ billions)			184
Total debt service (% of goods and services exports)	..	11.2	11.8
Short-term debt ($ billions)	13	16	31
Aid per capita ($)	2	9	9

Rwanda

Population (millions)	8	Population growth (%)	2.8
Surface area (1,000 sq. km)	26	National poverty rate (% pop.)	60
GNI ($ millions)	1,826	GNI per capita ($)	220

	1990	2002	2003
People			
Life expectancy at birth (years)	40	40	40
Fertility rate (births per woman)	7.1	5.7	5.7
Infant mortality rate (per 1,000 live births)	103	*118*	118
Under-five mortality rate (per 1,000)	173	*203*	203
Births attended by skilled health staff (% of total)	26	31	..
Child malnutrition, underweight (% of under age 5)	29	24	..
Child immunization, measles (% of ages 12–23 mon.)	83	69	90
HIV prevalence rate (% of ages 15–49)	..	5.1	5.1
Adult literacy, male (% of ages 15 and older)	63	75	..
Adult literacy, female (% of ages 15 and older)	44	63	..
Primary completion rate, total (% of age group)	44	37	..
Primary completion rate, female (% of age group)	44	36	..
Net primary enrollment (% of age group)	67	87	..
Net secondary enrollment (% of age group)	7	..	..
Environment			
Forests (1,000 sq. km)	5	*3*	..
Deforestation (average annual %, 1990–2000)		*3.9*	
Freshwater use (% of internal resources)			16
Carbon dioxide emissions (metric tons per capita)	0.1	*0.1*	..
Access to improved water source (% of total pop.)	58	73	..
Access to improved sanitation (% of urban pop.)	49	56	..
Energy use per capita (kg oil equivalent)	..	..	..
Electricity use per capita (kilowatt-hours)	..	..	..
Economy			
GDP ($ millions)	2,584	1,713	1,637
GDP growth (annual %)	–2.4	9.4	3.2
GDP implicit price deflator (annual % growth)	13.5	–1.1	4.6
Value added in agriculture (% of GDP)	33	42	42
Value added in industry (% of GDP)	25	22	22
Value added in services (% of GDP)	43	37	36
Exports of goods and services (% of GDP)	6	8	9
Imports of goods and services (% of GDP)	14	25	28
Gross capital formation (% of GDP)	15	19	20
Central government revenue (% of GDP)	10.8	..	..
Cash surplus/deficit (% of GDP)	–5.4	..	..
Technology and infrastructure			
Fixed-line and mobile subscribers (per 1,000 people)	2	16	..
Cost of 3-minute local call ($)	..	0.09	..
Personal computers (per 1,000 people)	..	..	..
Internet users (per 1,000 people)	..	3	..
Paved roads (% of total)	9.0	*8.3*	..
Aircraft departures (thousands)	1	..	..
Trade and finance			
Trade in goods (% of GDP)	15.4	15.1	18.3
Trade growth less GDP growth (avg. %, 1990–2003)			0.2
High-technology exports (% of manufactured exports)	..	1	25
Net barter terms of trade (2000 = 100)	40	69	..
Foreign direct investment ($ millions)	8	3	5
Present value of debt ($ millions)			972
Total debt service (% of goods and services exports)	14.2	11.5	14.4
Short-term debt ($ millions)	47	46	30
Aid per capita ($)	42	43	39

Samoa

East Asia & Pacific		Lower middle income	
Population (thousands)	178	Population growth (%)	1.0
Surface area (1,000 sq. km)	3	National poverty rate (% pop.)	..
GNI ($ millions)	257	GNI per capita ($)	1,440

	1990	2002	2003
People			
Life expectancy at birth (years)	66	69	70
Fertility rate (births per woman)	4.8	4.0	4.0
Infant mortality rate (per 1,000 live births)	33	21	19
Under-five mortality rate (per 1,000)	42	26	24
Births attended by skilled health staff (% of total)	76	100	..
Child malnutrition, underweight (% of under age 5)	..	2	..
Child immunization, measles (% of ages 12–23 mon.)	89	99	99
HIV prevalence rate (% of ages 15–49)	..	..	..
Adult literacy, male (% of ages 15 and older)	99	99	..
Adult literacy, female (% of ages 15 and older)	97	98	..
Primary completion rate, total (% of age group)	..	107	..
Primary completion rate, female (% of age group)	..	108	..
Net primary enrollment (% of age group)	..	95	..
Net secondary enrollment (% of age group)	..	61	..
Environment			
Forests (1,000 sq. km)	1	1	..
Deforestation (average annual %, 1990–2000)		2.1	
Freshwater use (% of internal resources)			..
Carbon dioxide emissions (metric tons per capita)	0.8	0.8	..
Access to improved water source (% of total pop.)	91	88	..
Access to improved sanitation (% of urban pop.)	100	100	..
Energy use per capita (kg oil equivalent)	..	..	..
Electricity use per capita (kilowatt-hours)	..	..	..
Economy			
GDP ($ millions)	201	241	268
GDP growth (annual %)	–4.4	1.5	3.5
GDP implicit price deflator (annual % growth)	..	2.9	4.6
Value added in agriculture (% of GDP)	..	..	..
Value added in industry (% of GDP)	..	..	..
Value added in services (% of GDP)	..	..	..
Exports of goods and services (% of GDP)	..	33	..
Imports of goods and services (% of GDP)	..	82	..
Gross capital formation (% of GDP)	..	..	..
Central government revenue (% of GDP)	..	..	..
Cash surplus/deficit (% of GDP)	..	..	..
Technology and infrastructure			
Fixed-line and mobile subscribers (per 1,000 people)	26	72	131
Cost of 3-minute local call ($)	0.04	0.03	0.04
Personal computers (per 1,000 people)	..	6.7	..
Internet users (per 1,000 people)	..	6	..
Paved roads (% of total)	..	42.0	..
Aircraft departures (thousands)	..	12	9
Trade and finance			
Trade in goods (% of GDP)	44.7	61.9	56.7
Trade growth less GDP growth (avg. %, 1990–2003)			4.2
High-technology exports (% of manufactured exports)	..	0	0
Net barter terms of trade (2000 = 100)	..	..	..
Foreign direct investment ($ millions)	7	0	0
Present value of debt ($ millions)			301
Total debt service (% of goods and services exports)	5.8	5.1	..
Short-term debt ($ millions)	0	78	196
Aid per capita ($)	298	212	186

San Marino

High income

Population (thousands)	28	Population growth (%)	..
Surface area (sq. km)	61	National poverty rate (% pop.)	..
GNI ($ millions)	..	GNI per capita ($)	..

	1990	2002	2003
People			
Life expectancy at birth (years)	..	..	..
Fertility rate (births per woman)	..	..	..
Infant mortality rate (per 1,000 live births)	9	5	4
Under-five mortality rate (per 1,000)	10	6	5
Births attended by skilled health staff (% of total)	..	..	..
Child malnutrition, underweight (% of under age 5)	..	..	..
Child immunization, measles (% of ages 12–23 mon.)	99	85	91
HIV prevalence rate (% of ages 15–49)	..	..	..
Adult literacy, male (% of ages 15 and older)	..	..	..
Adult literacy, female (% of ages 15 and older)	..	..	..
Primary completion rate, total (% of age group)	..	..	..
Primary completion rate, female (% of age group)	..	..	..
Net primary enrollment (% of age group)	..	..	..
Net secondary enrollment (% of age group)	..	..	..
Environment			
Forests (1,000 sq. km)	..	..	
Deforestation (average annual %, 1990–2000)		..	
Freshwater use (% of internal resources)			..
Carbon dioxide emissions (metric tons per capita)	..	..	..
Access to improved water source (% of total pop.)	..	..	..
Access to improved sanitation (% of urban pop.)	..	..	..
Energy use per capita (kg oil equivalent)	..	..	..
Electricity use per capita (kilowatt-hours)	..	..	..
Economy			
GDP ($ millions)	..	880	..
GDP growth (annual %)	..	2.3	..
GDP implicit price deflator (annual % growth)	..	..	..
Value added in agriculture (% of GDP)	..	..	..
Value added in industry (% of GDP)	..	..	..
Value added in services (% of GDP)	..	..	..
Exports of goods and services (% of GDP)	..	..	..
Imports of goods and services (% of GDP)	..	..	..
Gross capital formation (% of GDP)	..	..	..
Central government revenue (% of GDP)	..	46.4	..
Cash surplus/deficit (% of GDP)	..	1.3	..
Technology and infrastructure			
Fixed-line and mobile subscribers (per 1,000 people)	606	1,384	..
Cost of 3-minute local call ($)	0.10	0.06	..
Personal computers (per 1,000 people)	..	759.8	..
Internet users (per 1,000 people)	..	531	..
Paved roads (% of total)	..	..	..
Aircraft departures (thousands)	..	..	..
Trade and finance			
Trade in goods (% of GDP)	..	..	..
Trade growth less GDP growth (avg. %, 1990–2003)			..
High-technology exports (% of manufactured exports)	..	..	..
Net barter terms of trade (2000 = 100)	..	..	..
Foreign direct investment ($ millions)	..	..	..
Present value of debt ($ millions)			..
Total debt service (% of goods and services exports)	..	..	..
Short-term debt ($ millions)	..	..	..
Aid per capita ($)	..	..	..

São Tomé and Príncipe

Sub-Saharan Africa			Low income

Population (thousands)	157	Population growth (%)	2.1
Surface area (sq. km)	960	National poverty rate (% pop.)	..
GNI ($ millions)	48	GNI per capita ($)	300

	1990	2002	2003
People			
Life expectancy at birth (years)	62	66	66
Fertility rate (births per woman)	5.1	4.3	4.3
Infant mortality rate (per 1,000 live births)	75	75	75
Under-five mortality rate (per 1,000)	118	118	118
Births attended by skilled health staff (% of total)	..	79	..
Child malnutrition, underweight (% of under age 5)	..	13	..
Child immunization, measles (% of ages 12–23 mon.)	71	85	87
HIV prevalence rate (% of ages 15–49)	..	..	..
Adult literacy, male (% of ages 15 and older)	..	..	..
Adult literacy, female (% of ages 15 and older)	..	..	..
Primary completion rate, total (% of age group)	..	61	..
Primary completion rate, female (% of age group)	..	66	..
Net primary enrollment (% of age group)	..	97	..
Net secondary enrollment (% of age group)	..	29	..
Environment			
Forests (1,000 sq. km)	0	0	..
Deforestation (average annual %, 1990–2000)		0.0	
Freshwater use (% of internal resources)			..
Carbon dioxide emissions (metric tons per capita)	0.6	0.6	..
Access to improved water source (% of total pop.)	..	79	..
Access to improved sanitation (% of urban pop.)	..	32	..
Energy use per capita (kg oil equivalent)	..	..	..
Electricity use per capita (kilowatt-hours)	..	..	..
Economy			
GDP ($ millions)	58	54	59
GDP growth (annual %)	1.8	4.1	4.5
GDP implicit price deflator (annual % growth)	41.2	10.7	9.4
Value added in agriculture (% of GDP)	28	18	17
Value added in industry (% of GDP)	18	16	15
Value added in services (% of GDP)	55	67	68
Exports of goods and services (% of GDP)	14	37	38
Imports of goods and services (% of GDP)	72	85	83
Gross capital formation (% of GDP)	16	33	30
Central government revenue (% of GDP)	..	..	..
Cash surplus/deficit (% of GDP)	..	..	..
Technology and infrastructure			
Fixed-line and mobile subscribers (per 1,000 people)	19	54	78
Cost of 3-minute local call ($)	0.02	0.17	..
Personal computers (per 1,000 people)	..	..	..
Internet users (per 1,000 people)	..	44	99
Paved roads (% of total)	61.6	68.1	..
Aircraft departures (thousands)	1	1	1
Trade and finance			
Trade in goods (% of GDP)	43.4	67.3	82.4
Trade growth less GDP growth (avg. %, 1990–2003)			–0.1
High-technology exports (% of manufactured exports)	..	..	..
Net barter terms of trade (2000 = 100)	101	138	..
Foreign direct investment ($ millions)	0	3	10
Present value of debt ($ millions)			147
Total debt service (% of goods and services exports)	34.0	25.0	31.0
Short-term debt ($ millions)	16	23	9
Aid per capita ($)	475	169	239

Saudi Arabia

Middle East & North Africa   **Upper middle income**

Population (millions)	23	Population growth (%)	2.9
Surface area (1,000 sq. km)	2,150	National poverty rate (% pop.)	..
GNI ($ billions)	208	GNI per capita ($)	9,240

	1990	2002	2003
People			
Life expectancy at birth (years)	69	73	73
Fertility rate (births per woman)	6.6	5.3	5.3
Infant mortality rate (per 1,000 live births)	34	*24*	22
Under-five mortality rate (per 1,000)	44	*29*	26
Births attended by skilled health staff (% of total)	..	..	..
Child malnutrition, underweight (% of under age 5)	..	..	..
Child immunization, measles (% of ages 12–23 mon.)	88	97	96
HIV prevalence rate (% of ages 15–49)	..	..	..
Adult literacy, male (% of ages 15 and older)	76	84	..
Adult literacy, female (% of ages 15 and older)	50	69	..
Primary completion rate, total (% of age group)	57	61	..
Primary completion rate, female (% of age group)	52	61	..
Net primary enrollment (% of age group)	59	54	..
Net secondary enrollment (% of age group)	31	53	..
Environment			
Forests (1,000 sq. km)	15	*15*	..
Deforestation (average annual %, 1990–2000)		*0.0*	
Freshwater use (% of internal resources)			850
Carbon dioxide emissions (metric tons per capita)	11.3	*18.1*	..
Access to improved water source (% of total pop.)	90	..	..
Access to improved sanitation (% of urban pop.)	100	100	..
Energy use per capita (kg oil equivalent)	4,147	5,775	..
Electricity use per capita (kilowatt-hours)	3,181	5,275	..
Economy			
GDP ($ billions)	117	189	215
GDP growth (annual %)	8.3	0.1	7.2
GDP implicit price deflator (annual % growth)	13.1	2.9	6.1
Value added in agriculture (% of GDP)	6	5	5
Value added in industry (% of GDP)	49	51	55
Value added in services (% of GDP)	45	43	40
Exports of goods and services (% of GDP)	41	41	47
Imports of goods and services (% of GDP)	32	24	24
Gross capital formation (% of GDP)	15	20	19
Central government revenue (% of GDP)	..	..	..
Cash surplus/deficit (% of GDP)	..	..	..
Technology and infrastructure			
Fixed-line and mobile subscribers (per 1,000 people)	78	361	477
Cost of 3-minute local call ($)	*0.01*	0.04	0.05
Personal computers (per 1,000 people)	23.7	130.2	..
Internet users (per 1,000 people)	..	65	67
Paved roads (% of total)	40.6	*29.9*	..
Aircraft departures (thousands)	93	109	108
Trade and finance			
Trade in goods (% of GDP)	58.6	55.2	58.1
Trade growth less GDP growth (avg. %, 1990–2003)			..
High-technology exports (% of manufactured exports)	0	0	..
Net barter terms of trade (2000 = 100)	..	..	..
Foreign direct investment ($ millions)	..	..	..
Present value of debt ($ millions)			..
Total debt service (% of goods and services exports)	..	..	..
Short-term debt ($ millions)	..	..	..
Aid per capita ($)	3	1	1

Senegal

Sub-Saharan Africa | **Low income**

Population (millions)	10	Population growth (%)	2.3
Surface area (1,000 sq. km)	197	National poverty rate (% pop.)	..
GNI ($ millions)	5,563	GNI per capita ($)	540

	1990	2002	2003
People			
Life expectancy at birth (years)	50	52	52
Fertility rate (births per woman)	6.2	4.9	4.9
Infant mortality rate (per 1,000 live births)	90	*80*	78
Under-five mortality rate (per 1,000)	148	*139*	137
Births attended by skilled health staff (% of total)	..	41	..
Child malnutrition, underweight (% of under age 5)	*22*	23	..
Child immunization, measles (% of ages 12–23 mon.)	51	54	60
HIV prevalence rate (% of ages 15–49)	..	*0.8*	0.8
Adult literacy, male (% of ages 15 and older)	38	49	..
Adult literacy, female (% of ages 15 and older)	19	30	..
Primary completion rate, total (% of age group)	*42*	48	..
Primary completion rate, female (% of age group)	*33*	43	..
Net primary enrollment (% of age group)	47	58	..
Net secondary enrollment (% of age group)	..	..	..
Environment			
Forests (1,000 sq. km)	67	*62*	..
Deforestation (average annual %, 1990–2000)		*0.7*	
Freshwater use (% of internal resources)			5
Carbon dioxide emissions (metric tons per capita)	0.4	*0.4*	..
Access to improved water source (% of total pop.)	66	72	..
Access to improved sanitation (% of urban pop.)	52	70	..
Energy use per capita (kg oil equivalent)	305	319	..
Electricity use per capita (kilowatt-hours)	99	135	..
Economy			
GDP ($ millions)	5,699	5,037	6,496
GDP growth (annual %)	3.9	1.1	6.5
GDP implicit price deflator (annual % growth)	1.2	2.7	0.9
Value added in agriculture (% of GDP)	20	15	17
Value added in industry (% of GDP)	19	22	21
Value added in services (% of GDP)	61	63	62
Exports of goods and services (% of GDP)	25	30	28
Imports of goods and services (% of GDP)	30	40	40
Gross capital formation (% of GDP)	14	18	20
Central government revenue (% of GDP)	..	*17.8*	..
Cash surplus/deficit (% of GDP)	..	*–2.2*	..
Technology and infrastructure			
Fixed-line and mobile subscribers (per 1,000 people)	6	*77*	78
Cost of 3-minute local call ($)	*0.19*	*0.10*	0.20
Personal computers (per 1,000 people)	2.5	19.8	21.2
Internet users (per 1,000 people)	..	10	22
Paved roads (% of total)	27.2	*29.3*	..
Aircraft departures (thousands)	4	7	2
Trade and finance			
Trade in goods (% of GDP)	34.7	60.0	56.9
Trade growth less GDP growth (avg. %, 1990–2003)			–0.9
High-technology exports (% of manufactured exports)	..	5	9
Net barter terms of trade (2000 = 100)	172	96	..
Foreign direct investment ($ millions)	57	80	78
Present value of debt ($ millions)			1,916
Total debt service (% of goods and services exports)	20.0	11.6	10.4
Short-term debt ($ millions)	421	294	156
Aid per capita ($)	112	44	44

Serbia and Montenegro

Europe & Central Asia　　　　　　　　**Lower middle income**

Population (millions)	8	Population growth (%)	–0.7
Surface area (1,000 sq. km)	102	National poverty rate (% pop.)	..
GNI ($ billions)	16	GNI per capita ($)	1,910

	1990	2002	2003
People			
Life expectancy at birth (years)	72	73	73
Fertility rate (births per woman)	2.1	1.7	1.7
Infant mortality rate (per 1,000 live births)	23	13	12
Under-five mortality rate (per 1,000)	26	16	14
Births attended by skilled health staff (% of total)	..	99	..
Child malnutrition, underweight (% of under age 5)	..	2	..
Child immunization, measles (% of ages 12–23 mon.)	83	92	87
HIV prevalence rate (% of ages 15–49)	..	0.2	0.2
Adult literacy, male (% of ages 15 and older)	..	..	..
Adult literacy, female (% of ages 15 and older)	..	..	..
Primary completion rate, total (% of age group)	71	96	..
Primary completion rate, female (% of age group)	..	96	..
Net primary enrollment (% of age group)	69	76	..
Net secondary enrollment (% of age group)	62	83	..
Environment			
Forests (1,000 sq. km)	29	29	..
Deforestation (average annual %, 1990–2000)		0.0	
Freshwater use (% of internal resources)			30
Carbon dioxide emissions (metric tons per capita)	..	3.7	..
Access to improved water source (% of total pop.)	93	93	..
Access to improved sanitation (% of urban pop.)	97	97	..
Energy use per capita (kg oil equivalent)	1,435	1,981	..
Electricity use per capita (kilowatt-hours)	..	..	..
Economy			
GDP ($ billions)	..	16	21
GDP growth (annual %)	..	4.0	3.0
GDP implicit price deflator (annual % growth)	..	25.5	6.4
Value added in agriculture (% of GDP)	..	15	..
Value added in industry (% of GDP)	..	32	..
Value added in services (% of GDP)	..	53	..
Exports of goods and services (% of GDP)	..	21	22
Imports of goods and services (% of GDP)	..	44	45
Gross capital formation (% of GDP)	..	16	18
Central government revenue (% of GDP)	..	35.5	..
Cash surplus/deficit (% of GDP)	..	..	..
Technology and infrastructure			
Fixed-line and mobile subscribers (per 1,000 people)	166	489	581
Cost of 3-minute local call ($)	..	0.01	..
Personal computers (per 1,000 people)	..	27.1	..
Internet users (per 1,000 people)	..	38	79
Paved roads (% of total)	58.5	59.3	..
Aircraft departures (thousands)	57	20	22
Trade and finance			
Trade in goods (% of GDP)	..	54.8	48.5
Trade growth less GDP growth (avg. %, 1990–2003)			..
High-technology exports (% of manufactured exports)	3	..	..
Net barter terms of trade (2000 = 100)	..	..	..
Foreign direct investment ($ millions)	0	475	1,360
Present value of debt ($ billions)			13
Total debt service (% of goods and services exports)	..	4.6	13.6
Short-term debt ($ billions)	..	2	3
Aid per capita ($)	..	237	163

Seychelles

Sub-Saharan Africa   **Upper middle income**

Population (thousands)	84	Population growth (%)	1.4
Surface area (sq. km)	450	National poverty rate (% pop.)	..
GNI ($ millions)	626	GNI per capita ($)	7,490

	1990	2002	2003
People			
Life expectancy at birth (years)	70	73	73
Fertility rate (births per woman)	2.8	2.0	2.0
Infant mortality rate (per 1,000 live births)	17	*13*	11
Under-five mortality rate (per 1,000)	21	*17*	15
Births attended by skilled health staff (% of total)	..		
Child malnutrition, underweight (% of under age 5)	*6*	..	..
Child immunization, measles (% of ages 12–23 mon.)	86	98	99
HIV prevalence rate (% of ages 15–49)	..	..	..
Adult literacy, male (% of ages 15 and older)	..	..	91
Adult literacy, female (% of ages 15 and older)	..	..	92
Primary completion rate, total (% of age group)	..	118	..
Primary completion rate, female (% of age group)	..	116	..
Net primary enrollment (% of age group)	..	*99*	..
Net secondary enrollment (% of age group)	..	100	..
Environment			
Forests (1,000 sq. km)	0	*0*	..
Deforestation (average annual %, 1990–2000)		*0.0*	
Freshwater use (% of internal resources)			..
Carbon dioxide emissions (metric tons per capita)	1.6	*2.8*	..
Access to improved water source (% of total pop.)	..	87	..
Access to improved sanitation (% of urban pop.)	..	..	..
Energy use per capita (kg oil equivalent)	..	..	..
Electricity use per capita (kilowatt-hours)	..	..	..
Economy			
GDP ($ millions)	369	699	720
GDP growth (annual %)	7.0	0.3	–5.1
GDP implicit price deflator (annual % growth)	5.6	5.5	7.0
Value added in agriculture (% of GDP)	5	3	3
Value added in industry (% of GDP)	16	30	35
Value added in services (% of GDP)	79	67	62
Exports of goods and services (% of GDP)	62	78	77
Imports of goods and services (% of GDP)	67	81	77
Gross capital formation (% of GDP)	25	30	19
Central government revenue (% of GDP)	–1.9	41.3	..
Cash surplus/deficit (% of GDP)	..	–14.3	..
Technology and infrastructure			
Fixed-line and mobile subscribers (per 1,000 people)	124	823	851
Cost of 3-minute local call ($)	0.15	*0.14*	0.15
Personal computers (per 1,000 people)	..	160.8	..
Internet users (per 1,000 people)	..	140	..
Paved roads (% of total)	56.9	*84.5*	..
Aircraft departures (thousands)	16	22	19
Trade and finance			
Trade in goods (% of GDP)	65.7	92.7	98.3
Trade growth less GDP growth (avg. %, 1990–2003)			4.6
High-technology exports (% of manufactured exports)	1	..	..
Net barter terms of trade (2000 = 100)	78	100	..
Foreign direct investment ($ millions)	20	61	58
Present value of debt ($ millions)			563
Total debt service (% of goods and services exports)	9.0	15.6	14.0
Short-term debt ($ millions)	46	108	109
Aid per capita ($)	513	95	110

Sierra Leone

Sub-Saharan Africa   **Low income**

Population (millions)	5	Population growth (%)	1.9
Surface area (1,000 sq. km)	72	National poverty rate (% pop.)	70
GNI ($ millions)	808	GNI per capita ($)	150

	1990	2002	2003
People			
Life expectancy at birth (years)	35	37	37
Fertility rate (births per woman)	6.5	5.6	5.6
Infant mortality rate (per 1,000 live births)	175	167	166
Under-five mortality rate (per 1,000)	302	286	284
Births attended by skilled health staff (% of total)	..	42	..
Child malnutrition, underweight (% of under age 5)	29	27	..
Child immunization, measles (% of ages 12–23 mon.)	..	62	73
HIV prevalence rate (% of ages 15–49)	..	..	..
Adult literacy, male (% of ages 15 and older)	..	..	..
Adult literacy, female (% of ages 15 and older)	..	..	..
Primary completion rate, total (% of age group)	..	54	56
Primary completion rate, female (% of age group)	..	28	45
Net primary enrollment (% of age group)	41	..	..
Net secondary enrollment (% of age group)	..	..	..
Environment			
Forests (1,000 sq. km)	14	11	..
Deforestation (average annual %, 1990–2000)		2.9	
Freshwater use (% of internal resources)			0
Carbon dioxide emissions (metric tons per capita)	0.1	0.1	..
Access to improved water source (% of total pop.)	..	57	..
Access to improved sanitation (% of urban pop.)	..	53	..
Energy use per capita (kg oil equivalent)	..	..	..
Electricity use per capita (kilowatt-hours)	..	..	..
Economy			
GDP ($ millions)	650	783	793
GDP growth (annual %)	3.3	6.3	6.6
GDP implicit price deflator (annual % growth)	70.6	3.9	6.3
Value added in agriculture (% of GDP)	32	52	53
Value added in industry (% of GDP)	13	31	31
Value added in services (% of GDP)	55	16	16
Exports of goods and services (% of GDP)	22	18	22
Imports of goods and services (% of GDP)	24	41	49
Gross capital formation (% of GDP)	10	10	16
Central government revenue (% of GDP)	5.6	7.1	..
Cash surplus/deficit (% of GDP)	..	..	..
Technology and infrastructure			
Fixed-line and mobile subscribers (per 1,000 people)	3	18	..
Cost of 3-minute local call ($)	0.12	0.03	..
Personal computers (per 1,000 people)	..	..	..
Internet users (per 1,000 people)	..	2	..
Paved roads (% of total)	10.6	8.0	..
Aircraft departures (thousands)	1	0	0
Trade and finance			
Trade in goods (% of GDP)	44.2	40.0	49.8
Trade growth less GDP growth (avg. %, 1990–2003)			–5.5
High-technology exports (% of manufactured exports)	..	31	..
Net barter terms of trade (2000 = 100)	24	164	..
Foreign direct investment ($ millions)	32	2	3
Present value of debt ($ millions)			884
Total debt service (% of goods and services exports)	10.1	17.5	12.4
Short-term debt ($ millions)	148	16	23
Aid per capita ($)	15	67	56

Singapore

High income

Population (millions)	4	Population growth (%)		2.3
Surface area (sq. km)	680	National poverty rate (% pop.)		..
GNI ($ billions)	90	GNI per capita ($)		21,230

	1990	2002	2003
People			
Life expectancy at birth (years)	74	*78*	..
Fertility rate (births per woman)	1.9	1.4	1.4
Infant mortality rate (per 1,000 live births)	7	3	..
Under-five mortality rate (per 1,000)	8	5	..
Births attended by skilled health staff (% of total)	..	*100*	..
Child malnutrition, underweight (% of under age 5)	..	3	..
Child immunization, measles (% of ages 12–23 mon.)	84	91	88
HIV prevalence rate (% of ages 15–49)	..	0.2	0.2
Adult literacy, male (% of ages 15 and older)	94	97	..
Adult literacy, female (% of ages 15 and older)	83	*89*	..
Primary completion rate, total (% of age group)	..	..	..
Primary completion rate, female (% of age group)	..	..	..
Net primary enrollment (% of age group)	96	..	..
Net secondary enrollment (% of age group)	..	..	..
Environment			
Forests (1,000 sq. km)	0	*0*	..
Deforestation (average annual %, 1990–2000)		*0.0*	
Freshwater use (% of internal resources)			..
Carbon dioxide emissions (metric tons per capita)	13.8	*14.7*	..
Access to improved water source (% of total pop.)	..	..	..
Access to improved sanitation (% of urban pop.)	100	100	..
Energy use per capita (kg oil equivalent)	4,384	6,078	..
Electricity use per capita (kilowatt-hours)	4,130	7,039	..
Economy			
GDP ($ billions)	37	88	91
GDP growth (annual %)	9.0	3.3	1.1
GDP implicit price deflator (annual % growth)	4.4	0.6	–0.4
Value added in agriculture (% of GDP)	..	0	0
Value added in industry (% of GDP)	..	35	35
Value added in services (% of GDP)	..	65	65
Exports of goods and services (% of GDP)	..	..	..
Imports of goods and services (% of GDP)	..	..	..
Gross capital formation (% of GDP)	36	21	13
Central government revenue (% of GDP)	26.7	22.2	..
Cash surplus/deficit (% of GDP)	11.1	4.8	..
Technology and infrastructure			
Fixed-line and mobile subscribers (per 1,000 people)	363	1,258	1,303
Cost of 3-minute local call ($)	0.00	0.02	0.02
Personal computers (per 1,000 people)	65.6	622.0	..
Internet users (per 1,000 people)	2	504	509
Paved roads (% of total)	97.1	100.0	..
Aircraft departures (thousands)	31	72	64
Trade and finance			
Trade in goods (% of GDP)	307.6	273.7	297.8
Trade growth less GDP growth (avg. %, 1990–2003)			..
High-technology exports (% of manufactured exports)	40	60	59
Net barter terms of trade (2000 = 100)	116	94	..
Foreign direct investment ($ billions)	6	6	11
Present value of debt ($ millions)			..
Total debt service (% of goods and services exports)	..	..	..
Short-term debt ($ millions)	..	..	..
Aid per capita ($)	–1	2	2

Slovak Republic

Europe & Central Asia		Upper middle income

Population (millions)	5	Population growth (%)	0.2
Surface area (1,000 sq. km)	49	National poverty rate (% pop.)	..
GNI ($ billions)	27	GNI per capita ($)	4,940

	1990	2002	2003
People			
Life expectancy at birth (years)	71	73	73
Fertility rate (births per woman)	2.1	1.2	1.2
Infant mortality rate (per 1,000 live births)	14	8	7
Under-five mortality rate (per 1,000)	15	9	8
Births attended by skilled health staff (% of total)	..	..	..
Child malnutrition, underweight (% of under age 5)	..	..	..
Child immunization, measles (% of ages 12–23 mon.)	..	99	99
HIV prevalence rate (% of ages 15–49)	..	..	0.1
Adult literacy, male (% of ages 15 and older)	..	100	..
Adult literacy, female (% of ages 15 and older)	..	100	..
Primary completion rate, total (% of age group)	96	99	..
Primary completion rate, female (% of age group)	96	98	..
Net primary enrollment (% of age group)	..	87	..
Net secondary enrollment (% of age group)	..	87	..
Environment			
Forests (1,000 sq. km)	20	22	..
Deforestation (average annual %, 1990–2000)		–1.0	
Freshwater use (% of internal resources)			14
Carbon dioxide emissions (metric tons per capita)	8.4	6.6	..
Access to improved water source (% of total pop.)	100	100	..
Access to improved sanitation (% of urban pop.)	100	100	..
Energy use per capita (kg oil equivalent)	4,056	3,448	..
Electricity use per capita (kilowatt-hours)	4,432	4,222	..
Economy			
GDP ($ billions)	15	24	33
GDP growth (annual %)	–2.7	4.4	4.2
GDP implicit price deflator (annual % growth)	6.9	4.0	2.6
Value added in agriculture (% of GDP)	7	4	4
Value added in industry (% of GDP)	59	29	30
Value added in services (% of GDP)	33	67	67
Exports of goods and services (% of GDP)	27	72	78
Imports of goods and services (% of GDP)	36	79	80
Gross capital formation (% of GDP)	33	29	25
Central government revenue (% of GDP)	..	..	35.3
Cash surplus/deficit (% of GDP)	..	..	–3.3
Technology and infrastructure			
Fixed-line and mobile subscribers (per 1,000 people)	135	812	925
Cost of 3-minute local call ($)	0.03	0.12	..
Personal computers (per 1,000 people)	..	180.4	..
Internet users (per 1,000 people)	..	160	256
Paved roads (% of total)	98.7	87.3	..
Aircraft departures (thousands)	..	4	7
Trade and finance			
Trade in goods (% of GDP)	110.8	128.1	136.7
Trade growth less GDP growth (avg. %, 1990–2003)			6.8
High-technology exports (% of manufactured exports)	..	3	4
Net barter terms of trade (2000 = 100)	..	..	..
Foreign direct investment ($ millions)	0	4,123	571
Present value of debt ($ billions)			18
Total debt service (% of goods and services exports)	..	19.4	13.4
Short-term debt ($ billions)	..	4	8
Aid per capita ($)	1	29	30

Slovenia

High income

Population (millions)	2	Population growth (%)	0.1
Surface area (1,000 sq. km)	20	National poverty rate (% pop.)	..
GNI ($ billions)	24	GNI per capita ($)	11,920

	1990	2002	2003
People			
Life expectancy at birth (years)	73	76	76
Fertility rate (births per woman)	1.5	1.2	1.2
Infant mortality rate (per 1,000 live births)	8	5	4
Under-five mortality rate (per 1,000)	9	5	4
Births attended by skilled health staff (% of total)	100	..	..
Child malnutrition, underweight (% of under age 5)	..	..	..
Child immunization, measles (% of ages 12–23 mon.)	90	94	94
HIV prevalence rate (% of ages 15–49)	..	0.1	0.1
Adult literacy, male (% of ages 15 and older)	100	100	..
Adult literacy, female (% of ages 15 and older)	100	100	..
Primary completion rate, total (% of age group)	97	95	..
Primary completion rate, female (% of age group)	..	94	..
Net primary enrollment (% of age group)	..	93	..
Net secondary enrollment (% of age group)	..	93	..
Environment			
Forests (1,000 sq. km)	11	11	..
Deforestation (average annual %, 1990–2000)		–0.2	
Freshwater use (% of internal resources)			7
Carbon dioxide emissions (metric tons per capita)	6.2	7.3	..
Access to improved water source (% of total pop.)	..	..	..
Access to improved sanitation (% of urban pop.)	..	..	..
Energy use per capita (kg oil equivalent)	2,508	3,486	..
Electricity use per capita (kilowatt-hours)	4,371	5,907	..
Economy			
GDP ($ billions)	17	22	28
GDP growth (annual %)	–8.9	3.3	2.5
GDP implicit price deflator (annual % growth)	..	8.1	0.9
Value added in agriculture (% of GDP)	6	3	..
Value added in industry (% of GDP)	46	36	..
Value added in services (% of GDP)	49	61	..
Exports of goods and services (% of GDP)	84	58	60
Imports of goods and services (% of GDP)	74	56	60
Gross capital formation (% of GDP)	17	23	25
Central government revenue (% of GDP)	39.8	41.2	43.4
Cash surplus/deficit (% of GDP)	..	–2.7	–1.3
Technology and infrastructure			
Fixed-line and mobile subscribers (per 1,000 people)	211	1,341	1,278
Cost of 3-minute local call ($)	0.02	0.07	..
Personal computers (per 1,000 people)	32.5	300.6	..
Internet users (per 1,000 people)	..	376	..
Paved roads (% of total)	72.0	100.3	..
Aircraft departures (thousands)	4	15	16
Trade and finance			
Trade in goods (% of GDP)	102.4	96.2	95.9
Trade growth less GDP growth (avg. %, 1990–2003)			1.6
High-technology exports (% of manufactured exports)	3	5	6
Net barter terms of trade (2000 = 100)	..	..	..
Foreign direct investment ($ millions)	111	1,686	337
Present value of debt ($ millions)			..
Total debt service (% of goods and services exports)	..	..	..
Short-term debt ($ millions)	..	..	..
Aid per capita ($)	..	26	33

Solomon Islands

East Asia & Pacific			**Low income**

Population (thousands)	457	Population growth (%)	3.0
Surface area (1,000 sq. km)	29	National poverty rate (% pop.)	..
GNI ($ millions)	255	GNI per capita ($)	560

	1990	2002	2003
People			
Life expectancy at birth (years)	64	69	70
Fertility rate (births per woman)	5.9	5.3	5.3
Infant mortality rate (per 1,000 live births)	29	21	19
Under-five mortality rate (per 1,000)	36	25	22
Births attended by skilled health staff (% of total)	..	85	..
Child malnutrition, underweight (% of under age 5)	21	21	..
Child immunization, measles (% of ages 12–23 mon.)	70	78	78
HIV prevalence rate (% of ages 15–49)	..	..	..
Adult literacy, male (% of ages 15 and older)	..	..	..
Adult literacy, female (% of ages 15 and older)	..	..	..
Primary completion rate, total (% of age group)	61	..	..
Primary completion rate, female (% of age group)	..	..	..
Net primary enrollment (% of age group)	83	..	..
Net secondary enrollment (% of age group)	..	..	..
Environment			
Forests (1,000 sq. km)	26	25	..
Deforestation (average annual %, 1990–2000)		0.2	
Freshwater use (% of internal resources)			..
Carbon dioxide emissions (metric tons per capita)	0.5	0.4	..
Access to improved water source (% of total pop.)	..	70	..
Access to improved sanitation (% of urban pop.)	98	98	..
Energy use per capita (kg oil equivalent)	..	..	..
Electricity use per capita (kilowatt-hours)	..	..	..
Economy			
GDP ($ millions)	211	247	253
GDP growth (annual %)	1.8	−1.6	5.1
GDP implicit price deflator (annual % growth)	0.1	12.7	5.0
Value added in agriculture (% of GDP)	..	..	..
Value added in industry (% of GDP)	..	..	..
Value added in services (% of GDP)	..	..	..
Exports of goods and services (% of GDP)	47	31	..
Imports of goods and services (% of GDP)	73	33	..
Gross capital formation (% of GDP)	29		..
Central government revenue (% of GDP)	..	..	..
Cash surplus/deficit (% of GDP)	..	..	..
Technology and infrastructure			
Fixed-line and mobile subscribers (per 1,000 people)	15	17	16
Cost of 3-minute local call ($)	0.12	0.07	0.06
Personal computers (per 1,000 people)	..	40.5	..
Internet users (per 1,000 people)	..	5	5
Paved roads (% of total)	2.1	2.5	..
Aircraft departures (thousands)	11	13	10
Trade and finance			
Trade in goods (% of GDP)	76.2	42.6	56.2
Trade growth less GDP growth (avg. %, 1990–2003)			..
High-technology exports (% of manufactured exports)	..	..	..
Net barter terms of trade (2000 = 100)	..	..	..
Foreign direct investment ($ millions)	10	−1	−2
Present value of debt ($ millions)			146
Total debt service (% of goods and services exports)	11.9	4.8	..
Short-term debt ($ millions)	17	5	12
Aid per capita ($)	143	59	132

Somalia

Sub-Saharan Africa   **Low income**

Population (millions)	10	Population growth (%)	3.2
Surface area (1,000 sq. km)	638	National poverty rate (% pop.)	..
GNI ($ millions)	..	GNI per capita ($)	..

	1990	2002	2003
People			
Life expectancy at birth (years)	42	47	47
Fertility rate (births per woman)	7.3	6.9	6.9
Infant mortality rate (per 1,000 live births)	133	*133*	133
Under-five mortality rate (per 1,000)	225	*225*	225
Births attended by skilled health staff (% of total)	..	34	..
Child malnutrition, underweight (% of under age 5)	..	*26*	..
Child immunization, measles (% of ages 12–23 mon.)	30	45	40
HIV prevalence rate (% of ages 15–49)	..	..	..
Adult literacy, male (% of ages 15 and older)	..	..	..
Adult literacy, female (% of ages 15 and older)	..	..	..
Primary completion rate, total (% of age group)	..	..	..
Primary completion rate, female (% of age group)	..	..	..
Net primary enrollment (% of age group)	..	..	..
Net secondary enrollment (% of age group)	..	..	..
Environment			
Forests (1,000 sq. km)	83	*75*	..
Deforestation (average annual %, 1990–2000)		*1.0*	
Freshwater use (% of internal resources)			13
Carbon dioxide emissions (metric tons per capita)	0.0	..	..
Access to improved water source (% of total pop.)	..	29	..
Access to improved sanitation (% of urban pop.)	..	47	..
Energy use per capita (kg oil equivalent)	..	..	..
Electricity use per capita (kilowatt-hours)	..	..	..
Economy			
GDP ($ millions)	917	..	..
GDP growth (annual %)	..	..	..
GDP implicit price deflator (annual % growth)	215.5	..	..
Value added in agriculture (% of GDP)	65	..	..
Value added in industry (% of GDP)	..	..	..
Value added in services (% of GDP)	..	..	..
Exports of goods and services (% of GDP)	10	..	..
Imports of goods and services (% of GDP)	38	..	..
Gross capital formation (% of GDP)	16	..	..
Central government revenue (% of GDP)	..	..	..
Cash surplus/deficit (% of GDP)	..	..	..
Technology and infrastructure			
Fixed-line and mobile subscribers (per 1,000 people)	2	13	..
Cost of 3-minute local call ($)	..	..	..
Personal computers (per 1,000 people)	..	..	..
Internet users (per 1,000 people)	..	9	..
Paved roads (% of total)	11.1	*11.8*	..
Aircraft departures (thousands)	2	..	..
Trade and finance			
Trade in goods (% of GDP)	26.7	..	..
Trade growth less GDP growth (avg. %, 1990–2003)			..
High-technology exports (% of manufactured exports)	..	..	..
Net barter terms of trade (2000 = 100)	..	..	..
Foreign direct investment ($ millions)	6	0	1
Present value of debt ($ millions)			2,718
Total debt service (% of goods and services exports)	*47.6*	..	..
Short-term debt ($ millions)	285	677	735
Aid per capita ($)	69	21	18

South Africa

Sub-Saharan Africa			Lower middle income
Population (millions)	46	Population growth (%)	1.1
Surface area (1,000 sq. km)	1,219	National poverty rate (% pop.)	..
GNI ($ billions)	126	GNI per capita ($)	2,750

	1990	2002	2003
People			
Life expectancy at birth (years)	62	46	46
Fertility rate (births per woman)	3.3	2.8	2.8
Infant mortality rate (per 1,000 live births)	45	50	53
Under-five mortality rate (per 1,000)	60	63	66
Births attended by skilled health staff (% of total)	..	84	..
Child malnutrition, underweight (% of under age 5)	..	12	..
Child immunization, measles (% of ages 12–23 mon.)	79	78	83
HIV prevalence rate (% of ages 15–49)	..	20.9	15.6
Adult literacy, male (% of ages 15 and older)	82	87	..
Adult literacy, female (% of ages 15 and older)	80	85	..
Primary completion rate, total (% of age group)	81	99	..
Primary completion rate, female (% of age group)	85	102	..
Net primary enrollment (% of age group)	88	89	..
Net secondary enrollment (% of age group)	..	66	..
Environment			
Forests (1,000 sq. km)	90	89	..
Deforestation (average annual %, 1990–2000)		0.1	
Freshwater use (% of internal resources)			30
Carbon dioxide emissions (metric tons per capita)	8.3	7.4	..
Access to improved water source (% of total pop.)	83	87	..
Access to improved sanitation (% of urban pop.)	85	86	..
Energy use per capita (kg oil equivalent)	2,592	2,502	..
Electricity use per capita (kilowatt-hours)	3,676	3,860	..
Economy			
GDP ($ billions)	112	106	160
GDP growth (annual %)	–0.3	3.6	1.9
GDP implicit price deflator (annual % growth)	15.5	10.1	5.9
Value added in agriculture (% of GDP)	5	4	4
Value added in industry (% of GDP)	40	32	31
Value added in services (% of GDP)	55	64	65
Exports of goods and services (% of GDP)	24	34	28
Imports of goods and services (% of GDP)	19	30	26
Gross capital formation (% of GDP)	17	16	17
Central government revenue (% of GDP)	26.3	27.5	27.0
Cash surplus/deficit (% of GDP)	–3.5	–1.0	–2.5
Technology and infrastructure			
Fixed-line and mobile subscribers (per 1,000 people)	94	410	..
Cost of 3-minute local call ($)	0.07	0.09	0.15
Personal computers (per 1,000 people)	7.0	72.6	..
Internet users (per 1,000 people)	0	68	..
Paved roads (% of total)	29.8	20.9	..
Aircraft departures (thousands)	84	122	147
Trade and finance			
Trade in goods (% of GDP)	37.4	55.5	48.5
Trade growth less GDP growth (avg. %, 1990–2003)			3.0
High-technology exports (% of manufactured exports)	5	5	5
Net barter terms of trade (2000 = 100)	104	103	..
Foreign direct investment ($ millions)	–76	735	820
Present value of debt ($ billions)			29
Total debt service (% of goods and services exports)	..	12.3	9.0
Short-term debt ($ billions)	..	7	7
Aid per capita ($)	..	11	14

Spain

				High income
Population (millions)	41	Population growth (%)		0.4
Surface area (1,000 sq. km)	506	National poverty rate (% pop.)		..
GNI ($ billions)	700	GNI per capita ($)		17,040

	1990	2002	2003
People			
Life expectancy at birth (years)	77	79	80
Fertility rate (births per woman)	1.3	1.3	1.3
Infant mortality rate (per 1,000 live births)	8	4	4
Under-five mortality rate (per 1,000)	9	5	4
Births attended by skilled health staff (% of total)	..	..	..
Child malnutrition, underweight (% of under age 5)	..	..	..
Child immunization, measles (% of ages 12–23 mon.)	97	97	97
HIV prevalence rate (% of ages 15–49)	..	0.6	0.7
Adult literacy, male (% of ages 15 and older)	98	99	..
Adult literacy, female (% of ages 15 and older)	95	97	..
Primary completion rate, total (% of age group)	..	..	..
Primary completion rate, female (% of age group)	..	..	..
Net primary enrollment (% of age group)	100	100	..
Net secondary enrollment (% of age group)	..	94	..
Environment			
Forests (1,000 sq. km)	135	144	..
Deforestation (average annual %, 1990–2000)		–0.6	
Freshwater use (% of internal resources)			32
Carbon dioxide emissions (metric tons per capita)	5.5	7.0	..
Access to improved water source (% of total pop.)	..	..	..
Access to improved sanitation (% of urban pop.)	..	..	..
Energy use per capita (kg oil equivalent)	2,349	3,215	..
Electricity use per capita (kilowatt-hours)	3,239	5,048	..
Economy			
GDP ($ billions)	510	655	839
GDP growth (annual %)	3.8	2.0	2.4
GDP implicit price deflator (annual % growth)	7.3	4.4	4.2
Value added in agriculture (% of GDP)	6	3	3
Value added in industry (% of GDP)	35	30	30
Value added in services (% of GDP)	59	67	67
Exports of goods and services (% of GDP)	16	28	28
Imports of goods and services (% of GDP)	20	30	30
Gross capital formation (% of GDP)	27	25	26
Central government revenue (% of GDP)	..	27.9	..
Cash surplus/deficit (% of GDP)	..	0.3	..
Technology and infrastructure			
Fixed-line and mobile subscribers (per 1,000 people)	317	1,330	1,343
Cost of 3-minute local call ($)	0.04	0.07	..
Personal computers (per 1,000 people)	27.6	196.0	..
Internet users (per 1,000 people)	0	193	239
Paved roads (% of total)	74.0	99.0	..
Aircraft departures (thousands)	245	493	519
Trade and finance			
Trade in goods (% of GDP)	28.1	44.4	42.1
Trade growth less GDP growth (avg. %, 1990–2003)			6.0
High-technology exports (% of manufactured exports)	6	7	7
Net barter terms of trade (2000 = 100)	100	107	106
Foreign direct investment ($ billions)	14	37	26
Present value of debt ($ millions)			..
Total debt service (% of goods and services exports)	..	..	..
Short-term debt ($ millions)	..	..	..
Aid per capita ($)	..	..	..

Sri Lanka

South Asia		Lower middle income

Population (millions)	19	Population growth (%)	1.2
Surface area (1,000 sq. km)	66	National poverty rate (% pop.)	25
GNI ($ billions)	18	GNI per capita ($)	930

	1990	2002	2003
People			
Life expectancy at birth (years)	70	74	74
Fertility rate (births per woman)	2.5	2.0	2.0
Infant mortality rate (per 1,000 live births)	26	16	13
Under-five mortality rate (per 1,000)	32	20	15
Births attended by skilled health staff (% of total)	..	97	87
Child malnutrition, underweight (% of under age 5)	..	..	..
Child immunization, measles (% of ages 12–23 mon.)	80	99	99
HIV prevalence rate (% of ages 15–49)	..	0.1	0.1
Adult literacy, male (% of ages 15 and older)	93	95	..
Adult literacy, female (% of ages 15 and older)	85	90	..
Primary completion rate, total (% of age group)	103	98	..
Primary completion rate, female (% of age group)	103	95	..
Net primary enrollment (% of age group)	90	..	..
Net secondary enrollment (% of age group)	..	..	..
Environment			
Forests (1,000 sq. km)	23	19	..
Deforestation (average annual %, 1990–2000)		1.6	
Freshwater use (% of internal resources)			20
Carbon dioxide emissions (metric tons per capita)	0.2	0.6	..
Access to improved water source (% of total pop.)	68	78	..
Access to improved sanitation (% of urban pop.)	89	98	..
Energy use per capita (kg oil equivalent)	339	430	..
Electricity use per capita (kilowatt-hours)	160	297	..
Economy			
GDP ($ billions)	8	17	18
GDP growth (annual %)	6.4	4.0	5.9
GDP implicit price deflator (annual % growth)	20.1	8.2	5.0
Value added in agriculture (% of GDP)	26	21	19
Value added in industry (% of GDP)	26	26	26
Value added in services (% of GDP)	48	53	55
Exports of goods and services (% of GDP)	29	36	36
Imports of goods and services (% of GDP)	38	43	42
Gross capital formation (% of GDP)	23	21	22
Central government revenue (% of GDP)	21.0	16.4	..
Cash surplus/deficit (% of GDP)	–5.2	–7.6	..
Technology and infrastructure			
Fixed-line and mobile subscribers (per 1,000 people)	7	96	122
Cost of 3-minute local call ($)	0.02	0.03	0.03
Personal computers (per 1,000 people)	0.2	13.2	..
Internet users (per 1,000 people)	..	11	12
Paved roads (% of total)	32.0	..	81.0
Aircraft departures (thousands)	8	11	13
Trade and finance			
Trade in goods (% of GDP)	57.3	65.3	64.7
Trade growth less GDP growth (avg. %, 1990–2003)			2.5
High-technology exports (% of manufactured exports)	1	1	..
Net barter terms of trade (2000 = 100)	82	100	..
Foreign direct investment ($ millions)	43	197	229
Present value of debt ($ millions)			8,401
Total debt service (% of goods and services exports)	13.8	9.8	7.5
Short-term debt ($ millions)	405	507	471
Aid per capita ($)	45	18	35

St. Kitts and Nevis

Latin America & Caribbean		Upper middle income	
Population (thousands)	47	Population growth (%)	0.0
Surface area (sq. km)	360	National poverty rate (% pop.)	..
GNI ($ millions)	309	GNI per capita ($)	6,630

	1990	2002	2003
People			
Life expectancy at birth (years)	67	71	72
Fertility rate (births per woman)	2.7	2.1	2.1
Infant mortality rate (per 1,000 live births)	30	21	19
Under-five mortality rate (per 1,000)	36	25	22
Births attended by skilled health staff (% of total)	..	99	..
Child malnutrition, underweight (% of under age 5)	..	..	..
Child immunization, measles (% of ages 12–23 mon.)	99	99	98
HIV prevalence rate (% of ages 15–49)	..	..	..
Adult literacy, male (% of ages 15 and older)	..	..	..
Adult literacy, female (% of ages 15 and older)	..	..	..
Primary completion rate, total (% of age group)	..	118	..
Primary completion rate, female (% of age group)	..	125	..
Net primary enrollment (% of age group)	..	100	..
Net secondary enrollment (% of age group)	..	..	..
Environment			
Forests (1,000 sq. km)	0	0	..
Deforestation (average annual %, 1990–2000)		0.0	
Freshwater use (% of internal resources)			..
Carbon dioxide emissions (metric tons per capita)	1.6	2.4	..
Access to improved water source (% of total pop.)	99	99	..
Access to improved sanitation (% of urban pop.)	96	96	..
Energy use per capita (kg oil equivalent)	..	..	..
Electricity use per capita (kilowatt-hours)	..	..	..
Economy			
GDP ($ millions)	159	356	346
GDP growth (annual %)	2.3	2.1	0.0
GDP implicit price deflator (annual % growth)	8.7	1.4	–3.0
Value added in agriculture (% of GDP)	6	3	3
Value added in industry (% of GDP)	29	30	28
Value added in services (% of GDP)	65	67	69
Exports of goods and services (% of GDP)	52	46	37
Imports of goods and services (% of GDP)	83	71	56
Gross capital formation (% of GDP)	55	48	48
Central government revenue (% of GDP)	28.3	..	..
Cash surplus/deficit (% of GDP)	0.6	..	..
Technology and infrastructure			
Fixed-line and mobile subscribers (per 1,000 people)	197	606	..
Cost of 3-minute local call ($)	..	..	..
Personal computers (per 1,000 people)	..	191.5	..
Internet users (per 1,000 people)	..	60	..
Paved roads (% of total)	38.5	42.5	..
Aircraft departures (thousands)	..	..	..
Trade and finance			
Trade in goods (% of GDP)	86.7	64.6	79.0
Trade growth less GDP growth (avg. %, 1990–2003)			–2.0
High-technology exports (% of manufactured exports)	..	0	..
Net barter terms of trade (2000 = 100)	..	..	..
Foreign direct investment ($ millions)	49	80	53
Present value of debt ($ millions)			313
Total debt service (% of goods and services exports)	2.9	24.5	35.0
Short-term debt ($ millions)	1	2	2
Aid per capita ($)	193	610	0

St. Lucia

Latin America & Caribbean		Upper middle income

Population (thousands)	161	Population growth (%)	0.9
Surface area (sq. km)	620	National poverty rate (% pop.)	..
GNI ($ millions)	650	GNI per capita ($)	4,050

	1990	2002	2003
People			
Life expectancy at birth (years)	71	74	74
Fertility rate (births per woman)	3.3	2.1	2.1
Infant mortality rate (per 1,000 live births)	20	17	16
Under-five mortality rate (per 1,000)	24	19	18
Births attended by skilled health staff (% of total)	..	100	..
Child malnutrition, underweight (% of under age 5)	..	..	..
Child immunization, measles (% of ages 12–23 mon.)	82	98	90
HIV prevalence rate (% of ages 15–49)	..	..	..
Adult literacy, male (% of ages 15 and older)	..	..	..
Adult literacy, female (% of ages 15 and older)	..	..	..
Primary completion rate, total (% of age group)	111	114	..
Primary completion rate, female (% of age group)	107	111	..
Net primary enrollment (% of age group)	95	99	..
Net secondary enrollment (% of age group)	..	76	..
Environment			
Forests (1,000 sq. km)	0	0	..
Deforestation (average annual %, 1990–2000)		4.3	
Freshwater use (% of internal resources)			..
Carbon dioxide emissions (metric tons per capita)	1.2	2.1	..
Access to improved water source (% of total pop.)	98	98	..
Access to improved sanitation (% of urban pop.)	..	89	..
Energy use per capita (kg oil equivalent)	..	..	..
Electricity use per capita (kilowatt-hours)	..	..	..
Economy			
GDP ($ millions)	397	676	693
GDP growth (annual %)	23.5	2.2	1.7
GDP implicit price deflator (annual % growth)	3.2	1.2	0.7
Value added in agriculture (% of GDP)	15	6	5
Value added in industry (% of GDP)	18	18	18
Value added in services (% of GDP)	67	75	77
Exports of goods and services (% of GDP)	73	46	56
Imports of goods and services (% of GDP)	84	52	69
Gross capital formation (% of GDP)	26	23	29
Central government revenue (% of GDP)	..	..	..
Cash surplus/deficit (% of GDP)	..	..	..
Technology and infrastructure			
Fixed-line and mobile subscribers (per 1,000 people)	97	409	..
Cost of 3-minute local call ($)	..	0.09	..
Personal computers (per 1,000 people)	..	150.0	..
Internet users (per 1,000 people)	..	52	..
Paved roads (% of total)	4.6	5.2	..
Aircraft departures (thousands)	..	..	..
Trade and finance			
Trade in goods (% of GDP)	100.2	52.2	54.9
Trade growth less GDP growth (avg. %, 1990–2003)			..
High-technology exports (% of manufactured exports)	1	8	8
Net barter terms of trade (2000 = 100)	..	..	..
Foreign direct investment ($ millions)	45	31	32
Present value of debt ($ millions)			362
Total debt service (% of goods and services exports)	2.1	7.9	8.7
Short-term debt ($ millions)	7	204	133
Aid per capita ($)	92	211	92

St. Vincent & Grenadines

Latin America & Caribbean		Upper middle income	
Population (thousands)	109	Population growth (%)	0.0
Surface area (sq. km)	390	National poverty rate (% pop.)	..
GNI ($ millions)	361	GNI per capita ($)	3,310

	1990	2002	2003
People			
Life expectancy at birth (years)	70	73	73
Fertility rate (births per woman)	2.6	2.1	2.1
Infant mortality rate (per 1,000 live births)	22	21	23
Under-five mortality rate (per 1,000)	26	25	27
Births attended by skilled health staff (% of total)	..	100	..
Child malnutrition, underweight (% of under age 5)	..	..	..
Child immunization, measles (% of ages 12–23 mon.)	96	99	94
HIV prevalence rate (% of ages 15–49)	..	..	..
Adult literacy, male (% of ages 15 and older)	..	..	..
Adult literacy, female (% of ages 15 and older)	..	..	..
Primary completion rate, total (% of age group)	..	78	..
Primary completion rate, female (% of age group)	..	83	..
Net primary enrollment (% of age group)	..	90	..
Net secondary enrollment (% of age group)	..	58	..
Environment			
Forests (1,000 sq. km)	0	0	..
Deforestation (average annual %, 1990–2000)		1.5	
Freshwater use (% of internal resources)			..
Carbon dioxide emissions (metric tons per capita)	0.8	1.4	..
Access to improved water source (% of total pop.)	..	..	..
Access to improved sanitation (% of urban pop.)	..	..	..
Energy use per capita (kg oil equivalent)	..	..	..
Electricity use per capita (kilowatt-hours)	..	..	..
Economy			
GDP ($ millions)	198	361	371
GDP growth (annual %)	5.0	1.1	4.0
GDP implicit price deflator (annual % growth)	6.4	3.1	–1.1
Value added in agriculture (% of GDP)	21	10	9
Value added in industry (% of GDP)	23	25	24
Value added in services (% of GDP)	56	65	67
Exports of goods and services (% of GDP)	66	49	47
Imports of goods and services (% of GDP)	77	60	65
Gross capital formation (% of GDP)	30	30	34
Central government revenue (% of GDP)	25.6	..	..
Cash surplus/deficit (% of GDP)	..	..	..
Technology and infrastructure			
Fixed-line and mobile subscribers (per 1,000 people)	124	319	..
Cost of 3-minute local call ($)	0.09	0.09	..
Personal computers (per 1,000 people)	..	119.7	..
Internet users (per 1,000 people)	..	31	..
Paved roads (% of total)	27.7	70.0	..
Aircraft departures (thousands)	..	..	..
Trade and finance			
Trade in goods (% of GDP)	110.5	58.7	64.1
Trade growth less GDP growth (avg. %, 1990–2003)			–1.3
High-technology exports (% of manufactured exports)	..	0	..
Net barter terms of trade (2000 = 100)	..	..	..
Foreign direct investment ($ millions)	8	32	38
Present value of debt ($ millions)			192
Total debt service (% of goods and services exports)	2.9	7.3	..
Short-term debt ($ millions)	2	32	34
Aid per capita ($)	144	44	58

Sudan

Sub-Saharan Africa   **Low income**

Population (millions)	34	Population growth (%)	2.3
Surface area (1,000 sq. km)	2,506	National poverty rate (% pop.)	..
GNI ($ billions)	15	GNI per capita ($)	460

	1990	2002	2003
People			
Life expectancy at birth (years)	52	58	59
Fertility rate (births per woman)	5.4	4.4	4.4
Infant mortality rate (per 1,000 live births)	74	65	63
Under-five mortality rate (per 1,000)	120	97	93
Births attended by skilled health staff (% of total)	69	..	..
Child malnutrition, underweight (% of under age 5)	..	41	..
Child immunization, measles (% of ages 12–23 mon.)	57	49	57
HIV prevalence rate (% of ages 15–49)	..	1.9	2.3
Adult literacy, male (% of ages 15 and older)	60	71	..
Adult literacy, female (% of ages 15 and older)	32	49	..
Primary completion rate, total (% of age group)	44	49	..
Primary completion rate, female (% of age group)	39	45	..
Net primary enrollment (% of age group)	43	46	..
Net secondary enrollment (% of age group)	..	..	..
Environment			
Forests (1,000 sq. km)	712	616	..
Deforestation (average annual %, 1990–2000)		1.4	
Freshwater use (% of internal resources)			59
Carbon dioxide emissions (metric tons per capita)	0.1	0.2	..
Access to improved water source (% of total pop.)	64	69	..
Access to improved sanitation (% of urban pop.)	53	50	..
Energy use per capita (kg oil equivalent)	426	483	..
Electricity use per capita (kilowatt-hours)	51	74	..
Economy			
GDP ($ billions)	13	15	18
GDP growth (annual %)	–5.5	6.0	6.0
GDP implicit price deflator (annual % growth)	71.0	8.4	8.2
Value added in agriculture (% of GDP)	..	39	..
Value added in industry (% of GDP)	..	18	..
Value added in services (% of GDP)	..	43	..
Exports of goods and services (% of GDP)	..	15	16
Imports of goods and services (% of GDP)	..	13	12
Gross capital formation (% of GDP)	..	20	21
Central government revenue (% of GDP)	..	7.9	..
Cash surplus/deficit (% of GDP)	..	–0.4	..
Technology and infrastructure			
Fixed-line and mobile subscribers (per 1,000 people)	3	27	47
Cost of 3-minute local call ($)	0.02	0.03	0.03
Personal computers (per 1,000 people)	..	6.1	..
Internet users (per 1,000 people)	..	3	9
Paved roads (% of total)	33.8	36.3	..
Aircraft departures (thousands)	9	8	8
Trade and finance			
Trade in goods (% of GDP)	7.5	28.9	28.3
Trade growth less GDP growth (avg. %, 1990–2003)			5.6
High-technology exports (% of manufactured exports)	..	7	..
Net barter terms of trade (2000 = 100)	100	119	..
Foreign direct investment ($ millions)	0	713	1,349
Present value of debt ($ billions)			17
Total debt service (% of goods and services exports)	8.7	0.8	0.9
Short-term debt ($ millions)	4,155	6,277	6,832
Aid per capita ($)	33	11	19

Suriname

Latin America & Caribbean		Lower middle income	

Population (thousands)	438	Population growth (%)	1.1
Surface area (1,000 sq. km)	163	National poverty rate (% pop.)	..
GNI ($ millions)	998	GNI per capita ($)	2,280

	1990	2002	2003
People			
Life expectancy at birth (years)	69	70	70
Fertility rate (births per woman)	2.6	2.4	2.4
Infant mortality rate (per 1,000 live births)	35	31	30
Under-five mortality rate (per 1,000)	48	41	39
Births attended by skilled health staff (% of total)	..	85	91
Child malnutrition, underweight (% of under age 5)	..	13	..
Child immunization, measles (% of ages 12–23 mon.)	65	69	71
HIV prevalence rate (% of ages 15–49)	..	1.3	1.7
Adult literacy, male (% of ages 15 and older)	..	..	..
Adult literacy, female (% of ages 15 and older)	..	..	..
Primary completion rate, total (% of age group)	75	..	..
Primary completion rate, female (% of age group)	81	..	..
Net primary enrollment (% of age group)	78	97	..
Net secondary enrollment (% of age group)	..	63	..
Environment			
Forests (1,000 sq. km)	141	141	..
Deforestation (average annual %, 1990–2000)		0.0	
Freshwater use (% of internal resources)			1
Carbon dioxide emissions (metric tons per capita)	4.5	5.0	..
Access to improved water source (% of total pop.)	..	92	..
Access to improved sanitation (% of urban pop.)	99	99	..
Energy use per capita (kg oil equivalent)	..	..	..
Electricity use per capita (kilowatt-hours)	..	..	..
Economy			
GDP ($ millions)	399	945	1,154
GDP growth (annual %)	0.1	2.8	5.1
GDP implicit price deflator (annual % growth)	43.1	30.3	..
Value added in agriculture (% of GDP)	9	11	..
Value added in industry (% of GDP)	24	20	..
Value added in services (% of GDP)	67	69	..
Exports of goods and services (% of GDP)	42	21	..
Imports of goods and services (% of GDP)	44	45	..
Gross capital formation (% of GDP)	11	23	..
Central government revenue (% of GDP)	..	..	..
Cash surplus/deficit (% of GDP)	..	..	..
Technology and infrastructure			
Fixed-line and mobile subscribers (per 1,000 people)	92	389	472
Cost of 3-minute local call ($)	0.07	0.05	..
Personal computers (per 1,000 people)	..	45.5	..
Internet users (per 1,000 people)	..	42	44
Paved roads (% of total)	24.0	26.0	..
Aircraft departures (thousands)	2	2	4
Trade and finance			
Trade in goods (% of GDP)	236.5	111.8	98.3
Trade growth less GDP growth (avg. %, 1990–2003)			0.4
High-technology exports (% of manufactured exports)	..	0	..
Net barter terms of trade (2000 = 100)	..	..	..
Foreign direct investment ($ millions)	..	..	..
Present value of debt ($ millions)			..
Total debt service (% of goods and services exports)	..	..	..
Short-term debt ($ millions)	..	..	..
Aid per capita ($)	153	27	25

Swaziland

Sub-Saharan Africa   **Lower middle income**

Population (millions)	1	Population growth (%)	1.6
Surface area (1,000 sq. km)	17	National poverty rate (% pop.)	40
GNI ($ millions)	1,496	GNI per capita ($)	1,350

	1990	2002	2003
People			
Life expectancy at birth (years)	57	44	43
Fertility rate (births per woman)	5.3	4.2	4.2
Infant mortality rate (per 1,000 live births)	78	98	105
Under-five mortality rate (per 1,000)	110	142	153
Births attended by skilled health staff (% of total)	..	70	..
Child malnutrition, underweight (% of under age 5)	..	10	..
Child immunization, measles (% of ages 12–23 mon.)	85	94	94
HIV prevalence rate (% of ages 15–49)	..	38.2	38.8
Adult literacy, male (% of ages 15 and older)	74	82	..
Adult literacy, female (% of ages 15 and older)	70	80	..
Primary completion rate, total (% of age group)	69	75	..
Primary completion rate, female (% of age group)	72	77	..
Net primary enrollment (% of age group)	77	75	..
Net secondary enrollment (% of age group)	..	32	..
Environment			
Forests (1,000 sq. km)	5	5	..
Deforestation (average annual %, 1990–2000)		–1.2	
Freshwater use (% of internal resources)			..
Carbon dioxide emissions (metric tons per capita)	0.6	0.4	..
Access to improved water source (% of total pop.)	..	52	..
Access to improved sanitation (% of urban pop.)	..	78	..
Energy use per capita (kg oil equivalent)	..	..	..
Electricity use per capita (kilowatt-hours)	..	..	..
Economy			
GDP ($ millions)	859	1,186	1,845
GDP growth (annual %)	8.6	3.4	2.2
GDP implicit price deflator (annual % growth)	12.5	9.6	9.0
Value added in agriculture (% of GDP)	14	16	12
Value added in industry (% of GDP)	43	50	52
Value added in services (% of GDP)	43	35	36
Exports of goods and services (% of GDP)	77	91	84
Imports of goods and services (% of GDP)	76	100	94
Gross capital formation (% of GDP)	20	18	19
Central government revenue (% of GDP)	..	28.1	..
Cash surplus/deficit (% of GDP)	..	–0.9	..
Technology and infrastructure			
Fixed-line and mobile subscribers (per 1,000 people)	17	95	129
Cost of 3-minute local call ($)	0.05	0.04	0.05
Personal computers (per 1,000 people)	..	24.2	28.7
Internet users (per 1,000 people)	..	19	26
Paved roads (% of total)	53.6	..	..
Aircraft departures (thousands)	1	2	..
Trade and finance			
Trade in goods (% of GDP)	141.8	161.8	104.9
Trade growth less GDP growth (avg. %, 1990–2003)			1.2
High-technology exports (% of manufactured exports)	..	1	..
Net barter terms of trade (2000 = 100)	100	100	..
Foreign direct investment ($ millions)	30	45	44
Present value of debt ($ millions)			393
Total debt service (% of goods and services exports)	5.7	1.7	1.6
Short-term debt ($ millions)	5	68	54
Aid per capita ($)	70	21	24

Sweden

		High income
Population (millions)	9	Population growth (%)	0.4
Surface area (1,000 sq. km)	450	National poverty rate (% pop.)	..
GNI ($ billions)	259	GNI per capita ($)	28,910

	1990	2002	2003
People			
Life expectancy at birth (years)	78	80	80
Fertility rate (births per woman)	2.1	1.6	1.7
Infant mortality rate (per 1,000 live births)	6	3	3
Under-five mortality rate (per 1,000)	7	4	
Births attended by skilled health staff (% of total)	..	..	100
Child malnutrition, underweight (% of under age 5)	..	..	..
Child immunization, measles (% of ages 12–23 mon.)	96	94	94
HIV prevalence rate (% of ages 15–49)	..	0.1	0.1
Adult literacy, male (% of ages 15 and older)	..	..	..
Adult literacy, female (% of ages 15 and older)	..	..	..
Primary completion rate, total (% of age group)	96	101	..
Primary completion rate, female (% of age group)	96	101	..
Net primary enrollment (% of age group)	100	100	..
Net secondary enrollment (% of age group)	85	99	..
Environment			
Forests (1,000 sq. km)	271	271	..
Deforestation (average annual %, 1990–2000)		0.0	
Freshwater use (% of internal resources)			2
Carbon dioxide emissions (metric tons per capita)	5.7	5.3	..
Access to improved water source (% of total pop.)	100	100	..
Access to improved sanitation (% of urban pop.)	100	100	..
Energy use per capita (kg oil equivalent)	5,451	5,718	..
Electricity use per capita (kilowatt-hours)	14,061	14,742	..
Economy			
GDP ($ billions)	240	241	302
GDP growth (annual %)	1.0	2.1	1.6
GDP implicit price deflator (annual % growth)	8.8	1.4	2.3
Value added in agriculture (% of GDP)	3	2	2
Value added in industry (% of GDP)	32	28	28
Value added in services (% of GDP)	64	70	70
Exports of goods and services (% of GDP)	30	44	44
Imports of goods and services (% of GDP)	29	38	37
Gross capital formation (% of GDP)	24	17	16
Central government revenue (% of GDP)	..	37.7	..
Cash surplus/deficit (% of GDP)	..	0.3	..
Technology and infrastructure			
Fixed-line and mobile subscribers (per 1,000 people)	735	1,625	..
Cost of 3-minute local call ($)	0.04	0.11	..
Personal computers (per 1,000 people)	104.8	621.3	..
Internet users (per 1,000 people)	6	573	..
Paved roads (% of total)	71.0	78.6	..
Aircraft departures (thousands)	208	198	184
Trade and finance			
Trade in goods (% of GDP)	46.6	61.6	61.0
Trade growth less GDP growth (avg. %, 1990–2003)			4.3
High-technology exports (% of manufactured exports)	13	18	15
Net barter terms of trade (2000 = 100)	108	95	95
Foreign direct investment ($ billions)	2	12	3
Present value of debt ($ millions)			..
Total debt service (% of goods and services exports)	..	..	..
Short-term debt ($ millions)	..	..	..
Aid per capita ($)	..	..	..

Switzerland

High income

Population (millions)	7	Population growth (%)	0.8
Surface area (1,000 sq. km)	41	National poverty rate (% pop.)	..
GNI ($ billions)	299	GNI per capita ($)	40,680

	1990	2002	2003
People			
Life expectancy at birth (years)	77	80	80
Fertility rate (births per woman)	1.6	1.4	1.4
Infant mortality rate (per 1,000 live births)	7	5	4
Under-five mortality rate (per 1,000)	9	6	..
Births attended by skilled health staff (% of total)	..	..	..
Child malnutrition, underweight (% of under age 5)	..	..	..
Child immunization, measles (% of ages 12–23 mon.)	90	79	82
HIV prevalence rate (% of ages 15–49)	..	0.4	0.4
Adult literacy, male (% of ages 15 and older)	..	..	..
Adult literacy, female (% of ages 15 and older)	..	..	..
Primary completion rate, total (% of age group)	..	99	..
Primary completion rate, female (% of age group)	54	100	..
Net primary enrollment (% of age group)	84	99	..
Net secondary enrollment (% of age group)	80	87	..
Environment			
Forests (1,000 sq. km)	12	12	..
Deforestation (average annual %, 1990–2000)		–0.4	
Freshwater use (% of internal resources)			3
Carbon dioxide emissions (metric tons per capita)	6.4	5.4	..
Access to improved water source (% of total pop.)	100	100	..
Access to improved sanitation (% of urban pop.)	100	100	..
Energy use per capita (kg oil equivalent)	3,740	3,723	..
Electricity use per capita (kilowatt-hours)	6,997	7,381	..
Economy			
GDP ($ billions)	236	274	320
GDP growth (annual %)	3.7	0.2	–0.4
GDP implicit price deflator (annual % growth)	4.3	1.0	..
Value added in agriculture (% of GDP)	..	..	..
Value added in industry (% of GDP)	..	..	..
Value added in services (% of GDP)	..	..	..
Exports of goods and services (% of GDP)	36	44	..
Imports of goods and services (% of GDP)	34	37	..
Gross capital formation (% of GDP)	31	20	..
Central government revenue (% of GDP)	20.2	18.8	..
Cash surplus/deficit (% of GDP)	0.0	0.3	..
Technology and infrastructure			
Fixed-line and mobile subscribers (per 1,000 people)	592	1,534	..
Cost of 3-minute local call ($)	0.14	0.15	..
Personal computers (per 1,000 people)	87.3	708.7	..
Internet users (per 1,000 people)	6	351	..
Paved roads (% of total)	..	..	..
Aircraft departures (thousands)	152	243	189
Trade and finance			
Trade in goods (% of GDP)	56.6	62.5	60.8
Trade growth less GDP growth (avg. %, 1990–2003)			3.1
High-technology exports (% of manufactured exports)	12	21	22
Net barter terms of trade (2000 = 100)	..	..	..
Foreign direct investment ($ billions)	6	7	18
Present value of debt ($ millions)			..
Total debt service (% of goods and services exports)	..	..	..
Short-term debt ($ millions)	..	..	..
Aid per capita ($)	..	..	..

Syrian Arab Republic

Middle East & North Africa		Lower middle income

Population (millions)	17	Population growth (%)	2.3
Surface area (1,000 sq. km)	185	National poverty rate (% pop.)	..
GNI ($ billions)	20	GNI per capita ($)	1,160

	1990	2002	2003
People			
Life expectancy at birth (years)	66	70	70
Fertility rate (births per woman)	5.3	3.4	3.4
Infant mortality rate (per 1,000 live births)	35	*19*	16
Under-five mortality rate (per 1,000)	44	*22*	18
Births attended by skilled health staff (% of total)	..	..	..
Child malnutrition, underweight (% of under age 5)	..	7	..
Child immunization, measles (% of ages 12–23 mon.)	87	98	98
HIV prevalence rate (% of ages 15–49)	..	..	0.1
Adult literacy, male (% of ages 15 and older)	82	91	..
Adult literacy, female (% of ages 15 and older)	48	74	..
Primary completion rate, total (% of age group)	99	88	..
Primary completion rate, female (% of age group)	93	85	..
Net primary enrollment (% of age group)	92	98	..
Net secondary enrollment (% of age group)	43	43	..
Environment			
Forests (1,000 sq. km)	5	*5*	..
Deforestation (average annual %, 1990–2000)		*0.0*	
Freshwater use (% of internal resources)			171
Carbon dioxide emissions (metric tons per capita)	3.0	*3.3*	..
Access to improved water source (% of total pop.)	79	79	..
Access to improved sanitation (% of urban pop.)	97	97	..
Energy use per capita (kg oil equivalent)	984	1,063	..
Electricity use per capita (kilowatt-hours)	683	1,000	..
Economy			
GDP ($ billions)	12	20	21
GDP growth (annual %)	7.6	3.2	2.5
GDP implicit price deflator (annual % growth)	19.3	1.5	5.1
Value added in agriculture (% of GDP)	28	24	23
Value added in industry (% of GDP)	24	29	29
Value added in services (% of GDP)	48	47	48
Exports of goods and services (% of GDP)	28	43	40
Imports of goods and services (% of GDP)	28	33	33
Gross capital formation (% of GDP)	17	23	24
Central government revenue (% of GDP)	21.9	*23.9*	..
Cash surplus/deficit (% of GDP)	..	..	..
Technology and infrastructure			
Fixed-line and mobile subscribers (per 1,000 people)	41	147	..
Cost of 3-minute local call ($)	0.02	*0.01*	..
Personal computers (per 1,000 people)	..	19.4	..
Internet users (per 1,000 people)	0	2	..
Paved roads (% of total)	*72.0*	14.2	..
Aircraft departures (thousands)	11	13	7
Trade and finance			
Trade in goods (% of GDP)	53.7	52.7	48.6
Trade growth less GDP growth (avg. %, 1990–2003)			3.9
High-technology exports (% of manufactured exports)	..	1	1
Net barter terms of trade (2000 = 100)	..	..	..
Foreign direct investment ($ millions)	72	115	150
Present value of debt ($ billions)			21
Total debt service (% of goods and services exports)	21.8	3.3	4.2
Short-term debt ($ millions)	2,151	5,617	5,718
Aid per capita ($)	56	5	9

Tajikistan

Europe & Central Asia　　　　　　　　　　　　**Low income**

Population (millions)	6	Population growth (%)	0.6
Surface area (1,000 sq. km)	143	National poverty rate (% pop.)	..
GNI ($ millions)	1,343	GNI per capita ($)	210

	1990	2002	2003
People			
Life expectancy at birth (years)	69	67	66
Fertility rate (births per woman)	5.1	2.9	2.9
Infant mortality rate (per 1,000 live births)	92	80	76
Under-five mortality rate (per 1,000)	119	101	95
Births attended by skilled health staff (% of total)	..	71	..
Child malnutrition, underweight (% of under age 5)	..	..	..
Child immunization, measles (% of ages 12–23 mon.)	84	84	89
HIV prevalence rate (% of ages 15–49)	..	..	0.1
Adult literacy, male (% of ages 15 and older)	99	100	..
Adult literacy, female (% of ages 15 and older)	97	99	..
Primary completion rate, total (% of age group)	..	100	..
Primary completion rate, female (% of age group)	..	98	..
Net primary enrollment (% of age group)	77	85	..
Net secondary enrollment (% of age group)	..	79	..
Environment			
Forests (1,000 sq. km)	4	4	..
Deforestation (average annual %, 1990–2000)		–0.5	
Freshwater use (% of internal resources)			18
Carbon dioxide emissions (metric tons per capita)	3.7	0.6	..
Access to improved water source (% of total pop.)	..	58	..
Access to improved sanitation (% of urban pop.)	..	71	..
Energy use per capita (kg oil equivalent)	1,631	518	..
Electricity use per capita (kilowatt-hours)	2,954	2,236	..
Economy			
GDP ($ millions)	2,629	1,235	1,553
GDP growth (annual %)	–0.6	9.1	10.2
GDP implicit price deflator (annual % growth)	6.2	21.6	9.9
Value added in agriculture (% of GDP)	33	29	23
Value added in industry (% of GDP)	38	25	20
Value added in services (% of GDP)	29	46	56
Exports of goods and services (% of GDP)	28	64	60
Imports of goods and services (% of GDP)	35	78	79
Gross capital formation (% of GDP)	25	18	19
Central government revenue (% of GDP)	..	11.4	..
Cash surplus/deficit (% of GDP)	..	–0.2	..
Technology and infrastructure			
Fixed-line and mobile subscribers (per 1,000 people)	45	39	45
Cost of 3-minute local call ($)	0.00	0.01	0.01
Personal computers (per 1,000 people)	..	..	..
Internet users (per 1,000 people)		1	1
Paved roads (% of total)	71.6	..	..
Aircraft departures (thousands)	..	6	7
Trade and finance			
Trade in goods (% of GDP)	..	118.2	108.1
Trade growth less GDP growth (avg. %, 1990–2003)			5.8
High-technology exports (% of manufactured exports)	..	42	..
Net barter terms of trade (2000 = 100)	..	..	..
Foreign direct investment ($ millions)	0	36	32
Present value of debt ($ millions)			937
Total debt service (% of goods and services exports)	0.0	11.3	9.1
Short-term debt ($ millions)	0	60	82
Aid per capita ($)	2	27	23

Tanzania

Sub-Saharan Africa			**Low income**
Population (millions)	36	Population growth (%)	2.0
Surface area (1,000 sq. km)	945	National poverty rate (% pop.)	36
GNI ($ billions)	11	GNI per capita ($)	300

	1990	2002	2003
People			
Life expectancy at birth (years)	50	43	43
Fertility rate (births per woman)	6.3	5.0	5.0
Infant mortality rate (per 1,000 live births)	102	*104*	104
Under-five mortality rate (per 1,000)	163	*165*	165
Births attended by skilled health staff (% of total)	44	36	..
Child malnutrition, underweight (% of under age 5)	*29*	29	..
Child immunization, measles (% of ages 12–23 mon.)	80	89	97
HIV prevalence rate (% of ages 15–49)	..	*9.0*	8.8
Adult literacy, male (% of ages 15 and older)	76	85	..
Adult literacy, female (% of ages 15 and older)	51	69	..
Primary completion rate, total (% of age group)	*62*	58	58
Primary completion rate, female (% of age group)	63	59	57
Net primary enrollment (% of age group)	50	69	..
Net secondary enrollment (% of age group)	..	..	..
Environment			
Forests (1,000 sq. km)	397	*388*	..
Deforestation (average annual %, 1990–2000)		*0.2*	
Freshwater use (% of internal resources)			1
Carbon dioxide emissions (metric tons per capita)	0.1	*0.1*	..
Access to improved water source (% of total pop.)	38	73	..
Access to improved sanitation (% of urban pop.)	51	54	..
Energy use per capita (kg oil equivalent)	385	408	..
Electricity use per capita (kilowatt-hours)	51	62	..
Economy			
GDP ($ billions)	4	10	10
GDP growth (annual %)	7.0	7.2	7.1
GDP implicit price deflator (annual % growth)	22.4	6.5	5.7
Value added in agriculture (% of GDP)	46	45	45
Value added in industry (% of GDP)	18	16	16
Value added in services (% of GDP)	36	39	39
Exports of goods and services (% of GDP)	13	17	18
Imports of goods and services (% of GDP)	37	25	27
Gross capital formation (% of GDP)	26	19	19
Central government revenue (% of GDP)	..	..	..
Cash surplus/deficit (% of GDP)	..	..	..
Technology and infrastructure			
Fixed-line and mobile subscribers (per 1,000 people)	3	24	29
Cost of 3-minute local call ($)	0.02	0.12	..
Personal computers (per 1,000 people)	..	4.2	5.7
Internet users (per 1,000 people)	..	2	7
Paved roads (% of total)	37.0	*4.2*	..
Aircraft departures (thousands)	8	4	6
Trade and finance			
Trade in goods (% of GDP)	31.9	26.2	33.2
Trade growth less GDP growth (avg. %, 1990–2003)			–0.7
High-technology exports (% of manufactured exports)	..	1	2
Net barter terms of trade (2000 = 100)	107	131	..
Foreign direct investment ($ millions)	0	240	248
Present value of debt ($ millions)			2,165
Total debt service (% of goods and services exports)	32.9	6.7	5.1
Short-term debt ($ millions)	520	710	831
Aid per capita ($)	46	35	47

Thailand

East Asia & Pacific   **Lower middle income**

Population (millions)	62	Population growth (%)	0.6
Surface area (1,000 sq. km)	513	National poverty rate (% pop.)	13
GNI ($ billions)	136	GNI per capita ($)	2,190

	1990	2002	2003
People			
Life expectancy at birth (years)	69	69	69
Fertility rate (births per woman)	2.3	1.8	1.8
Infant mortality rate (per 1,000 live births)	34	25	23
Under-five mortality rate (per 1,000)	40	29	26
Births attended by skilled health staff (% of total)	..	99	69
Child malnutrition, underweight (% of under age 5)	..	..	..
Child immunization, measles (% of ages 12–23 mon.)	80	94	94
HIV prevalence rate (% of ages 15–49)	..	1.7	1.5
Adult literacy, male (% of ages 15 and older)	95	95	..
Adult literacy, female (% of ages 15 and older)	89	91	..
Primary completion rate, total (% of age group)	..	86	..
Primary completion rate, female (% of age group)	..	87	..
Net primary enrollment (% of age group)	76	86	..
Net secondary enrollment (% of age group)	..	..	..
Environment			
Forests (1,000 sq. km)	159	148	..
Deforestation (average annual %, 1990–2000)		0.7	
Freshwater use (% of internal resources)			16
Carbon dioxide emissions (metric tons per capita)	1.7	3.3	..
Access to improved water source (% of total pop.)	81	85	..
Access to improved sanitation (% of urban pop.)	95	97	..
Energy use per capita (kg oil equivalent)	789	1,353	..
Electricity use per capita (kilowatt-hours)	690	1,626	..
Economy			
GDP ($ billions)	85	127	143
GDP growth (annual %)	11.2	5.3	6.9
GDP implicit price deflator (annual % growth)	5.8	0.7	2.0
Value added in agriculture (% of GDP)	12	9	10
Value added in industry (% of GDP)	37	43	44
Value added in services (% of GDP)	50	48	46
Exports of goods and services (% of GDP)	34	65	66
Imports of goods and services (% of GDP)	42	57	59
Gross capital formation (% of GDP)	41	24	25
Central government revenue (% of GDP)	..	..	19.5
Cash surplus/deficit (% of GDP)	..	..	2.0
Technology and infrastructure			
Fixed-line and mobile subscribers (per 1,000 people)	25	365	499
Cost of 3-minute local call ($)	0.12	0.07	0.07
Personal computers (per 1,000 people)	4.2	39.8	..
Internet users (per 1,000 people)	0	78	111
Paved roads (% of total)	55.3	98.5	..
Aircraft departures (thousands)	70	98	94
Trade and finance			
Trade in goods (% of GDP)	65.7	105.3	109.4
Trade growth less GDP growth (avg. %, 1990–2003)			2.8
High-technology exports (% of manufactured exports)	21	31	30
Net barter terms of trade (2000 = 100)	119	90	
Foreign direct investment ($ millions)	2,444	953	1,949
Present value of debt ($ billions)			51
Total debt service (% of goods and services exports)	16.9	23.2	15.6
Short-term debt ($ billions)	8	12	11
Aid per capita ($)	14	5	–16

Timor-Leste

East Asia & Pacific			Low income
Population (thousands)	877	Population growth (%)	5.3
Surface area (1,000 sq. km)	15	National poverty rate (% pop.)	..
GNI ($ millions)	372	GNI per capita ($)	460

	1990	2002	2003
People			
Life expectancy at birth (years)	..	62	62
Fertility rate (births per woman)	..	7.8	7.6
Infant mortality rate (per 1,000 live births)	110	91	87
Under-five mortality rate (per 1,000)	160	130	124
Births attended by skilled health staff (% of total)	..	24	..
Child malnutrition, underweight (% of under age 5)	..	43	..
Child immunization, measles (% of ages 12–23 mon.)	..	47	60
HIV prevalence rate (% of ages 15–49)	..	..	..
Adult literacy, male (% of ages 15 and older)	..	..	..
Adult literacy, female (% of ages 15 and older)	..	..	..
Primary completion rate, total (% of age group)	..	..	..
Primary completion rate, female (% of age group)	..	..	..
Net primary enrollment (% of age group)	..	..	..
Net secondary enrollment (% of age group)	..	..	..
Environment			
Forests (1,000 sq. km)	5	5	..
Deforestation (average annual %, 1990–2000)		0.6	
Freshwater use (% of internal resources)			..
Carbon dioxide emissions (metric tons per capita)	..	..	..
Access to improved water source (% of total pop.)	..	52	..
Access to improved sanitation (% of urban pop.)	..	65	..
Energy use per capita (kg oil equivalent)	..	..	..
Electricity use per capita (kilowatt-hours)	..	..	..
Economy			
GDP ($ millions)	..	381	341
GDP growth (annual %)	..	3.0	–3.0
GDP implicit price deflator (annual % growth)	..	–6.7	–10.4
Value added in agriculture (% of GDP)	..	26	..
Value added in industry (% of GDP)	..	18	..
Value added in services (% of GDP)	..	56	..
Exports of goods and services (% of GDP)	..	..	..
Imports of goods and services (% of GDP)	..	..	..
Gross capital formation (% of GDP)	..	25	..
Central government revenue (% of GDP)	..	..	..
Cash surplus/deficit (% of GDP)	..	..	..
Technology and infrastructure			
Fixed-line and mobile subscribers (per 1,000 people)	..	..	..
Cost of 3-minute local call ($)	..	..	..
Personal computers (per 1,000 people)	..	..	..
Internet users (per 1,000 people)	..	..	..
Paved roads (% of total)	..	..	..
Aircraft departures (thousands)	..	..	..
Trade and finance			
Trade in goods (% of GDP)	..	..	..
Trade growth less GDP growth (avg. %, 1990–2003)			..
High-technology exports (% of manufactured exports)	..	..	..
Net barter terms of trade (2000 = 100)	..	..	..
Foreign direct investment ($ millions)			..
Present value of debt ($ millions)			..
Total debt service (% of goods and services exports)	..	..	..
Short-term debt ($ millions)	..	..	..
Aid per capita ($)	0	264	172

Togo

Sub-Saharan Africa   **Low income**

Population (millions)	5	Population growth (%)	2.1
Surface area (1,000 sq. km)	57	National poverty rate (% pop.)	..
GNI ($ millions)	1,528	GNI per capita ($)	310

	1990	2002	2003
People			
Life expectancy at birth (years)	50	50	50
Fertility rate (births per woman)	6.6	4.9	4.9
Infant mortality rate (per 1,000 live births)	88	*80*	78
Under-five mortality rate (per 1,000)	152	*142*	140
Births attended by skilled health staff (% of total)	*31*	49	..
Child malnutrition, underweight (% of under age 5)	*25*	*25*	..
Child immunization, measles (% of ages 12–23 mon.)	73	58	58
HIV prevalence rate (% of ages 15–49)	..	*4.3*	4.1
Adult literacy, male (% of ages 15 and older)	60	74	..
Adult literacy, female (% of ages 15 and older)	29	45	..
Primary completion rate, total (% of age group)	40	78	..
Primary completion rate, female (% of age group)	26	63	..
Net primary enrollment (% of age group)	75	91	..
Net secondary enrollment (% of age group)	18	*27*	..
Environment			
Forests (1,000 sq. km)	7	*5*	..
Deforestation (average annual %, 1990–2000)		*3.4*	
Freshwater use (% of internal resources)			1
Carbon dioxide emissions (metric tons per capita)	0.2	*0.4*	..
Access to improved water source (% of total pop.)	49	51	..
Access to improved sanitation (% of urban pop.)	71	71	..
Energy use per capita (kg oil equivalent)	290	324	..
Electricity use per capita (kilowatt-hours)	..	..	..
Economy			
GDP ($ millions)	1,628	1,476	1,759
GDP growth (annual %)	–0.2	4.1	2.7
GDP implicit price deflator (annual % growth)	3.0	1.5	–3.2
Value added in agriculture (% of GDP)	34	38	41
Value added in industry (% of GDP)	23	19	22
Value added in services (% of GDP)	44	43	37
Exports of goods and services (% of GDP)	33	34	34
Imports of goods and services (% of GDP)	45	52	47
Gross capital formation (% of GDP)	27	19	19
Central government revenue (% of GDP)	..	..	..
Cash surplus/deficit (% of GDP)	..	..	..
Technology and infrastructure			
Fixed-line and mobile subscribers (per 1,000 people)	3	45	56
Cost of 3-minute local call ($)	0.18	0.10	..
Personal computers (per 1,000 people)	..	30.8	32.0
Internet users (per 1,000 people)	0	41	42
Paved roads (% of total)	21.2	*31.6*	..
Aircraft departures (thousands)	1	1	..
Trade and finance			
Trade in goods (% of GDP)	52.1	69.0	57.3
Trade growth less GDP growth (avg. %, 1990–2003)			–1.5
High-technology exports (% of manufactured exports)	*1*	1	1
Net barter terms of trade (2000 = 100)	133	104	..
Foreign direct investment ($ millions)	18	54	20
Present value of debt ($ millions)			1,338
Total debt service (% of goods and services exports)	11.9	2.1	1.9
Short-term debt ($ millions)	113	198	176
Aid per capita ($)	75	11	9

Tonga

East Asia & Pacific			Lower middle income

Population (thousands)	102	Population growth (%)	0.4
Surface area (sq. km)	750	National poverty rate (% pop.)	..
GNI ($ millions)	152	GNI per capita ($)	1,490

	1990	2002	2003
People			
Life expectancy at birth (years)	69	71	71
Fertility rate (births per woman)	4.2	3.4	3.4
Infant mortality rate (per 1,000 live births)	23	17	15
Under-five mortality rate (per 1,000)	27	21	19
Births attended by skilled health staff (% of total)	92	92	..
Child malnutrition, underweight (% of under age 5)	..	..	
Child immunization, measles (% of ages 12–23 mon.)	86	90	99
HIV prevalence rate (% of ages 15–49)	..	..	
Adult literacy, male (% of ages 15 and older)	..	..	
Adult literacy, female (% of ages 15 and older)	..	..	
Primary completion rate, total (% of age group)	121	107	..
Primary completion rate, female (% of age group)	111	108	..
Net primary enrollment (% of age group)	92	91	..
Net secondary enrollment (% of age group)	83	72	..
Environment			
Forests (1,000 sq. km)	0	0	..
Deforestation (average annual %, 1990–2000)		0.0	
Freshwater use (% of internal resources)			..
Carbon dioxide emissions (metric tons per capita)	0.8	1.2	..
Access to improved water source (% of total pop.)	100	100	..
Access to improved sanitation (% of urban pop.)	98	98	..
Energy use per capita (kg oil equivalent)	..	..	..
Electricity use per capita (kilowatt-hours)	..	..	..
Economy			
GDP ($ millions)	113	139	163
GDP growth (annual %)	–2.0	1.6	2.5
GDP implicit price deflator (annual % growth)	12.2	8.0	14.6
Value added in agriculture (% of GDP)	36	29	..
Value added in industry (% of GDP)	14	15	..
Value added in services (% of GDP)	50	56	..
Exports of goods and services (% of GDP)	34	13	..
Imports of goods and services (% of GDP)	65	58	..
Gross capital formation (% of GDP)	18	21	..
Central government revenue (% of GDP)	..	..	..
Cash surplus/deficit (% of GDP)	..	..	..
Technology and infrastructure			
Fixed-line and mobile subscribers (per 1,000 people)	46	147	..
Cost of 3-minute local call ($)	0.08	0.05	..
Personal computers (per 1,000 people)	..	20.2	..
Internet users (per 1,000 people)	..	29	..
Paved roads (% of total)	..	27.0	..
Aircraft departures (thousands)	4	4	5
Trade and finance			
Trade in goods (% of GDP)	64.4	76.0	67.0
Trade growth less GDP growth (avg. %, 1990–2003)			..
High-technology exports (% of manufactured exports)	..	..	..
Net barter terms of trade (2000 = 100)	..	..	
Foreign direct investment ($ millions)	0	2	3
Present value of debt ($ millions)			59
Total debt service (% of goods and services exports)	2.9	2.5	..
Short-term debt ($ millions)	9	1	1
Aid per capita ($)	310	220	270

Trinidad and Tobago

Latin America & Caribbean		Upper middle income	

Population (millions)	1	Population growth (%)	0.7
Surface area (1,000 sq. km)	5	National poverty rate (% pop.)	..
GNI ($ billions)	10	GNI per capita ($)	7,790

	1990	2002	2003
People			
Life expectancy at birth (years)	71	72	72
Fertility rate (births per woman)	2.4	1.8	1.8
Infant mortality rate (per 1,000 live births)	21	17	17
Under-five mortality rate (per 1,000)	24	20	20
Births attended by skilled health staff (% of total)	..	96	..
Child malnutrition, underweight (% of under age 5)	..	6	..
Child immunization, measles (% of ages 12–23 mon.)	70	87	88
HIV prevalence rate (% of ages 15–49)	..	3.0	3.2
Adult literacy, male (% of ages 15 and older)	98	99	..
Adult literacy, female (% of ages 15 and older)	96	98	..
Primary completion rate, total (% of age group)	100	91	..
Primary completion rate, female (% of age group)	102	91	..
Net primary enrollment (% of age group)	91	91	..
Net secondary enrollment (% of age group)	..	70	..
Environment			
Forests (1,000 sq. km)	3	3	..
Deforestation (average annual %, 1990–2000)		0.8	
Freshwater use (% of internal resources)			8
Carbon dioxide emissions (metric tons per capita)	13.9	20.5	..
Access to improved water source (% of total pop.)	92	91	..
Access to improved sanitation (% of urban pop.)	100	100	..
Energy use per capita (kg oil equivalent)	4,770	7,121	..
Electricity use per capita (kilowatt-hours)	2,553	4,330	..
Economy			
GDP ($ billions)	5	9	11
GDP growth (annual %)	1.5	6.8	13.2
GDP implicit price deflator (annual % growth)	15.5	–5.7	5.6
Value added in agriculture (% of GDP)	3	1	1
Value added in industry (% of GDP)	45	44	49
Value added in services (% of GDP)	52	55	50
Exports of goods and services (% of GDP)	45	50	50
Imports of goods and services (% of GDP)	29	46	41
Gross capital formation (% of GDP)	13	17	19
Central government revenue (% of GDP)	..	..	..
Cash surplus/deficit (% of GDP)	..	..	..
Technology and infrastructure			
Fixed-line and mobile subscribers (per 1,000 people)	141	528	..
Cost of 3-minute local call ($)	0.05	0.04	0.04
Personal computers (per 1,000 people)	4.2	79.5	..
Internet users (per 1,000 people)	..	106	..
Paved roads (% of total)	46.2	51.1	..
Aircraft departures (thousands)	22	23	18
Trade and finance			
Trade in goods (% of GDP)	60.6	84.9	78.2
Trade growth less GDP growth (avg. %, 1990–2003)			3.9
High-technology exports (% of manufactured exports)	1	2	..
Net barter terms of trade (2000 = 100)	..	..	..
Foreign direct investment ($ millions)	109	791	616
Present value of debt ($ millions)			3,084
Total debt service (% of goods and services exports)	19.3	5.6	4.1
Short-term debt ($ millions)	127	865	890
Aid per capita ($)	15	–6	–2

Tunisia

Sub-Saharan Africa		Lower middle income
Population (millions)	10	Population growth (%)	1.2
Surface area (1,000 sq. km)	164	National poverty rate (% pop.)	..
GNI ($ billions)	22	GNI per capita ($)	2,240

	1990	2002	2003
People			
Life expectancy at birth (years)	70	73	73
Fertility rate (births per woman)	3.5	2.0	2.0
Infant mortality rate (per 1,000 live births)	41	22	19
Under-five mortality rate (per 1,000)	52	28	24
Births attended by skilled health staff (% of total)	69	90	..
Child malnutrition, underweight (% of under age 5)	10	4	..
Child immunization, measles (% of ages 12–23 mon.)	93	94	90
HIV prevalence rate (% of ages 15–49)	..	0.1	0.1
Adult literacy, male (% of ages 15 and older)	72	83	..
Adult literacy, female (% of ages 15 and older)	47	63	..
Primary completion rate, total (% of age group)	75	99	101
Primary completion rate, female (% of age group)	70	99	102
Net primary enrollment (% of age group)	94	97	..
Net secondary enrollment (% of age group)	..	68	..
Environment			
Forests (1,000 sq. km)	5	5	..
Deforestation (average annual %, 1990–2000)		–0.2	
Freshwater use (% of internal resources)			70
Carbon dioxide emissions (metric tons per capita)	1.6	1.9	..
Access to improved water source (% of total pop.)	77	82	..
Access to improved sanitation (% of urban pop.)	95	90	..
Energy use per capita (kg oil equivalent)	679	846	..
Electricity use per capita (kilowatt-hours)	604	1,019	..
Economy			
GDP ($ billions)	12	21	25
GDP growth (annual %)	8.0	1.7	5.6
GDP implicit price deflator (annual % growth)	4.5	2.3	2.2
Value added in agriculture (% of GDP)	16	10	12
Value added in industry (% of GDP)	30	29	28
Value added in services (% of GDP)	54	60	60
Exports of goods and services (% of GDP)	44	45	43
Imports of goods and services (% of GDP)	51	49	47
Gross capital formation (% of GDP)	32	25	25
Central government revenue (% of GDP)	30.7	29.9	29.4
Cash surplus/deficit (% of GDP)	–3.2	–2.4	–2.4
Technology and infrastructure			
Fixed-line and mobile subscribers (per 1,000 people)	37	169	310
Cost of 3-minute local call ($)	0.08	0.02	0.02
Personal computers (per 1,000 people)	2.6	30.7	40.5
Internet users (per 1,000 people)	..	52	64
Paved roads (% of total)	76.1	65.4	..
Aircraft departures (thousands)	13	19	19
Trade and finance			
Trade in goods (% of GDP)	73.5	78.0	75.6
Trade growth less GDP growth (avg. %, 1990–2003)			0.2
High-technology exports (% of manufactured exports)	2	4	4
Net barter terms of trade (2000 = 100)	109	104	..
Foreign direct investment ($ millions)	76	795	541
Present value of debt ($ billions)			16
Total debt service (% of goods and services exports)	24.5	13.5	13.0
Short-term debt ($ millions)	634	598	812
Aid per capita ($)	48	27	31

Turkey

Population (millions)	71	Population growth (%)	1.5
Surface area (1,000 sq. km)	775	National poverty rate (% pop.)	..
GNI ($ billions)	198	GNI per capita ($)	2,800

	1990	2002	2003
People			
Life expectancy at birth (years)	66	69	69
Fertility rate (births per woman)	3.0	2.5	2.4
Infant mortality rate (per 1,000 live births)	64	*38*	33
Under-five mortality rate (per 1,000)	78	*45*	39
Births attended by skilled health staff (% of total)	..	81	..
Child malnutrition, underweight (% of under age 5)	..	8	..
Child immunization, measles (% of ages 12–23 mon.)	78	82	75
HIV prevalence rate (% of ages 15–49)	..	..	..
Adult literacy, male (% of ages 15 and older)	89	94	..
Adult literacy, female (% of ages 15 and older)	66	79	..
Primary completion rate, total (% of age group)	..	98	95
Primary completion rate, female (% of age group)	..	90	88
Net primary enrollment (% of age group)	89	*88*	..
Net secondary enrollment (% of age group)	42	..	..
Environment			
Forests (1,000 sq. km)	100	*102*	..
Deforestation (average annual %, 1990–2000)		*–0.2*	
Freshwater use (% of internal resources)			16
Carbon dioxide emissions (metric tons per capita)	2.6	*3.3*	..
Access to improved water source (% of total pop.)	81	93	..
Access to improved sanitation (% of urban pop.)	96	94	..
Energy use per capita (kg oil equivalent)	944	1,083	..
Electricity use per capita (kilowatt-hours)	801	1,458	..
Economy			
GDP ($ billions)	151	184	240
GDP growth (annual %)	9.3	7.9	5.8
GDP implicit price deflator (annual % growth)	58.2	44.1	21.3
Value added in agriculture (% of GDP)	18	13	13
Value added in industry (% of GDP)	30	24	22
Value added in services (% of GDP)	52	63	65
Exports of goods and services (% of GDP)	13	29	28
Imports of goods and services (% of GDP)	18	31	31
Gross capital formation (% of GDP)	24	21	23
Central government revenue (% of GDP)	13.7	*23.7*	..
Cash surplus/deficit (% of GDP)	–3.0	*–7.9*	..
Technology and infrastructure			
Fixed-line and mobile subscribers (per 1,000 people)	122	629	662
Cost of 3-minute local call ($)	0.07	0.13	0.14
Personal computers (per 1,000 people)	5.3	44.6	..
Internet users (per 1,000 people)	..	62	85
Paved roads (% of total)	..	41.6	..
Aircraft departures (thousands)	44	106	104
Trade and finance			
Trade in goods (% of GDP)	23.4	47.6	48.2
Trade growth less GDP growth (avg. %, 1990–2003)			6.8
High-technology exports (% of manufactured exports)	1	2	2
Net barter terms of trade (2000 = 100)	109	98	..
Foreign direct investment ($ millions)	684	1,038	1,562
Present value of debt ($ billions)			153
Total debt service (% of goods and services exports)	29.4	46.5	38.5
Short-term debt ($ billions)	10	16	23
Aid per capita ($)	22	6	2

Turkmenistan

Europe & Central Asia		Lower middle income	

Population (millions)	5	Population growth (%)	1.5
Surface area (1,000 sq. km)	488	National poverty rate (% pop.)	..
GNI ($ millions)	5,442	GNI per capita ($)	1,120

	1990	2002	2003
People			
Life expectancy at birth (years)	66	65	64
Fertility rate (births per woman)	4.2	2.7	2.7
Infant mortality rate (per 1,000 live births)	80	77	79
Under-five mortality rate (per 1,000)	97	99	102
Births attended by skilled health staff (% of total)	..	97	..
Child malnutrition, underweight (% of under age 5)	..	12	..
Child immunization, measles (% of ages 12–23 mon.)	76	88	97
HIV prevalence rate (% of ages 15–49)	..	..	0.1
Adult literacy, male (% of ages 15 and older)	..	..	..
Adult literacy, female (% of ages 15 and older)	..	..	..
Primary completion rate, total (% of age group)	..	..	..
Primary completion rate, female (% of age group)	..	..	..
Net primary enrollment (% of age group)	..	..	..
Net secondary enrollment (% of age group)	..	..	..
Environment			
Forests (1,000 sq. km)	38	38	..
Deforestation (average annual %, 1990–2000)		0.0	
Freshwater use (% of internal resources)			2,380
Carbon dioxide emissions (metric tons per capita)	7.2	7.5	..
Access to improved water source (% of total pop.)	..	71	..
Access to improved sanitation (% of urban pop.)	..	77	..
Energy use per capita (kg oil equivalent)	2,914	3,465	..
Electricity use per capita (kilowatt-hours)	1,419	1,371	..
Economy			
GDP ($ millions)	3,232	4,606	6,201
GDP growth (annual %)	0.7	19.8	16.9
GDP implicit price deflator (annual % growth)	6.3	11.0	5.0
Value added in agriculture (% of GDP)	32	25	..
Value added in industry (% of GDP)	30	44	..
Value added in services (% of GDP)	38	30	..
Exports of goods and services (% of GDP)	..	41	..
Imports of goods and services (% of GDP)	..	42	..
Gross capital formation (% of GDP)	40	27	..
Central government revenue (% of GDP)	..	..	..
Cash surplus/deficit (% of GDP)	..	..	..
Technology and infrastructure			
Fixed-line and mobile subscribers (per 1,000 people)	60	79	..
Cost of 3-minute local call ($)	..	..	..
Personal computers (per 1,000 people)	..	..	..
Internet users (per 1,000 people)	..	2	..
Paved roads (% of total)	73.5	81.2	..
Aircraft departures (thousands)	..	24	25
Trade and finance			
Trade in goods (% of GDP)	..	107.9	98.9
Trade growth less GDP growth (avg. %, 1990–2003)			3.6
High-technology exports (% of manufactured exports)	..	5	..
Net barter terms of trade (2000 = 100)	..	..	..
Foreign direct investment ($ millions)	0	100	100
Present value of debt ($ millions)			0
Total debt service (% of goods and services exports)	..	31.8	..
Short-term debt ($ billions)	..	0	0
Aid per capita ($)	2	8	6

Uganda

Sub-Saharan Africa **Low income**

Population (millions)	25	Population growth (%)	2.7
Surface area (1,000 sq. km)	241	National poverty rate (% pop.)	44
GNI ($ millions)	6,244	GNI per capita ($)	250

	1990	2002	2003
People			
Life expectancy at birth (years)	47	43	43
Fertility rate (births per woman)	7.0	6.0	6.0
Infant mortality rate (per 1,000 live births)	93	85	81
Under-five mortality rate (per 1,000)	160	145	140
Births attended by skilled health staff (% of total)	38	39	..
Child malnutrition, underweight (% of under age 5)	23	23	..
Child immunization, measles (% of ages 12–23 mon.)	52	77	82
HIV prevalence rate (% of ages 15–49)	..	5.1	4.1
Adult literacy, male (% of ages 15 and older)	69	79	..
Adult literacy, female (% of ages 15 and older)	43	59	..
Primary completion rate, total (% of age group)	..	64	63
Primary completion rate, female (% of age group)	..	59	58
Net primary enrollment (% of age group)	53	..	..
Net secondary enrollment (% of age group)	..	14	..
Environment			
Forests (1,000 sq. km)	51	42	..
Deforestation (average annual %, 1990–2000)		2.0	
Freshwater use (% of internal resources)			1
Carbon dioxide emissions (metric tons per capita)	0.0	0.1	..
Access to improved water source (% of total pop.)	44	56	..
Access to improved sanitation (% of urban pop.)	54	53	..
Energy use per capita (kg oil equivalent)	..	..	..
Electricity use per capita (kilowatt-hours)	..	..	..
Economy			
GDP ($ millions)	4,304	5,861	6,297
GDP growth (annual %)	6.5	6.8	4.7
GDP implicit price deflator (annual % growth)	44.4	–3.9	10.1
Value added in agriculture (% of GDP)	57	31	32
Value added in industry (% of GDP)	11	22	21
Value added in services (% of GDP)	32	47	46
Exports of goods and services (% of GDP)	7	12	12
Imports of goods and services (% of GDP)	19	27	26
Gross capital formation (% of GDP)	13	20	21
Central government revenue (% of GDP)	..	12.2	..
Cash surplus/deficit (% of GDP)	..	–4.6	..
Technology and infrastructure			
Fixed-line and mobile subscribers (per 1,000 people)	2	18	33
Cost of 3-minute local call ($)	0.04	0.21	..
Personal computers (per 1,000 people)	..	3.3	4.0
Internet users (per 1,000 people)	..	4	5
Paved roads (% of total)	..	6.7	..
Aircraft departures (thousands)	2	0	0
Trade and finance			
Trade in goods (% of GDP)	10.2	26.5	28.8
Trade growth less GDP growth (avg. %, 1990–2003)			3.1
High-technology exports (% of manufactured exports)	..	12	8
Net barter terms of trade (2000 = 100)	146	87	..
Foreign direct investment ($ millions)	0	187	194
Present value of debt ($ millions)			1,894
Total debt service (% of goods and services exports)	81.4	6.3	7.1
Short-term debt ($ millions)	140	159	148
Aid per capita ($)	38	26	38

Ukraine

Europe & Central Asia		Lower middle income	

Population (millions)	48	Population growth (%)	–0.7
Surface area (1,000 sq. km)	604	National poverty rate (% pop.)	..
GNI ($ billions)	47	GNI per capita ($)	970

	1990	2002	2003
People			
Life expectancy at birth (years)	70	68	68
Fertility rate (births per woman)	1.8	1.2	1.2
Infant mortality rate (per 1,000 live births)	18	17	15
Under-five mortality rate (per 1,000)	22	21	20
Births attended by skilled health staff (% of total)	..	100	..
Child malnutrition, underweight (% of under age 5)	..	3	..
Child immunization, measles (% of ages 12–23 mon.)	90	99	99
HIV prevalence rate (% of ages 15–49)	..	1.2	1.4
Adult literacy, male (% of ages 15 and older)	100	100	..
Adult literacy, female (% of ages 15 and older)	99	100	..
Primary completion rate, total (% of age group)	56	..	59
Primary completion rate, female (% of age group)	57	..	..
Net primary enrollment (% of age group)	80	84	..
Net secondary enrollment (% of age group)	..	85	..
Environment			
Forests (1,000 sq. km)	93	96	..
Deforestation (average annual %, 1990–2000)		–0.3	
Freshwater use (% of internal resources)			49
Carbon dioxide emissions (metric tons per capita)	11.5	6.9	..
Access to improved water source (% of total pop.)	..	98	..
Access to improved sanitation (% of urban pop.)	100	100	..
Energy use per capita (kg oil equivalent)	4,187	2,684	..
Electricity use per capita (kilowatt-hours)	3,578	2,229	..
Economy			
GDP ($ billions)	81	42	50
GDP growth (annual %)	–6.3	5.2	9.4
GDP implicit price deflator (annual % growth)	16.4	5.1	6.9
Value added in agriculture (% of GDP)	26	15	14
Value added in industry (% of GDP)	45	38	40
Value added in services (% of GDP)	30	47	46
Exports of goods and services (% of GDP)	28	55	53
Imports of goods and services (% of GDP)	29	51	48
Gross capital formation (% of GDP)	27	19	19
Central government revenue (% of GDP)	..	29.2	..
Cash surplus/deficit (% of GDP)	..	0.3	..
Technology and infrastructure			
Fixed-line and mobile subscribers (per 1,000 people)	136	300	..
Cost of 3-minute local call ($)	..	0.00	..
Personal computers (per 1,000 people)	1.9	19.0	..
Internet users (per 1,000 people)	..	19	..
Paved roads (% of total)	93.7	96.8	..
Aircraft departures (thousands)	45	27	33
Trade and finance			
Trade in goods (% of GDP)	..	82.4	93.1
Trade growth less GDP growth (avg. %, 1990–2003)			3.7
High-technology exports (% of manufactured exports)	..	5	..
Net barter terms of trade (2000 = 100)	..	..	..
Foreign direct investment ($ millions)	0	693	1,424
Present value of debt ($ billions)			16
Total debt service (% of goods and services exports)	..	13.7	12.5
Short-term debt ($ millions)	93	578	1,230
Aid per capita ($)	6	10	7

United Arab Emirates

High income

Population (millions)	4	Population growth (%)	7.4
Surface area (1,000 sq. km)	84	National poverty rate (% pop.)	..
GNI ($ millions)	..	GNI per capita ($)	..

	1990	2002	2003
People			
Life expectancy at birth (years)	74	75	75
Fertility rate (births per woman)	4.1	3.0	3.0
Infant mortality rate (per 1,000 live births)	12	8	7
Under-five mortality rate (per 1,000)	14	9	8
Births attended by skilled health staff (% of total)	..	..	..
Child malnutrition, underweight (% of under age 5)	..	..	..
Child immunization, measles (% of ages 12–23 mon.)	80	94	94
HIV prevalence rate (% of ages 15–49)	..	..	..
Adult literacy, male (% of ages 15 and older)	71	76	..
Adult literacy, female (% of ages 15 and older)	71	81	..
Primary completion rate, total (% of age group)	107	71	..
Primary completion rate, female (% of age group)	111	72	..
Net primary enrollment (% of age group)	99	83	..
Net secondary enrollment (% of age group)	58	71	..
Environment			
Forests (1,000 sq. km)	2	3	..
Deforestation (average annual %, 1990–2000)		–2.8	
Freshwater use (% of internal resources)			1,050
Carbon dioxide emissions (metric tons per capita)	34.3	18.1	..
Access to improved water source (% of total pop.)	..	..	..
Access to improved sanitation (% of urban pop.)	100	100	..
Energy use per capita (kg oil equivalent)	10,061	9,609	..
Electricity use per capita (kilowatt-hours)	8,092	9,656	..
Economy			
GDP ($ millions)	34,132	70,960	..
GDP growth (annual %)	17.5	1.8	..
GDP implicit price deflator (annual % growth)	5.8	0.7	..
Value added in agriculture (% of GDP)	2	..	..
Value added in industry (% of GDP)	64	..	..
Value added in services (% of GDP)	35	..	..
Exports of goods and services (% of GDP)	65	67	..
Imports of goods and services (% of GDP)	40	67	..
Gross capital formation (% of GDP)	20	30	..
Central government revenue (% of GDP)	..	10.0	..
Cash surplus/deficit (% of GDP)	..	0.1	..
Technology and infrastructure			
Fixed-line and mobile subscribers (per 1,000 people)	224	1,010	1,017
Cost of 3-minute local call ($)	0.00	0.00	0.00
Personal computers (per 1,000 people)	29.4	129.0	..
Internet users (per 1,000 people)	..	260	275
Paved roads (% of total)	94.2	100.0	..
Aircraft departures (thousands)	19	55	70
Trade and finance			
Trade in goods (% of GDP)	101.8	119.4	..
Trade growth less GDP growth (avg. %, 1990–2003)			..
High-technology exports (% of manufactured exports)	0	2	..
Net barter terms of trade (2000 = 100)	..	..	..
Foreign direct investment ($ millions)	..	..	..
Present value of debt ($ millions)			..
Total debt service (% of goods and services exports)	..	..	..
Short-term debt ($ millions)	..	..	..
Aid per capita ($)	2	1	1

United Kingdom

High income

Population (millions)	59	Population growth (%)	0.2
Surface area (1,000 sq. km)	243	National poverty rate (% pop.)	..
GNI ($ billions)	1,680	GNI per capita ($)	28,320

	1990	2002	2003
People			
Life expectancy at birth (years)	76	78	78
Fertility rate (births per woman)	1.8	1.6	1.6
Infant mortality rate (per 1,000 live births)	8	5	5
Under-five mortality rate (per 1,000)	10	7	5
Births attended by skilled health staff (% of total)	..	99	..
Child malnutrition, underweight (% of under age 5)	..	..	..
Child immunization, measles (% of ages 12–23 mon.)	87	83	80
HIV prevalence rate (% of ages 15–49)	..	0.2	0.2
Adult literacy, male (% of ages 15 and older)	..	..	..
Adult literacy, female (% of ages 15 and older)	..	..	..
Primary completion rate, total (% of age group)	..	..	..
Primary completion rate, female (% of age group)	..	..	..
Net primary enrollment (% of age group)	98	100	..
Net secondary enrollment (% of age group)	81	96	..
Environment			
Forests (1,000 sq. km)	26	28	..
Deforestation (average annual %, 1990–2000)		–0.6	
Freshwater use (% of internal resources)			8
Carbon dioxide emissions (metric tons per capita)	9.9	9.6	..
Access to improved water source (% of total pop.)	..	..	..
Access to improved sanitation (% of urban pop.)	..	..	..
Energy use per capita (kg oil equivalent)	3,686	3,824	..
Electricity use per capita (kilowatt-hours)	4,768	5,618	..
Economy			
GDP ($ billions)	990	1,564	1,795
GDP growth (annual %)	0.8	1.6	2.2
GDP implicit price deflator (annual % growth)	7.6	3.3	3.1
Value added in agriculture (% of GDP)	2	1	1
Value added in industry (% of GDP)	35	27	27
Value added in services (% of GDP)	63	72	72
Exports of goods and services (% of GDP)	24	26	25
Imports of goods and services (% of GDP)	27	29	28
Gross capital formation (% of GDP)	20	16	16
Central government revenue (% of GDP)	..	36.1	36.0
Cash surplus/deficit (% of GDP)	..	–1.7	–3.7
Technology and infrastructure			
Fixed-line and mobile subscribers (per 1,000 people)	460	1,431	..
Cost of 3-minute local call ($)	0.26	0.18	..
Personal computers (per 1,000 people)	107.7	405.7	..
Internet users (per 1,000 people)	1	423	..
Paved roads (% of total)	100.0	100.0	..
Aircraft departures (thousands)	671	925	891
Trade and finance			
Trade in goods (% of GDP)	41.2	40.1	38.7
Trade growth less GDP growth (avg. %, 1990–2003)			3.5
High-technology exports (% of manufactured exports)	24	31	26
Net barter terms of trade (2000 = 100)	101	102	104
Foreign direct investment ($ billions)	34	29	21
Present value of debt ($ millions)			..
Total debt service (% of goods and services exports)	..	..	..
Short-term debt ($ millions)	..	..	..
Aid per capita ($)	..	..	..

United States

High income

Population (millions)	291	Population growth (%)	0.8
Surface area (1,000 sq. km)	9,629	National poverty rate (% pop.)	..
GNI ($ billions)	11,013	GNI per capita ($)	37,870

	1990	2002	2003
People			
Life expectancy at birth (years)	75	77	77
Fertility rate (births per woman)	2.1	2.0	2.0
Infant mortality rate (per 1,000 live births)	9	7	..
Under-five mortality rate (per 1,000)	11	8	..
Births attended by skilled health staff (% of total)	99	99	..
Child malnutrition, underweight (% of under age 5)	..	..	..
Child immunization, measles (% of ages 12–23 mon.)	90	91	93
HIV prevalence rate (% of ages 15–49)	..	0.6	0.6
Adult literacy, male (% of ages 15 and older)	..	..	..
Adult literacy, female (% of ages 15 and older)	..	..	..
Primary completion rate, total (% of age group)	..	..	..
Primary completion rate, female (% of age group)	..	..	..
Net primary enrollment (% of age group)	97	93	..
Net secondary enrollment (% of age group)	85	85	..
Environment			
Forests (1,000 sq. km)	2,221	2,260	..
Deforestation (average annual %, 1990–2000)		–0.2	
Freshwater use (% of internal resources)			17
Carbon dioxide emissions (metric tons per capita)	19.3	19.8	..
Access to improved water source (% of total pop.)	100	100	..
Access to improved sanitation (% of urban pop.)	100	100	..
Energy use per capita (kg oil equivalent)	7,722	7,943	..
Electricity use per capita (kilowatt-hours)	10,550	12,183	..
Economy			
GDP ($ billions)	5,757	10,429	10,949
GDP growth (annual %)	1.9	2.2	3.1
GDP implicit price deflator (annual % growth)	3.9	1.5	..
Value added in agriculture (% of GDP)	2	2	..
Value added in industry (% of GDP)	28	23	..
Value added in services (% of GDP)	70	75	..
Exports of goods and services (% of GDP)	10	10	..
Imports of goods and services (% of GDP)	11	14	..
Gross capital formation (% of GDP)	18	18	..
Central government revenue (% of GDP)	..	18.1	17.4
Cash surplus/deficit (% of GDP)	..	–2.6	–3.7
Technology and infrastructure			
Fixed-line and mobile subscribers (per 1,000 people)	569	1,134	1,164
Cost of 3-minute local call ($)	0.09	0.00	..
Personal computers (per 1,000 people)	217.9	658.9	..
Internet users (per 1,000 people)	8	551	..
Paved roads (% of total)	58.2	58.8	..
Aircraft departures (thousands)	6,849	8,117	7,789
Trade and finance			
Trade in goods (% of GDP)	15.8	18.2	18.5
Trade growth less GDP growth (avg. %, 1990–2003)			4.4
High-technology exports (% of manufactured exports)	33	32	31
Net barter terms of trade (2000 = 100)	101	104	103
Foreign direct investment ($ billions)	48	72	40
Present value of debt ($ millions)			..
Total debt service (% of goods and services exports)	..	..	..
Short-term debt ($ millions)	..	..	..
Aid per capita ($)	..	..	..

Uruguay

Latin America & Caribbean		Upper middle income	
Population (millions)	3	Population growth (%)	0.6
Surface area (1,000 sq. km)	176	National poverty rate (% pop.)	..
GNI ($ billions)	13	GNI per capita ($)	3,820

	1990	2002	2003
People			
Life expectancy at birth (years)	73	75	75
Fertility rate (births per woman)	2.5	2.2	2.2
Infant mortality rate (per 1,000 live births)	20	15	12
Under-five mortality rate (per 1,000)	24	17	14
Births attended by skilled health staff (% of total)	..	100	..
Child malnutrition, underweight (% of under age 5)	6	..	..
Child immunization, measles (% of ages 12–23 mon.)	97	92	95
HIV prevalence rate (% of ages 15–49)	..	0.3	0.3
Adult literacy, male (% of ages 15 and older)	96	97	..
Adult literacy, female (% of ages 15 and older)	97	98	..
Primary completion rate, total (% of age group)	95	95	92
Primary completion rate, female (% of age group)	97	98	93
Net primary enrollment (% of age group)	92	90	..
Net secondary enrollment (% of age group)	..	72	..
Environment			
Forests (1,000 sq. km)	8	13	..
Deforestation (average annual %, 1990–2000)		–5.0	
Freshwater use (% of internal resources)			1
Carbon dioxide emissions (metric tons per capita)	1.3	1.6	..
Access to improved water source (% of total pop.)	..	98	..
Access to improved sanitation (% of urban pop.)	95	95	..
Energy use per capita (kg oil equivalent)	725	747	..
Electricity use per capita (kilowatt-hours)	1,220	1,834	..
Economy			
GDP ($ billions)	9	12	11
GDP growth (annual %)	0.3	–11.0	2.5
GDP implicit price deflator (annual % growth)	106.8	18.7	17.9
Value added in agriculture (% of GDP)	9	9	13
Value added in industry (% of GDP)	35	27	27
Value added in services (% of GDP)	56	64	60
Exports of goods and services (% of GDP)	24	22	26
Imports of goods and services (% of GDP)	18	20	23
Gross capital formation (% of GDP)	12	12	13
Central government revenue (% of GDP)	23.8	25.2	..
Cash surplus/deficit (% of GDP)	0.5	–4.7	..
Technology and infrastructure			
Fixed-line and mobile subscribers (per 1,000 people)	134	472	..
Cost of 3-minute local call ($)	0.04	0.17	..
Personal computers (per 1,000 people)	..	110.1	..
Internet users (per 1,000 people)	..	119	..
Paved roads (% of total)	74.0	90.0	..
Aircraft departures (thousands)	5	8	7
Trade and finance			
Trade in goods (% of GDP)	32.7	31.2	39.2
Trade growth less GDP growth (avg. %, 1990–2003)			2.3
High-technology exports (% of manufactured exports)	..	3	2
Net barter terms of trade (2000 = 100)	116	100	..
Foreign direct investment ($ millions)	0	175	275
Present value of debt ($ billions)			12
Total debt service (% of goods and services exports)	40.8	40.3	26.3
Short-term debt ($ millions)	1,201	1,600	1,445
Aid per capita ($)	17	4	5

Uzbekistan

Europe & Central Asia		Low income

Population (millions)	26	Population growth (%)	1.3
Surface area (1,000 sq. km)	447	National poverty rate (% pop.)	28
GNI ($ billions)	11	GNI per capita ($)	420

	1990	2002	2003
People			
Life expectancy at birth (years)	69	67	67
Fertility rate (births per woman)	4.1	2.3	2.3
Infant mortality rate (per 1,000 live births)	65	59	57
Under-five mortality rate (per 1,000)	79	71	69
Births attended by skilled health staff (% of total)	..	96	..
Child malnutrition, underweight (% of under age 5)	..	8	..
Child immunization, measles (% of ages 12–23 mon.)	84	97	99
HIV prevalence rate (% of ages 15–49)	..	0.1	0.1
Adult literacy, male (% of ages 15 and older)	99	100	..
Adult literacy, female (% of ages 15 and older)	98	99	..
Primary completion rate, total (% of age group)	..	103	103
Primary completion rate, female (% of age group)	..	103	102
Net primary enrollment (% of age group)	78	..	..
Net secondary enrollment (% of age group)	..	..	..
Environment			
Forests (1,000 sq. km)	19	20	..
Deforestation (average annual %, 1990–2000)		–0.2	
Freshwater use (% of internal resources)			363
Carbon dioxide emissions (metric tons per capita)	5.3	4.8	..
Access to improved water source (% of total pop.)	89	89	..
Access to improved sanitation (% of urban pop.)	73	73	..
Energy use per capita (kg oil equivalent)	2,098	2,047	..
Electricity use per capita (kilowatt-hours)	1,878	1,670	..
Economy			
GDP ($ billions)	13	10	10
GDP growth (annual %)	1.6	4.2	4.4
GDP implicit price deflator (annual % growth)	4.0	45.2	24.2
Value added in agriculture (% of GDP)	33	35	35
Value added in industry (% of GDP)	33	22	22
Value added in services (% of GDP)	34	44	43
Exports of goods and services (% of GDP)	29	31	37
Imports of goods and services (% of GDP)	48	28	30
Gross capital formation (% of GDP)	32	21	17
Central government revenue (% of GDP)	..	..	..
Cash surplus/deficit (% of GDP)	..	..	..
Technology and infrastructure			
Fixed-line and mobile subscribers (per 1,000 people)	69	74	80
Cost of 3-minute local call ($)	0.00	0.01	..
Personal computers (per 1,000 people)	..	..	..
Internet users (per 1,000 people)	..	11	19
Paved roads (% of total)	79.0	87.3	..
Aircraft departures (thousands)	..	23	22
Trade and finance			
Trade in goods (% of GDP)	..	52.6	58.6
Trade growth less GDP growth (avg. %, 1990–2003)			–1.6
High-technology exports (% of manufactured exports)	..	..	..
Net barter terms of trade (2000 = 100)	..	..	..
Foreign direct investment ($ millions)	0	65	70
Present value of debt ($ millions)			4,765
Total debt service (% of goods and services exports)	..	25.2	21.3
Short-term debt ($ millions)	0	331	221
Aid per capita ($)	3	7	8

Vanuatu

East Asia & Pacific		Lower middle income	
Population (thousands)	210	Population growth (%)	2.2
Surface area (1,000 sq. km)	12	National poverty rate (% pop.)	..
GNI ($ millions)	248	GNI per capita ($)	1,180

	1990	2002	2003
People			
Life expectancy at birth (years)	64	69	69
Fertility rate (births per woman)	5.5	4.3	4.3
Infant mortality rate (per 1,000 live births)	52	35	31
Under-five mortality rate (per 1,000)	70	44	38
Births attended by skilled health staff (% of total)	..	..	..
Child malnutrition, underweight (% of under age 5)	..	..	..
Child immunization, measles (% of ages 12–23 mon.)	66	44	48
HIV prevalence rate (% of ages 15–49)	..	..	..
Adult literacy, male (% of ages 15 and older)	..	..	..
Adult literacy, female (% of ages 15 and older)	..	..	..
Primary completion rate, total (% of age group)	85	96	..
Primary completion rate, female (% of age group)	84	97	..
Net primary enrollment (% of age group)	71	93	..
Net secondary enrollment (% of age group)	..	28	..
Environment			
Forests (1,000 sq. km)	4	4	..
Deforestation (average annual %, 1990–2000)		–0.1	
Freshwater use (% of internal resources)			..
Carbon dioxide emissions (metric tons per capita)	0.4	0.4	..
Access to improved water source (% of total pop.)	60	60	..
Access to improved sanitation (% of urban pop.)	..	78	..
Energy use per capita (kg oil equivalent)	..	..	..
Electricity use per capita (kilowatt-hours)	..	..	..
Economy			
GDP ($ millions)	151	234	283
GDP growth (annual %)	0.0	–0.3	2.0
GDP implicit price deflator (annual % growth)	8.2	2.1	4.0
Value added in agriculture (% of GDP)	21	15	..
Value added in industry (% of GDP)	12	9	..
Value added in services (% of GDP)	67	76	..
Exports of goods and services (% of GDP)	49	47	..
Imports of goods and services (% of GDP)	77	61	..
Gross capital formation (% of GDP)	35	21	..
Central government revenue (% of GDP)	27.5	22.2	..
Cash surplus/deficit (% of GDP)	–8.2	–0.8	..
Technology and infrastructure			
Fixed-line and mobile subscribers (per 1,000 people)	18	57	69
Cost of 3-minute local call ($)	0.13	0.22	0.25
Personal computers (per 1,000 people)	..	14.8	..
Internet users (per 1,000 people)	..	35	36
Paved roads (% of total)	21.6	23.9	..
Aircraft departures (thousands)	0	2	1
Trade and finance			
Trade in goods (% of GDP)	76.3	46.5	46.6
Trade growth less GDP growth (avg. %, 1990–2003)			..
High-technology exports (% of manufactured exports)	20	1	..
Net barter terms of trade (2000 = 100)	..	..	..
Foreign direct investment ($ millions)	13	15	19
Present value of debt ($ millions)			68
Total debt service (% of goods and services exports)	2.1	1.5	1.4
Short-term debt ($ millions)	10	14	15
Aid per capita ($)	338	134	154

Venezuela, RB

Latin America & Caribbean **Upper middle income**

Population (millions)	26	Population growth (%)	1.8
Surface area (1,000 sq. km)	912	National poverty rate (% pop.)	..
GNI ($ billions)	90	GNI per capita ($)	3,490

	1990	2002	2003
People			
Life expectancy at birth (years)	71	74	74
Fertility rate (births per woman)	3.4	2.7	2.7
Infant mortality rate (per 1,000 live births)	23	20	18
Under-five mortality rate (per 1,000)	27	23	21
Births attended by skilled health staff (% of total)	..	94	..
Child malnutrition, underweight (% of under age 5)	8	4	..
Child immunization, measles (% of ages 12–23 mon.)	61	83	82
HIV prevalence rate (% of ages 15–49)	..	0.6	0.7
Adult literacy, male (% of ages 15 and older)	90	94	..
Adult literacy, female (% of ages 15 and older)	88	93	..
Primary completion rate, total (% of age group)	81	90	..
Primary completion rate, female (% of age group)	86	92	..
Net primary enrollment (% of age group)	88	91	..
Net secondary enrollment (% of age group)	19	59	..
Environment			
Forests (1,000 sq. km)	517	495	..
Deforestation (average annual %, 1990–2000)		0.4	
Freshwater use (% of internal resources)			1
Carbon dioxide emissions (metric tons per capita)	5.8	6.5	..
Access to improved water source (% of total pop.)	..	83	..
Access to improved sanitation (% of urban pop.)	..	71	..
Energy use per capita (kg oil equivalent)	2,224	2,141	..
Electricity use per capita (kilowatt-hours)	2,279	2,472	..
Economy			
GDP ($ billions)	49	95	85
GDP growth (annual %)	6.5	–8.9	–9.4
GDP implicit price deflator (annual % growth)	41.7	33.1	36.8
Value added in agriculture (% of GDP)	5	4	4
Value added in industry (% of GDP)	61	39	41
Value added in services (% of GDP)	34	56	54
Exports of goods and services (% of GDP)	39	29	31
Imports of goods and services (% of GDP)	20	17	15
Gross capital formation (% of GDP)	10	14	9
Central government revenue (% of GDP)	23.7	22.2	23.5
Cash surplus/deficit (% of GDP)	2.9	–3.1	–4.0
Technology and infrastructure			
Fixed-line and mobile subscribers (per 1,000 people)	77	369	384
Cost of 3-minute local call ($)	0.02	0.04	0.02
Personal computers (per 1,000 people)	10.3	60.9	..
Internet users (per 1,000 people)	0	34	60
Paved roads (% of total)	35.6	33.6	..
Aircraft departures (thousands)	82	161	106
Trade and finance			
Trade in goods (% of GDP)	51.1	38.1	38.6
Trade growth less GDP growth (avg. %, 1990–2003)			2.4
High-technology exports (% of manufactured exports)	4	3	4
Net barter terms of trade (2000 = 100)	90	89	..
Foreign direct investment ($ millions)	451	782	2,520
Present value of debt ($ billions)			41
Total debt service (% of goods and services exports)	23.3	25.5	30.1
Short-term debt ($ millions)	2,000	4,590	4,345
Aid per capita ($)	4	2	3

Vietnam

East Asia & Pacific		Low income

Population (millions)	81	Population growth (%)	1.1
Surface area (1,000 sq. km)	332	National poverty rate (% pop.)	29
GNI ($ billions)	39	GNI per capita ($)	480

	1990	2002	2003
People			
Life expectancy at birth (years)	65	70	70
Fertility rate (births per woman)	3.6	1.9	1.9
Infant mortality rate (per 1,000 live births)	38	23	19
Under-five mortality rate (per 1,000)	53	30	23
Births attended by skilled health staff (% of total)	..	85	..
Child malnutrition, underweight (% of under age 5)	45	34	..
Child immunization, measles (% of ages 12–23 mon.)	85	96	93
HIV prevalence rate (% of ages 15–49)	..	0.3	0.4
Adult literacy, male (% of ages 15 and older)	94	94	..
Adult literacy, female (% of ages 15 and older)	87	87	..
Primary completion rate, total (% of age group)	..	104	95
Primary completion rate, female (% of age group)	..	102	95
Net primary enrollment (% of age group)	90	94	..
Net secondary enrollment (% of age group)	..	65	..
Environment			
Forests (1,000 sq. km)	93	98	..
Deforestation (average annual %, 1990–2000)		–0.5	
Freshwater use (% of internal resources)			15
Carbon dioxide emissions (metric tons per capita)	0.3	0.7	..
Access to improved water source (% of total pop.)	72	73	..
Access to improved sanitation (% of urban pop.)	46	84	..
Energy use per capita (kg oil equivalent)	367	530	..
Electricity use per capita (kilowatt-hours)	93	374	..
Economy			
GDP ($ billions)	6	35	39
GDP growth (annual %)	5.1	7.0	7.2
GDP implicit price deflator (annual % growth)	42.1	4.0	5.4
Value added in agriculture (% of GDP)	39	23	22
Value added in industry (% of GDP)	23	38	40
Value added in services (% of GDP)	39	38	38
Exports of goods and services (% of GDP)	36	55	60
Imports of goods and services (% of GDP)	45	60	68
Gross capital formation (% of GDP)	13	33	35
Central government revenue (% of GDP)	..	19.1	..
Cash surplus/deficit (% of GDP)	..	..	..
Technology and infrastructure			
Fixed-line and mobile subscribers (per 1,000 people)	1	72	88
Cost of 3-minute local call ($)	..	0.02	0.02
Personal computers (per 1,000 people)	0.1	9.8	..
Internet users (per 1,000 people)	..	3	43
Paved roads (% of total)	23.5	25.1	..
Aircraft departures (thousands)	2	43	48
Trade and finance			
Trade in goods (% of GDP)	79.7	101.3	115.0
Trade growth less GDP growth (avg. %, 1990–2003)			15.0
High-technology exports (% of manufactured exports)	..	2	..
Net barter terms of trade (2000 = 100)	..	..	..
Foreign direct investment ($ millions)	180	1,400	1,450
Present value of debt ($ billions)			14
Total debt service (% of goods and services exports)	..	6.0	3.4
Short-term debt ($ millions)	1,780	784	1,289
Aid per capita ($)	3	16	22

Virgin Islands (U.S.)

High income

Population (thousands)	112	Population growth (%)	1.1
Surface area (sq. km)	340	National poverty rate (% pop.)	..
GNI ($ millions)	..	GNI per capita ($)	..

	1990	2002	2003
People			
Life expectancy at birth (years)	74	78	78
Fertility rate (births per woman)	2.6	2.2	2.2
Infant mortality rate (per 1,000 live births)	..	..	..
Under-five mortality rate (per 1,000)	..	..	..
Births attended by skilled health staff (% of total)	..	..	..
Child malnutrition, underweight (% of under age 5)	..	..	..
Child immunization, measles (% of ages 12–23 mon.)	..	..	..
HIV prevalence rate (% of ages 15–49)	..	..	..
Adult literacy, male (% of ages 15 and older)	..	..	..
Adult literacy, female (% of ages 15 and older)	..	..	..
Primary completion rate, total (% of age group)	..	..	..
Primary completion rate, female (% of age group)	..	..	..
Net primary enrollment (% of age group)	..	..	..
Net secondary enrollment (% of age group)	..	..	..
Environment			
Forests (1,000 sq. km)	0	0	..
Deforestation (average annual %, 1990–2000)		0.0	
Freshwater use (% of internal resources)			..
Carbon dioxide emissions (metric tons per capita)	81.1	121.2	..
Access to improved water source (% of total pop.)	..	..	..
Access to improved sanitation (% of urban pop.)	..	..	..
Energy use per capita (kg oil equivalent)	..	..	..
Electricity use per capita (kilowatt-hours)	..	..	..
Economy			
GDP ($ millions)	1,565	..	..
GDP growth (annual %)	..	..	..
GDP implicit price deflator (annual % growth)	4.1	..	..
Value added in agriculture (% of GDP)	..	..	..
Value added in industry (% of GDP)	..	..	..
Value added in services (% of GDP)	..	..	..
Exports of goods and services (% of GDP)	..	..	..
Imports of goods and services (% of GDP)	..	..	..
Gross capital formation (% of GDP)	..	..	..
Central government revenue (% of GDP)	..	..	..
Cash surplus/deficit (% of GDP)	..	..	..
Technology and infrastructure			
Fixed-line and mobile subscribers (per 1,000 people)	457	1,010	..
Cost of 3-minute local call ($)	..	0.00	..
Personal computers (per 1,000 people)	..	..	..
Internet users (per 1,000 people)	..	273	..
Paved roads (% of total)	..	..	..
Aircraft departures (thousands)	..	..	..
Trade and finance			
Trade in goods (% of GDP)	..	..	..
Trade growth less GDP growth (avg. %, 1990–2003)			..
High-technology exports (% of manufactured exports)	..	..	..
Net barter terms of trade (2000 = 100)	..	..	..
Foreign direct investment ($ millions)	..	..	..
Present value of debt ($ millions)			..
Total debt service (% of goods and services exports)	..	..	..
Short-term debt ($ millions)	..	..	..
Aid per capita ($)	..	..	..

West Bank and Gaza

Middle East & North Africa		Lower middle income	
Population (millions)	3	Population growth (%)	4.1
Surface area (1,000 sq. km)	6	National poverty rate (% pop.)	..
GNI ($ millions)	3,734	GNI per capita ($)	1,110

	1990	2002	2003
People			
Life expectancy at birth (years)	*69*	73	73
Fertility rate (births per woman)	*6.3*	4.9	4.9
Infant mortality rate (per 1,000 live births)	..	..	..
Under-five mortality rate (per 1,000)	..	..	..
Births attended by skilled health staff (% of total)	..	..	..
Child malnutrition, underweight (% of under age 5)	..	..	..
Child immunization, measles (% of ages 12–23 mon.)	..	..	..
HIV prevalence rate (% of ages 15–49)	..	..	..
Adult literacy, male (% of ages 15 and older)	..	..	..
Adult literacy, female (% of ages 15 and older)	..	..	..
Primary completion rate, total (% of age group)	..	106	..
Primary completion rate, female (% of age group)	..	107	..
Net primary enrollment (% of age group)	..	..	..
Net secondary enrollment (% of age group)	..	..	..
Environment			
Forests (1,000 sq. km)	..	..	
Deforestation (average annual %, 1990–2000)		..	
Freshwater use (% of internal resources)			..
Carbon dioxide emissions (metric tons per capita)	..	..	
Access to improved water source (% of total pop.)	..	..	..
Access to improved sanitation (% of urban pop.)	..	..	..
Energy use per capita (kg oil equivalent)	..	..	..
Electricity use per capita (kilowatt-hours)	..	..	..
Economy			
GDP ($ millions)	..	3,396	3,454
GDP growth (annual %)	..	−19.1	−1.7
GDP implicit price deflator (annual % growth)	..	17.2	7.0
Value added in agriculture (% of GDP)	..	6	6
Value added in industry (% of GDP)	..	13	12
Value added in services (% of GDP)	..	80	82
Exports of goods and services (% of GDP)	..	12	10
Imports of goods and services (% of GDP)	..	47	49
Gross capital formation (% of GDP)	..	4	3
Central government revenue (% of GDP)	..	..	..
Cash surplus/deficit (% of GDP)	..	..	..
Technology and infrastructure			
Fixed-line and mobile subscribers (per 1,000 people)	*41*	180	220
Cost of 3-minute local call ($)	..	0.05	..
Personal computers (per 1,000 people)	..	36.2	..
Internet users (per 1,000 people)	..	30	40
Paved roads (% of total)	..	..	..
Aircraft departures (thousands)	..	..	..
Trade and finance			
Trade in goods (% of GDP)	..	..	..
Trade growth less GDP growth (avg. %, 1990–2003)			−3.1
High-technology exports (% of manufactured exports)	..	..	..
Net barter terms of trade (2000 = 100)	..	..	..
Foreign direct investment ($ millions)	..	..	..
Present value of debt ($ millions)			..
Total debt service (% of goods and services exports)	..	..	..
Short-term debt ($ millions)	..	..	..
Aid per capita ($)	..	500	289

Yemen, Rep.

Middle East & North Africa		Low income

Population (millions)	19	Population growth (%)	3.0
Surface area (1,000 sq. km)	528	National poverty rate (% pop.)	42
GNI ($ billions)	10	GNI per capita ($)	520

	1990	2002	2003
People			
Life expectancy at birth (years)	52	57	58
Fertility rate (births per woman)	7.5	6.0	6.0
Infant mortality rate (per 1,000 live births)	98	84	82
Under-five mortality rate (per 1,000)	142	117	113
Births attended by skilled health staff (% of total)	16	22	..
Child malnutrition, underweight (% of under age 5)	30	46	..
Child immunization, measles (% of ages 12–23 mon.)	69	65	66
HIV prevalence rate (% of ages 15–49)	..	..	0.1
Adult literacy, male (% of ages 15 and older)	55	69	..
Adult literacy, female (% of ages 15 and older)	13	29	..
Primary completion rate, total (% of age group)	..	65	66
Primary completion rate, female (% of age group)	..	46	48
Net primary enrollment (% of age group)	52	72	..
Net secondary enrollment (% of age group)	..	35	..
Environment			
Forests (1,000 sq. km)	5	4	..
Deforestation (average annual %, 1990–2000)		1.8	
Freshwater use (% of internal resources)			73
Carbon dioxide emissions (metric tons per capita)	0.7	0.5	..
Access to improved water source (% of total pop.)	69	69	..
Access to improved sanitation (% of urban pop.)	59	76	..
Energy use per capita (kg oil equivalent)	228	221	..
Electricity use per capita (kilowatt-hours)	108	152	..
Economy			
GDP ($ billions)	5	10	11
GDP growth (annual %)	2.0	3.6	3.8
GDP implicit price deflator (annual % growth)	17.1	5.2	9.2
Value added in agriculture (% of GDP)	24	15	15
Value added in industry (% of GDP)	27	40	40
Value added in services (% of GDP)	49	44	45
Exports of goods and services (% of GDP)	14	38	31
Imports of goods and services (% of GDP)	20	39	36
Gross capital formation (% of GDP)	15	17	17
Central government revenue (% of GDP)	18.9	23.9	..
Cash surplus/deficit (% of GDP)	–7.8	–2.3	..
Technology and infrastructure			
Fixed-line and mobile subscribers (per 1,000 people)	11	49	..
Cost of 3-minute local call ($)	0.01	0.02	..
Personal computers (per 1,000 people)	..	7.4	..
Internet users (per 1,000 people)	..	1	..
Paved roads (% of total)	9.1	11.5	..
Aircraft departures (thousands)	14	16	15
Trade and finance			
Trade in goods (% of GDP)	46.9	60.7	66.4
Trade growth less GDP growth (avg. %, 1990–2003)			2.2
High-technology exports (% of manufactured exports)	..	..	..
Net barter terms of trade (2000 = 100)	..	..	..
Foreign direct investment ($ millions)	–131	114	–89
Present value of debt ($ millions)			3,790
Total debt service (% of goods and services exports)	5.6	3.3	3.1
Short-term debt ($ millions)	1,192	341	229
Aid per capita ($)	34	31	13

Zambia

Sub-Saharan Africa		Low income

Population (millions)	10	Population growth (%)	1.5
Surface area (1,000 sq. km)	753	National poverty rate (% pop.)	73
GNI ($ millions)	3,982	GNI per capita ($)	380

	1990	2002	2003
People			
Life expectancy at birth (years)	49	37	36
Fertility rate (births per woman)	6.3	5.1	5.0
Infant mortality rate (per 1,000 live births)	101	102	102
Under-five mortality rate (per 1,000)	180	182	182
Births attended by skilled health staff (% of total)	51	43	..
Child malnutrition, underweight (% of under age 5)	25	28	..
Child immunization, measles (% of ages 12–23 mon.)	90	84	84
HIV prevalence rate (% of ages 15–49)	..	16.7	15.6
Adult literacy, male (% of ages 15 and older)	79	86	..
Adult literacy, female (% of ages 15 and older)	59	74	..
Primary completion rate, total (% of age group)	..	60	69
Primary completion rate, female (% of age group)	..	55	64
Net primary enrollment (% of age group)	79	68	..
Net secondary enrollment (% of age group)	..	23	..
Environment			
Forests (1,000 sq. km)	398	312	..
Deforestation (average annual %, 1990–2000)		2.4	
Freshwater use (% of internal resources)			2
Carbon dioxide emissions (metric tons per capita)	0.3	0.2	..
Access to improved water source (% of total pop.)	50	55	..
Access to improved sanitation (% of urban pop.)	64	68	..
Energy use per capita (kg oil equivalent)	703	639	..
Electricity use per capita (kilowatt-hours)	761	583	..
Economy			
GDP ($ millions)	3,288	3,697	4,335
GDP growth (annual %)	–0.5	3.3	5.1
GDP implicit price deflator (annual % growth)	106.4	19.9	20.1
Value added in agriculture (% of GDP)	21	22	23
Value added in industry (% of GDP)	51	26	27
Value added in services (% of GDP)	28	52	50
Exports of goods and services (% of GDP)	36	24	21
Imports of goods and services (% of GDP)	37	29	28
Gross capital formation (% of GDP)	17	23	26
Central government revenue (% of GDP)	20.4	19.1	..
Cash surplus/deficit (% of GDP)	..	–0.4	..
Technology and infrastructure			
Fixed-line and mobile subscribers (per 1,000 people)	8	21	29
Cost of 3-minute local call ($)	0.06	0.09	..
Personal computers (per 1,000 people)	..	7.5	8.5
Internet users (per 1,000 people)	..	5	6
Paved roads (% of total)	16.6	22.0	..
Aircraft departures (thousands)	7	5	5
Trade and finance			
Trade in goods (% of GDP)	76.9	59.1	56.4
Trade growth less GDP growth (avg. %, 1990–2003)			1.3
High-technology exports (% of manufactured exports)	..	2	..
Net barter terms of trade (2000 = 100)	207	93	..
Foreign direct investment ($ millions)	203	82	100
Present value of debt ($ millions)			4,519
Total debt service (% of goods and services exports)	14.9	25.4	27.8
Short-term debt ($ millions)	1,414	108	128
Aid per capita ($)	62	63	54

Zimbabwe

Sub-Saharan Africa | **Low income**

Population (millions)	13	Population growth (%)	0.8
Surface area (1,000 sq. km)	391	National poverty rate (% pop.)	..
GNI ($ millions)	..	GNI per capita ($)	..

	1990	2002	2003
People			
Life expectancy at birth (years)	56	39	39
Fertility rate (births per woman)	4.8	3.7	3.6
Infant mortality rate (per 1,000 live births)	53	73	78
Under-five mortality rate (per 1,000)	80	117	126
Births attended by skilled health staff (% of total)	70	73	..
Child malnutrition, underweight (% of under age 5)	12	13	..
Child immunization, measles (% of ages 12–23 mon.)	87	58	80
HIV prevalence rate (% of ages 15–49)	..	24.9	24.6
Adult literacy, male (% of ages 15 and older)	87	94	..
Adult literacy, female (% of ages 15 and older)	75	86	..
Primary completion rate, total (% of age group)	96	81	..
Primary completion rate, female (% of age group)	93	78	..
Net primary enrollment (% of age group)	86	80	..
Net secondary enrollment (% of age group)	..	38	..
Environment			
Forests (1,000 sq. km)	222	190	..
Deforestation (average annual %, 1990–2000)		1.5	
Freshwater use (% of internal resources)			9
Carbon dioxide emissions (metric tons per capita)	1.6	1.2	..
Access to improved water source (% of total pop.)	77	83	..
Access to improved sanitation (% of urban pop.)	69	69	..
Energy use per capita (kg oil equivalent)	911	751	..
Electricity use per capita (kilowatt-hours)	888	831	..
Economy			
GDP ($ millions)	8,784	17,750	..
GDP growth (annual %)	7.0	−5.6	..
GDP implicit price deflator (annual % growth)	14.7	107.5	..
Value added in agriculture (% of GDP)	16	17	..
Value added in industry (% of GDP)	33	24	..
Value added in services (% of GDP)	50	59	..
Exports of goods and services (% of GDP)	23	24	..
Imports of goods and services (% of GDP)	23	22	..
Gross capital formation (% of GDP)	17	8	..
Central government revenue (% of GDP)	24.1	29.5	..
Cash surplus/deficit (% of GDP)	−2.6	−5.2	..
Technology and infrastructure			
Fixed-line and mobile subscribers (per 1,000 people)	13	55	58
Cost of 3-minute local call ($)	0.05	0.04	..
Personal computers (per 1,000 people)	0.2	51.6	52.7
Internet users (per 1,000 people)	..	43	..
Paved roads (% of total)	14.0	47.4	..
Aircraft departures (thousands)	10	5	4
Trade and finance			
Trade in goods (% of GDP)	40.7	20.1	..
Trade growth less GDP growth (avg. %, 1990–2003)			4.8
High-technology exports (% of manufactured exports)	2	3	..
Net barter terms of trade (2000 = 100)	98	101	..
Foreign direct investment ($ millions)	−12	26	20
Present value of debt ($ millions)			4,415
Total debt service (% of goods and services exports)	23.1	..	..
Short-term debt ($ millions)	591	501	718
Aid per capita ($)	33	15	14

Glossary

Access to an improved water source is the percentage of the population with reasonable access to an adequate amount of water from an improved source, such as a household connection, public standpipe, borehole, protected well or spring, or rainwater collection. Unimproved sources include vendors, tanker trucks, and unprotected wells and springs. Reasonable access is defined as the availability of at least 20 liters a person a day from a source within 1 kilometer of the dwelling. (World Health Organization/United Nations Children's Fund Joint Monitoring Programme)

Access to improved sanitation facilities is the percentage of the population with at least adequate excreta disposal facilities (private or shared, but not public) that can effectively prevent human, animal, and insect contact with excreta. Improved facilities range from simple but protected pit latrines to flush toilets with a sewerage connection. To be effective, facilities must be correctly constructed and properly maintained. (World Health Organization/United Nations Children's Fund Joint Monitoring Programme)

Aid per capita is official development assistance and official aid received from members of the OECD, Development Assistance Committee and other official donors. (Organisation for Economic Co-operation and Development)

Aircraft departures are the number of domestic and international takeoffs of air carriers registered in the country. (International Civil Aviation Organization)

Births attended by skilled health staff are the percentage of deliveries attended by personnel trained to give the necessary supervision, care, and advice to women during pregnancy, labor and the postpartum period, to conduct deliveries on their own, and to care for newborns. (World Health Organization)

Carbon dioxide emissions are emissions stemming from the burning of fossil fuels and the manufacture of cement. They include carbon dioxide produced during consumption of solid, liquid, and gas fuels and gas flaring. (Carbon Dioxide Information Analysis Center)

Cash surplus/deficit is revenue (including grants) minus expense, minus net acquisition of nonfinancial assets. In the earlier version nonfinancial assets were included under revenue and expenditure in gross terms. This is the closest to the earlier overall budget balance (still missing is the lending minus repayments which have been brought below as a financing item under net acquisition of financial assets). (International Monetary Fund)

Central government revenue is cash receipts from taxes, social contributions, and other revenue such as fines, fees, rent, and income from property sales. Grants are also considered revenue but are excluded here.

Child immunization, measles is the percentage of children ages 12–23 months at the time of the survey who received a dose of measles vaccine by 12 months, or at any time before the interview date. A child is considered adequately immunized against measles after receiving one dose of vaccine. (World Health Organization and United Nations Children's Fund)

Child malnutrition is the percentage of children under age five whose weight for age are more than two standard deviations below the median for the international reference population ages 0–59 months. The reference population, adopted by the World Health Organization in 1983, is based on children from the United States, who are assumed to be well nourished. (World Health Organization)

Cost of 3-minute local call is the cost of a three-minute peak-rate, fixed-line call within the same exchange area using the subscriber's equipment (that is, not from a public phone). (International Telecommunication Union)

Deforestation is the permanent conversion of natural forest areas to other uses, including shifting cultivation, permanent agriculture, ranching, settlements, and infrastructure development. Deforested areas do not include areas logged but intended for regeneration or areas degraded by fuelwood gathering, acid precipitation, or forest fires. Negative numbers indicate an increase in forest area. (Food and Agriculture Organization)

Electricity use per capita is the production of power plants and combined heat and power plants less transmission, distribution, and transformation losses and own use by heat and power plants. (International Energy Agency)

Energy use per capita is the apparent consumption of commercial energy, which is equal to indigenous production plus imports and stock changes, minus exports and fuels supplied to ships and aircraft engaged in international transportation. (International Energy Agency)

Europe EMU is the 12 participating member countries of the European Monetary Union (EMU) comprising Austria, Belgium, Finland, France, Germany, Greece, Ireland, Italy, Luxembourg, the Netherlands, Portugal, and Spain

Exports of goods and services are the value of all goods and other market services provided to the rest of the world, including the value of merchandise, freight, insurance, transport, travel, royalties, license fees, and other services. Labor and property income (formerly called factor services) are excluded as are transfer payments. (World Bank, Organisation for Economic Co-operation and Development, United Nations)

Fertility rate is the number of children that would be born to a woman if she were to live to the end of her childbearing years and bear children in accordance with current age-specific fertility rates. (World Bank)

Fixed-line and mobile phone subscribers: fixed lines are telephone lines connecting a customer's equipment to the public switched telephone network. Mobile telephones refer to users of portable telephones subscribing to an automatic public mobile telephone service using cellular technology that provides access to the public switched telephone network, per 1,000 people. (International Telecommunication Union)

Foreign direct investment is net inflows of investment to acquire a lasting management interest (10 percent or more of voting stock) in an enterprise operating in an economy other than that of the investor. It is the sum of equity capital, reinvestment of earnings, other long-term capital, and short-term capital as shown in the balance of payments. (World Bank, International Monetary Fund)

Forests are land under natural or planted stands of trees, whether productive or not. (Food and Agriculture Organization)

Freshwater use is estimates of total freshwater withdrawals for domestic, industrial, and agricultural use not counting evaporation losses from storage basins. Total resources refer to internal renewable resources, which include internal flows of rivers and groundwater from rainfall in the country, but do not include river flows from other countries. Withdrawals also include water from desalination plants in countries where they are a significant source, and can exceed 100 percent of total renewable resources where extraction from non-renewable aquifers or desalination plants is considerable or where there is significant water reuse. (World Resources Institute)

GDP (gross domestic product) is the gross domestic product at purchaser prices is the sum of the gross value added by all resident producers in the economy plus any product taxes and minus any subsidies not included in the value of the products. It is calculated without making deductions for depreciation of fabricated assets or for depletion and degradation of natural resources. (World Bank, Organisation for Economic Co-operation and Development, United Nations)

GDP growth is the one-year rate of growth in real gross domestic product. (World Bank, Organisation for Economic Cooperation and Development, United Nations)

GDP implicit price deflator is the one-year rate of price change in the economy as a whole. (World Bank, Organisation for Economic Cooperation and Development, United Nations)

GNI (gross national income) is gross domestic product (GDP) plus net receipts of primary income (employee compensation and property income) from abroad. GDP is the sum of value added by all resident producers plus any product taxes (less subsidies) not included in the valuation of output. (World Bank)

GNI per capita is gross national income divided by midyear population. (World Bank)

Gross capital formation is outlays on additions to the fixed assets of the economy plus net changes in the level of inventories. Fixed assets include land improvements (fences, ditches, drains, and so on); plant, machinery, and equipment purchases; and the construction of roads, railways, and the like, including schools, offices, hospitals, private residential dwellings, and commercial and industrial buildings. Inventories are stocks of goods held by firms to meet temporary or unexpected fluctuations in production or sales and "work in progress." According to the 1993 System of National Accounts, net acquisitions of valuables are also considered capital formation. (World Bank, Organisation for Economic Co-operation and Development, United Nations)

High-technology exports are products with high research and development intensity. They include high-technology products such as those in aerospace, computers, pharmaceuticals, scientific instruments, and electrical machinery. (United Nations COMTRADE database)

HIV prevalence rate is the percentage of people ages 15–24 who are infected with HIV. (Joint United Nations Programme on HIV/AIDS/World Health Organization)

Imports of goods and services are the value of all goods and other market services received from the rest of the world, including the value of merchandise, freight, insurance, transport, travel, royalties, license fees, and other services. Labor and property income (formerly called factor services) are excluded, as are transfer payments. (World Bank, Organisation for Economic Co-operation and Development, United Nations)

Infant mortality rate is the number of infants dying before reaching one year of age, per 1,000 live births in a given year. (United Nations, United Nations International Children's Emergency Fund)

Internet users are people with access to the worldwide network. (International Telecommunication Union)

Life expectancy is the number of years a newborn infant would live if prevailing patterns of mortality at the time of its birth were to stay the same throughout its life. (World Bank)

Literacy, female is the percentage of females ages 15 and older who can, with understanding, read and write a short, simple statement about their everyday life. (United Nations Educational, Scientific, and Cultural Organization)

Literacy, total is the percentage of people ages 15 and older who can, with understanding, read and write a short, simple statement about their everyday life. (United Nations Educational, Scientific, and Cultural Organization)

Net barter terms of trade is the ratio of the export price index to the corresponding import price index measured relative to the base year 1995. (United Nations Conference on Trade and Development, International Monetary Fund)

Net primary enrollment is the ratio of the number of children of official primary school age (as defined by the national education system) who are enrolled in school to the population of the official primary school age. Based on the International Standard Classification of Education (ISCED). Net enrollment ratios exceeding 100 indicate discrepancies between the estimates of school age population and reported enrollment data. Note: There is a break in series between 1997 and 1998 due to the change from International Standard Classification of Education (ISCED) 1976 to ISCED97. (United Nations Educational, Scientific, and Cultural Organization)

Net secondary enrollment is the ratio of the number of children of official secondary school age (as defined by the national education system) who are enrolled in school to the population of the official secondary school age. Based on the International Standard Classification of Education (ISCED). Net enrollment ratios exceeding 100 indicate discrepancies between the estimates of school age population and reported enrollment data. Note: There is a break in series between 1997 and 1998 due to the change from ISCED76 to ISCED97. (United Nations Educational, Scientific, and Cultural Organization)

Paved roads are those surfaced with crushed stone (macadam) and hydrocarbon binder or bituminized agents, with concrete, or with cobblestones, as a percentage of all the country's roads, measured in length. (International Road Federation)

Personal computers are self-contained computers designed to be used by a single individual. (International Telecommunication Union)

Population is midyear estimates of all residents regardless of legal status or citizenship, except for refugees not permanently settled in the country of asylum who are generally considered part of the population of their country of origin. (World Bank)

Population growth is the one-year rate of growth in total population. (World Bank)

Poverty rate is the percentage of the population living below the national poverty line. National estimates are based on population-weighted subgroup estimates from household surveys. (World Bank)

Present value of debt is the sum of short-term external debt plus the discounted sum of total debt service payments due on public, publicly guaranteed, and private nonguaranteed long-term external debt over the life of existing loans. (World Bank)

Primary completion rate, total is the number of students successfully completing (or graduating from) the last year of primary school in a given year, divided by the number of children of official graduation age in the population. (World Bank, Education group)

Primary completion rate, female is the number of female students successfully completing (or graduating from) the last year of primary school in a given year, divided by the number of children of official graduation age in the population. (World Bank, Education group)

Short-term debt is all debt having an original maturity of one year or less and interest in arrears on long-term debt. (World Bank)

Surface area is a country's total area, including areas under inland bodies of water and some coastal waterways. (Food and Agriculture Organization)

Total debt service is the sum of principal repayments and interest actually paid in foreign currency, goods, or services on long-term debt, interest paid on short-term debt, and repayments (repurchases and charges) to the International Monetary Fund. The exports of goods and services denominator includes income and workers' remittances received. (World Bank)

Trade growth less GDP growth is the difference between annual growth in trade of goods and services and annual growth in GDP. Growth rates are calculated using constant price series taken from national accounts and are expressed as a percentage. (World Bank)

Trade in goods as share of GDP is the sum of merchandise exports and imports measured in current U.S. dollars divided by the value of GDP in U.S. dollars. (World Trade Organization, World Bank)

Under-five mortality rate is the probability that a newborn baby will die before reaching the age of five, if subject to current age-specific mortality rates. (United Nations, United Nations International Children's Emergency Fund)

Urban population is the midyear population of areas defined as urban in each country and reported to the United Nations. (United Nations)

Value added in agriculture is the net output of agriculture (International Standard Industrial Classification divisions 1-5 including forestry and fishing) after adding up all outputs and subtracting intermediate inputs. (World Bank, Organisation for Economic Co-operation and Development, United Nations)

Value added in industry is the net output of industry (International Standard Individual Classification divisions 10-45, which include mining, manufacturing, construction, electricity, water, and gas) after adding up all outputs and subtracting intermediate inputs. (World Bank, Organisation for Economic Co-operation and Development, United Nations)

Value added in services is the net output of services (International Standard Industrial Classification divisions 50-99) after adding up all outputs and subtracting intermediate inputs. This sector is derived as a residual and may not properly reflect the sum of service output, including banking and financial services. (World Bank, Organisation for Economic Co-operation and Development, United Nations)